Empirically Based Interventions Targeting Social Problems

John S. Wodarski • Laura M. Hopson

Editors

Empirically Based Interventions Targeting Social Problems

 Springer

Editors
John S. Wodarski
College of Social Work
University of Tennessee
Knoxville, TN, USA

Laura M. Hopson
School of Social Work
The University of Alabama
Tuscaloosa, AL, USA

ISBN 978-3-030-28489-3   ISBN 978-3-030-28487-9   (eBook)
https://doi.org/10.1007/978-3-030-28487-9

This Springer imprint is published by the registered company Springer Nature Switzerland AG
The registered company address is: Gewerbestrasse 11, 6330 Cham, Switzerland

Contents

Contributors

Robert Bidwell Department of Pediatrics, University of Hawaii, Honolulu, HI, USA

Anna Celeste Burke The Ohio State University, Columbus, OH, USA

Namkee Choi Steve Hicks School of Social Work, The University of Texas at Austin, Austin, TX, USA

Sherry Cummings College of Social Work, University of Tennessee, Knoxville, TN, USA

Sarah V. Curtis College of Social Work, University of Tennessee, Knoxville, TN, USA

Catherine N. Dulmus School of Social Work, University of Buffalo, Buffalo, NY, USA

M. E. Betsy Garrison School of Human Environmental Sciences, University of Arkansas, Fayetteville, AR, USA

M. Sebrena Jackson School of Social Work, University of Alabama, Tuscaloosa, AL, USA

Nancy P. Kropf Georgia State University, Atlanta, GA, USA

Jan Ligon School of Social Work, Andrew Young School of Policy Studies, Georgia State University, Atlanta, GA, USA

Peter Lyons School of Social Work, Andrew Young School of Policy Studies, Georgia State University, Atlanta, GA, USA

Eberhard Mann Department of Pediatrics, University of Hawaii, Honolulu, HI, USA

Charles W. Mueller Department of Psychology, University of Hawai'i at Mānoa, Honolulu, HI, USA

Scott Okamoto School of Social Work, College of Health and Society, Hawai'i Pacific University, Honolulu, HI, USA

Lisa A. Rapp School of Educational Social Services, Saint Leo University, St. Leo, FL, USA

Shanae Shaw School of Social Work, University of Alabama, Tuscaloosa, AL, USA

John S. Wodarski College of Social Work, University of Tennessee, Knoxville, TN, USA

Fan Yang Dongbei University of Finance and Economics, Dalian Shi, Liaoning Sheng, China

About the Editors

John S. Wodarski, PhD, is professor of social work at the University of Tennessee College of Social Work in Knoxville. Dr. Wodarski has over 40 years of experience teaching graduate and undergraduate social work students. His main interests include child, adolescent, and young adult health behaviors, including research on violence, substance abuse, depression, sexuality, HIV and viral hepatitis prevention, and employment. He has written over 65 textbooks and has contributed to over 50 additional texts.

Laura M. Hopson, PhD, is an associate professor at the University of Alabama School of Social Work in Tuscaloosa. Dr. Hopson has over 10 years of experience teaching social work students and practitioners. Her research focuses on prevention of health risk behaviors and academic failure among vulnerable adolescents, especially ethnic minority adolescents from economically disadvantaged households. Her work also examines barriers to implementing evidence-based practices in community agencies and strategies for overcoming these barriers. She has authored or coauthored over 50 publications in journals and texts and coauthored the book *Research Methods for Evidence-Based Practice* with John S. Wodarski.

Chapter 1
Social Problems: A Cost-Effective Psychosocial Prevention Paradigm

John S. Wodarski

The cost of social problems and the negative consequences are extensive and well documented. From a cost-benefit perspective, the largely remedial, as opposed to practice, interventions the social service system has chosen are extremely costly and highly unproductive for both client and practitioner in terms of targets, timing of intervention, ages, and contexts. Social, cognitive, and academic skills that individuals must master should provide the focus for intervention from a life-span development perspective. A review and analysis centering on social problems underscores the need for cost-effective, evidence-based, and preventive efforts. First, the personal and societal costs of child abuse, educational outcomes, violence in the schools, teenage sexuality, HIV/AIDS, drug abuse, crime, urban decline and homelessness, unemployment, marital conflict, race, retirement, and hospice are analyzed. Subsequent chapters review the personal, social, economic, and political benefits of prevention. Preventive models of service delivery are elucidated. The chapter concludes with specific applications and discussions.

Prevention Versus Remediation

Much has been written about many problem behaviors of the young and the undesirable consequences thereof. Teenagers' experimentation with drugs and alcohol can lead to overindulgence and abuse. Serious short-term and long-term effects include risk taking and daredevil behaviors that increase risks to mental and physical health, including accidents, which are a leading cause of death among adolescents. Likewise, risk taking may increase the incidence of irresponsible sexual activity, which eventuates in venereal disease, unwanted pregnancy, and premature

J. S. Wodarski (✉)
College of Social Work, University of Tennessee, Knoxville, TN, USA
e-mail: jwodarsk@utk.edu

© Springer Nature Switzerland AG 2019
J. S. Wodarski, L. M. Hopson (eds.), *Empirically Based Interventions Targeting Social Problems*, https://doi.org/10.1007/978-3-030-28487-9_1

parenthood. Prevention during the adolescent developmental period would reduce these serious physical and social problems (Sood & Berkowitz, 2016; Tremblay, 2006).

These problems usually intensify later and become harder to alter, thereby increasing the need for investments of time and money. Prevention provides a view of the person that is optimistic. The approach is economic and mass-oriented rather than individual-oriented, and it seeks to build health from the start rather than to repair damage that has already been done.

The life skills training intervention model is proposed as the treatment of choice. This model has rationale and elements in common with other prevention programs that are based on a public health orientation. Such prevention programs consist of three essential components: education, skills training, and practice in applying skills. The Teams-Games-Tournaments (TGT) model consists of the same components as other prevention programs, except for an additional component: It uses peers as parallel teachers (Buckholdt & Wodarski, 1978; Wodarski, Wodarski, & Parris, 2004). Data to support social workers' use of the life skills and Teams-Games-Tournaments models are reviewed later in this chapter. Other applicable intervention models will also be mentioned. For example, the use of the Internet and games as a way of helping adolescents prepare for life (McGonigal, 2011).

The prevention approach to intervention has implications for the traditional role of the human services practitioner and for the timing of the intervention. The prevention approach places major emphasis on the teaching and skills-building components of the intervention process (Benson, Leffert, Scales, & Blyth, 2012; Catalano et al., 2012; Swearer, Espelage, Vaillancourt, & Hymel, 2010). Practitioners do not take a passive role in the intervention process, but instead attempt to help clients learn how to exert control over their own behaviors and over the environments in which they live. Professional knowledge, expertise, and understanding of human behavior theory and personality development are used by the practitioner in the conceptualization and implementation of intervention strategies. Since their training equips them to evaluate scientifically any prevention procedure they have instituted, there is continual assessment of the prevention process.

Need for Prevention Programs

Deficit-ridden state and local governments are cutting back prevention programs in order to balance their budgets. However, this proves to be cost-ineffective on every level. One informative example of this unfortunate policy is the curtailing of family planning services and teen pregnancy programs. Specifically, savings in public medical costs alone are estimated to be $5.68 for each $1 spent in contraceptive services to the typical clinic patient (Frost, Zolna, & Frohwirth, 2013). Savings in income support and social services are greater yet. Approximately 13.9% women of reproductive age have no insurance (Guttmacher Institute, 2015). State insurance commissioners should pressure planning services. Teens, single women, and poor women, who have the highest incidence of low-birth-weight (LBW) babies, are most likely to use publicly funded family services (Guttmacher Institute, 2016a) and these women tend to have far more unwanted pregnancies (Guttmacher Institute, 2016b).

Examples of Incidence and Cost of Social Problems

Child Abuse

When the battered child syndrome was first promulgated, it was estimated to be affecting about 300 hospitalized children (Kempe, Silverman, Steele, Droegemueller, & Silver, 1962). This proved to be a gross underestimation of the true extent of the problem. Since the 1960s, the number of reported victims of all types of maltreatment has steadily increased. By 1984, 1.7 million children were reported as victims, 2.4 million were reported in 1989, and 2.9 million were reported in 1993 (Ards & Harrel, 1993; Curtis, Boyd, Liepold, & Petit, 1995; McCurdy & Daro, 1993; National Center on Child Abuse and Neglect (NCCAN), 1988; NCCAN, 1995). Allowing for duplicated counts, an estimated 2.3 million individual children were subjects of report in 1993 (NCCAN, 1995). Of these, just over 1000 were fatalities related to child maltreatment (NCCAN, 1995). Curtis and his colleagues have estimated, based on several national reports, that approximately 18,000 serious disabilities and 141,000 serious injuries arise annually from maltreatment (Curtis et al., 1995). In 1993, about 24% of victims suffered from physical abuse and about 48% from neglect (NCCAN, 1995). The most recent national statistics estimated 1670 children die of abuse or neglect at a rate of 2.25 per 100,000 children (U.S. Department of Health and Human Services (U.S. DHHS), 2017). In relation to age groups of those reported as maltreated, the youngest group, aged birth to 1 year, is more likely than any other age group to be subjected to maltreatment, composing 24.2% of the victims (U.S. DHHS, 2017). Children from families with low socioeconomic status were five times more likely to experience child maltreatment than children from families with higher incomes (Sedlak et al., 2010); children in a single parent home have over a 70% chance of being victimized than children with both parents in the home. Other risk factors have been identified as well.

Educational Outcomes

The future economic viability of the USA is in jeopardy due to poor educational outcomes for a large percentage of its young citizens. With 25% truancy and drop-out rates for elementary, middle, and high school students, we can expect that not enough educated individuals will be available to fill the jobs in the twenty-first century (Cabrera & LaNasa, 2001).

Furthermore, a number of reports, e.g., *Measuring Up: The National Report Card on Higher Education* (National Center for Public Policy and Higher Education, 2008), *A Nation at Risk: The Imperative for Educational Reform* (The National Commission on Excellence in Education, 1983), *The Death and Life of the Great American School System* (Ravitch, 2010), *Winning the Future: A 21st Century Contract with America* (Gingrich, 2006), *Waiting for "Superman"* (Chilcott & Guggenheim, 2010), and *Time to Start Thinking: America in the Age of Decent* (Luce, 2012), document the number of US citizens who enroll in post-secondary education and graduate at 33%. These numbers are sorely inadequate to fill 20 million jobs expected to be available by the year 2030 for individuals with college degrees (Friedman & Mandelbaum, 2011; Moore et al., 2010).

Violence in Schools

Since 1992, the rates of violent crimes in America's schools have steadily declined (Bureau of Justice Statistics, 2008; Hahn et al., 2007; U.S. Department of Justice, 2007; University of Virginia, 2007). Violent crimes rarely occur in schools (Hahn et al., 2007). However, the Department of Health and Human Services (2008) identifies youth violence as a significant public health problem. Despite the hint that violent crimes are more prevalent in communities as opposed to school houses, which have been beefed-up with armed, resource officers, the National Center for Education Statistics (2016) indicates that in the 2013–2014 academic year 65% of public schools reported one or more serious violent incidents. In 2014, among students ages 12–18, there were about 850,100 nonfatal victimizations at school, which included 363,700 theft victimizations and 486,400 violent victimizations (Morgan, Musu-Gillette, Robers, & Zhang, 2015). Furthermore, research indicates that 740,000 violent crimes were committed against children at school in 2003 (Hahn et al., 2007). Therefore, the portion of youth violence that does occur in schools warrants attention.

Teenage Sexuality

Each teenage pregnancy translates into a significant cost to the taxpayer, which is a major cause for concern. In 1985, for example, teenage pregnancy cost each US taxpayer $16.65 in Aid to Families with Dependent Children, Medicaid, and food stamps (Guttmacher Institute, 1985). In another example, the city of Baltimore spent about $179,500,000 in 1987 on AFDC, Medicaid, and food stamps for families that were begun when the mother was a teenager. Had these births been delayed until the mother was at least 20 years old, Baltimore would have saved almost

$72,000,000 in public outlays (Santelli, Rosenblatt, & Birn, 1990). The cost borne by Medicaid for a birth to a teenager age 14 or younger has been calculated as $3494; the cost for 15–17 year olds is $3224; and for 18–19 year olds, it is $2696, exclusive of pediatric care (Armstrong & Waszak, 1990). While the prevalence of teenage pregnancy has steadily declined since the late 1980s, the cost of this social problem to taxpayers continues to be of major concern. In 2010, taxpayers spent a total of $10.9 billion on costs related to teenage pregnancy, birth, and teenage motherhood. Each child born to a teenage mother today costs US taxpayers $1682 (The National Campaign to Prevent Teen and Unplanned Pregnancy, 2011).

HIV/AIDS

There are approximately 33.4 million people living with HIV/AIDS worldwide (UN, 2010). In the most vulnerable countries, less than 10% of those living with AIDS are even aware of their status. Currently, in sub-Saharan Africa, 22.5 million people are living with HIV. This is two-thirds of all people with AIDS and of this number 59% are women (WHO, 2011). In Eastern Europe and Central Asia, the percentage of people living with HIV/AIDS has increased over 20% between the years of 2003 and 2005 (WHO, 2006). There are now over one million individuals living with the HIV infection in the USA (CDC, 2012). Since the first cases of HIV/AIDS were seen in the USA nearly 30 years ago, over 575,000 Americans have lost their lives to AIDS (The White House Office of National AIDS Policy, 2010). Fortunately, with the use of medications such as highly active antiretroviral therapy (HAART), the mortality and morbidity related to HIV/AIDS has experienced a reduced rate of increase (Montaner et al., 2014).

Within the USA, the youth population has seen an increasing number of infections. There were 4205 adolescents diagnosed with HIV in 2002, and by 2009 the number had doubled to 8300 new infections in adolescents aged 13–24 years (CDC, 2012). In addition, adolescents are the fastest growing segment of the population newly diagnosed with HIV in the USA. Many adolescents may acquire the infection and are not diagnosed until later. The latency period for the HIV infection can be as long as 10 years (CDC, 2010a, 2010b). In 2008, the CDC estimated that of the 68,600 adolescents living with HIV, nearly 60% were unaware they were infected (CDC, 2012). Within the adolescent population in the USA, males tend to acquire the virus more often than females. White men who have sex with men (MSM) accounted for 61% of the new HIV diagnoses in 2009 (CDC, 2011). While gay and bisexual men continue to be the most affected population, the trend toward more transmissions occurring through heterosexual activity and intravenous drug use has occurred for several decades. Females most often acquire the disease through heterosexual activity (71%). Most startlingly in the USA, the disproportionately large number of HIV/AIDS infections found in African Americans. In 2009, this race accounted for more than 44% of new HIV/AIDS cases. Minority races, women, and children are becoming more and more represented in those with the virus. Considering geographic data within the USA, urban areas contain large proportion of HIV infections; however, rural area infection rates are increasing. New York City houses 13.6% of the adolescents with HIV. Other epicenters in descending order are Houston, Los Angeles, Miami, Philadelphia, Washington, D.C., and Chicago.

There are certain groups of adolescents who are at particular risk for HIV infection such as economically vulnerable adolescents, female, gay and bisexual males, homeless and runaway adolescents, and other high risk homosexuals and intravenous drug users (Bermudez et al., 2016; Dellar, Dlamini, & Karim, 2015; Gallagher, Denning, Allen, Nakashima, & Sullivan, 2007). The number of studies related to prevention of HIV infections in these populations have increased in the past decade.

Drug Abuse

In the President's Report of The Economic Costs of Drug Abuse in the United States (Office of the President, 2004) conducted by The Lewin Group, statistics were compiled from years 1992–2002 and costs reported for this period. The reported overall cost of drug abuse exacts more than $740 billion annually (National Institute on Drug Abuse, 2017). This is a 5.34% annual increase. A breakdown looks like this: health care costs comprising treatment, prevention programs, and medical consequences (HIV/AIDS, Hepatitis B and C, and drug-exposed infant) total more than $15.8 billion; productivity losses (premature death, abuse related illness, institutionalization, etc.) more than $128.6 billion; and costs of other effects which addresses the criminal costs (police protection, supply reduction measures, and state and federal corrections) comprised an additional $36.4 billion (Lewin Group, 2004, pp. ix–xi). However, careful scrutiny of these figures suggests gross exaggeration, e.g., they include private legal defense, abuse related figures in both the health care table and the productivity table; incarceration is listed in the productivity table and in the other effects table; and there is a category listed as crime careers accounting for more than $27 billion that appears to be a mystery. One possible explanation for these dubious figures might be to justify the costs incurred in the President's War on Terrorism.

In another study sponsored by the National Institute on Alcohol Abuse and Alcoholism, Sacks, Gonzales, Bouchery, Tomedi, and Brewer (2015) put the total economic costs at $$249.0 billion in 2010. 88,000 deaths are attributed to AOD problems. In 2012, there were estimably 23.1 million Americans in need of AOD treatment, and only about 2.5 million people (1%) were able to receive treatment (National Institute on Drug Abuse).

Crime

The Federal Bureau of Investigation's Uniform Crime Reporting Program (UCR), which captures 94% of the US population, found that in 2010 there were 1,246,248 violent crimes and 9,082,887 property crimes (Federal Bureau of Investigation [FBI], 2011). In 2010, the rate of violent crime victimization (excluding murder) for US residents age 12 or older was about 15 in 1000. The rate for property crime victimization was about 120 in 1000 (Bureau of Justice Statistics [BJS], 2011). The rate for intimate partner violence was 0.8 per 1000 for men and 3.1 per 1000 for women.

There are estimated to have been 13.1 million arrests (except traffic violations), which translate to 4257.6 arrests per 100,000 people for those 29 offenses tracked (FBI, 2011). For violent crimes, the arrest rate was 179.2 per 100,000 people, whereas for property crimes, the rate was 538.5 per 100,000 persons. In 2010, the clearance rate for violent crime was 47.2% and for property crimes, 18.3% (FBI, 2011).

Looking at several kinds of crime committed between 1996 and 2001, there were 1,551,143 occurrences of family violence according to the UCR program. Of these, 29.6% were within girlfriend/boyfriend relationships, while 24.4 occurred between spouses. Between 1996 and 2001, there were 20,955 people assaulted who were related to the perpetrator (National Criminal Justice Reference Service [NCJRS], 2006). In 2015, the number of children victimized by sexual and physical abuse and neglect was approximately 700,000, with younger children being at greater risk (National Children's Alliance, 2015).

Substance abuse is implicated in this relative-as-perpetrator category of crime, as it is in many other kinds of crime. In a study conducted by the Arrestee Drug Abuse Monitoring Program, 60% of arrestees tested positive for one or more drugs at the time of arrest (Office of National Drug Control Policy [ONDCP], 2011). In 2002, perpetrators of violent crimes were believed by their victims to have been drinking in approximately one million instances. Multiple studies have consistently revealed the high rates of alcohol use among perpetrators (Cafferky, Mendez, Anderson, & Stith, 2016).

The costs of crime include those which are tangible and hence calculable monetarily, such costs being related to property loss, medical expenses, public safety programs, and private security strategies. Much more difficult to calculate are the intangible costs, such as the pain and suffering caused by the criminal events, as well as the subsequent diminishment of the quality of life for victims and their families.

Tangible costs are considerable. Crime cost victims as much as $15 billion in economic losses for victims and $179 billion in assorted government expenditures in 2007. In 2003, nearly half of the billions that victims received went to medical expenses while 12% went to mental health counseling (National Center for Victims of Crime [NCVC], 2004). Considering the costs of domestic or intimate partner violence alone, the Centers for Disease Control and Prevention (CDCP) determined that the 2003 health-related costs stemming from physical assault, rape, homicide, and stalking were at least $5.8 billion annually (CDCP, 2003). The UCR also found that in 2010, the tangible costs of property crimes other than arson were approximately $16.21 billion (FBI, 2011). A single serious violent crime could cost up to $17 million (DeLisi et al., 2010).

There are many other costs as well, such as the costs to keep the US corrections system going. In 2001, this was estimated to be in excess of $38 billion (NCVC, 2004). In 2000, the national budget for reduction of drug use alone was 9936.6 million, with an anticipated request for fiscal year 2007 being 12,655.8 million (BJS, 2007). This is just part of the annual cost of alcohol abuse, at about $150 million, and drug abuse, at about $96 million (McDonald & Finn, 2000).

Urban Decline and Family Homelessness

One of our most serious social problems, which has worsened in the recent decades, is the deterioration of housing and other living conditions in central cities and the resulting homelessness, especially among families with children. The number of the homeless is a matter of dispute between governments and advocates for the homeless due to inconsistent definitions, methodologies, and samples studied (Kondratas, 1991; Mihaly, 1991; Morrison, 1989; Newman, 2001; Tsemberis, McHugo, Williams, Hanrahan, & Stefancic, 2007). The number may not be in the millions, as estimated by homeless advocates, but most parties agree that it is as least in the hundreds of thousands, even without counting the rising number of families living doubled up with friends or relatives (Dyrness, Spoto, & Thompson, 2003). Other homeless families can be found living in cars and abandoned buildings (Fertig & Reingold, 2008). Moreover, all data indicate that poor families, headed up mostly minority, young, single mothers with children, people with mental health and substance use problem, occupy an increasing share of the rank and file of the homeless (Brown et al., 2016; Eisenberg & Keil, 2000; Rossi, 1994). A major cause of homelessness is poverty. Families make up approximately one-third of all homeless and are the fastest-growing group of homeless (Rosenheck, Bassuk, & Solomon, 2001). Children are estimated to make up between one-third and one half of the members of homeless families (Mihaly, 1991). Most studies of the homeless indicate that the number of homeless families and extremely poor families with children who are precariously housed and thus at risk of homelessness is also increasing.

The cost of human suffering due to homelessness is manifested in tens of thousands of poor families with children sleeping in temporary shelters or living doubled up with equally poor relatives or friends. Homeless children exhibit a host of academic, physical, and psychological problems that interfere with their proper development (Bassuk & Rosenberg, 1990; Bassuk, Richard, & Tsertsvadze, 2015;

Chiu, DiMarco, & Prokop, 2013; National Alliance to End Homelessness, 2000; Rafferty, 1995; Schanzer, Dominguez, Shrout, & Canton, 2007; Thompson, Zittel-Palamara, & Maccio, 2004). Insecurity, instability, and uncertainty about the next meal and bed undoubtedly cause enormous stress and anguish and overwhelm adults and children alike. Homeless and near-homeless families who move from one dangerous neighborhood to another in deteriorating central cities are also susceptible to crime and violence on the city streets. The overall physical health of children and adults alike living the shelters can lead to health problems such as respiratory and intestinal infections (Schanzer et al., 2007).

Unemployment

Unemployment refers to the inability to gain entry into the labor market or to the "involuntary withdrawal from the workforce due to plant closures, layoffs, or other types of dismissals" (Leana & Feldman, 1991, p. 65). Since the mid-1970s, the US economy has undergone dramatic changes, contributing to relatively high unemployment rates and large numbers of workers confronted with job loss. Between 1981 and 1988 alone, estimates are that 10.8 million US workers experienced unemployment (Fraze, 1988). In July 2012, the Bureau of Labor Statistics found that 12.8 million people were unemployed. In the 1980s and 1990s, it has also become increasingly difficult for young people to negotiate the transition from school to work (Mann, Miller, & Baum, 1995; Sum, Fogg, & Taggert, 1988). This is particularly true for young people with little education or training, but even those with college degrees find job acquisition more challenging (Sum et al., 1988). The current employment rate is 4.4% in 2017 (U.S. Department of Labor, 2017). A 5.2% unemployment rate in 2024is projected by US Department of Labor (2015), meaning many more individuals will face unemployment.

Efforts to put a dollar amount on costs of unemployment typically include estimates of lost productivity, reduced consumption, and additional subsidy provided by taxpayers for unemployment compensation and other benefits for the unemployed. Needless to say, any such estimate runs into billions of dollars quickly. One recent study found that counties with higher unemployment rates had higher rates of depression hospitalizations as unemployment appeared to be risk factor for hospitalization. These high cost hospitalizations add to the overall social costs for the unemployed (Fortney et al., 2007). A 1% rise in unemployment, for example, has been estimated to add $55 billion to the federal deficit. Given the range of health, social, and psychological problems associated with unemployment, such dollar estimates fall short of representing the full impact of unemployment on individuals, their families, and the larger community.

Marital Conflict

Presumably, all marriages involve some degree of marital conflict, given that life is inherently stressful and that all relationships involve some degree of dissension. According to the National Survey of Family Growth, 48% of marriages will end in divorce before the 20th anniversary (CDC, 2010a, 2010b). The majority of these cases will involve at least one child under the age of 18 (Ganong, Coleman, Markham, & Rothrauff, 2011).

For several years now, marital conflict has been identified as a risk factor for health and mental problems and a major disruption in the workplace (Snyder, Heyman, & Haynes, 2005). Choi and Marks (2008) suggest that separation and divorce have strong negative consequences for the mental and physical health of both spouses. Lower marital quality has been linked to high levels of depression and a lower quality of life (Amato, 2014; Choi & Marks, 2008). Bray and Jouriles (1995) discussed the cost-effectiveness of marital therapy and noted that the majority of marital therapies that have been empirically evaluated are relatively brief in duration and below the standard 20-session limit imposed by health insurance companies. Using an average cost of $60 to $100 per session, an average course of marital therapy would cost between $600 and $1000. As stated by Bray and Jouriles, "Even twice this amount seems certainly less than the cost of a divorce and pales in comparison to the costs of many medical procedures" (1995, p. 469).

Race

Social work has historically emphasized the importance of diversity in the worker client relationship. However, most of the recent research in the profession has emphasized the study of other aspects of social work practice. At the same time, disciplines such as psychology and psychiatry have produced research with greater emphasis on relationship factors such as race and gender, on the therapeutic alliance, and on counseling outcomes. Greene, Jensen, and Harper-Jones (1996) indicate that "virtually all therapeutic approaches are equally effective and that the one thing essential to therapeutic success, regardless of theoretical orientation, is a good working relationship between the clinician and the client" (p. 172). Coady (1993) notes that "over the past two decades, the most striking and consistent empirical findings in individual psychotherapeutic research have been the nonsignificant outcome differences among various therapies" (p. 292).

Empirical evidence indicates that race and gender are key variables that affect the helping relationship and can produce clinician bias. For example, psychiatric evaluations are primarily based on a patient's history, basic personality, and current mental state. According to Wade (1993), the emphasis given to one item of information or the importance attached to an incident is dependent on the beliefs, value judgments, understanding, and knowledge of the psychiatrist. Diagnosis and subsequent care can often be a result of the differences in race, gender, age, and ethnicity between worker and client (Krieger, 2014).

Cultural conditioning, which even social workers are not immune from, has been shown to create racial biases that people may or may not be aware of (Abelson, Dasgupta, Park, & Banaji, 1998; Banaji, Hardin, & Rothman, 1993; Thyer, Myers, Wodarski, & Harrison, 2010). Other studies have supported the contention that racial bias exists in the assessment, diagnosis, and treatment of mental illness (Jenkins-Hall & Sacco, 1991; Jones, 1982; Whaley, 2001). Accumulating research has revealed that racial and cultural bias significantly contributes in the psychiatric misdiagnosis of African Americans (Whaley & Geller, 2003, 2007).

For example, some studies indicate that white professionals may misconstrue uncooperative behavior among Latinos as evidence of psychosis (Rendon, 1974; Smith Kline Corporation, 1978). Others suggest that instances of paranoid behavior exhibited by blacks when interacting with white therapists are indicative of coping behavior exhibited by many African Americans in response to discriminatory life experiences (Pavkov, Lewis, & Lyons, 1989). Trierweiler et al. (2006) found that Non-African American therapists generally rated their black clients as more psychologically impaired than did black therapists. Furthermore, when diagnosed with psychotic or affective disorders, minority-race clients are more likely to be labeled as having a chronic syndrome than an acute episode (Sata, 1990).

Retirement

Since the turn of the last century, the increase in the number of older adults has been dramatic. In the early 1900s, when the current cohort of elders was born, only 5% of the population was over the age of 65 (Aging America, 1991). In 2010, there were nearly 50 million people over the age of 62, which is 16.2% of the population. That is a 21.1% increase from 2000 (U.S. Census Bureau, 2010). The trend toward an increasingly older population is expected to continue, as a greater number of adults live into late life. Because of their multiple needs that often include medical, social, and financial assistance, social work practitioners in all service settings can expect to work with greater numbers of older adults in coming years.

Due to the diversity of practice issues in work with older clients, various approaches focus on different practice outcomes. Certain interventions have prevention objectives, with goals of keeping older adults as physically, socially, and psychologically healthy as possible. Other intervention approaches are remedial, with the goal of restoring functioning after the onset of a certain type of problematic condition (e.g., death of a spouse, onset of chronic health problem). Finally, some approaches provide support in progressive and irreversible situations, such as dementia care or terminal illness. Intervention approaches discussed in this chapter are practice with individual clients, groups and families of older adults, and community prevention programs.

Hospice

The National Hospice and Palliative Care Organization released a hospice census in 2012 which estimates various pieces of demographic data for hospice patients. It is estimated that 1.58 million patients were served by hospice in 2010, and 41.9% of all deaths in the USA occurred under the care of a hospice program. In 2010, the average length of time that a patient received hospice care was 67.4 days; 56.1% of hospice patients were female, and 43.9% were male; 82.7% were 65 years of age or above, and 17.3% were 64 or below; 77.3% were White/Caucasian; 5.7% reported Hispanic or Latino origin; 35.6% maintained a cancer diagnosis, and 64.4% maintained a non-cancer diagnosis (National Hospice and Palliative Care Organization, 2012).

References

Abelson, R. P., Dasgupta, N., Park, J., & Banaji, M. R. (1998). Perceptions of the collective other. *Personality and Social Psychology Review, 2*, 243–250.

Aging America: Trends and projections. (1991). Washington, DC: U.S. Senate Special Committee on Aging, American Association of Retired Persons, the Federal Council on the Aging, and the U.S. Administration on Aging.

Amato, P. R. (2014). The consequences of divorce for adults and children: An update. *Društvena istraživanja-Časopis za opća društvena pitanja, 1*, 5–24.

Ards, S., & Harrel, A. (1993). Reporting of child maltreatment: A secondary analysis of the national incidence surveys. *Child Abuse and Neglect, 17*, 337–344.

Armstrong, E., & Waszak, C. (1990). *Teenage pregnancy and too-early childbearing; public costs, personal consequences.* Washington, DC: Center for Population Options.

Banaji, M. R., Hardin, C., & Rothman, A. J. (1993). Implicit stereotyping in person judgment. *Journal of Personality and Social Psychology, 65*, 272–281.

Bassuk, E. L., Richard, M. K., & Tsertsvadze, A. (2015). The prevalence of mental illness in homeless children: A systematic review and meta-analysis. *Journal of the American Academy of Child & Adolescent Psychiatry, 54*(2), 86–96.

Bassuk, E. L., & Rosenberg, L. (1990). Psychosocial characteristics of homeless children and children with homes. *Pediatrics, 85*(3), 257–261.

Benson, P. L., Leffert, N., Scales, P. C., & Blyth, D. A. (2012). Beyond the "village" rhetoric: Creating healthy communities for children and adolescents. *Applied Developmental Science, 16*(1), 3–23.

Bermudez, L. G., Jennings, L., Ssewamala, F. M., Nabunya, P., Mellins, C., & McKay, M. (2016). Equity in adherence to antiretroviral therapy among economically vulnerable adolescents living with HIV in Uganda. *AIDS Care, 28*(sup2), 83–91.

Bray, J. H., & Jouriles, E. N. (1995). Treatment of marital conflict and prevention of divorce. *Journal of Marital and Family Therapy, 21*(4), 461–473.

Brown, R. T., Goodman, L., Guzman, D., Tieu, L., Ponath, C., & Kushel, M. B. (2016). Pathways to homelessness among older homeless adults: Results from the HOPE HOME study. *PLoS One, 11*(5), e0155065.

Buckholdt, D. R., & Wodarski, J. S. (1978). The effects of different reinforcement systems on cooperative behaviors exhibited by children in classroom contexts. *Journal of Research and Development in Education, 12*, 50–68.

Bureau of Justice Statistics. (2007). *Drug control budget*. Retrieved February 14, 2007, from http://www.ojp.usdoj.gov/bjs/dcf/dcb.htm

Bureau of Justice Statistics. (2008). *Indicators of school crime and safety: 2007*. Retrieved October 13, 2008, from http://www.ojp.usdoj.gov/bjs/cvict_c.htm#school

Bureau of Justice Statistics. (2011). *Criminal victimization, 2010*. Retrieved from http://bjs.ojp.usdoj.gov/index.cfm?ty=pbdetail&iid=2224

Cabrera, A. F., & LaNasa, S. M. (2001). On the path to college: Three critical tasks facing America's disadvantaged. *Research in Higher Education, 42*(2), 119–149.

Cafferky, B. M., Mendez, M., Anderson, J. R., & Stith, S. M. (2016). Substance use and intimate partner violence: A meta-analytic review. *Psychology of Violence, 8*.

Catalano, R. F., Fagan, A. A., Gavin, L. E., Greenberg, M. T., Irwin, C. E., Ross, D. A., & Shek, D. T. (2012). Worldwide application of prevention science in adolescent health. *The Lancet, 379*(9826), 1653–1664.

Centers for Disease Control and Prevention. (2003). *Costs of intimate partner violence against women in the United States*. Atlanta, GA: U.S. Department of Health and Human Services.

Centers for Disease Control and Prevention. (2010a). *Weekly morbidity and mortality reports*. Retrieved from http://www.cdc.gov/mmwr/pdf/wk/mm5924.pdf

Centers for Disease Control and Prevention. (2010b). *National survey of family growth*. Atlanta, GA: CDC.

Centers for Disease Control and Prevention. (2011). *Estimates of new HIV infections in the United States, 2006-2009*. Retrieved from http://www.cdc.gov/nchhstp/newsroom/docs/HIV-Infections-2006-2009.pdf

Centers for Disease Control and Prevention. (2012). *HIV testing among adolescents: What schools and education agencies can do*. Retrieved from http://www.cdc.gov/healthyyouth/sexualbe-haviors/pdf/hivtesting_adolescents.pdf

Chilcott, L., & Guggenheim, D. (2010). *Waiting for 'Superman' [motion picture]*. Los Angeles, CA: Walden Media and Participant Media.

Chiu, S. H., DiMarco, M. A., & Prokop, J. L. (2013). Childhood obesity and dental caries in homeless children. *Journal of Pediatric Health Care, 27*(4), 278–283.

Choi, H., & Marks, N. F. (2008). Marital conflict, depressive symptoms, and functional impairment. *Journal of Marriage and Family, 70*, 377–390.

Coady, N. (1993, May). The worker-client relationship revisited. *Families in Society: The Journal of Contemporary Human Services*, 292–297.

Curtis, P. A., Boyd, J. D., Liepold, M., & Petit, M. (1995). *Child abuse and neglect: A look at the states*. Washington, DC: Child Welfare League of America.

DeLisi, M., Koloski, A., Sween, M., Hachmeister, E., Moore, M., & Drury, A. (2010). Murder by numbers: Monetary costs imposed by a sample of homicide offenders. *Journal of Forensic Psychiatry & Psychology, 21*, 501–513.

Dellar, R. C., Dlamini, S., & Karim, Q. A. (2015). Adolescent girls and young women: Key populations for HIV epidemic control. *Journal of the International AIDS Society, 18*, 64–70.

Department of Health and Human Services, Centers for Disease Control and Prevention. (2008). *Youth violence: Fact sheet*. Retrieved October 11, 2008, from http://www.cdc.gov/ncipc/fact-sheets/yvfacts.htm

Dyrness, G. R., Spoto, P., & Thompson, M. (2003). *Crisis on the streets: Homeless women and children in Los Angeles*. Los Angeles, CA: University of Southern California Center for Religion and Civic Culture.

Eisenberg, E., & Keil, J. (2000). Growth, construction, and housing prices. *Housing Economics, 48*(9), 1056–5140.

Federal Bureau of Investigation. (2011). *Crime in the United States, 2010*. Retrieved May 14, 2012, from http://www.fbi.gov/about-us/cjis/ucr/crime-in-the-u.s/2010/crime-in-the-u.s.-2010

Fertig, A. R., & Reingold, D. A. (2008). Homelessness among at-risk families with children in twenty American cities. *Social Service Review, 82*(3), 485–510.

Fortney, J., Rushton, G., Wood, S., Zhang, L., Xu, S., Dong, F., & Rost, K. (2007). Community-level risk factors for depression hospitalizations. *Administration and Policy in Mental Health and Mental Health Services Research, 34*, 343–352.

Fraze, J. (1988). Displaced workers: Oakies of the 80's. *Personnel Administrator, 33*, 42–51.

Friedman, T. L., & Mandelbaum, M. (2011). *That used to be us: How America fell behind in the world it invented and how we can come back.* New York, NY: Picador.

Frost, J. J., Zolna, M. R., & Frohwirth, L. (2013). *Contraceptive needs and services, 2010.* New York, NY: Guttmacher Institute.

Gallagher, K. M., Denning, P. D., Allen, D. R., Nakashima, A. K., & Sullivan, P. S. (2007). Use of rapid behavioral assessments to determine the prevalence of HIV risk behaviors in high-risk populations. *Public Health Reports, 122*(1), 56–62.

Ganong, L. H., Coleman, M., Markham, M., & Rothrauff, T. (2011). Predicting postdivorce coparental communication. *Journal of Divorce and Remarriage, 52*(1), 1–18.

Gingrich, N. (2006). *Winning the future: A 21st century contract with America.* Washington, DC: Regnery Publishing.

Greene, G., Jensen, C., & Harper-Jones, D. (1996). A constructivist perspective on clinical social work with ethnically diverse clients. *Social Work, 41*(2), 172–180.

Guttmacher Institute. (1985). *Report on adolescent pregnancy.* New York, NY: Author.

Guttmacher Institute. (2015). *Fewer U.S. women of reproductive age were uninsured in 2014.* Retrieved from https://www.guttmacher.org/article/2015/09/fewer-us-women-reproductive-age-were-uninsured-2014

Guttmacher Institute. (2016a). *Publicly funded family planning services in the United States.* Retrieved from https://www.guttmacher.org/fact-sheet/publicly-funded-family-planning-services-united-states

Guttmacher Institute. (2016b). *Unintended pregnancy in the United States.* Retrieved from https://www.guttmacher.org/fact-sheet/unintended-pregnancy-united-states

Hahn, R., Fuqua-Whitley, D., Wethington, H., Lowy, J., Crosby, A., Fullilove, M., … Task Force on Community Preventive Services. (2007). Effectiveness of universal school-based programs to prevent violent and aggressive behavior: a systematic review. *American Journal of Preventive Medicine, 33*(2), 114–129.

Jenkins-Hall, K., & Sacco, W. P. (1991). Effect of client race and depression on evaluations by white therapists. *Journal of Social and Clinical Psychology, 10*, 322–333.

Jones, E. E. (1982). Psychotherapists' impressions of treatment outcome as a function of race. *Journal of Clinical Psychology, 38*, 722–731.

Kempe, C., Silverman, F., Steele, B., Droegemueller, W., & Silver, H. (1962). The battered child syndrome. *Journal of the American Medical Association, 181*, 17–24.

Kondratas, A. (1991). Ending homelessness: Policy challenges. *American Psychologist, 46*(1), 1226–1231.

Krieger, N. (2014). Discrimination and health inequities. *International Journal of Health Services, 44*(4), 643–710.

Leana, C. R., & Feldman, D. C. (1991). Gender differences in responses to unemployment. *Journal of Vocational Behavior, 38*(1), 65–77.

Lewin Group. (2004). *Costs of serving homeless individuals in nine cities: Chart book.* Prepared for The Partnership to End Long-Term Homelessness.

Luce, E. (2012). *Time to start thinking: America in the age of descent.* New York, NY: Atlantic Monthly Press.

Mann, A. R., Miller, D. A., & Baum, M. (1995). Coming of age in hard times. *Journal of Health & Social Policy, 6*(3), 41–57.

McCurdy, K., & Daro, D. (1993). *Current trends in child abuse reporting and fatalities: The results of the 1992 Annual Fifty State Survey* (Working paper number 808). Chicago, IL: National Center on Child Abuse Prevention Research.

McDonald, D., & Finn, P. (2000). *Crime and justice trends in the United States during the past three decades.* Cambridge, MA: Abt Associates.

McGonigal, J. (2011). *Reality is broken: Why games make us better and how they can change the world*. New York, NY: Penguin Press HC.

Mihaly, L. (1991). Beyond numbers: Homeless families with children. In H. Kryder-Coe, L. M. Salmon, & J. M. Molnar (Eds.), *Homeless children and youth: A new American dilemma* (pp. 11–32). New Brunswick, NJ: Transaction.

Montaner, J. S., Lima, V. D., Harrigan, P. R., Lourenço, L., Yip, B., Nosyk, B., ... Hogg, R. S. (2014). Expansion of HAART coverage is associated with sustained decreases in HIV/AIDS morbidity, mortality and HIV transmission: The "HIV treatment as prevention" experience in a Canadian setting. *PLoS One, 9*(2), e87872.

Moore, G. W., Slate, J. R., Edmonson, S. L., Combs, J. P., Bustamante, R., & Onwueglowzie, A. J. (2010). High school students and their lack of preparedness for college: A statewide study. *Education and Urban Society, 42*(7), 817–838.

Morgan, R. E., Musu-Gillette, L., Robers, S., & Zhang, A. (2015). *Indicators of school crime and safety: 2014*. Washington, DC: National Center for Education Statistics, U.S. Department of Education, and Bureau of Justice Statistics, Office of Justice Programs, U.S. Department of Justice

Morrison, K. (1989). Correlations between definitions of the homeless mentally ill population. *Hospital and Community Psychiatry, 40*(9), 952–954.

National Alliance to End Homelessness. (2000). *A plan, not a dream: How to end homelessness in ten years*. Washington, DC: National Alliance to End Homelessness.

The National Campaign to Prevent Teen and Unplanned Pregnancy. (2011). *Counting it up: The public costs of teen childbearing: Key data*. Washington, DC: The National Campaign to Prevent Teen and Unplanned Pregnancy.

National Center for Education Statistics. (2016). *Indicators of school crime and safety: 2015*. Retrieved from https://nces.ed.gov/pubs2016/2016079.pdf

National Center for Public Policy and Higher Education. (2008). *Measuring up: The national report card on higher education*. Retrieved November 8, 2012, from http://measuringup2008. highereducation.org/print/NCPPHEMUNationalRpt.pdf

National Center for Victims of Crime. (2004). *Cost of crime*. Retrieved March 24, 2007, from http://www.ncvc.org/ncvc/main.aspx?dbName=DocumentViewer&DocumentID=38710

National Center on Child Abuse and Neglect. (1988). *Research symposium on child neglect*. Washington, DC: Author.

National Center on Child Abuse and Neglect. (1995). *Child maltreatment 1993 reports from the states to the National Center on Child Abuse and Neglect*. Washington, DC: U.S. Government Publishing Office.

National Children's Alliance. (2015). *National statistics on child abuse*. Retrieved from http://www.nationalchildrensalliance.org/media-room/media-kit/national-statistics-child-abuse

National Commission on Excellence in Education. (1983). *A nation at risk: The imperative for educational reform*. Retrieved October 25, 2012, from http://datacenter.spps.org/uploads/SOTW_A_Nation_At_Risk_1983.pdf

National Criminal Justice Reference Service. (2006). *Family violence—facts and figures*. Retrieved on February 13, 2007, from http://www.ncjrs.gov/spotlight/family_violence/facts.html

National Hospice and Palliative Care Organization. (2012). NHPCO facts and figures: Hospice care in America. Alexandria, VA: National Hospice and Palliative Care Organization.

National Institute on Drug Abuse. (2017). *Trends and statistics*. Retrieved from https://www.drugabuse.gov/related-topics/trends-statistics

Newman, S. J. (2001). Housing attributes and serious mental illness: Implications for research and practice. *Psychiatric Services, 52*(10), 1309–1370.

Office of National Drug Control Policy. (2011). *Arrestee drug abuse monitoring program II: Annual report*. Retrieved from http://www.whitehouse.gov/ondcp/arrestee-drug-abuse-monitoring-program

Office of the President. (2004). *The economic costs of drug abuse in the United States* (pp. v–xii). Washington, DC: Executive Office.

Pavkov, T., Lewis, D., & Lyons, J. (1989). Psychiatric diagnoses and racial bias: An empirical investigation. *Professional Psychology: Research and Practice, 20*(6), 364–368.

Rafferty, Y. (1995). The legal rights and educational problems of homeless children and youth. *Educational Evaluation and Policy Analysis, 17*(1), 39–61.

Ravitch, D. (2010). *The death and life of the great American school system: How testing and choice are undermining education.* New York, NY: Basic Books.

Rendon, M. (1974). Transcultural aspects of Puerto Rican mental illness. *International Journal of Social Psychiatry, 20,* 297–309.

Rosenheck, R., Bassuk, E., & Solomon, A. (2001). *Special populations of homeless Americans.* Retrieved April 1, 2007, from www.aspe.hhs.gov/progsys/homeless/symposium/2-Spclpop.htm

Rossi, P. H. (1994). Troubling families: Family homelessness in America. *American Behavioral Scientist, 37*(3), 342–395.

Sacks, J. J., Gonzales, K. R., Bouchery, E. E., Tomedi, L. E., & Brewer, R. D. (2015). 2010 National and state costs of excessive alcohol consumption. *American Journal of Preventive Medicine, 49*(5), e73–e79. PMID: 26477807.

Santelli, J., Rosenblatt, L., & Birn, A. E. (1990). Estimates of public cost for teenage childbearing in Baltimore city in FY 1987. *Maryland Medical Journal, 39*(5), 459–464.

Sata, L. (1990, April). *Working with persons from Asian backgrounds.* Paper presented at the Cross-Cultural Psychotherapy Conference, Hahnemann University, Philadelphia, PA.

Schanzer, B., Dominguez, B., Shrout, P. E., & Canton, C. L. M. (2007). Homelessness, health status, and health care use. Research and practice. *American Journal of Public Health, 97*(3), 464–469.

Sedlak, A. J., Mettenburg, J., Basena, M., Peta, I., McPherson, K., & Greene, A. (2010). *Fourth national incidence study of child abuse and neglect (NIS-4).* Washington, DC: US Department of Health and Human Services. Retrieved July 9, 2010.

Smith Kline Corporation. (1978). *Cultural issues in contemporary psychiatry: The Asian American.* Philadelphia, PA: Author.

Snyder, D. K., Heyman, R. E., & Haynes, S. N. (2005). Evidence-based approaches to assessing couple distress. *Psychological Assessment, 17*(3), 288–307.

Sood, A. B., & Berkowitz, S. J. (2016). Prevention of youth violence: A public health approach. *Child and Adolescent Psychiatric Clinics of North America, 25*(2), 243–256.

Sum, A., Fogg, N., & Taggert, R. (1988). *Withered dreams: The decline in the economic fortunes of young, non-college educated male adults and their families* (report to the William T. Grant Foundation Commission on Family, Work, and Citizenship). New York, NY: William T. Grant Foundation.

Swearer, S. M., Espelage, D. L., Vaillancourt, T., & Hymel, S. (2010). What can be done about school bullying? Linking research to educational practice. *Educational Researcher, 39*(1), 38–47.

Thompson, S. J., Zittel-Palamara, K. M., & Maccio, E. M. (2004). Runaway youth utilizing crisis shelter services: Predictors of presenting problems. *Child and Youth Care Forum, 33,* 387–403.

Thyer, B. A., Myers, L. L., Wodarski, J. S., & Harrison, D. F. (2010). *Cultural diversity and social work practice.* Springfield, IL: Charles C Thomas Publishers.

Tremblay, R. E. (2006). Prevention of youth violence: Why not start at the beginning? *Journal of Abnormal Child Psychology, 34*(4), 480–486.

Trierweiler, S., Neighbors, H. W., Munday, C., Thompson, E., Jackson, J., & Binion, V. (2006). Differences in patterns of symptom attribution in diagnosing schizophrenia between African American and non-African American clinicians. *American Journal of Orthopsychiatry, 76,* 154–160.

Tsemberis, S., McHugo, G., Williams, V., Hanrahan, P., & Stefancic, A. (2007). Measuring homelessness and residential stability: The residential time-line follow-back inventory. *Journal of Community Psychology, 35*(1), 29–42.

U.S. Census Bureau. (2010). *USA QuickFacts.* Retrieved from http://quickfacts.census.gov/qfd/states/00000.html

U.S. Department of Health and Human Services, Administration for Children and Families, Administration on Children, Youth and Families, Children's Bureau. (2017). *Child maltreatment 2015*. Retrieved from http://www.acf.hhs.gov/programs/cb/research-data-technology/statistics-research/child-maltreatment

U.S. Department of Justice. (2007). *Crime in schools and colleges: A study of offenders and arrestees reported via national incident-based reporting system data* (The Card Report: Crime Analysis, Research and Development Unit). Washington, DC: Noonan, J. H., & Vavra, M. C. Retrieved October 11, 2008, from http://www.fbi.gov/ucr/schoolviolence/2007/schoolviolence.pdf

U.S. Department of Labor. (2015). *Employment projections 2014-24*. Retrieved from https://www.bls.gov/news.release/pdf/ecopro.pdf

U.S. Department of Labor. (2017). *The employment situation—April 2017*. Retrieved from https://www.bls.gov/news.release/pdf/empsit.pdf

United Nations Department of Public Information. (2010). *Millennium development goals: Goal 6: Combat HIV/AIDS, malaria and other diseases*. Retrieved from http://www.un.org/millenniumgoals/pdf/MDG_FS_6_EN.pdf

University of Virginia. (2007). *Violence in schools*. Retrieved October 11, 2008, from http://youth-violence.edschool.virginia.edu/violence-in-schools/national-statistics.html

Wade, J. C. (1993). Institutional racism: An analysis of the mental health system. *American Journal of Orthopsychiatry, 63*(4), 536–544.

Whaley, A. L. (2001). Cultural mistrust and mental health services for African Americans: A review and meta-analysis. *The Counseling Psychologist, 29*, 513–531.

Whaley, A. L., & Geller, P. A. (2003). Ethnic/racial differences in psychiatric disorders: A test of four hypotheses. *Ethnicity & Disease, 13*, 499–512.

Whaley, A. L., & Geller, P. A. (2007). Toward a cognitive process model of ethnic/racial biases in clinical judgment. *Review of General Psychology, 11*, 75–96.

The White House Office of National AIDS Policy. (2010). *National HIV/AIDS strategy for the United States*. Retrieved from http://www.whitehouse.gov/sites/default/files/uploads/NHAS.pdf

Wodarski, J. S., Wodarski, L. A., & Parris, H. N. (2004). Adolescent preventive health and teams-games-tournaments: A research and development paradigm entering its fourth decade of research. *Journal of Evidence-Based Social Work, 1*(1), 101–123.

World Health Organization. (2006). Young people and HIV: The evidence is clear-act now! Study identifies prevention interventions set to go. *Indian Journal of Medical Sciences, 60*(9), 394–397.

World Health Organization. (2011). *HIV in the WHO African region: Progress towards achieving universal access to priority health sector interventions*. Brazzaville, Republic of Congo: WHO Regional Office for Africa.

Chapter 2
Child Maltreatment

M. Sebrena Jackson and Peter Lyons

Overview

Our understanding of child maltreatment has increased markedly since the radiologist Caffey (1946) first noticed a correlation between multiple long bone fractures and subdural hematoma in infants. This was followed by Kempe's contribution, which focused attention on the battered child syndrome in the 1960s (Kempe, Silverman, Steele, Droegemueller, & Silver, 1962). Currently, the literature recognizes four major types of maltreatment: physical abuse, physical neglect, emotional maltreatment, and sexual abuse (Oshri, Sutton, Clay-Warner, & Miller, 2015). Child physical abuse and neglect, the twin foci of this chapter, are often coterminal, but independent entities, with separate, albeit similar, etiologies and trajectories (Walker, 2010). In reviewing the empirical literature on the treatment of physical abuse and neglect, one should make frequent distinctions between the two (e.g., physical abuse as event, neglect as condition; physical abuse as commission, neglect as omission). However, in this context, the two are dealt with simultaneously, as many studies have combined both types of maltreatment. In addition, physical abuse and neglect are often comorbid manifestations (Higgins, 2004; Luke & Banerjee, 2013).

According to Fantuzzo, Stevenson, Kabir, and Perry (2007), child maltreatment is a national problem that threatens the development of our most vulnerable children. Child maltreatment is a significant problem in the USA. Its significance derives from a combination of its prevalence and the serious consequences of maltreatment for individuals, families, neighborhoods, and for society as a whole. It has

M. S. Jackson (✉)
School of Social Work, University of Alabama, Tuscaloosa, AL, USA
e-mail: msjackson5@ua.edu

P. Lyons
School of Social Work, Andrew Young School of Policy Studies, Georgia State University, Atlanta, GA, USA

© Springer Nature Switzerland AG 2019
J. S. Wodarski, L. M. Hopson (eds.), *Empirically Based Interventions Targeting Social Problems*, https://doi.org/10.1007/978-3-030-28487-9_2

been suggested that child abuse is fundamental in three ways: first, it is correlated with a broad range of other social problems; second, it is a sensitive marker of the strength of the social fabric; third, it denies the worth of children (Melton, Thompson, & Small, 2002; Thompson, 2015). It is clear that for abused individuals there are very profound negative sequelae. These include psychological, social, academic, and emotional problems and deficits (Arnow, 2003; Lereya, Copeland, Costello, & Wolke, 2015).

The *child* protective service agencies (CPS) have difficult decisions today that include but are not limited to: (1) assessing the safety of those children who are found to be at risk of *maltreatment*, (2) determining which types of services are immediately needed to keep children safe, and (3) which conditions necessitate children being placed in out-of-home custody for their immediate protection (DePanfilis, 2005). It is crucial that social/cultural acceptability and parental satisfaction be assessed in relation to the services being offered when working with families who are at risk of, or reported for, child abuse or neglect. Families may be more resistant to treatment as a result of their embarrassment and/or denial, making it imperative for CPS staff to be approachable and nonthreatening and that services are delivered in acceptable and meaningful ways (Taban & Lutzker, 2001). Successful intervention with parents of children under the care of CPS is key. However, intervention among such families is a complex matter secondary to the multiple and diverse problems these families face (Fraser & Allen-Meares, 2004; Russell, Gockel, & Harris, 2006). Effective support of such families is essential and has been found to require a range of interventions, including attending to the parenting capacity of the parents (Russell et al., 2006).

Incidence

When the battered child syndrome was first promulgated, it was estimated to affect about 300 hospitalized children (Kempe et al., 1962). This proved to be a gross underestimation of the true extent of the problem. Since the 1960s, the number of reported victims of all types of maltreatment has steadily increased. By 1984, 1.7 million children were reported as victims, 2.4 million were reported in 1989, 2.9 million were reported in 1993, and 3.7 million in 2011. In the year 2016, 4 million children were deemed appropriate referrals for further investigation by Child Protective Services (Ards & Harrel, 1993; Child Welfare Information Getaway [CWIG], 2019; Curtis, Boyd, Liepold, & Petit, 1995; McCurdy & Daro, 1993; National Center on Child Abuse and Neglect (NCCAN), 1995; NCCAN, 1988). Allowing for unduplicated counts, an estimated 3.4 million children were reported in 2016 (CWIG, 2013). Of these, a nationally estimated 1750 fatalities were directly attributed to child abuse and neglect (CWIG, 2019). In 2016, about 18% of victims suffered from physical abuse, 74.8% from neglect, and approximately 8.5% were sexually abused (CWIG, 2019). In relation to age groups of those reported as maltreated, the youngest group, aged birth to 1 year, is more likely than any other age group to be subjected to maltreatment (U.S. Department of Health and Human Services [DHHS], 2017).

Children from families with the lowest income levels (below $15,000) were over 22 times more likely to be abused or neglected than children from families with higher incomes (Fantuzzo et al., 2007); children in a single parent home have over a 70% chance of being victimized than children with both parents in the home (Fantuzzo et al., 2007). Other risk factors have been identified as well.

Definition of Child Abuse and Neglect

This proliferation of reports is also a function of the malleable definition of the phenomenon. The Child Abuse Prevention and Treatment Act (CAPTA) of 1974, while establishing broad parameters for defining child abuse and neglect, allows autonomy of the individual states to articulate their own definitions. Consequently, there is some agreement in extreme cases about what is and what is not child maltreatment. This precision fades, however, with the complexity of cases, in which decisions are often not between optimal parenting and abuse, but between shades of behavior (Wayne, 2008). According to Vig and Kaminer (2002), many children experience more than one type of maltreatment, and there can be considerable overlap among categories. Also, states vary in their definitions of maltreatment as well as in their reporting procedures.

Abuse has been defined as the degree to which parents may use inappropriate or aversive strategies to control their child or children; *neglect* has been defined as the degree to which parents provide little stimulation or structure or fail to provide minimal standards of nurturing and caregiving in the crucial areas of education, nutrition, supervision, health care, emotional availability, and general safety (Erickson & Egeland, 2002). This definition encapsulates the twin concepts of commission (abuse) and omission (neglect) that often characterize these two phenomena.

Hutchison and Charlesworth (2000) have suggested that these definitions of maltreatment have been developed to meet four interrelated purposes: social policy and planning, legal regulations, research, and case management. Confusion surrounding the definition of maltreatment is in part a function of the variety of competing explanations for its causes. It is generally recognized that maltreatment is multi-causal and multi-determined, although there is no such agreement about the relative weight or combination of these variable contributors (Black, Heyman, & Smith Slep, 2001; Lyons, Doueck, & Wodarski, 1996). The definitional consequences of these competing ontologies for the treatment of physical abuse and neglect are manifold. Selection of treatment is often determined by theoretical subscription or orientation, thus setting the parameters for intervention. In order to minimize these impediments, it is important that a uniform, commonly understood definition of the parameters used to define child maltreatment be developed. Standardization of maltreatment variables will help to promote equality in child experience across jurisdictions and geographical regions, may contribute to a shortened duration in child welfare proceedings, and allow for enhanced individualization of a carefully selected treatment plan (Chaffin & Friedrich, 2004).

Objectives of Risk Assessment

According to Morton and Salovitz, the primary objective of risk assessment processes is to identify, from cases referred to child welfare authorities, the subgroup of children at high risk of future abuse or neglect so that action may be taken to prevent it (Morton & Salovitz, 2006). A second identification relates to the probable severity of subsequent maltreatment (2006). The most important aspect of risk assessment in child maltreatment cases is estimating the probability of recurrence. Since child protection agencies are not adequately resourced to serve all children and families in which a report is substantiated, risk assessment has been suggested as a rational way to triage those families and children most in need of a service intervention (2006).

Child welfare practitioners are employing formal and structured risk assessment processes to predict child vulnerability or to improve case decision making (Macdonald, 2001). However, research has yet to prove conclusively which set of risk factors are most critical for evaluating risk within a family and community, nor has it resolved the controversy regarding the importance of professional training and experience in risk assessment procedures and processes (2001).

Risk Factors

According to Vig and Kaminer (2002), causes of child maltreatment are complex and stressors of various kinds interact with family, parent, and child characteristics to mediate the risk of maltreatment for children with and without disabilities. Resources for intervention and respite may not be available for the complex and numerous family issues associated with child maltreatment (2002).

Parental substance abuse is a major contributing factor to increasing child welfare caseloads (Freisthler, 2004). For almost half of the 8.3 million children living with a substance-abusing parent, alcohol was the substance of abuse; an additional 28% live with a parent who abused a combination of both alcohol and illicit drugs (2004). The issue remains important as neglected and abused children of parents with substance use disorders stay in the child welfare system longer and experience poorer outcomes (U.S. Department of Health and Human Services, 2014).

Numerous additional parental and family characteristics have been linked to child maltreatment. Research indicates that abusive mothers are significantly younger upon having their first child than mothers who do not abuse their children (Mersky, Berger, Reynolds, & Gromoske, 2009). Maternal depression has been linked to child maltreatment in several studies (Silverstein, Augustyn, Young, &

Zuckerman, 2009; Whitson, Martinez, Ayala, & Kaufman, 2011; Windham et al., 2004). Social isolation of families is an additional problem associated with various types of child maltreatment (Dubowitz & Bennett, 2007). Lower levels of community integration, participation in social activities, and limited use of formal or informal community organizations are all linked to increased rates of child abuse (Maguire-Jack & Showalter, 2016). Additional factors include but are not limited to: life stress (Crouch & Behl, 2001); past history of using corporal punishment (2001); approval of violence (Widom, Czaja, & Dutton, 2014), and parental experience of suffering from abuse as a child (Widom, Czaja, & DuMont, 2015).

Although any single problem may present as primary in a family, the reality is that child maltreatment often exists within families experiencing multiple problems across multiple systems (Kazak et al., 2010). It is unclear how many of these families exist. However, it is safe to say that combinations of the stressors mentioned above and others (e.g., unemployment, poor housing, single parenting, mental illness) may lead to violence and abuse in the home.

Assessment Methods

The non-solitary nature of child abuse and neglect suggests that a multimethod, multisource assessment and intervention is required for maximum efficiency. There are also special circumstances surrounding the assessment of child maltreatment (e.g., social desirability in self-report measures and reactivity in observation), which reinforce the need to seek convergent findings across multiple sources to ensure the most accurate results. Reliable and accurate assessment tools are necessary to prevent future maltreatment and to compensate for human judgment error and bias during the assessment process (Shlonsky & Wagner, 2005). It is recommended that the clinician select from a variety of assessment procedures dictated by the unique features of each individual case.

The primary concern in any assessment of child abuse and neglect must be the assessment of immediate risk to the child. This is particularly salient in light of the findings from an analysis of National Child Abuse and Neglect Data System (NCANDS) correlates, which found that as many as 22% of families reported for child maltreatment, were re-reported (Fluke, Shusterman, Hollinshead, & Yuan, 2008). Younger children, those with disabilities, children of white or mixed race, and those with parents who abused drugs or alcohol were at an increased risk for repeated maltreatment. Interestingly, families who received services were also at an increased risk for repeated episodes of maltreatment, creating the need for further risk assessment in those families who receive services while a CPS case is investigated (2008).

Currently, several empirically derived risk assessment instruments are available, each offering its own strengths and limitations in use and application of the risk of child maltreatment (e.g., Baird & Wagner, 2000; Macdonald, 2001; Shlonsky & Wagner, 2005). Important, none of these tools alone provide a sufficient level of predictive accuracy to allow for sole dependence in decision making (Macdonald, 2001). In addition, these models have been derived to substantiate reports to Child Protection Services, rather than for use in a clinical setting, although they may provide a useful adjunct to clinical judgment (Shlonsky & Wagner, 2005).

Having addressed the initial determination of child safety, the next step is to determine the contextual assessment of parental and family functioning competency to implement the most effective case management and treatment plan (Shlonsky & Wagner, 2005). The family functioning assessment collects data based upon what the parent or caregiver understands, believes, knows, does, or has the capacity to do. This implies that, in addition to parental assumptions about child needs and their knowledge of parenting, the current and potential future behavior of the parent becomes central to clinical assessment. Furthermore, given the understanding that child maltreatment occurs within the complex integration of multiple levels of environment and systems, it is important to examine and explore the influential impact of multiple factors such as the family's culture, community, and socioeconomic status, in addition to the immediate and direct variables of influence (Gambrill & Shlonsky, 2000).

Structured Clinical Interviews

The modal form of clinical assessment is the interview, and to the extent that certain factors concerning individual qualities and relationships, coping skills, and the person-in-environment perspective are addressed, this is an appropriate method of data collection. However, as a vehicle for obtaining information regarding situations of family violence, the interview often suffers from respondent distortion; self-serving, or social desirability bias and poor recall (Austin, 2001). In an effort to guide clinicians in the assessment of abusive families, Ammerman and his colleagues devised the Child Abuse and Neglect Interview Schedule (CANIS) (Ammerman, Hersen, & Van Hasselt, 1988). This was originally developed for use with disabled children. Revised in 1993, it is designed to assess maltreating behaviors such as corporal punishment, physical abuse, and history of maltreatment, and is applicable to the general population (Matulis, Resick, Rosner, & Steil, 2014; Stowman & Donohue, 2005).

Structured interviews may also incorporate various combinations of existing instruments. In choosing empirical measures, the clinician should have a clear understanding of the purpose of the assessment, the type of information required for relevance, the interventions available, and the family's strengths and cultural background, as well as the applicability of measures within diverse populations. A complete review of measures is beyond the scope of this chapter; however, research is available on the empirical assessment measures available for clinical use in child abuse and neglect (e.g., Baird & Wagner, 2000; Shlonsky & Wagner, 2005). Factors often included in assessment tools include: parental assessment, child assessment, family level measures, marital assessment, environmental level measures, and ecological measures. Also important when selecting assessment tools for child maltreatment within the clinical environment is the availability of the desired tool and the length of time required to administer each component.

Computerized Assessment Methods

The advent and availability of personal computers has made the collection and analysis of client information a much more accessible task. There are many computer programs available for clinical use; however, most are not inclusive of psychometric information. Two measures with extensive psychometric information available are listed below: both are available in computerized format.

One measure of general individual and family functioning is the Multi-Problem Screening Inventory (MPSI) (Hudson, 1990), which provides the clinician with a 334-item scale measuring across 27 dimensions of family and individual functioning. Subscales additionally address the scope of child problems, family problems, and numerous other issues.

A measure more directly focused on the individual child is the Child Well-Being Scale (Magura & Moses, 1986) a multidimensional measure of potential threats to a child's well-being. These scales include both child and family measures and were originally designed as an outcome measure for child welfare services, rather than for use in clinical assessment. However, a computerized form of the scales has been in use as a clinical decision-making tool since the early 1990s (Lyons & Doueck, 2009).

Self-Report Methods

In cases of child abuse and neglect, there is an almost inevitable influence of the social desirability bias in self-report measures, deriving from the significance of assessment and treatment for the parent's future capacity to continue in their parenting role. This reinforces the need for triangulation in assessment to ensure accuracy and veracity. The Child Abuse Potential Inventory (CAPI) (Chan, 2012; Milner, 1986), the most extensively researched instrument of its kind, has a validity index designed to detect biases or random response patterns. This 160-item inventory is intended to differentiate between physically abusive and non-physically abusive parents. The scale includes items measuring distress, rigidity, child problems, family problems, unhappiness, loneliness, negative self-concept, and negative concept of the child. The CAPI is one of the few instruments available with published validation and cross-validation information. This measure also has cross-validated data available in Spanish. Unlike many other instruments, it can be effective in predicting future maltreatment even in the absence of any previous maltreatment or abusive behaviors (Chan, 2012).

Although not yet as extensively researched as the CAPI, several other self-report instruments are worthy of note. The Parenting Stress Index (PSI) (Abidin, 1986; Haskett, Ahern, Ward, & Allaire, 2006) is designed to assess the extent of parenting-related stressors. Historically used more as a program evaluation tool, it has also been used successfully with abusive parents. In more recent applications, it has been shown to be successful in predicting child behavior up to 1 year post-assessment with the Childrearing subscale showing predictive accuracy of abusive history of the parent (Haskett et al., 2006).

The Parent Opinion Questionnaire is an 80-item instrument designed to assess the extent to which parents may hold unrealistic expectations about the developmental abilities of their children (Azar, Robinson, Hekimian, & Twentyman, 1984). Azar and her colleagues found significant scoring differences on this instrument with abusive as opposed to non-abusive parents (1984). This questionnaire has since been used in conjunction with other measurements as an informative method of collecting data used to determine the most effective treatment method for maltreating families (Sanders et al., 2004).

Observation Methods

Several observational procedures are available for assessment of selected behaviors or qualities of the parent–child interaction. One such tool is the 100-item Home Observation Measurement of the Environment (HOME) (Caldwell & Bradley, 1978), which assesses the quality of stimulation in the child's environment. Four versions of this instrument are available based on the age of the child to be observed: birth to age 3; ages 3–6; ages 6–10; and ages 10–15. This scale consists of some self-report items; however, the majority are based on observation of the parent and child. Special training is required to effectively administer, but the HOME has been used successfully with psychometric validation (Totsika & Sylva, 2004).

An observational system designed specifically to evaluate parent control strategies was developed by Schaffer and Crooke (1979, 1980). Examination of the parent–child interaction system using this model yields the classic, tripartite, antecedent child behavior-parent control-consequent child behavior model (Wodarski, 2015, p. 105). Various methods of control mechanisms are examined, including the motive, appropriateness, and timing of responses and communications. This observational model is based on the premise that parental control mechanisms create the boundaries for social regulation in children (Schaffer, 2006).

Some caution is merited in the use of observational methods, as they require extensive training for reliable use. In addition, many were developed for research, rather than clinical purposes. Notwithstanding, the items they reflect are often vital to understanding the nature of parent–child behaviors during observations. Haynes and Horn (1982) noted that reactive effects may not preclude the validity of such assessments. In contrast, some research suggests that demand characteristics do impact observational assessment by depressing the frequency of negative interactions

(Kavanaugh, Youngblade, Reid, & Fagot, 1988). Clearly, there is a need for caution in the interpretation of observational measures. Wolfe, Edwards, Manion, and Koverola (1988) have suggested that this type of observation is most reliably performed in the family home or a structured setting such as a clinic, and that interactions should optimally involve the whole family, taking place over multiple sessions.

Rating Scales

The Childhood Level of Living Scale (CLLS) (Polansky, Chalmers, Buttenweiser, & Williams, 1981) is a 99-item behavior rating scale developed as a measure for scaling the essential elements of child care and neglect of a child under age seven. Subscales include positive child care, state of home repair, negligence, household maintenance, health care, encouraging competence, consistency of discipline, and parental coldness. This scale is particularly useful in assessing chronicity and severity of caretaking deficits (Stowman & Donohue, 2005).

Physiological Methods

Interference of the social desirability bias is decreased when additional and correlational measures are also included. Physiological arousal responses are often introduced to enhance the reliability and accuracy of self-reporting or observational assessments. Physiological measurements of arousal may be taken in response to audio or videotaped material or in vivo exposure to problematic child behavior, infant crying, and so forth (Joosen, Mesman, Bakermans-Kranenburg, & van Ijzendoorn, 2013). As an adjunct, to complement parent self-report, physiological measures may compensate for underreporting or a failure to recognize negative responses.

Family Strengths

The family or individual need concentration of many assessment measures means they are often focused on the identification of existing deficits. This may color the perspectives of the clinician, and further contribute to the stigmatization of already demoralized parents. Therefore, it is crucial that clinicians take into account the strengths and potential resources possessed by families. It is important for the clinician to assess the strengths from both a standardized assessment model, in addition to an assessment to include the family's own perception of the strengths and resiliency factors they possess. This simple assessment may identify existing problematic parenting features, as well as become the foundation towards building parenting competence in future work (Cash, 2001).

Effective Social Work Interventions

Unlike neglect, which is often a readily observable condition, child abuse is most often a private phenomenon. This makes it almost impossible to observe, at least until after the event. Consequently, most child abuse treatment programs are aimed at the amelioration of the correlates of maltreatment, such as parent–child conflict, anger, vulnerability to stress and social isolation, rather than maltreatment per se.

Reflecting the multi-causal nature of child abuse and neglect, many of the empirically validated interventions that follow consist of multiple components offered simultaneously to parents, children, and/or families, in both group and nongroup settings. Additionally, many of the studies contrast two types of interventions (CBT and Multi-Systemic therapy, casework and play therapy, parent training and family therapy, etc.). Therefore, the following sections are divided between child-focused interventions, parent-focused interventions, and multiple-component interventions. However, overlap and duplication of one or other components has led to some arbitrary allocation based on the predominant component.

CPS Intervention with Modern Views

A modern view of child protection services implies that to help young people, simply intervening on their behalf is not sufficient. It suggests that involving parents in the intervention process is essential to ensure that they are most likely to fulfill their role as parent to their children in the fullest possible way (Saint-Jacques, Drapeau, Lessard, & Beaudoin, 2006). The social service philosophy in child protection services has changed in recent years—the idea of taking over for parents who are "incapable of taking care of their children" is now considered passé (Saint-Jacques et al., 2006). There have been several empirical studies which have demonstrated that the presence and active involvement of parents is essential and that, in most situations, the child's original family remains the environment most conducive to his or her development; any interruption in that primary relationship results in a negative effect on the child (Chen & Chan, 2016). In regard to child sexual abuse, participation of a non-offending parent may be particularly important in recovery (Elliott & Carnes, 2001).

The idea of parent involvement can be found across many different social work perspectives, including ecological, family preservation, network intervention, strengths perspective, or empowerment. By focusing on parents' skills and strengths, rather than on their shortcomings, parent involvement is the springboard for a process of empowerment (Saint-Jacques et al., 2006). Practices whose goals are to involve parents within an empowerment perspective must be based on values, knowledge, skills, attitudes, and behavior that are not only adopted by the practitioners, but also conveyed by the establishment in which they work (Saint-Jacques et al., 2006).

Research has shown that both parent and child reap benefits from parent involvement. One example can be seen in the case of foster care. Parent involvement decreases the length of time the child is placed in alternative custody and facilitates the child's reintegration into the family unit (Saint-Jacques et al., 2006). Parent involvement is an essential condition for improving parenting skills (2006). However, if parents are to get involved, practitioners must encourage parent participation (2006). Since each family is different, caseworkers need many different strategies for involving parents (2006).

In relation to CPS involvement, Saint-Jacques et al. (2006) state that the main components of successful intervention should include initiate contact, introduce oneself, clarify one's role and social service philosophy, inform parents of the program, inform parents of their rights and responsibilities in participation, encourage parents to visit the residential treatment center and to take the child home for visits during the placement period, let parents know how their child is doing during the placement period, draw up a case plan in collaboration with the parents and encourage them to actively participate in its implementation, give parents homework in order to encourage them to take responsibility for the changes that need to be made, telephone regularly to check on their progress and well-being, praise parents for the strategies they use that prove effective, help parents to reinterpret their situation in a more positive light, share one's personal experiences, emotions, or difficulties, take time, offer to arrange transportation for parents if needed, check whether parents are satisfied with the services, and to receive feedback about additional services the parent feels might be helpful for them (2006).

Child-Focused Interventions

There is a large body of research demonstrating the negative effects of various types of maltreatment on child outcome (Wang & Holton, 2007). Such negative effects have been shown to affect nearly every domain of the child's development, including academic, social relations, critical thinking skills, problem solving, substance abuse, stress management, self-esteem, sexual identity and development, mental health, physical health, and even future parenting methods, just to name a few (2007). Research has even been able to highlight the exponential effects on child outcome when a child is a victim of more than one type of abuse, with promising risk predictability specific to the types and combination of abuse patterns (Arata, Langhinrichsen-Rohling, Bowers, & O'Farrill-Swails, 2005).

Although it is appropriate that parents should be held accountable for child abuse and neglect and that a significant proportion of societal efforts should be targeted at helping them alter their maltreating behavior, there is still an unprecedented obligation to keep the needs and safety of the child as the utmost priority. Whether a child remains with his or her family, or is placed into alternative custody, there is no doubt that the child has suffered undue hardship and will be in need of treatment to help them cope with the situation they have experienced and their comprehension of the circumstances.

Promising treatment methods include those that focus on the individual child and the specific effects of maltreatment and subsequent events. Neurobiological impacts of early abuse can alter the way a victim responds to stressful stimuli, which can further impact the child's socialization patterns and coping skills (Stirling & Amaya-Jackson, 2008). Treatment methods that include peer relation skills and promotion of the victim's self-concept have been shown to be most effective towards the long-term outcome of the child (2008).

Therapeutic day programs have been shown to provide an efficient setting to incorporate the various interventions ideal for the child's recovery (Kanine, Tunno, Jackson, & O'Connor, 2015; Ware, Novotny, & Coyne, 2001). Although length of program duration or participation may vary based on program procedures or psychopathology of the individual child, effective components include a structured, child-centered environment, group setting to promote positive peer relations, emotional identification and expression skill-building, activities to promote self-esteem and self-efficacy, and an academic component that encompasses all of these qualities (2001). In addition, the day program setting is staffed by therapists and counselors who are experienced in crisis intervention and therapeutic de-escalation techniques to address potentially volatile situations or outbursts, should the need arise (2001).

Fantuzzo, Manz, Atkins, and Meyers (2005) applied a form of classroom-based therapy called Resilient Peer Treatment (RPT) on a group of 82 socially withdrawn Head Start students, both maltreated and non-maltreated. Data was collected from both teachers and independent observers in a blind manner to the existence of maltreatment history and treatment condition of the children. Both groups of children showed higher rates of collaborative play among peers within the treatment setting. This study also found promising results in the ability to generalize the treatment results to a general classroom free-play session. These results were confirmed by teachers, who confirmed increased interactive peer play and improved social skills (2005). The results of these studies are promising, since children of maltreatment often have a hard time relating to and cooperating with their peers, resulting in potentially disruptive behaviors.

In addition to the specific methods of child-focused therapy with demonstrated efficacy for child abuse victim populations, a study by Cloitre, Chase Stovall-McClough, Miranda, and Chemtob (2004) has also highlighted the importance of several additional factors that promote positive outcome. These factors include the strength and sincerity of the therapeutic alliance between the clinician and the child as well as the acquisition of mood regulation skills in the part of the child, especially the ability to regulate and respond to negative emotional cues relating to traumatic memories of the incidences of maltreatment (2004).

Among some controversy is the practice of play therapy in children who have experienced maltreatment. Widely used by child therapists in practice, the body of evidence on this type of treatment efficacy has been inconsistent in empirical validation. In a meta-analysis of the literature on play therapy, Bratton, Ray, Rhine, and Jones (2005) concluded that play therapy can indeed be effective as a treatment method, when certain criteria were met: developmental appropriateness for maturational age of the child, imagery that is humanistic and realistic (to demonstrate healthy boundaries and conflict resolution situations), and, when possible, to include the parents or caregivers of the child. Important to the practice of play therapy is the therapist's role to make sure the child takes precedent over anything else; the therapeutic healing lies within the child's perception of his or her own importance and ability to control the immediate world around them (Macdonald, 2001). The therapist's role is to encourage the child dictate the direction of the healing and therapeutic recovery by facilitating an environment that allows the child to feel valued and respected (2001).

Renner and Slack (2006) conducted a study to assess the extent to which intimate partner violence and different forms of child maltreatment occur within and across childhood and adulthood for a high-risk group of women. Low-income adult women were interviewed (with the benefit of hindsight) on their experiences with intimate partner violence and child maltreatment in childhood and adulthood. Both intra- and intergenerational relationships between multiple forms of family violence were identified. The outcome of this study favored assessments of those children identified for one form of victimization to determine if other forms of victimization were present; also, interventions should address learned behaviors or beliefs associated with continued or future victimization (Widom et al., 2014).

Parent-Focused Interventions

Parent Training

The form of intervention for parents appearing most frequently in the empirical literature is parent training. This has been presented in videotaped demonstrations, discussion, modeling, and role playing and is most typically allied with contingency contracts. Sessions often include information on human development, child management, and problem solving, as well as instruction, modeling, and rehearsal, and self-control strategies (relaxation training and use of self-statements). The training is based on a social learning model targeted at problems in child management and child development, and in the literature has often been accompanied by home visits in order to facilitate generalization.

With a purpose of revealing the effect of a Parent–Child Interaction Therapy (PCIT) model, Mersky, Topitzes, Grant-Savela, Brondino, and McNeil (2016) conducted a randomized trial. The researchers assign the sample of 102 foster kids to three conditions: brief PCIT, extended PCIT, or waiting list. Both samples in brief and extended PCIT groups received 2 days of PCIT training and 8 weeks of telephone consultation. An additional booster training and 6 weeks of consolation were provided the extended PCIT group. This results showed that participants in both brief and extend PCIT groups demonstrated a greater reduction in externalizing and internalizing scores over time.

Project SafeCare was a 4-year intervention program consisting of parent training that was facilitated within the home of the participants (Gershater-Molko, Lutzker, & Wesch, 2003). Participants were taken by referral from the local Department of Children's Services and a local hospital, and were referred based on the criteria of experiencing child maltreatment, or being at-risk of such experience. Within the homes of the participants, parents were provided training and education in treating their children's illnesses, maximizing their own health care skills, parenting training focusing on maintaining positive parent–child interactions, and maintaining safe home environments. Acquired skills were tested and reinforced based on role-play situations, physical data collection on number of home hazards, and observed number and quality of parent–child interactions. Results of Project SafeCare showed significant results across all measured domains of child well-being (2003). Project SafeCare has been adjusted and implemented in different countries and has exhibited significant effects at home setting (Gardner, Hodson, Churchill, & Cotmore, 2014; Self-Brown et al., 2015).

Many of the parent-training programs available are designed for households where both parents are present. Research has shown that single-parent households often do not inherit the full benefit of such curricula, in addition to also bearing the burden of the challenges of being a single-parent home (Briggs, Miller, Orellana, Briggs, & Cox, 2013). In an effort to more effectively reach this growing demographic of families, Briggs et al. combined behavior parent training curricula with an additional curriculum that provided specific insight to the unique components of single parent training to three single parent–child dyads. While the participants in this study were chosen based on the status of single-parent households described as being exposed to distressing family circumstances, and not necessarily those having experienced child maltreatment, the findings showed promising results that indeed may be generalizable to the families of child maltreatment. Of the three single-parent child dyads, two of these showed marked improvement after having completed the combined parent training curriculum training. Improvements included more effective parental reinforcement, increased attention behaviors, and decreased child noncompliant behaviors (2013). Parental reinforcement behavior is often a component in parenting training programs when child maltreatment has been identified, and child noncompliant behavior has been shown to increase instances of maltreatment; the ability to demonstrate effectiveness at targeting these behaviors indeed creates an opportunity for further research into the incorporation of this curriculum into the child welfare treatment arsenal.

One of the issues of concern in the treatment of child abuse and neglect is the impact of the legal system on therapeutic accessibility. Irueste-Montes and Montes (1988) examined the effects of voluntary versus court-mandated participation in a child abuse and neglect treatment program. Treatment consisted of a weekly parent training group and a therapeutic day care program for the child. Based on pre- and post-improvements for each group, and facilitation of an observational checklist, the authors concluded that both groups of parents increased the level of praise directed at their children and reduced their level of criticism, but continued to attend to their children's annoying behavior. In other words, the court-ordered nature of some of the parents' involvement did not adversely impact their participation.

Multisystemic therapy is based upon the belief that behavior problems are both multi-determined and multidimensional (Brunk, Henggeler, & Whelan, 1987). Given the multiple barriers often experienced by families who come into contact with Child Welfare Services, this theory seems appropriate. In an attempt to determine efficacy of a multi-systemic therapy approach, 86 families being followed by Child Protective Services due to physical abuse were randomly assigned to two groups of treatment methods: the first receiving Multisystemic Therapy for Child Abuse and Neglect (MST-CAN), the other group receiving Enhanced Outpatient Treatment (EOT) (Swenson, Schaeffer, Henggeler, Faldowski, & Mayhew, 2010). Both treatments were delivered by trained therapists in a community mental health center. At post-treatment follow-up, MST-CAN was found more effective at reducing child mental health symptoms, reducing parent psychiatric distress, and improving social supports for parents (2010). Effects found during this examination showed promising application for child abuse prevention efforts to be delivered within community-based settings that target multiple issues within one environment.

In response to risk factors associated with child maltreatment, much of the intervention literature has focused on child behavior management; the central focus being increased child compliance with parental requests and reduction of child behavior problems (Fantuzzo et al., 2007). Recently, developers of these programs have focused on other aspects of parental well-being, including improvement of parent social skills, expanding social networks and resources of maltreating offenders, and teaching coping skills to reduce the negative impact of daily stressors (Fantuzzo et al., 2007).

Evaluation of Parenting Interventions

In the evaluation of parenting interventions, there is definitional variation in terms such as "parenting training" or "parenting program," which have been used to describe a wide range of program intensities from brief didactic teaching to long-term, comprehensive, multifaceted interventions into diverse aspects of a family's life (Russell et al., 2006). It has been found that parents experience a range of problems when child maltreatment is identified as the primary issue: family disorganization, distrust of child protection services, poverty, physical and/or mental health problems, and/or addictions (Russell et al., 2006). Thus, interventions frequently include a range of other services to target the multiple challenges experienced by parents, sometimes referred to as family preservation services or intensive family preservation services (Russell et al., 2006). According to Russell et al., when families are exposed to different intensities of multiple interventions, evaluation of such service requires a more individualized approach that seeks to understand the components of interventions that parents find beneficial or detrimental (2006).

Behavioral and Cognitive-Behavioral Interventions

Runyon, Deblinger, Ryan, and Thakkar-Kolar (2004) confirm the importance of parent education and skills training as a component of effective treatment for maltreating families; however, they introduce the additional concept of an integrated cognitive-behavioral intervention for both the parent and the child in order to challenge the misattributions of the behavior and response patterns of each individual. Runyon and colleagues describe maltreating behavior as an escalating event that leads to increased distorted thinking that is followed by increased tactics by the parent to control or coerce the desired behavior in the child (2004). Throughout this process, the child in turn becomes conditioned to expect escalated behavior responses from the parent–child relationship and in turn learns maladaptive behaviors as an anticipatory response. Indeed, this heightened response may be interpreted by the parent as defiant behavior, with the parent responding harshly according to the child's learned cognitions (2014).

In order to incorporate all of the necessary components of an integrated cognitive-behavioral approach according to Runyon et al. (2004), parents are first taught the normative adaptive coping skills and nonviolent discipline strategies that are typical of the parent education curriculum. In addition, cognitive coping and appropriate child development education is included, as an accessory to help parents challenge their own misattributions of child maladaptive behavior that lead to aroused negative reactions and perpetuated violence. As therapeutic progression continues, parents learn to bring these new skills into an anger-management and self-control setting, where they can further learn to dispute the negative perceptions of their child's behavior and instead implement developmentally appropriate parenting strategies in a calm (and thus more effective) manner (2004). Initially, these learned skills are taught through modeling of the desired skills by the therapists. Parents then demonstrate these skills in a controlled setting, where they can refine them and receive performance feedback from the therapists. As parents learn to implement these strategies within the home, they are further reinforced by the positive changes in their child's behavior and responses (2004).

Whiteman, Fanshell, and Grundy (1987) reported a study with 14 people from a public agency who had "some credible evidence" of physical abuse and 40 people from a private agency who were thought to be at risk of abuse. Subjects were divided into four different treatment conditions and a control group. The control group continued to receive service from the agencies, but did not receive the treatment interventions: cognitive restructuring, relaxation procedures, problem solving, and a composite package consisting of all three interventions. Treatment took place in the client's own home and was provided by doctoral students, all of whom had graduate degrees in social work.

Results indicated that the composite treatment was the most effective in alleviating anger. However, the authors suggest that the relaxation technique might be omitted from the composite package, as individually it was the least effective. This treatment package is very encouraging, because the gains were made in only six sessions (Whiteman et al., 1987).

A recent study (Kolko, 2002) combined the monitoring of high-risk behaviors during the course of treatment with a comparison of child and parent CBT and family therapy. Participants were randomly assigned to one of the two treatment conditions. CBT was provided for both children and parents by separate therapists using similar treatment protocols. Treatment for the children covered stressors, coping with violence, self-control, and interpersonal skills. The parent treatment included stress and the use of physical punishment, attributions, self-control techniques, and behavioral principles. The family therapy conditions emphasized family functioning and relationships, the enhancement of cooperation, motivation, and an understanding of coercive behavior.

In addition to 12 one-hour-per-week clinic sessions, each condition involved home sessions following every one or two clinic sessions (Kolko, 2002). These home sessions provided the opportunity for review and application of the skills and knowledge developed in the clinic sessions.

Participants in this study consisted of 38 physically abused children from age 6 to –13 and their caregivers. Twenty-nine of the families were referred by CPS. Results indicated that CBT parents and children reported less use of physical discipline during treatment and greater reduction in family problems. In addition, the average length of time until the first use of force or physical discipline was nearly twice as long for the CBT condition (Kolko, 2002).

After a review of the literature identified multiple agreed-upon antecedents to abusive behavior, Azar and Weinzierl (2005) specifically chose to focus on the parent-factors that contributed to a higher risk for maltreatment. Unique to this focus was that Azar and Weinzierl followed the patterns of other maltreatment theorists, in that they did not separate the specific behaviors of parents that lead to neglect or abuse, but instead focused on the broad spectrum of skill deficits that result in inadequate parenting and increased risk of harm to children (2004). The authors present effective intervention points for using cognitive-behavioral restructuring to help the parent identify misattributions of intent (2004).

The premise of cognitive restructuring treatment is the appropriation of parental schemas (developmentally appropriate expectations of the child), effective executive function (ability to assess a situation and apply appropriate behavior modification), and the ability to assess the results of applied tactics to determine efficacy and need for any modification (Azar & Weinzierl, 2005). The authors assert that, even when the most effective parenting skills are learned, the presence of contextual stress can exhaust the parent's ability to execute any one of these processes effectively and the overwhelm the judgment of a well-intentioned parent (2004). In the presence of multiple stressors and challenges for a parent, a child's poor behavior can become overgeneralized into the broader context of the environmental stressors, a misattribution that can cause the parent to react more harshly than what may be appropriate for a specific situation. The therapeutic restructuring in this event includes helping a parent to understand when an overgeneralization has occurred. This was achieved primarily through gentle challenging of an assessment, usually by asking the parent to consider alternative explanations for their child's negative behavior.

Another point of intervention for cognitive restructuring occurs in the perceived control of a parent is thought to be challenged (Azar & Weinzierl, 2005). When parents hold schemas that their role as a parent is to hold the position of power, they can become sensitized to any situation where they perceive that this ultimate control is being challenged, and again, this can result in an over dominant tactic by the parent to regain the power they feel they should possess. Related, another common point of misinterpretation between child and parent that often results in escalating behavior is the use of rule-setting and consistency. Indeed, this is often addressed in parenting education curriculum as well, establishing the need for establishing behavior rules that are developmentally appropriate, contextually appropriate, consistent, and environmentally generalizable. The mutual understanding between the parent and the child over rules of engagement can be a source of misinterpretation and thus increased escalating behaviors.

Finally, this analysis of effective cognitive-behavioral interventions revealed that for many parents at high risk of child maltreatment offenses, the skill deficits exist well before the individual becomes a parent (Azar & Weinzierl, 2005). This finding reiterates the theory that maltreatment behaviors exist within a much broader context than simple parenting inadequacies and thus requires additional interventions to target the full spectrum of contributory behaviors. Social skills that lead to harsher parenting practices such as low coping skills, low interpersonal skills, misguided child development comprehension, and self-regulation can be identified early and contribute to the unrealistic expectations these individuals develop as they become parents. Targeting the unrealistic cognitions present prior to parenting may indeed prevent occurrences of maltreatment from happening (Allen & Hoskowitz, 2016).

Ecological, Family-Centered Perspective

The need to provide effective social services for children and their families at high risk for substance abuse problems has been a growing concern at the federal, state, and local community levels according to Ruffolo, Evans, and Lukens (2003). New models of human service delivery have surfaced (Ruffolo et al., 2003) that (1) encourage the provision of services that deal holistically with the multiple needs of children and families; (2) bring multiple agencies together to provide coordinated services; and (3) develop partnerships between vulnerable families and service providers. The delivery of services that deal holistically with the multiple needs of children and families in the social services system has increasingly focused attention on addressing individual (both biological and psychological), family, neighbor-hood, and broader contextual conditions that produce childhood problems (Ruffolo et al., 2003).

Ecobehavioral Interventions (Project 12 Ways)

Several studies from Project 12 Ways, a multifaceted, in-home assessment and treat-ment service for children of neglect, are worthy of note. Many of the interventions described to ameliorate neglect are, of necessity, very practical in nature; however, this should in no way detract from their contribution to improved well-being for the children involved. For example, in an effort to examine the effect of SafeCare (SC), a promising home-based model for child maltreatment prevention based on Ecobehavioral Interventions, on reductions in future child maltreatment report, researchers conducted a randomized clinical trial. The results exhibited that partici-pants in SC are more likely to remain in service (Silovsky et al., 2011).

Two studies that improved the home safety and cleanliness of client families utilized a treatment and education program also from Project 12 Ways (Barone, Greene, & Lutzker, 1986; Tertinger, Greene, & Lutzker, 1984). The first of these (Tertinger et al., 1984) targeted the reduction of hazards, such as poisons, fire, elec-tricity, suffocation, and firearms. The program was generally successful in the reduction of serious hazards in the homes of six families. The treatment component in this study was to provide these families with educational information about haz-ards, ensuring they are inaccessible to children and determining the number and type of hazards present in the home. An elaboration of this program (Barone et al., 1986) used a 35-mm slide presentation rather than the personalized educational component, as well as stickers, a home safety review manual, safety plates, and electrical tape. Using a multiple-baseline design across the homes and unannounced follow-up visits, the researchers were able to report zero hazards in each home post-intervention.

A common feature of child neglect is the inability or unwillingness of parents to adequately provide a clean home environment. Three families presenting with this problem were assessed using a specifically designed measure, the Checklist for Environments to Assess Neglect (CLEAN; Watson-Perczel, Lutzker, Greene, & McGimpsey, 1988). In a successful effort to improve the personal hygiene and cleanliness of the families who had been adjudicated for child neglect, the authors established multiple baselines using various behavioral techniques, feedback, posi-tive reinforcement, and shaping. Conditions in all three homes were improved upon several months of targeted interactions with each family.

Application of a multifaceted, ecobehavioral approach to the prevention of phys-ical child abuse has also been reported (Campbell, O'Brien, Bickett, & Lutzker, 1983). In-home treatment, consisting of stress reduction, parent training, and behav-ioral marital counseling, was assessed in a single-subject design and determined to be effective in reduction of the mother's migraine headaches and the development of a less coercive environment.

An overall examination of the ecobehavioral services provided by Project 12 Ways (Lutzker & Rice, 1984) looked at the recidivism data from a random sample of former clients, compared with a sample of non-Project clients. Both groups were involved with CPS and had at least one previous incident of child abuse or neglect, or were considered at high risk for such behavior. Results of this study indicated that families who had received service from the Project were less likely to be reported for repeat incidents in the 1-year follow-up period.

Social Network Interventions

A framework for understanding child maltreatment in terms of complex and interacting factors from the individual to the societal level can aid in conceptualizing and implementing prevention efforts (Geeraert, Van den Noortgate, Grietens, & Onghena, 2004; Hay & Jones, 1994). In order to succeed in preventative measures, it will be necessary to also increase the level of investment placed in both the family and the community to be served (Hay & Jones, 1994). At each level of the individual, family, community, environment, culture, and society are both risk and protective factors which have unlimited possibilities of cross-interaction potentially leading to child maltreatment (Geeraert et al., 2004; Hay & Jones, 1994).

In a National Center for Child Abuse & Neglect (NCCAN)-funded study, Gaudin and his colleagues (Gaudin, Wodarski, Arkinson, & Avery, 1990/1991) assessed the effectiveness of social network interventions to reduce neglect, increase the size and supportiveness of informal support networks, and improve parenting knowledge and skills (Gaudin et al., 1990/1991). A culturally diverse sample of families from existing CPS caseloads, in which neglect had been verified, were randomly assigned to one of two conditions. The control group (36 families) received traditional agency services. The treatment group (52 families) received a multicomponent intervention consisting of: (a) direct interventions in the family members' existing relationships to improve the family support network, (b) mutual aid groups, (c) volunteers, (d) the development of relationships with "functionally adequate" (p. 105) neighbors, and (e) social skills training. The median intervention period was 10 weeks and the range was 2–23 months.

Results indicated that the combination of the Social Network Intervention Program combined with intensive casework, advocacy, and case management was successful at 6- and 12-month follow-ups in strengthening informal networks and in improving the parenting efficacy of low-socioeconomic status (SES), neglectful families in both urban and rural settings. The authors stress that, although the research had initially posited the use of the program as an alternative to conventional casework, their experience with this program suggested that it would be more appropriately utilized as an adjunct to traditional services.

Children who are physically maltreated are at risk of a range of adverse outcomes in both childhood and adulthood, according to Jaffee, Caspi, Moffitt, Polo-Tomas, and Taylor (2007). However, some children who experience maltreatment manage to function well despite their history of adversity (2007). Jaffee et al. (2007) also found that for those children who are residing in multi-problem families, personal resources may not be sufficient to promote their adaptive functioning.

Summary

The empirical literature on the treatment of physical abuse and neglect consists of several broad types: child-focused interventions aimed at social and cognitive development; parent-focused interventions; and multiservice or multicomponent treatments. However, the current empirical evidence is still preliminary. These studies contained numerous methodological weaknesses, often arising from the sensitivity and difficulty of research in this area. There was considerable variance in terms of how physical abuse and neglect were reported. This was also true for demographic characteristics of clients, referral sources, and the severity and duration of maltreatment. A major problem with several of the studies was the lack of follow-up to determine the maintenance of any change identified in the treatment phase. The small sample sizes and absence of appropriate controls all contribute to the need for healthy caution in selecting interventions. Differential dropout rates were also a major problem, as group differences may have been due to differences in the remaining participants rather than the treatment itself. Unfortunately, but predictably, the extant research seems to indicate that those likely to remain in treatment are the most motivated and thus the least chronic child abusers (Juretic, 2008).

There are also significant gaps in our own knowledge. For example, most of the studies involving parents were targeted towards mothers, even though fathers and other caregivers are associated with significant numbers of abusive incidents (NCCAN, 1995; Sedlak et al., 2010). There were not any empirical interventions dealing with macrolevel or socioeconomic variables, although the multiservice and social network interventions may have something to offer in this regard in the future. Substance abuse and culturally diverse treatments are also noticeably absent. Even the intervention with the most empirical support (parent training) necessitates being able to specify the cause of maltreatment and the intervention recipient is only assumed to be capable of learning the appropriate skills in the first place. As an illustration, none of these interventions is clinically tested with a client who is seriously psychiatrically disturbed. In fact, this was an exclusion criterion in many of the studies.

With the possible exception of parent training, the current state of the empirical literature makes it virtually impossible to determine the precise impact of individual treatment components. In addition, treatment success has been defined differently, often measured by the learning of a particular behavior, skill, or knowledge, rather than its utilization in a real-world setting, or by the assessment of future abuse. In essence, most of these studies focused on corollary outcomes and because none of these studies identified abuse as the dependent variable, there are no substantial conclusions to be drawn about which treatment was responsible for eliminating abuse. Progress has undoubtedly been made, however, with behavioral and cognitive-behavioral interventions clearly emerging as the treatment of choice for many child, parent, and family-level problems associated with child abuse and neglect.

References

Abidin, R. R. (1986). *Parenting stress index manual*. Charlottesville, VA: Pediatric Psychology Press.

Allen, B., & Hoskowitz, N. A. (2016). Structured trauma-focused CBT and unstructured play/experiential techniques in the treatment of sexually abused children: a field study with practicing clinicians. *Child Maltreatment, 22*, 112–120.

Ammerman, R. T., Hersen, M., & Van Hasselt, V. B. (1988). *The child abuse and neglect interview schedule (CANIS)*. Pittsburgh, PA: Western Pennsylvania School for Blind Children.

Arata, C. M., Langhinrichsen-Rohling, J., Bowers, D., & O'Farrill-Swails, L. (2005). Single versus multi-type maltreatment: An examination of the long-term effects of child abuse. *Journal of Aggression, Maltreatment & Trauma, 11*(4), 29–52.

Ards, S., & Harrel, A. (1993). Reporting of child maltreatment: A secondary analysis of the national incidence surveys. *Child Abuse and Neglect, 17*, 337–344.

Arnow, B. A. (2003). Relationships between childhood maltreatment, adult health and psychiatric outcomes, and medical utilization. *The Journal of Clinical Psychiatry, 65*, 10–15.

Austin, W. G. (2001). Partner violence and risk assessment in child custody evaluations. *Family Court Review, 39*(4), 483–496.

Azar, S. T., Robinson, D. R., Hekimian, E., & Twentyman, C. T. (1984). Unrealistic expectation and problem-solving ability in maltreating and comparison mothers. *Journal of Consulting and Clinical Psychology, 52*, 687–691.

Azar, S. T., & Weinzierl, K. M. (2005). Child maltreatment and childhood injury research: A cognitive behavioral approach. *Journal of Pediatric Psychology, 30*(7), 598–614.

Baird, C., & Wagner, D. (2000). The relative validity of actuarial-and consensus-based risk assessment systems. *Children and Youth Services Review, 22*(11), 839–871.

Barone, V. J., Greene, B. F., & Lutzker, J. R. (1986). Home safety with families being treated for child abuse and neglect. *Behavior Modification, 10*(1), 93–114.

Black, D. A., Heyman, R. E., & Smith Slep, A. M. (2001). Risk factors for child physical abuse. *Aggression and Violent Behavior, 6*(2), 121–188.

Bratton, S. C., Ray, D., Rhine, T., & Jones, L. (2005). The efficacy of play therapy with children: A meta-analytic review of treatment outcomes. *Professional Psychology: Research and Practice, 36*(4), 376.

Briggs, H. E., Miller, K. M., Orellana, E. R., Briggs, A. C., & Cox, W. H. (2013). Effective single-parent training group program: Three system studies. *Research on Social Work Practice, 23*(6), 680–693.

Brunk, M., Henggeler, S. W., & Whelan, J. P. (1987). Comparison of multi-systemic therapy and parent-training in the treatment of child abuse and neglect. *Journal of Consulting and Clinical Psychology, 55*, 171–178.

Caffey, J. (1946). Multiple fractures in the long bones of infants suffering chronic subdural hematoma. *American Journal of Roentgenology, 56*, 163–173.

Caldwell, B. M., & Bradley, R. H. (1978). *Home observation for measurement of the environment.* Little Rock, AR: University of Arkansas.

Campbell, R. V., O'Brien, S., Bickett, A. D., & Lutzker, J. R. (1983). In-home parent training, treatment of migraine headaches, and marital counseling as an eco-behavioral approach to prevent child abuse. *Journal of Behavior Therapy and Experimental Psychiatry, 14*, 147–154.

Cash, S. J. (2001). Risk assessment in child welfare: The art and science. *Children and Youth Services Review, 23*(11), 811–830.

Chaffin, M., & Friedrich, B. (2004). Evidence-based treatments in child abuse and neglect. *Children and Youth Services Review, 26*(11), 1097–1113.

Chan, K. L. (2012). Evaluating the risk of child abuse: The child abuse risk assessment scale. *Journal of Interpersonal Violence, 27*(5), 951–973.

Chen, M., & Chan, K. L. (2016). Effects of parenting programs on child maltreatment prevention: A meta-analysis. *Trauma, Violence, & Abuse, 17*(1), 88–104.

Child Welfare Information Gateway. (2013). *Child maltreatment 2011: Summary of key findings.* Washington, DC: U.S. Department of Health and Human Services, Children's Bureau.

Child Welfare Information Gateway [CWIG] (2019). *Child maltreatment 2017: Summary of key findings.* Washington, DC: U.S. Department of Health and Human Services, Administration for Children and Families, Children's Bureau.

Cloitre, M., Chase Stovall-McClough, K., Miranda, R., & Chemtob, C. M. (2004). Therapeutic alliance, negative mood regulation, and treatment outcome in child abuse-related posttraumatic stress disorder. *Journal of Consulting and Clinical Psychology, 72*(3), 411.

Crouch, J. L., & Behl, L. E. (2001). Relationships among parental beliefs in corporal punishment, reported stress, and physical child abuse potential. *Child Abuse and Neglect, 25*(3), 413–419.

Curtis, P. A., Boyd, J. D., Liepold, M., & Petit, M. (1995). *Child abuse and neglect: A look at the states.* Washington, DC: Child Welfare League of America.

Depanfilis, D. (2005). Child protective services. In G. P. Mallon & P. M. Hess (Eds.), *Child welfare for the 21st century: A handbook of practices, policies, and programs* (pp. 290–301). New York, NY: Columbia University Press.

Dubowitz, H., & Bennett, S. (2007). Physical abuse and neglect of children. *Lancet, 369*, 1891–1899.

Elliott, A. N., & Carnes, C. N. (2001). Reactions of nonoffending parents to the sexual abuse of their child: A review of the literature. *Child Maltreatment, 6*(4), 314–331.

Erickson, M. F., & Egeland, B. (2002). Child neglect. In M. JEB, L. Berliner, J. Briere, C. T. Hendrix, C. Jenny, & T. A. Reid (Eds.), *The APSAC handbook on child maltreatment* (Vol. 2, pp. 3–20). Thousand Oaks, CA: Sage Publications.

Fantuzzo, J., Manz, P., Atkins, M., & Meyers, R. (2005). Peer-mediated treatment of socially withdrawn maltreated preschool children: Cultivating natural community resources. *Journal of Clinical Child and Adolescent Psychology, 34*(2), 320–325.

Fantuzzo, J. W., Stevenson, H., Kabir, S. A., & Perry, M. A. (2007). An investigation of a community-based intervention for socially isolated parents with a history of child maltreatment. *Journal of Family Violence, 22*(2), 81–89.

Fluke, J. D., Shusterman, G. R., Hollinshead, D. M., & Yuan, Y. Y. T. (2008). Longitudinal analysis of repeated child abuse reporting and victimization: Multistate analysis of associated factors. *Child Maltreatment, 13*(1), 76–88.

Fraser, M. W., & Allen-Meares, P. (2004). Intervention with children and adolescents: New hope and enduring challenges. In *Intervention with children and adolescents: An interdisciplinary perspective* (pp. 532–544). Boston, MA: Pearson Allyn & Bacon.

Freisthler, B. (2004). A spatial analysis of social disorganization, alcohol access, and rates of child maltreatment in neighborhoods. *Children and Youth Services Review, 26*(9), 803–819.

Gambrill, E., & Shlonsky, A. (2000). Risk assessment in context. *Children and Youth Services Review, 22*(11), 813–837.

Gardner, R., Hodson, D., Churchill, G., & Cotmore, R. (2014). Transporting and implementing the SafeCare® home-based programme for parents, designed to reduce and mitigate the effects of child neglect: An initial progress report. *Child Abuse Review, 23*(4), 297–303.

Gaudin, J. M., Wodarski, J. S., Arkinson, M. K., & Avery, L. S. (1990/1991). Remedying child neglect: Effectiveness of social network interventions. *Journal of Applied Social Science, 15*, 97–123.

Geeraert, L., Van den Noortgate, W., Grietens, H., & Onghena, P. (2004). The effects of early prevention programs for families with young children at risk for physical child abuse and neglect: A meta-analysis. *Child Maltreatment, 9*(3), 277–291.

Gershater-Molko, R. M., Lutzker, J. R., & Wesch, D. (2003). Project SafeCare: Improving health, safety, and parenting skills in families reported for, and at-risk for child maltreatment. *Journal of Family Violence, 18*(6), 377–386.

Haskett, M. E., Ahern, L. S., Ward, C. S., & Allaire, J. C. (2006). Factor structure and validity of the parenting stress index-short form. *Journal of Clinical Child and Adolescent Psychology, 35*(2), 302–312.

Hay, T., & Jones, L. (1994). Societal interventions to prevent child abuse and neglect. *Child Welfare, 73*(5), 379–403.

Haynes, S. N., & Horn, W. F. (1982). Reactivity in behavioral observation: A review. *Behavioral Assessment, 4*, 369–385.

Higgins, D. (2004). Differentiating between child maltreatment experiences. *Family Matters, 69*, 50–55.

Hudson, W. W. (1990). *The multi-problem screening inventory*. Tempe, AZ: WALMYR.

Hutchison, E. D., & Charlesworth, L. W. (2000). Securing the welfare of children: Policies past, present, and future. *Families in Society: The Journal of Contemporary Social Services, 81*(6), 576–585.

Irueste-Montes, A. M., & Montes, F. (1988). Court-ordered vs. voluntary treatment of abusive and neglectful parents. *Child Abuse & Neglect, 12*, 33–39.

Jaffee, S. R., Caspi, A., Moffitt, T. E., Polo-Tomas, M., & Taylor, A. (2007). Individual, family, and neighborhood factors distinguish resilient from non-resilient maltreated children: A cumulative stressors model. *Child Abuse & Neglect, 31*(3), 231–253.

Joosen, K. J., Mesman, J., Bakermans-Kranenburg, M. J., & van Ijzendoorn, M. H. (2013). Maternal overreactive sympathetic nervous system responses to repeated infant crying predicts risk for impulsive harsh discipline of infants. *Child Maltreatment, 18*(4), 252–263.

Juretic, M. A. (2008). *Predictors of treatment success for parents of abused children* (Doctoral dissertation). University of Utah.

Kanine, R. M., Tunno, A. M., Jackson, Y., & O'Connor, B. M. (2015). Therapeutic day treatment for young maltreated children: A systematic literature review. *Journal of Child & Adolescent Trauma, 8*(3), 187–199.

Kavanaugh, K. A., Youngblade, L., Reid, J. B., & Fagot, B. (1988). Interactions between children and abusive versus control parents. *Journal of Clinical Child Psychology, 17*, 132–142.

Kazak, A. E., Hoagwood, K., Weisz, J. R., Hood, K., Kratochwill, T. R., Vargas, L. A., & Banez, G. A. (2010). A meta-systems approach to evidence-based practice for children and adolescents. *American Psychologist, 65*(2), 85.

Kempe, C., Silverman, F., Steele, B., Droegemueller, W., & Silver, H. (1962). The battered child syndrome. *Journal of the American Medical Association, 181*, 17–24.

Kolko, D. J. (2002). Child physical abuse. In M. JEB, L. Berliner, J. Briere, C. T. Hendrix, C. Jenny, & T. A. Reid (Eds.), *The APSAC handbook on child maltreatment* (Vol. 2, pp. 21–54). Thousand Oaks, CA: Sage Publications.

Lereya, S. T., Copeland, W. E., Costello, E. J., & Wolke, D. (2015). Adult mental health consequences of peer bullying and maltreatment in childhood: Two cohorts in two countries. *The Lancet Psychiatry, 2*(6), 524–531.

Luke, N., & Banerjee, R. (2013). Differentiated associations between childhood maltreatment experiences and social understanding: A meta-analysis and systematic review. *Developmental Review, 33*(1), 1–28.

Lutzker, J. R., & Rice, J. M. (1984). Project 12 ways: Measuring outcome of a large in home service for treatment and prevention of child abuse and neglect. *Child Abuse & Neglect, 8*(4), 519–524.

Lyons, P., & Doueck, H. J. (2009). Child well-being scales as a predictor of casework activity and services in child protection. *Journal of Public Child Welfare, 3*(2), 139–158.

Lyons, P., Doueck, H. J., & Wodarski, J. S. (1996). Risk assessment for child protective services: A review of the empirical literature on instrument performance. *Social Work Research, 20*(3), 143–152.

Macdonald, G. M. (2001). *Effective interventions for child abuse and neglect: An evidence-based approach to planning and evaluating interventions*. Chichester, England: Wiley.

Maguire-Jack, K., & Showalter, K. (2016). The protective effect of neighborhood social cohesion in child abuse and neglect. *Child Abuse & Neglect, 52*, 29–37.

Magura, S., & Moses, B. S. (1986). *Outcome measures for child welfare services: Theory and applications*. Washington, DC: Child Welfare League of America.

Matulis, S., Resick, P. A., rosner, R., & Steil, R. (2014). Developmentally adapted cognitive processing therapy for adolescents suffering from posttraumatic stress disorder after childhood sexual or physical abuse: A pilot study. *Clinical Child and Family Psychology Review, 17*(2), 173–190.

McCurdy, K., & Daro, D. (1993). *Current trends in child abuse reporting and fatalities: The results of the 1992 Annual Fifty State Survey* (working paper number 808). Chicago, IL: National Center on Child Abuse Prevention Research.

Melton, G. B., Thompson, R. A., & Small, M. A. (2002). *Toward a child-centered, neighborhood-based child protection system: A report of the consortium on children, families, and the law*. Westport, CT: Praeger Publishers/Greenwood Publishing Group.

Mersky, J. P., Berger, L. M., Reynolds, A. J., & Gromoske, A. N. (2009). Risk factors for child and adolescent maltreatment: A longitudinal investigation of a cohort of inner-city youth. *Child Maltreatment, 14*(1), 73–88.

Mersky, J. P., Topitzes, J., Grant-Savela, S. D., Brondino, M. J., & McNeil, C. B. (2016). Adapting parent–child interaction therapy to foster care: Outcomes from a randomized trial. *Research on Social Work Practice, 26*(2), 157–167.

Milner, J. S. (1986). Assessing child maltreatment: The role of testing. *Journal of Sociology and Social Welfare, 13*, 64–76.

Morton, T. D., & Salovitz, B. (2006). Evolving a theoretical model of child safety in maltreating families. *Child Abuse & Neglect, 30*(12), 1317–1327.

National Center on Child Abuse and Neglect. (1988). *Study findings. Study of national incidence and prevalence of child abuse and neglect: 1988* (DHHS# 105-85 1702). Washington, DC: U.S. Government Publishing Office.

National Center on Child Abuse and Neglect. (1995). *Child maltreatment 1993 reports from the states to the National Center on Child Abuse and Neglect*. Washington, DC: U.S. Government Printing Office.

Oshri, A., Sutton, T. E., Clay-Warner, J., & Miller, J. D. (2015). Child maltreatment types and risk behaviors: Associations with attachment style and emotion regulation dimensions. *Personality and Individual Differences, 73*, 127–133.

Polansky, N. A., Chalmers, M. A., Buttenweiser, E., & Williams, B. (1981). *Damaged parents: An anatomy of child neglect*. Chicago, IL: University of Chicago Press.

Renner, L. M., & Slack, K. S. (2006). Intimate partner violence and child maltreatment: Understanding intra-and intergenerational connections. *Child Abuse & Neglect, 30*(6), 599–617.

Ruffolo, M. C., Evans, M. E., & Lukens, E. P. (2003). Primary prevention programs for children in the social service system. *The Journal of Primary Prevention, 23*(4), 425–450.

Runyon, M. K., Deblinger, E., Ryan, E. E., & Thakkar-Kolar, R. (2004). An overview of child physical abuse developing an integrated parent-child cognitive-behavioral treatment approach. *Trauma, Violence, & Abuse, 5*(1), 65–85.

Russell, M., Gockel, A., & Harris, B. (2006). Parent perspectives on intensive intervention for child maltreatment. *Child and Adolescent Social Work Journal, 24*, 101–120.

Saint-Jacques, M., Drapeau, S., Lessard, G., & Beaudoin, A. (2006). Parent involvement practices in child protection: A matter of know-how and attitude. *Child and Adolescent Social Work Journal, 23*(2), 196–215.

Sanders, M. R., Pidgeon, A. M., Gravestock, F., Connors, M. D., Brown, S., & Young, R. W. (2004). Does parental attributional retraining and anger management enhance the effects of the triple P-positive parenting program with parents at risk of child maltreatment? *Behavior Therapy, 35*(3), 513–535.

Schaffer, H. R. (2006). The mutuality of parental control in early childhood. *Childhood Socialization*, 45–64.

Schaffer, H. R., & Crooke, C. K. (1979). Maternal control techniques in a directed play situation. *Child Development, 50*, 989–996.

Schaffer, H. R., & Crooke, C. K. (1980). Child compliance and maternal control techniques. *Developmental Psychology, 16*, 54–61.

Sedlak, A. J., Mettenburg, J., Basena, M., Peta, I., McPherson, K., & Greene, A. (2010). *Fourth national incidence study of child abuse and neglect (NIS-4)*. Washington, DC: US Department of Health and Human Services. Retrieved July 9, 2010.

Self-Brown, S., Cowart-Osborne, M., Baker, E., Thomas, A., Boyd, C., Jr., Chege, E., … Lutzker, J. (2015). Dad2K: An adaptation of SafeCare to enhance positive parenting skills with at-risk fathers. *Child & Family Behavior Therapy, 37*(2), 138–155.

Shlonsky, A., & Wagner, D. (2005). The next step: Integrating actuarial risk assessment and clinical judgment into an evidence-based practice framework in CPS case management. *Children and Youth Services Review, 27*(4), 409–427.

Silovsky, J. F., Bard, D., Chaffin, M., Hecht, D., Burris, L., Owora, A., … Lutzker, J. (2011). Prevention of child maltreatment in high-risk rural families: A randomized clinical trial with child welfare outcomes. *Children and Youth Services Review, 33*(8), 1435–1444.

Silverstein, M., Augustyn, M., Young, R., & Zuckerman, B. (2009). *Archives of Disease in Childhood, 94*, 138–143.

Stirling, J., & Amaya-Jackson, L. (2008). Understanding the behavioral and emotional consequences of child abuse. *Pediatrics, 122*(3), 667–673.

Stowman, S. A., & Donohue, B. (2005). Assessing child neglect: A review of standardized measures. *Aggression and Violent Behavior, 10*(4), 491–512.

Swenson, C. C., Schaeffer, C. M., Henggeler, S. W., Faldowski, R., & Mayhew, A. M. (2010). Multisystemic therapy for child abuse and neglect: A randomized effectiveness trial. *Journal of Family Psychology, 24*(4), 497.

Taban, N., & Lutzker, J. R. (2001). Consumer evaluation of an ecobehavioral program for prevention and intervention of child maltreatment. *Journal of Family Violence, 16*(3), 323–330.

Tertinger, D. A., Greene, B. F., & Lutzker, J. R. (1984). Home safety: Development and validation of one component of an ecobehavioral approach. *Journal of Applied Behavior Analysis, 17*, 159–174.

Thompson, R. A. (2015). Social support and child protection: Lessons learned and learning. *Child Abuse & Neglect, 41*, 19–29.

Totsika, V., & Sylva, K. (2004). The HOME observation for measurement of the environment revisited. *Child and Adolescent Mental Health, 9*(1), 25–35.

U.S. Department of Health and Human Services. (2014). *Parental substance abuse and the child welfare system*. Retrieved from http://www.childwelfare.gov/pubs/factsheets/parentalsubabuse.cfm

U.S. Department of Health and Human Services, Administration for Children and Families, Administration on Children, Youth and Families, Children's Bureau. (2017). *Child maltreat-*

ment 2015. Retrieved from http://www.acf.hhs.gov/programs/cb/research-data-technology/statistics-research/child-maltreatment

Vig, S., & Kaminer, R. (2002). Maltreatment and developmental disabilities in children. *Journal of Developmental and Physical Disabilities, 14*(4), 371–386.

Walker, L. E. (2010). Child physical abuse and neglect. In *Handbook of clinical psychology competencies* (pp. 1515–1540). New York, NY: Springer.

Wang, C. T., & Holton, J. (2007). *Total estimated cost of child abuse and neglect in the United States.* Chicago, IL: Prevent Child Abuse America.

Ware, L. M., Novotny, E. S., & Coyne, L. (2001). A therapeutic nursery evaluation study. *Bulletin of the Menninger Clinic, 65*(4), 522–548.

Watson-Perczel, M., Lutzker, J. R., Greene, B. F., & McGimpsey, B. J. (1988). Assessment and modification of home cleanliness among families adjudicated for child neglect. *Behavior Modification, 12*(1), 57–81.

Wayne, R. H. (2008). The best interests of the child: A silent standard—will you know it when you hear it? *Journal of Public Child Welfare, 2*(1), 33–49.

Whiteman, M., Fanshell, D., & Grundy, J. F. (1987). Cognitive-behavioral intervention aimed at anger of parents at risk of child abuse. *Social Work, 32*(6), 469–474.

Whitson, M. A., Martinez, A., Ayala, C., & Kaufman, J. S. (2011). Predictors of parenting and infant outcomes for impoverished adolescent parents. *Journal of Family Social Work, 14*, 284–297.

Widom, C. S., Czaja, S., & Dutton, M. A. (2014). Child abuse and neglect and intimate partner violence victimization and perpetration: A prospective investigation. *Child Abuse & Neglect, 38*(4), 650–663.

Widom, C. S., Czaja, S. J., & DuMont, K. A. (2015). Intergenerational transmission of child abuse and neglect: Real or detection bias? *Science, 347*(6229), 1480–1485.

Windham, A. M., Rosenberg, L., Fuddy, L., McFarlane, E., Sia, C., & Duggan, A. K. (2004). Risk of mother-reported child abuse in the first 3 years of life. *Child Abuse & Neglect, 28*(6), 645–667.

Wodarski, J. S. (2015). Assessment and Practice. In J. S. Wodarski, M. J. Holosko, & M. D. Feit (Eds.). *Evidence-Informed Assessment and Practice in Child Welfare.* New York: Springer.

Wolfe, D. A., Edwards, B., Manion, I., & Koverola, C. (1988). Early interventions for parents at risk of child abuse and neglect: A preliminary investigation. *Journal of Consulting and Clinical Psychology, 56*, 40–47.

Chapter 3
Educationally Disadvantaged Children

Catherine N. Dulmus, John S. Wodarski, and Fan Yang

The future economic viability of the USA is in jeopardy due to poor educational outcomes for a large percentage of its young citizens. With 25% truancy and drop-out rates for elementary, middle, and high school students, we can expect that not enough educated individuals will be available to fill the jobs in the twenty-first century (Cabrera & La Nasa, 2001). Furthermore, a number of reports, e.g., *Measuring Up: The National Report Card on Higher Education* (National Center for Public Policy and Higher Education, 2008), *A Nation at Risk: The Imperative for Educational Reform* (National Commission on Excellence in Education, 1983), *The Death and Life of the Great American School System* (Ravitch, 2010), *Winning the Future: A 21st Century Contract with America* (Gingrich, 2006), *Waiting for "Superman"* (Chilcott & Guggenheim, 2010), and *Time to Start Thinking: America in the Age of Decent* (Luce, 2012), document the number of US citizens who enroll in post-secondary education and graduate at 33%. These numbers are sorely inadequate to fill 20 million jobs expected to be available by the year 2030 for individuals with college degrees (Friedman & Mandelbaum, 2011; Moore et al., 2010).

School spending figures place the USA first in the world among industrialized countries in the dollar amount spent per child on public education. In 2008–2009, the amount the school systems spent rose 46% comparatively from 10 years before (National Center for Education Statistics, 2012). Unfortunately, the USA also continues to lead other developed countries in rates of teen pregnancy, single parenthood, and poverty (Hobbs & Lippman, 1990). These problems, along with substance

C. N. Dulmus (✉)
School of Social Work, University of Buffalo, Buffalo, NY, USA
e-mail: cdulmus@buffalo.edu

J. S. Wodarski
College of Social Work, University of Tennessee, Knoxville, TN, USA

F. Yang
Dongbei University of Finance and Economics, Dalian Shi, Liaoning Sheng, China

© Springer Nature Switzerland AG 2019

J. S. Wodarski, L. M. Hopson (eds.), *Empirically Based Interventions Targeting Social Problems*, https://doi.org/10.1007/978-3-030-28487-9_3

abuse, truancy, and violence in our schools, place America's youth at risk of dropping out without obtaining the minimal education and skills that the job market demands of them today. The Glory of Education Reform (2013) state:

> The term at-risk is often used to describe students or groups of students who are considered to have a higher probability of failing academically or dropping out of school. The term may be applied to students who face circumstances that could jeopardize their ability to complete school, such as homelessness, incarceration, teenage pregnancy, serious health issues, domestic violence, transiency (as in the case of migrant-worker families), or other conditions, or it may refer to learning disabilities, low test scores, disciplinary problems, grade retentions, or other learning-related factors that could adversely affect the educational performance and attainment of some students. While educators often use the term at-risk to refer to general populations or categories of students, they may also apply the term to individual students who have raised concerns—based on specific behaviors observed over time—that indicate they are more likely to fail or drop out.

Shanker (1994) reports that the biggest problem facing US educators today is massive underachievement among all students throughout the system, at all levels. An April 1983 report entitled *A Nation at Risk* was released which warned that the USA is "menaced by a rising tide of mediocrity" in its schools and education system and that the nation had best make every effort to set matters right or it will be in serious trouble (Finn & Walberg, 1994).

Students in the USA continue to rank near the bottom of industrialized countries in achievement scores. The school-year length remains at 175–180 days, the shortest among industrialized nations even though research supports a longer school year. Current per-student costs peaked in 2008–2009 academic year at $11,621. After that, the cost decreased each year and reached $11,011 at the academic year of 2014–2015 (Kena et al., 2016).

Children who do not complete their high school educations have disadvantages in a high-tech society such as that of the USA. Although a variety of risk factors are associated with dropping out of school, this chapter's discussion is limited to the following: underachievement, truancy, teen pregnancy, substance abuse, juvenile violence, and poverty. In addition, empirically based interventions are discussed.

The future economic viability of the USA is in jeopardy due to poor educational outcomes for a large percentage of its young citizens. That is in terms of 25% truancy and dropout rates. The outcome will be that not enough educated individuals will be available to fill jobs in the twenty-first century (Cabrera & La Nasa, 2001).

A number of reports, Measuring Up, Before it's too Late, Nation at Risk, The Death and Life of the Great American School System, Winning the Future, Waiting for Superman, and Time to Start Thinking: America in the Age of Descent, state that the number of US Citizens who enroll in post-secondary education and graduate is 33%. This graduation rate is not adequate to fill 20 million jobs that are going to be available by the year 2030 for individuals with college degrees (Friedman & Mandelbaum, 2011).

Overview

Public schools in the USA were instituted after the War of Independence by political and educational leaders of the time in order to educate the new nation's children to assume the responsibilities of citizenship in a democracy (Goodlad, 1994). The US Constitution leaves to the states the responsibility for developing and guiding public education. This has resulted in a great variability in the programs and practices of the thousands of school in the USA, with certain school districts providing better education than others for their students.

School conditions must be considered when examining educationally disadvantaged children. Sometimes school conditions can actually create disadvantages for at-risk student through inappropriate instruction, competitive learning environments, ability grouping, and hostile classroom environments (Manning & Baruth, 1995).

Societal factors also contribute to the problem, as children and adolescents are often pushed to engage in adult behaviors and consumer habits. The tendency of US society to be racist and sexist and to discriminate against culturally diverse groups, females, and people with disabilities adds to the educational disadvantages of these children and adolescents. Personal factors associated with educational disadvantages on the part of an individual student might include a lower self-concept, a lower ability level, a lack of motivation, and a decision to experiment with drugs and alcohol (Collins, McLeod, & Kenway, 2000).

Certainly, social workers are concerned about educationally disadvantaged children. School social workers' days are often spent addressing problems that interfere with student learning among such children. Educationally disadvantaged children fill social workers' caseloads in a variety of social work settings. Often, many of the adults social workers encounter were once educationally disadvantaged children themselves. Children in stable environments are more likely to have positive outcomes and children in unstable or detrimental home environments had more deleterious outcomes. Some noted effects of these outcomes are delayed development (Rubin, O'Reilly, Luan, & Localio, 2007), poor academic achievement, and lack of interpersonal skills (Jones, 2004). Studies have found that children with stable environments perform better academically, are more likely to have positive relationships with peers, and have fewer behavior problems (Jones, 2004).

Dropping Out of School

Experts increasingly realize that completion of high school is the absolute minimum educational level necessary to prepare youngsters for the vast majority of jobs in the modern US economy. During 2014, 6.5% of students dropped out of school (Kena et al., 2016). Levin and Belfield (2007) report that the average high school dropout costs $260,000 in lost productivity and forgone taxes during the course of his or her lifetime.

In 2013, 17% of 16 to 24 year olds who were status dropouts were unemployed and 42% were not in the labor force (McFarland, Stark, & Cui, 2016). There is an overrepresentation among school dropouts of students from some minority groups, which has contributed to growing concern that large segments of the US population may be isolated from mainstream social, political, and economic life if they fail to attain the basic education represented by the high school diploma (Natriello, 1995).

Natriello (1995) reports that factors associated with dropping out of school are many, but can be classified by at least three different types of antecedents: characteristics of individual students, characteristics of their schools, and the wider environments in which both the students and the schools exist. Characteristics of individuals that can be linked to nonattendance at school include racial and ethnic minority status, poor school performance, low self-esteem, low socioeconomic status, delinquency, a history of substance abuse, pregnancy, a non-English-speaking family, a single-parent family, and a family that is less involved in the educational process (Balfanz et al., 2014; De Witte, Cabus, Thyssen, Groot, & van den Brink, 2013). The lack of a "caring culture" within the school is another reason for children dropping out. This can be circumvented by the school system creating an environment where the child is respected and important. The steps to create a caring culture include seeing the child as unique, being empathetic and non-reactive were among the list (Cassidy & Bates, 2005).

The USA has a dropout rate of 6.5% at 2014 (Kena et al., 2016). Smith (1988) estimates that 12 million youngsters will become high school dropouts by the year 2000. The implications are serious. Students who drop out are five times more likely to face unemployment than those with diplomas, and those from diverse cultures fare even worse in the job market (McFarland et al., 2016). In the year 2000, the dropout rate among high school students in the USA is 9.8% or 1.6 million (U.S. Bureau of the Censes, 2000).

The following section examines specific risk factors associated with an increase in the number of children who drop out of school, becoming educationally disadvantaged youth.

Risk Factors

Underachievers

As previously stated, the achievement scores of students in the USA continue to rank near the bottom among those of students from industrialized countries. Underachievement, or failing to achieve at one's potential, is a common problem facing both students at risk for educational disadvantages and their educators (Manning & Baruth, 1995) In 1985, 30.3% of 15-year-old males and 25.2% of

15-year-old females were one or more grade level behind in school (Children's Defense Fund, 1988). Murphy (1990) reports that 18% of US high school seniors read at least 4 years below grade level, approximately 13% of 17 year olds may be functionally illiterate, and 50% of 13 year olds do not have a good grasp of elemental scientific concepts. Among high school seniors, nearly 40% lack the ability to draw logical inferences from written material, 20% cannot write a persuasive essay, and 33% cannot correctly solve multi-step mathematical problems. Up to 20% of all students are retained in grade at least once at some time in their school careers (Meisels & Liaw, 1993), and, on average, 25% of students drop out of high school (National Center for Education Statistics, 1991). Underachieving students who do not learn to their potential are often educationally disadvantaged children. They do not acquire the necessary knowledge and skills to be gainfully employed upon graduating from school, which negatively impacts their future.

Poverty

The USA has the highest poverty rate of all industrialized nations. Poverty in childhood can translate into poorer health condition, weaker school performance, and greater chances in adulthood (Smeeding & Thévenot, 2016). In 2007, 13 million children were in poverty, and this number will likely continue to grow (Griffith et al., 2010). The USA ranks first among developed nations in rates of children poverty, with a rate of over 20% (Smeeding & Thévenot, 2016). Child poverty varies with age. In most nations, including the USA, the youngest children have the highest poverty rates (Smeeding & Thévenot, 2016). One fourth of the children in the USA spent part or all their early, developmentally critical years living in poverty (Erwin, 1996).

The task of educating children of poverty has long been recognized as difficult. Knapp and Shields (1990) state:

> Many of these children and adolescents perform poorly on academic tasks. Likewise, the school, serving large numbers of these children and adolescents, faces a variety of problems that pose barriers to providing high-quality education such as high rates of mobility among learners' families, a high prevalence of severe emotional and behavioral problems among students, large number of students with limited English proficiency, low staff morale, and inadequate facilities and resources. (p. 19)

It is no wonder that poor teenagers are three times more likely to drop out of school than nonpoor teenagers (Children's Defense Fund, 1991). Children from impoverished families normally enter schools with limited resources decreasing the opportunities they have to reach their potential. This extends the risk factors poverty creates for these children (Skiba, Poloni-Staudinger, Simmons, Feggins-Azziz, & Chung, 2005). Carlson (2006) found that poverty significantly predicts the "direct exposure to school violence" (p. 91).

Teen Pregnancy

About half of American teenagers are sexually active by the time they leave high school, and one in four young women has experienced a pregnancy (Kenny, 1987). By the age of 19, a majority of adolescents have engaged in sexual activity (Upadhya & Ellen, 2011). Between 1960 and 1993, the birth rate for American teenagers rose nearly 200% (Schinke, 1997). It was estimated in 1985 that roughly 1 million teenage girls become pregnant every year, resulting in 600,000 live births and 378,500 pregnancies terminated by abortion (Guttmacher Institute, 1985). Presently, 1 in 10 babies is born to an unmarried teenage mother in the USA (Center for the Study of Social Policy, 1993). The USA has the highest rate of both teenage pregnancy and sexually transmitted diseases among developed nations (Stanger-Hall & Hall, 2011).

Schinke (1997) reports the social costs of teenage childbearing and parenthood as tremendous, stating, "Teenage mothers have more health problems, attain less education, and realize lower wages" (p. 5). Of unmarried teens who give birth, 73% will be on welfare within 4 years (Carnegie Council on Adolescent Development, 1989). Barth, Middleton, and Wagman (1989) summarized the evidence on youth pregnancy, stating that 20% of all teens have unintended pregnancies, with teenage pregnancy remaining the major reason for students leaving school. Eighty percent of all teenage mothers report that their pregnancies were not wanted.

Teenage mothers are more likely to become welfare recipients, less likely to finish high school, and less likely to marry than other women (Ellwood, 1988). Forty-seven percent of girls who drop out of school because they are pregnant never return to school (Schorr, 1988). When adolescents' schooling is disrupted by pregnancy, their financial futures are limited not only for themselves, but also for their offspring.

Juvenile Violence

The USA has the highest homicide rate in the world (Fingerhut & Kleinman, 1990). In 2014, each day in the USA, 12 children are murdered, and 69 children are arrested for violent crimes (Center for Disease Control, 2016). Children and adolescents are twice as likely as adults to be victims of crime (Manning & Baruth, 1995). One survey found that from 1982 to 1984, youths from age 12 to 19 were the victims of 1.8 million violent crimes and 3.7 million thefts per year (Vandrer Zanden, 1989). The Office of Technology Assessment (1991) reports that adolescents in the USA are more likely to be victims of violent crimes than individuals from other age groups.

In recent years, youths age 18 and younger have accounted for about 20% of all arrests for violent crimes in the USA, 44% of all arrests for serious property violations, and 39% of overall arrests for serious crime (Manning & Baruth, 1995). Earls (1994) reports that 20% of all adolescents report having engaged in at least one violent act prior to age 18. Incidents of violence committed by adolescents have now become almost routine and commonplace. How does this increase in juvenile violence impact education in US schools?

Manning and Baruth (1995) report that approximately 28,200 students are physically attacked in US secondary schools each month. In addition, almost 8% of middle school and high school students missed at least 1 day of school per month because they were afraid to go to school. About one-third of all violent crimes against younger teenagers and 83% of the thefts occur in school, whereas older teenagers are the victims of 14% of the violent crime and 42% of the thefts at school (Vandrer Zanden, 1989). In the USA, one in four students report of being victims of bullying and one in five students admit to bullying other students (Lumsden, 2002). It is reported that each day, approximately 160,000 students stay home from school due to the fear of being bullied (Vail, 1999).

In recent years, school violence has extended to cyber bullying. The implications of bullying have amplified as teenagers have increased their use of technology. Sixty-three percent of teenagers access the internet daily and 88% of adolescents use text messaging. Changes in mood, mental health problems, substance abuse, and school difficulties all increase with cyber bullying. The effects can be even more detrimental than traditional bullying (Mishna, Khoury-Kassabri, Gadalla, & Daciuk, 2012). How can young people focus on achieving an education when they are victims or perpetrators of violence in their school?

Truancy

Truancy is defined as an unlawful absence from school without the parents' knowledge or permission (Hersov & Berg, 1980). Schultz (1987) defines truancy as excessive unexcused absences. Truancy directly affects student, educational institutions, and society in general (Bell, Rosen, & Dynlacht, 1994). It is estimated that 10–19% of school children are truant (Sommer, 1985). Nearly 11% of eighth graders and 16% of tenth graders reported recent truancy (Henry, 2007). Truancy tends to be a large problem in urban areas, with some school systems reporting thousands of unexcused absences daily (Spencer, 2009).

The most obvious and immediate implication of truancy is reflected in the truant's academic deficits. If students are not attending school, it is virtually impossible for them to receive the instruction they need to earn passing grades and graduate from high school (Bell et al., 1994). Also associated with truancy are juvenile criminal behavior, loitering, vandalism, and drug and alcohol abuse (Schultz, 1987). Truancy is further associated with lower status occupations, less stable career patterns, and more unemployment in adulthood (Gray, Smith, & Rutter, 1980). Truancy is highly correlated with school dropout rates (Rutter, Maugham, Mortimore, & Ouston, 1979). Truancy is the principal risk factor for many of the other problems disadvantaged youth are facing including teenage pregnancy, substance abuse, and social isolation (Spencer, 2009). Teasley (2004) suggests that social factors, personal factors, developmental factors, family and parental factors, and neighborhood and community factors may contribute toward truant behaviors.

Substance Abuse

The use and abuse of alcohol and other drugs by adolescents are significant problems today and continue to drain communities in the USA of human potential and financial resources (Johnson, O'Malley, & Bachman, 1994). In 2016, 17.6% eighth graders consumed alcohol daily, 0.7% used marijuana daily, and 0.9% used cigarette daily (National Institute on Drug Abuse, 2016). By 2003, nearly 51% of high school students said they used illicit drugs and 28% reported drinking alcohol heavily with five or more drinks in a row (Sabri, Williams, Smith, Jang, & Hall, 2010). In a recent national survey, 51% of high school seniors reported using alcohol in the past 30 days (Johnson et al., 1994).

Substance use among adolescents appears to be influenced by a multitude of factors, including peers, family, school environment, and community (Lee et al., 2014; Sneed, Mehdiyoun, Matsumura, & Hess, 2015). Education-related risk factors for substance abuse include poor school performance and lack of commitment to school, low perceived expectations for education or career options, the marginal quality of the educational environment, and limited access to educational and career options (Dryfoos, 1990).

Effective Interventions

Educationally disadvantaged children should be assessed for identified risk factors, and empirically proven interventions, as they exist, should be carried out (Dulmus & Wodarski, 1997). To date, preventative interventions to address many risk factors are suggested by the literature. The prevention approach to intervention has implications for the traditional role of social work practitioners and the timing of the intervention (Wodarski, Smokowski, & Feit, 1996). The prevention approach places major emphasis on the teaching and skills-building components of the intervention process (Wodarski & Bagarozzi, 1979). Social workers do not take a passive role in the intervention process, but instead attempt to help clients learn how to exert control over their own behaviors and over the environments in which they live (Wodarski et al., 1996). Prevention is especially appropriate to dealing with the problems of adolescence. The following section reviews prevention approaches to handling the issues of poverty, teen pregnancy, juvenile violence, truancy, and substance abuse as they affect educationally disadvantaged children. A study found, although to a limited degree, that the school's physical environment contributes to reduction of problem behaviors among students (Kumar, O'Malley, & Johnston, 2008). Kumar et al. (2008) states "a positive school environment appears to encourage their [students] involvement in school by significantly decreasing the likelihood of truant behavior" (p. 479). Cassidy and Bates (2005) agree with a positive school environment and when a school cares for a student, they are reducing the risk of school failure, and dropping out of school.

Poverty

The best single predictor of future academic performance is early academic performance. Children in poverty enter school at a deficit when compared to middle class children. For example, poor children's vocabulary consists of 4000 words compared to 12,000 for middle class children. By the age of 4, children from professional families have heard 45 million words, middle class children have heard 26 million words, and children in poverty have only heard 13 million words (Roseberry-McKibbin, 2008). The disadvantage children in poverty face can be eased by preschool.

Prevention of learning problems depends on early intervention and should occur before children from low-income households, who are at greater risk for such problems, reach elementary school (Durlak, 1995). Head Start, an early education program targeted for preschool children living in poverty, has been successful in addressing academic problems associated with poverty (Lacy, 2014). Head Start is based on encouraging or developing the inherent adaptive abilities of children. A multi-component program includes early childhood education, home visits, parenting educating, and socialization, which may assist some children in developing or maintaining resiliency. Even Start, a federally funded demonstration project, is a family literacy program that holds promise for children and families from disadvantaged backgrounds. Although it is a similar to Head Start, it is more comprehensive and intensive, working with the entire family until the youngest child reaches age 8. This provides long-term programming and support to vulnerable children and their families (Dulmus & Wodarski, 1997). The outcomes for the child have been improved ability to read at grade level, school attendance, grade retention and promotion. There are also benefits for the parents and families by children participating in preschool programs like Even Start (Chico, 2011).

Teen Pregnancy

Schinke (1997) reports that, to date, most teen pregnancy prevention programs have been ineffective. Although programs have focused on trying to help teenagers avoid unprotected intercourse in an attempt to delay childbearing, a report from the US General Accounting Office (1995) concludes that teen pregnancy prevention programs have not been successful in preventing first or subsequent pregnancies.

Effective school-based prevention programs identified by Bennett and Assefi (2005) share five common components: (a) focusing on behavioral goals that lead to pregnancy prevention, (b) using learning principles to guide intervention, (c) informing youths about risks and prevention of unprotected intercourse through experiential activities, (d) addressing social and media influences, and (e) reinforcing norms against unprotected sex. Each of these components, combined with cognitive-behavioral approaches, such as educational materials and skills-building exercises, has had limited success in teen pregnancy prevention programs.

Schinke (1997) states, "New directions are needed to meet the challenges of reaching, engaging, and impacting today's youth with pregnancy prevention content" (p. 8). He further states that teen pregnancy involves multiple dimensions that require multiple solutions. He suggests that matching prevention programs to different adolescent populations, grouped according to risk, may hold greater promise. Further research is necessary to develop such programs.

Juvenile Violence

Both micro and macro approaches are currently recommended to address risk factors associated with juvenile violence. In a systematic review, Vries, Hoeve, Assink, Stams, and Asscher (2015) examined 39 juvenile violence prevention programs and revealed that parenting skills and behavioral contracting are significantly associated with better program outcomes. In addition, programs involving juveniles, parents, and siblings showed better effect that programs targeting the juveniles only. The setting has an impact on the outcome. Programs carried in the courts have less effect than programs in direct environments like schools, homes, community, and ambulant setting. Programs containing these components yielded better results.

Psychoeducation on bullying needs to be an ongoing goal within the school system. Teachers and students should learn the warning signs of bullying and know how to respond to the violence. With teachers knowing how to respond, they can take responsibility of stopping the bullying rather than referring the student to a counselor or social worker. The teacher is in closer vicinity of the students throughout the day, making them a crucial element in the reduction of bullying (Newman-Carlson & Horne, 2004). Research and psychoeducation needs to be targeted toward new forms of bullying, such as cyber-bullying, so school professionals will know how to respond (Mishna et al., 2012).

Rapp and Wodarski (1997) report that individual and family interventions will do little to ameliorate juvenile violence without the help of the community, which necessitates the need for macro interventions also. They recommend after-school recreational activities, sports clinics, job skills and training workshops, educational tutoring, and social activities as means of prevention. The use of metal detectors and an increase in security personnel in schools have been shown to decrease the incidents of weapons possession and conflicts between students (Wilson & Howell, 1995). Additional recommended macro approaches to prevent juvenile violence include community policing and legislation specific to the sale and possession of firearms (Rapp & Wodarski, 1997).

Truancy

Because truancy is a problem with multiple causes and impacts, interventions for truant behavior have been targeted at three areas: the individual truant, the family of the truant, and the educational institution (Bell et al., 1994).

Individual interventions to date have targeted low self-esteem, conduct disorders, nonconformist behaviors, lower academic abilities, and lack of motivation (Bell et al., 1994). In-school suspension incorporating counseling, writing therapy, and contingency contracting (Miller, 1986) and supportive instruction (Grala & McCauley, 1976) have been shown to improve school attendance and attitudes toward school.

A family intervention typically attempts to either alter a dysfunctional family situation or simply achieve more parental involvement in the child's education (Bell et al., 1994). School-based interventions have decreased truancy through lottery systems for perfect attendance (Rogers, 1980), contingency contracting (Brooks, 1974), and revised attendance policies (Duckworth, 1988). It is important that any truancy prevention program be multimodal, incorporating the individual, the family, and the school.

Another effective intervention is Check & Connect, a model created by the Institute on Community Integration, University of Minnesota. This model is designed to promote student engagement, support regular attendance, and improve the likelihood of school completion (Maynard, Kjellstrand, & Thompson, 2014).

Another area for prevention measures is working with youth who are bilingual. A major risk factor of being truant is English being a youth's second language. This risk factor among others should be targeted and addressed before truancy becomes an issue. The risk factors can be eased by the emotional support provided by the school personal (Spencer, 2009). A caring culture in a school setting helps children rise above their current deficits (Cassidy & Bates, 2005).

Substance Abuse

Although some progress has been made in the prevention of adolescent substance abuse, the problem remains a critical one for society (Wodarski & Smyth, 1994). When concentrating on the prevention of adolescent substance abuse, it is essential that intervention goals be clearly defined and that an appropriate target audience for intervention be selected (Bukowski, 1991). Programs would be more successful if they emphasized early interventions, drug resistance skills training, parent involvement, peer involvement, healthy school climate, social and life skills training, and communitywide planning, intervention, and coordination (Schinke, Botvin, & Orlandi, 1991). In addition, current research points toward a prevention model that is a multifaceted, ecological approach to dysfunctional adolescent behavior as holding much promise (Norman & Turner, 1993).

Because children and adolescents spend the major portion of their youth in the school setting, schools may be the sensible place to implement prevention programs (Wodarski & Smyth, 1994). A unique adolescent education program that is easily administered in a school setting is Teams-Games-Tournaments, or TGT (Wodarski, 1988). The TGT technique is an innovative, small group technique. Research (Chambers & Abrami, 1991; Niehoff & Mesch, 1991; Wodarski, 1988; Wodarski,

Wodarski, & Parris, 2004) has shown the TGT method to be a highly effective prevention strategy for alcohol and drug abuse. The TGT technique has been developed and proved an effective classroom method for adolescents. According to the developer, and supported by research data, TGT is especially helpful in teaching adolescents about behavior that puts them at high risk for educational disadvantage. It is also helpful in teaching adolescents how to make better decisions regarding these behaviors. Using the TGT technique, all students have an opportunity to succeed because all students compete against members of other teams who are at similar achievement levels. Points earned by low achievers are just as valuable to the overall team as points earned by high achievers. By using peer influence in a positive way (Swadi & Zeitlin, 1988), TGT capitalizes on one of the primary elements in an adolescent's life, thereby increasing social attachments and facilitating the acquisition of knowledge and behavior change (Wodarski & Wodarski, 1993). When compared with those receiving traditional instruction or no instruction, participants in the TGT method achieved superior results on the self-report indexes; they increased their drug and alcohol knowledge; and they showed a reduction in drinking behavior, positive shifts relating to drinking and driving, reduced impulsivity, and improved self-concept (Wodarski, 1988).

Macro approaches are also necessary in the prevention of substance abuse among youth. Raising the alcohol purchase age to 21 has resulted in a decrease in alcohol-related highway deaths to date among both adults and youth. Data suggest that in states where a lower blood-alcohol limit for adolescent drinking drivers has been legislated, alcohol-related crashes among youth have decreased (Hingson, 1993). Researchers continue to advocate for a raise in the age of alcohol consumption to reduce the violence surrounding the usage (Martin & Bryant, 2001).

When looking at the macro level, social workers need to engage communities in the process of reducing youths use of substances. CASASTART is a program which targets youth in urban areas. It is school and neighborhood based, allowing the intervention to be applied in all areas in which the adolescent interacts. It works with children from the ages of 8–13, to prevent aggression and further substance use. The program offers help in various forms, such as social support, family services, educational services, after-school and summer recreational activities, mentoring incentives, community policing, and criminal/juvenile justice interventions. The children are provided with case managers for up to 2 years and the services are adjusted for the individual person. The children who complete CASASTART (Striving Together to Achieve Rewarding Tomorrows, formerly known as Children at Risk) are less likely to use marijuana and alcohol, and other substance related activities (Lisha, Pokhrel, & Sussman, 2014).

Another community program is Communities That Care (CTC). This program has adopted a public health approach which is adjusted for the specific community. The goal is to reduce the identified risk factors in the community by promoting the protective factors. The members of the community are the ones who identify the risk and protective factors and who determine what steps need to be pursued, allowing the members to be the expert of their community. Community leaders are identified, trained, and begin the process of forming a board and task groups. After the board identifies the strengths and weaknesses of the community in relation to substance abuse, task groups implement evidence-based interventions in which they have been trained. CTC has been proven to be successful with several hundred communities utilizing it and many communities continue CTC beyond the first 4 years (Brown, Hawkins, Arthur, & Briney, 2011; Hawkins, Catalano, & Arthur, 2002).

Parental monitoring is a key factor which may prevent drug involvement or decrease drug use in adolescents even after a drug pattern has been established (Liddle et al., 2001). Improving or adding protective factors may buffer the risk factors that are influencing drug use (Liddle et al., 2001). Newer treatment strategies such as multisystemic therapy (MST), functional therapy, motivational interviewing, community reinforcement, the 12-step approach, and cognitive-behavioral therapy show reduction in drug abuse but studies done have not been able to determine which is superior in short- and long-term outcomes (Kaminer, 2001; Van Der Stouwe, Asscher, Stams, Deković, & Van Der Laan, 2014). MST is able to focus on multiple risk factors rather than some interventions that are limited to the amount of risk factors (Henggeler, Schoenwald, Rowland, & Cunningham, 2002). MST has been applied to adolescents with serious clinical problems such as substance abuse, chronic and violent offenders, mistreat family members, and sexual offenders (Henggeler & Lee, 2003). MST aims at the importance of improving protective factors which can maintain therapeutic change (Henggeler et al., 2002).

The literature indicates that a multifaceted, comprehensive approach to substance abuse among youth, incorporating multiple systems, is recommended.

Conclusion

Many adolescents are not completing high school today for a variety of reasons. Others are graduating but lack necessary literacy skills to obtain gainful employment. The impact this has on both the individual and society as a whole is astounding. Multifaceted prevention programs are recommended to address many of the risk factors associated with educationally disadvantaged children, in an attempt to decrease the number of students who drop out of school and to increase the literacy skills among our youth. Social workers must continue to address the risk factors associated with educationally disadvantaged children in the USA and develop empirically based interventions to assist their young clients.

Comprehensive, research-based mentoring programs, substantial in length and emphasizing skills development, are believed to be the most viable means to achieve higher graduation rates (DuBois, Portillo, Rhodes, Silverthorn, & Valentine, 2011). These programs are intended to improve the educational and employment outlook for at-risk US youth through the initiation of a comprehensive intervention designed to improve university enrollment and graduations rates. The intervention emphasizes life skills development and employment preparation delivered through a collegiate mentoring program. These programs propose a holistic approach that responds not only to the problem of preparing high-risk youths for college but prepares them for subsequent employment as well.

References

Balfanz, R., Bridgeland, J. M., Fox, J. H., DePaoli, J. L., Ingram, E. S., & Maushard, M. (2014). *Building a grad nation: Progress and challenge in ending the high school dropout epidemic. Annual update 2014*. Washington, DC: Civic Enterprises.

Barth, R. P., Middleton, K., & Wagman, E. (1989). A skill building approach to preventing teenage pregnancy. *Theory Into Practice, 28*(3), 183–190.

Bell, A. J., Rosen, L. A., & Dynlacht, D. (1994). Truancy intervention. *The Journal of Research and Development in Education, 27*(3), 203–211.

Bennett, S. E., & Assefi, N. P. (2005). School-based teenage pregnancy prevention programs: A systematic review of randomized controlled trials. *Journal of Adolescent Health, 36*(1), 72–81.

Brooks, B. D. (1974). Contingency contracts with truants. *Personnel and Guidance Journal, 52*, 316–320.

Brown, E. C., Hawkins, J. D., Arthur, M. W., & Briney, J. S. (2011). Prevention service system transformation using communities that care. *Journal of Community Psychology, 39*(2), 183–201.

Bukowski, W. J. (1991). A framework for drug abuse prevention research. In C. G. Leukefeld & W. J. Bukoski (Eds.), *Drug abuse prevention intervention research: Methodological issues.* (NIDA Research Monograph 107, DHHS Pub. No. ADM 91-1761, pp. 7–28). Rockville, MD: National Institute on Drug Abuse.

Cabrera, A. F., & La Nasa, S. M. (2001). On the path to college: Three critical tasks facing America's disadvantaged. *Research in Higher Education, 42*(2), 119–149.

Carlson, K. T. (2006). Poverty and youth violence exposure: Experiences in rural communities. *Children & Schools, 28*(2), 87–96.

Carnegie Council on Adolescent Development. (1989). *Turning points: Preparing American youth for the 21st century*. Washington, DC: Author.

Cassidy, W., & Bates, A. (2005). "Drop-outs" and "push-outs": Finding hope at a school that actualizes the ethic of care. *American Journal of Education, 112*(1), 66–102.

Center for Disease Control. (2016). *Youth violence facts at a glance 2016*. Retrieved from https://www.cdc.gov/violenceprevention/pdf/yv-datasheet.pdf

Center for the Study of Social Policy. (1993). *Kids count data book 1993: State profiles of child well-being*. Washington, DC: Author.

Chambers, B., & Abrami, P. C. (1991). The relationship between student team learning outcomes and achievement, causal attributions, and affect. *Journal of Educational Psychology, 8*(1), 140–146.

Chico, G. J. (2011, January 14). *Early childhood education: Even start family literacy program*. Retrieved from http://www.isbe.state.il.us/earlychi/html/even_start_family_literacy.htm

Chilcott, L., & Guggenheim, D. (2010). *Waiting for 'Superman'* [motion picture]. Los Angeles, CA: Walden Media and Participant Media.

Children's Defense Fund. (1988). *Making the middle grades work*. Washington, DC: Author.

Children's Defense Fund. (1991). *Child poverty in America*. Washington, DC: Author.

Collins, C. W., McLeod, J., & Kenway, J. (2000). *Factors influencing the educational performance of males and females in school and their initial destinations after leaving school*. Canberra, ACT: Department of Education, Training and Youth Affairs.

De Witte, K., Cabus, S., Thyssen, G., Groot, W., & van den Brink, H. M. (2013). A critical review of the literature on school dropout. *Educational Research Review, 10*, 13–28.

Dryfoos, J. G. (1990). *Adolescents at risk: Prevalence and prevention*. New York, NY: Oxford University Press.

DuBois, D. L., Portillo, N., Rhodes, J. E., Silverthorn, N., & Valentine, J. C. (2011). How effective are mentoring programs for youth? A systematic assessment of the evidence. *Psychological Science, 12*(2), 57–91.

Duckworth, K. (1988). Coping with student absenteeism. *The Practitioner, 14*, 1–14.

Dulmus, C. N., & Wodarski, J. S. (1997). Prevention of childhood mental disorders: A literature review reflecting hope and a vision for the future. *Child and Adolescent Social Work Journal, 14*(3), 181–198.

Durlak, J. A. (1995). *School-based prevention programs for children and adolescents.* Thousand Oaks, CA: Sage.

Earls, F. (1994). Violence and today's youth. *The Future of Children, 4,* 10–23.

Ellwood, D. T. (1988). *Poor support: Poverty in the American family.* New York, NY: Basic Books.

Erwin, E. J. (1996). *Putting children first: Visions for a brighter future for young children and their families.* Baltimore, MD: Paul H. Brookes.

Fingerhut, L. A., & Kleinman, J. C. (1990). International and interstate comparisons of homicide among young males. *Journal of the American Medical Association, 265,* 3292–3295.

Finn, C. E., & Walberg, H. J. (1994). *Radical education reforms.* Berkeley, CA: McCutchan.

Friedman, T. L., & Mandelbaum, M. (2011). *That used to be us: How America fell behind in the world it invented and how we can come back.* New York, NY: Picador.

Gingrich, N. (2006). *Winning the future: A 21st century contract with America.* Washington, DC: Regnery Publishing.

The Glory of Education Reform. (2013). *At-risk.* Retrieved from http://edglossary.org/at-risk/

Goodlad, J. I. (1994). *What schools are for?* (2nd ed.). Bloomington, IN: Phi Delta Educational Foundation.

Grala, C., & McCauley, C. (1976). Counseling truants back to school: Motivation combined with a program for action. *Journal of Child Psychology and Psychiatry and Allied Disciplines, 24,* 607–611.

Gray, G., Smith, A., & Rutter, M. (1980). School attendance and the first year of employment. In L. Hersov & I. Berg (Eds.), *Out of school* (pp. 321–339). New York, NY: Wiley.

Griffith, A. K., Hurley, K. D., Trout, A. L., Synhorst, L., Epstein, M. H., & Allen, E. (2010). Assessing the strengths of young children at risk: Examining use of the preschool behavioral and emotional rating scale with a head start population. *Journal of Early Intervention, 32*(4), 274–285.

Guttmacher Institute. (1985). *Report on adolescent pregnancy.* New York, NY: Author.

Hawkins, J. D., Catalano, R. F., & Arthur, M. W. (2002). Promoting science-based prevention in communities. *Addictive Behaviors, 27,* 951–976.

Henggeler, S. W., & Lee, T. (2003). Multisystemic treatment of serious clinical problems. In A. E. Kazdin & J. R. Weisz (Eds.), *Evidence-based psychotherapies for children and adolescents* (pp. 301–322). New York, NY: Guilford Press.

Henggeler, S. W., Schoenwald, S. K., Rowland, M. D., & Cunningham, P. B. (2002). *Serious emotional disturbance in children and adolescents: Multisystemic therapy.* New York, NY: Guildford Press.

Henry, K. L. (2007). Who's skipping school: Characteristics of truants in 8th and 10th grade. *Journal of School Health, 77,* 29–35.

Hersov, L. A., & Berg, I. (Eds.). (1980). *Out of school.* New York, NY: Wiley.

Hingson, R. (1993, June). *The effect of lowered BAC limits in state per se DUI laws on crash statistics.* Paper presented at the annual conference of the Research Society on Alcoholism, San Antonio, TX.

Hobbs, F., & Lippman, L. (1990). *Children's well-being: An international comparison.* Washington, DC: U.S. Bureau of the Census.

Johnson, L. D., O'Malley, P. M., & Bachman, J. G. (1994). *National survey results on drug use from The Monitoring of the Future Study, 1975–1993: Vol. I, Secondary school students.* (National Institute on Drug Abuse. NIH Publication No. 94-3809). Washington, DC: U.S. Government Printing Office.

Jones, B. H. (2004). Safety and stability for foster children: A developmental perspective. *The Future of Children, 14*(1), 30–48.

Kaminer, Y. (2001). Adolescent substance abuse treatment: Where do we go from here? *Psychiatric Services, 52*(2), 147–149.

Kena, G., Hussar, W., McFarland, J., de Brey, C., Musu-Gillette, L., Wang, X., … Barmer, A. (2016). *The condition of education 2016. NCES 2016-144.* Washington, DC: National Center for Education Statistics.

Kenny, A. M. (1987). Teen pregnancy: An issue for schools. *Phi Delta Kappan, 68*(10), 728–736.

Knapp, M. S., & Shields, P. M. (1990). Reconceiving instruction for the disadvantaged. *Phi Delta Kappan, 72,* 753–758.

Kumar, R., O'Malley, P. M., & Johnston, L. D. (2008). Association between physical environment of secondary schools and student problem behavior: A national study, 2000–2003. *Environment and Behavior, 40*(4), 455–486.

Lacy, G. (2014). *Head start social services: How African American mothers use and perceive them.* New York, NY: Routledge.

Lee, J. O., Hill, K. G., Guttmannova, K., Hartigan, L. A., Catalano, R. F., & Hawkins, J. D. (2014). Childhood and adolescent predictors of heavy episodic drinking and alcohol use disorder at ages 21 and 33: A domain-specific cumulative risk model. *Journal of Studies on Alcohol and Drugs, 75*(4), 684–694.

Levin, H. M., & Belfield, C. R. (2007). Educational interventions to raise high school graduation rates. In C. R. Belfield & H. M. Levin (Eds.), *The price we pay: Economic and social consequences of inadequate education* (pp. 177–199). Washington, DC: Brookings Institution Press.

Liddle, H. A., Dakof, G. A., Parker, K., Diamond, G. S., Barrett, K., & Tejeda, M. (2001). Multidimensional family therapy for adolescent drug abuse: Results of a randomized clinical trial. *American Journal of Drug and Alcohol Abuse, 27*(4), 651–688.

Lisha, N. E., Pokhrel, P., & Sussman, S. (2014). Drug use prevention during childhood. In *Encyclopedia of primary prevention and health promotion* (pp. 648–661). New York, NY: Springer.

Luce, E. (2012). *Time to start thinking: America in the age of descent.* New York, NY: Atlantic Monthly Press.

Lumsden, L. (2002). *Preventing bullying.* Retrieved October 9, 2008, from http://eric.ed.gov/ERICDocs/data/ericdocs2sql/content_storage_01/0000019b/80/19/f3/5b.pdf

Manning, M. L., & Baruth, L. G. (1995). *Students at risk.* Boston, MA: Allyn & Bacon.

Martin, S. E., & Bryant, K. (2001). Gender differences in the association of alcohol intoxication and illicit drug abuse among persons arrested for violent and property offenses. *Journal of Substance Abuse, 13,* 563–581.

Maynard, B. R., Kjellstrand, E. K., & Thompson, A. M. (2014). Effects of check and connect on attendance, behavior, and academics: A randomized effectiveness trial. *Research on Social Work Practice, 24*(3), 296–309.

McFarland, J., Stark, P., & Cui, J. (2016). *Trends in high school dropout and completion rates in the United States: 2013. NCES 2016117REV.* Washington, DC: National Center for Education Statistics.

Meisels, S. J., & Liaw, F. R. (1993). Failure in grade: Do retained students catch up? *Journal of Educational Research, 87,* 69–77.

Miller, D. (1986). Effects of a program of therapeutic discipline on the attitude, attendance, and insight of truant adolescents. *Journal of Experimental Education, 55,* 49–53.

Mishna, F., Khoury-Kassabri, M., Gadalla, T., & Daciuk, J. (2012). Risk factors for involvement in cyber bullying: Victims, bullies, and bully-victims. *Children and Youth Services Review, 34,* 63–70.

Moore, G. W., Slate, J. R., Edmonson, S. L., Combs, J. P., Bustamante, R., & Onwueglowzie, A. J. (2010). High school students and their lack of preparedness for college: A statewide study. *Education and Urban Society, 42*(7), 817–838.

Murphy, J. (Ed.). (1990). *The educational reform movement of the 1980's.* Berkeley, CA: McCutchan.

National Center for Education Statistics. (2012). *The condition of education.* Washington, DC: U.S. Government Printing Office.

National Center for Public Policy and Higher Education. (2008). *Measuring up: The national report card on higher education.* Retrieved November 8, 2012, from http://measuringup2008. highereducation.org/print/NCPPHEMUNationalRpt.pdf

National Commission on Excellence in Education. (1983). *A nation at risk: The imperative for educational reform.* Retrieved October 25, 2012, from http://datacenter.spps.org/uploads/ SOTW_A_Nation_At_Risk_1983.pdf

National Institute on Drug Abuse. (2016). *Monitoring the future survey: High school and youth trends.* Retrieved from https://www.drugabuse.gov/publications/drugfacts/monitoring-future-survey-high-school-youth-trends

Natriello, G. (1995). Dropouts: Definitions, causes, consequences, and remedies. In P. W. Cookson & B. Schneider (Eds.), *Transforming schools* (pp. 107–127). New York, NY: Garland.

Newman-Carlson, D., & Horne, A. M. (2004). Bully busters: A psychoeducational intervention for reducing bullying behavior in middle school students. *Journal of Counseling & Development, 82,* 259–267.

Niehoff, B. P., & Mesch, D. J. (1991). Effects of reward structures on academic performance and group processes in a classroom setting. *Journal of Psychology, 125*(4), 457–467.

Norman, E., & Turner, S. (1993). Adolescent substance abuse prevention programs: Theories, models, and research in the encouraging 80's. *Journal of Primary Prevention, 14*(1), 3–20.

Office of Technology Assessment. (1991). *Adolescent health.* U.S. Congress. Washington, DC: Author.

Rapp, L. A., & Wodarski, J. S. (1997). Juvenile violence: The high risk factors, current interventions, and implications for social work practice. *Journal of Applied Social Sciences, 22,* 3–14.

Ravitch, D. (2010). *The death and life of the great American school system: How testing and choice are undermining education.* New York, NY: Basic Books.

Rogers, D. C. (1980). Stepping up school attendance. *NASSP Bulletin, 64,* 21–25.

Roseberry-McKibbin, C. (2008). *Increasing language skills of students from low-income backgrounds: Practical strategies for professionals.* San Diego, CA: Plural Publishing.

Rubin, D. M., O'Reilly, A. L. R., Luan, X., & Localio, A. R. (2007). The impact of placement stability on behavioral well-being for children in foster care. *Pediatrics, 119*(2), 336–344.

Rutter, M., Maugham, B., Mortimore, P., & Ouston, J. (1979). *Fifteen thousand hours: Secondary schools and their effects on children.* London, England: Open Books.

Sabri, B., Williams, J. K., Smith, D. C., Jang, M., & Hall, J. A. (2010). Substance abuse treatment outcomes for adolescents with violent behaviors. *Journal of Social Work Practice in the Addictions, 10*(1), 44–62.

Schinke, S. P. (1997). Preventing teenage pregnancy. *Journal of Human Behavior in the Social Environment, 1*(1), 53–66.

Schinke, S. P., Botvin, G. J., & Orlandi, M. A. (1991). *Substance abuse in children and adolescents: Evaluation and intervention.* Newbury Park, CA: Sage.

Schorr, E. B. (1988). *Within our reach: Breaking the cycle of disadvantaged.* New York, NY: Doubleday.

Schultz, R. M. (1987). Truancy: Issues and interventions. *Behavioral Disorders, 12,* 175–130.

Shanker, A. (1994). National standards. In C. E. Finn & H. J. Walberg (Eds.), *Radical education reforms* (pp. 3–27). Berkeley, CA: McCutchan.

Skiba, R. J., Poloni-Staudinger, L., Simmons, A. B., Feggins-Azziz, R., & Chung, C. (2005). Unproven links: Can poverty explain ethnic disproportionity in special education? *The Journal of Special Education, 39,* 130–144.

Smeeding, T., & Thévenot, C. (2016). Addressing child poverty: How does the United States compare with other nations? *Academic Pediatrics, 16*(3), S67–S75.

Smith, R. (1988). *America's shame, America's hope: Twelve million youth at risk.* New York, NY: Charles Stewart Mott.

Sneed, C. D., Mehdiyoun, N. F., Matsumura, S. H., & Hess, R. A. (2015). Smoking on school property as a risk factor for substance use among adolescent smokers. *The Journal of Psychology, 149*(1), 19–28.

Sommer, B. (1985). What's different about truants? A comparison study of eighth-graders. *Journal of Youth and Adolescence, 14*, 411–423.

Spencer, A. M. (2009). School attendance patterns, unmet educational needs, and truancy: A chronological perspective. *Remedial and Special Education, 30*, 309–319.

Stanger-Hall, K. F., & Hall, D. W. (2011). Abstinence-only education and teen pregnancy rates: Why we need comprehensive sex education in the US. *PLoS One, 6*(10), e24658.

Swadi, H., & Zeitlin, H. (1988). Peer influence and adolescent substance abuse: A promising side? *British Journal of Addiction, 83*(2), 153–157.

Teasley, M. L. (2004). Absenteeism and truancy: Risk, protection, and best practice implications for school social workers. *Children and Schools, 26*(2), 117–128.

U.S. Bureau of the Censes. (2000). Retrieved October 9, 2008, from http://www.census.gov/main/www/cen2000.html

U.S. General Accounting Office. (1995). *Welfare dependency: Coordinated community efforts can better serve young at-risk teen girls*. Gaithersburg, MD: Author.

Upadhya, K. K., & Ellen, J. M. (2011). Social disadvantage as a risk for first pregnancy among adolescent females in the United States. *Journal of Adolescent Health, 49*, 538–541.

Vail, K. (1999). Words that wound. *American School Board Journal, 186*, 37–40.

Van Der Stouwe, T., Asscher, J. J., Stams, G. J. J., Deković, M., & Van Der Laan, P. H. (2014). The effectiveness of multisystemic therapy (MST): A meta-analysis. *Clinical Psychology Review, 34*(6), 468–481.

Vandrer Zanden, J. W. (1989). *Human development* (4th ed.). New York, NY: Alfred A. Knopf.

Vries, S. L., Hoeve, M., Assink, M., Stams, G. J. J., & Asscher, J. J. (2015). Practitioner review: Effective ingredients of prevention programs for youth at risk of persistent juvenile delinquency–recommendations for clinical practice. *Journal of Child Psychology and Psychiatry, 56*(2), 108–121.

Wilson, J., & Howell, J. (1995). Comprehensive strategy for serious, violent, and chronic juvenile offenders. In J. Howell, B. Krisberg, J. Hawkins, & J. Wilson (Eds.), *Serious, violent, and chronic juvenile offenders*. Thousand Oaks, CA: Sage.

Wodarski, J. S. (1988). Teaching adolescents about alcohol and driving. *Journal of Alcohol and Drug Education, 33*(3), 54–67.

Wodarski, J. S., & Bagarozzi, D. A. (1979). *Behavioral social work*. New York, NY: Human Services Press.

Wodarski, J. S., Smokowski, P. R., & Feit, M. D. (1996). Adolescent preventative health: A cost-beneficial social and life group paradigm. In J. S. Wodarski, M. D. Feit, & J. R. Ferrari (Eds.), *Adolescent health care* (pp. 1–40). New York, NY: Haworth Press.

Wodarski, J. S., & Smyth, N. J. (1994). Adolescent substance abuse: A comprehensive approach to prevention intervention. *Journal of Child & Adolescent Substance Abuse, 3*(3), 33–58.

Wodarski, J. S., & Wodarski, L. A. (1993). *Curriculums and practical aspects of implementation: Preventive health services for adolescents*. Lanham, MD: University Press of America.

Wodarski, J. S., Wodarski, L. A., & Parris, H. (2004). Teams-games-tournaments: Four decades of research. *Journal of Evidence-Based Social Work, 1*(1), 101–124.

Chapter 4
Violence in Schools

Lisa A. Rapp and John S. Wodarski

Overview

In the past decade, school violence has become a serious concern in the USA. Violent crimes are still a rare event on school grounds however, intense media coverage of violent events versus positive news clips about students and schools has fueled rampant fear about school violence. Data supports some of this attention as violent crimes have now become more prevalent in schools than in communities. According to the National Center for Education Statistics (2018), the rate of violent victimization was 38.1 per 1000 students at school and 26.2 per 1000 students away from school. Yet, only 2.7% of students report being the victim of any form of crime at school. The issue of school violence is multi-faceted and quite complicated. Consequently, the Department of Health and Human Services, Centers for Disease Control and Prevention (2018) identify youth violence as a significant public health problem. This chapter focuses on various types of undesirable and delinquent behaviors of American youth that school social workers are purposed to address and eradicate.

Aggressive behavior, such as bullying, is a daily occurrence at school and can lead to violence in schools (Mongan, Hatcher, & Masche, 2009; Wike & Fraser, 2009). Accordingly, this form of child-abuse-by-peer (or teacher) can build isolation, frustration, and anger for children, especially adolescents, who are already overwhelmed with managing peer pressure and other stage development tasks, including experimenting with various adult identities and coping with new, intense emotions. In extreme circumstances, such as school shootings, victimized students

L. A. Rapp (✉)
School of Educational Social Services, Saint Leo University, St. Leo, FL, USA
e-mail: Lisa.Rapp-McCall@saintleo.edu

J. S. Wodarski
College of Social Work, University of Tennessee, Knoxville, TN, USA

© Springer Nature Switzerland AG 2019
J. S. Wodarski, L. M. Hopson (eds.), *Empirically Based Interventions Targeting Social Problems*, https://doi.org/10.1007/978-3-030-28487-9_4

feel trapped and think that the system can no longer protect them. The destructive logic and indiscriminate violence that can result is powerfully described by Pittaro (2007):

"School shooters are often angry with those who bullied, belittled, or ostracized the shooter for days, weeks, or months leading up to the attacks" (Vossekuil, Reddy, Fein, Borum, & Modzeleski, 2000). The research suggests that shooters often create a list of potential targets, but are willing to take innocent lives in the process as demonstrated in the randomness of the typical shooter's aim and direction in the widespread attacks. This is very similar to the cognitive restructuring process that terrorists use to justify the killing of innocent lives.

Media attention increases awareness of the problem of school shootings, but a narrow focus on the most heinous forms of violence only amplifies fear of the worst-case-scenario while inadvertently minimizing lesser forms of aggression. Consequently, terror and insidious forms of aggression have proliferated in high schools, junior high schools, and even elementary schools.

Trends

Historically, characteristics of students' misbehavior have changed. Prior to the 1980s, students' misbehavior was considered only a minor problem. Horseplay, gum chewing, and tardiness were concerns that led to detention. By the late 1980s, however, serious concern from parents and educators increased as school crime and assaults rose by 35% in New York City schools, and weapons became more popular than pencils. In the early 1990s, statistics indicated that approximately three million crimes occur every year on school campuses. That is equal to 16,000 per day or one crime every 6 s (Soriano, Soriano, & Jimenez, 1991). Surprisingly, the greatest number of school crime increased at the elementary school level. In 1991, one in five elementary school teachers reported being physically threatened by students. During this period, approximately 5200 of the nation's secondary school teachers were physically assaulted at school each month. In 1992, 14% of high school students were threatened with a weapon at school (Soriano et al., 1991). Investigators at the University of Michigan in 1993 found that 29% of eighth grades were threatened at school; 19% of those threatened were threatened with a weapon (Batsche & Knoff, 1994). Several school shootings occurred in the mid-1990s, including in small-town American schools such as Heath High School in West Paducah, Kentucky. At the end of the decade, the Columbine High School massacre resulted in 15 lost lives. The 1990s were a particularly violent period of time in America's schools.

Although the above information creates a general awareness of the historical upsurge in school violence, defining school violence in the twenty-first century requires an examination of the major forms of aggression and what path is warranted to create substantive change. The range of violent behaviors in schools is vast. Because of the need to identify and ultimately address specific and inappropriate behaviors, a thorough examination of these various types of behaviors in schools is warranted.

In addition, to elaborating on various types of detrimental behaviors occurring within the school, it is just as important to understand that the school environment or the culture and climate of the learning institution plays an intricate role in the level of violence found at the school. Studies have found that peer relationships, teacher/staff relationships, student support, pecking orders, codes of honor, and codes of silence have an impact on cognitive and non-cognitive student outcomes (Thapa, Cohen, Guffey, & Higgins-D'Alessandro, 2013).

A hostile environment is a detriment to school performance, as fear impedes learning for both the victim and perpetrator. Furthermore, dangerous school environments contribute to truancy, gangs, substance abuse, and school avoidant behaviors. In 2015, approximately 5% of students reported that they avoided one school activity or class because they thought someone might attack or harm them (National Center for Education Statistics, 2018).

Bullying

Bullying can be defined as a chronic form of aggression in which one or more students physically, psychologically, or sexually harass another student repeatedly and over a period of time. This form of aggression also includes teachers who victimize students (Whitted & Dupper, 2008). The initial bullying episode is typically unprovoked, and the victim perceives the perpetrator as being more powerful than himself or herself (Booren, Handy, & Power, 2011). Data from the National Crime Victimization Survey from 2015 found 21% of students reported being bullied at school with females reporting higher levels of bullying than males (National Center for Education Statistics, 2018).

Cyberbullying is a more recent form of bullying that involves the use of popular social media sites, such as Snapchat, Instagram, and Twitter but can also include emails, texts, and instant messaging. Using these methods, bullies extend the scope and frequency of harassment beyond the physical school building and can bully a victim 24/7. Cyberbullying can provide the bully with anonymity and/or a far wider audience, therefore causing more damage and humiliation. Approximately 16% of students were cyberbullied in 2015 (Albin, 2012; National Center for Education Statistics, 2018).

These startling statistics mandate a collaborative effort with parents, teachers, and school social workers. This form of aggression often starts in later elementary school with the highest rate occurring during middle school. Bullying may start with simple name calling, but it can be a precursor to future behavior, including physical and sexual assault (Stein, 1995). In more than two thirds of the cases, the school shooters felt persecuted, bullied, threatened, attacked, or injured by others prior to the incident. In fact, some of the boys had experienced bullying and harassment that was long-standing and severe (Borum, Cornell, Modzeleski, & Jimerson, 2010).

Many times, bullying is ignored by school staff, who believe it to be a normal part of development. Our American culture subscribes to the motto "fight your own battles," which perpetuates the bystander effect. According to Bright (2005), neutrality, which consists of watching passively as incidences occur, reinforces bullying behavior 75% of the time. Moreover, the US Secret Service, National Threat Assessment Center (2002) reported that many school shootings were actually encouraged by bystanders:

> In many cases, other students were involved in some capacity. The attackers acted alone in at least two-thirds of the cases. However, in almost half of the cases, friends or fellow students influenced or encouraged the attacker to act… The attacker shared his plan with two friends who convinced him to actually shoot students at the school to persuade others to leave him alone. Several days later, he did just that. The attacker schemed to shoot fellow students in the lobby of his school at a specific time in the morning. On the morning of the attack, he asked three others to meet him in the mezzanine overlooking the lobby, where only a few students could be found every morning. The students told so many others that by the time the attacker opened fire in the lobby—killing 2 and injuring 2—a total of 24 students were in the mezzanine watching the attack. One student brought a camera to record the event. (p. 14)

However, bullying could be addressed in its beginning stages preventing many future i.ncidents. An awareness of person-in-environment contexts is of paramount importance in considering prevention programs. Whole-school interventions programs, which seek to involve parents, educators, staff, and students, systemically, are the most effective interventions to reduce bullying (Swearer, Espelage, Vaillancourt, & Hymel, 2010; Vreeman & Carroll, 2007). The culture and climate of the school must be assessed and modified. Subtle rules about codes of silence and views that bullying is "typical" developmental milestones need to be reformed. Research on whole-school interventions indicates that "there are fewer bullying episodes among students in schools that are described as having more positive student-teacher relationships" (Richard, Schneider, & Mallet, 2011). Universal programming should be delivered to the entire school population but specialty intervention programs should be delivered to bullies separately. In these programs, bullies are taught improved social skills, coping skills, empathy, and are provided mental health counseling as necessary.

Whether its cyberbullying or bullying in-person, chronic bullying, has been found to cause physical health and mental health problems, academic issues, substance abuse, delinquency, as well as suicidal ideation (Swearer et al., 2010). Houbre, Tarquinio, and Thuillier (2006) conducted a study in France which examined the relationship between bullying and behavioral problems and psychosomatic disorders. A positive correlation was indicated for both the victims and perpetrators. More obvious bullying symptoms, such as fear, anxiety, and depression, are quite common as are shame, anger, hostility, and aggression. Many times youth respond to bullying by unhealthy withdrawal, including skipping school, running away, or committing suicide.

Overall, bullying results in a decline in academic achievement, pervasive fear and avoidance of school, and a range of other physical and emotional problems. Schools have no choice but to address and attempt to mitigate in-person and cyber-bullying and schools which can modify their culture, climate, and inclusivity in a holistic manner have the best chance at achieving this outcome.

Physical Aggression

Physical aggression by a student can be inflicted with or without a weapon, and its effects to victims can be serious and long-term. Victims often report distress, anxiety, depression, fear, problems concentrating, sleep issues, among other symptoms after a physical victimization (Averdijk, 2011). In addition, physical aggression can cause fear of school in students. Approximately, 6% of students did not go to school on one or more days in the 30 days preceding the study because they felt unsafe at school or on their way to or from school. Unfortunately, physical aggression is a relatively common experience at school (Department of Health and Human Services, 2018). A 2015 study found 39% of schools reported at least one student threat of physical attack without a weapon, compared with 9% of schools that reported such a threat with a weapon (National Center for Education Statistics, 2018). A nationally representative study of 9th–12th grade students found 10% of male students and 5% of female students reported being in a physical fight on school property in the 12 months preceding the survey (Department of Health and Human Services, 2018).

Statistics that relate to physical aggression are under-reported. Often times, the victim is too ashamed to come forward, school administrators do not contact the police in every incident, and there is no national database for homicides that are committed on school grounds (Furlong & Morrison, 1994).

Aggressive students usually have exhibited aggression at home and in the community. Many have had traumatic backgrounds and most often, but not exclusively, these incidents occur in school districts where there are high levels of unemployment, crime, transience, and poverty (Department of Health and Human Services, 2018).

Minority Youth Violence

Studies on violence, both in the community and on or around school grounds, indicate that youths of color are most often victimized by violence. Racial minorities, including African Americans and Latinos, are disproportionately involved in violence on school grounds and more often interact with deviant peers (Antunes & Ahlin, 2018; Soriano et al., 1991). Nationally, Latino males have the highest homicide victimization rate. Native American males have a homicide victimization rate which is three to four times higher than that of Whites (Hechinger, 1992). Black/ African Americans and Latino American students who are victimized at school are at greater risk of dropping out before completion of high school (Jiang & Peguero, 2017).

These minority students most often live in neighborhoods with the highest percentages of homelessness, poverty, joblessness, crowded schools, disorder, and individuals who embody racial stereotypes, factors that have been repeatedly linked to violence. Particular cultures are not to be considered the cause of violence. However, when differences (e.g., values, cultures, and ethnicities) come together in an environment where youths are striving to develop a core identity, notions of racism, classism, and sexism are often exploited. These variables are frequently used to incite violence.

American schools are rapidly changing to include diverse ethnic groups and multiple languages. Cultural diversity and cross-cultural communication is now part of the curriculum of many schools. Parents are encouraged to teach their children about differences. The importance of outreach to parents is a key to reducing or eliminating factors that spread minority violence in their schools and communities (Wright & Fitzpatrick, 2006).

Violence Toward Lesbian, Gay, Bisexual, Transgendered, and Questioning Youth

Studies have shown that although violence in schools is not uncommon for youth, LGBTQ youth endure more bullying and violence than non-LGBTQ youth (Espelage, Merrin, & Hatchel, 2016). The National School Climate study, completed in 2013, noted that 74% of LGBT youth were verbally harassed, 36% were physically harassed and 16% were physically assaulted due to their sexual orientation or gender expression (Kosciw, Greytak, Palmer, & Boesen, 2014). Other studies conducted across the country indicate that LGBTQ adolescents endure a wide range of violent victimization, including harassment, threats, verbal abuse, sexual assault, and murder more often than their heterosexual counterparts (National Gay and Lesbian Task Force Policy Institute, 2018).

These victimizations are concerning as they often result in serious consequences like social isolation, academic issues, mental health problems, and suicidal ideation and attempts (Espelage et al., 2016). Sexual minority youth have been found to be significantly more likely to report physical and sexual abuse than heterosexual youth, and bisexual teens of both genders were more than twice as likely than heterosexual teens to report abuse (Saewyc et al., 2006). As minorities, these youth also have fewer social supports and are therefore more vulnerable as targets of abuse (Espelage et al., 2016). For some youth who have not formally disclosed their sexual orientation, victimization may rush disclosure to peers who lack the maturity to safeguard the information. Consequently, these youth often experience a secondary victimization through their attempts to obtain help. In fact, the abuse can come from teachers and other staff members as well. More than 1 in 20 youth reported that they had suffered some form of victimization from their teachers (Pilkington & D'Augelli, 1995). Schools are increasingly protecting LGBTQ youths who choose to disclose their sexual orientation. Training for educators, staff, and students, as well as curricula designed to encourage empathy and reduce violence, can be incorporated through a whole-school approach.

Juvenile Gangs

According to Goldstein, Glick, Carthen, and Blancero (1994), there are approximately 2000 gangs in the USA located throughout urban, suburban, and rural settings. The National Crime Victimization Survey (NCVS), from 2013, found 12% of students in the USA reporting the presence of gangs at their school, down from the 1995 estimate of 28% (Zhang, Musu-Gillette, & Oudekerk, 2016). Youths join gangs for many reasons, including peer friendship, pride, sense of identity, increased self-esteem, excitement, attempts to gain resources to drugs, and family tradition (Currie, 2010; Goldstein & Soriano, 1994). Most of these motivations are normal development tasks for all adolescents. However, juveniles often join gangs for safety reasons, that is, as a response to violence that permeates a school or community (Carson & Esbensen, 2017).

Despite the decrease in gangs, schools continue to have concerns about gangs in schools as they pose safety, drug, crime, and violence problems (Carson & Esbensen, 2017). Typically, gangs tend to generate problems off school grounds and in the community however, gangs permeate school confines and create serious dangers for students and school personnel. That is, gang clashes occurring within the school building, on campus, or in close proximity of the school are both violent and distracting. Oftentimes, gangs use schools as prime recruiting grounds for membership and as a "staging" area to highlight defiance and build reputations (Carson & Esbensen, 2017). Most conflicts occur when members of opposing gangs attend the same school. Gang conflicts often involve weapons, which lead to clashes that have lethal results. Drive-by shootings, assaults at school, and in-house burglaries are all common behaviors of contemporary gangs.

Younger students are usually more common prey for gang recruitment. For the uncooperative youth, refusal to join the gang often results in threats, coercion, and even assault and battery. Besides potentiating physical harm, gang behaviors can also induce fear and anxiety in children and school staff. Severe and chronic threats and violence can result in acute and long-term trauma, anxiety, depression, feelings of hopelessness, and aggression (Carson & Esbensen, 2017). Students in schools that face these problems will have difficulty not only on an academic level, but also on an interpersonal and behavioral level. In other words, violence breeds multiple and complex psychosocial problems for youth and adult victims.

Gun Violence

Misuse of firearms has contributed significantly to the substantial increase in the number and severity of violent incidents in the past few years. Mortality due to firearms has been endemic and stable over the past 18 years, with approximately 90 people a day dying from gunshot wounds (Centers for Disease Control and Prevention, 2016). Firearm deaths occur mostly among young adults aged 17–25 years and account for 80% of all homicides and 45% of all suicides within this age group (Centers for Disease Control and Prevention, 2016). In recent years, there has been an increase in mass school shootings and this has been partly blamed on the easy access and use of automatic and semiautomatic weapons.

There are approximately 200 million privately owned guns in the USA, and it has been estimated that 270,000 are brought to school every day (Center to Prevent Handgun Violence, 1990). The CDC reports 4% of the 9th through 12th grade students surveyed reported carrying a weapon to school in the preceding month and 6% were threatened or injured by a weapon on school grounds in the past year. Sixty-eight percent of school shooters obtained their gun from their own homes or that of a relative (Bradycampaign.org). Those students who did not own a handgun reported that they could obtain one quickly and without much hassle. In fact, about 1.7 million youth live in homes with unlocked, loaded firearms. Handgun ownership has been related to involvement in defiant behavior, gang membership, drug use, assault, and suicide (Bradycampaign.org).

Over one million high school students are threatened or injured with a firearm at school (Bradycampaign.org). These statistics have led school administrators to employ security guards, metal detectors, and trained dogs. These procedures have been somewhat successful in the reduction of the number of weapons within school buildings, but they have not stopped the overall violence in schools. Parents and youth greatly overestimate the number of youth carrying guns to school. It is believed that marketing campaigns could be used to help lower the perception of gun carrying among adolescents who could in turn lower actual rates of gun carrying in school (Hemenway, Vriniotis, Johnson, Miller, & Azrael, 2011).

Substance Use

In 2016, 10% of individuals aged 12 and over used an illegal substance in the past month and 7.5% had a substance use disorder (Substance Abuse and Mental Health Services Administration, 2017). Drug use has been found to directly link to crime and violent behavior. Both gun violence and use of illegal substances have similar risk factors and substance use impairs judgment, increases impulsivity and aggression (Banks et al., 2017). Drugs also increase violence in an indirect manner by users committing violence to protect turf (Jensen, 2000). Drugs present a critical motivation as well as a tremendous economic opportunity for youths who reside in impoverished communities. Many youths view the drug trade as their only hope of financial gain, despite its dangers and illegality.

Jensen (2000) reports that drug sales are strongly associated with violence and occur most often around inner-city schools. Drugs have been a problem in schools for many years. Their presence has been related to violence in two ways: (a) Drugs have caused increased incidences of violence and (b) drugs have exacerbated the level of aggression that already existed. Schools need to be aware of the factors that lure adolescents toward controlled substances. They need to be prepared to handle substance abuse and substance selling—in addition to gangs, guns, and violence. These are the ingredients that, when combined, result in the victimization of student and school personnel. One study found that selling or using drugs was greatly correlated with carrying a handgun among adolescent males (Vaughn et al., 2012).

Assessment

A formal assessment of the type, frequency, location, and level of violence that is occurring in and around school grounds is required before a school system can begin to implement interventions and system wide changes in policy and practice. Every school district will be different—some schools may have only minor violence problems that need to be addressed before major problems occur, while other schools will require swift, potent interventions. Some schools may require interventions that will confront the issues of violence against minorities and substance abuse, while other schools may require interventions for bullying and homophobia.

A comprehensive evaluation should include an assessment of bullying, weapons, substance abuse, gangs, and physical altercations. Assessments should also include review of the violent acts against minorities, women, and homosexuals. Assessments should describe when and where violence occurs (e.g., at school events, on the bus, or on the way home from school). Attendance records and discipline records should be analyzed as well as the overall school climate (Stephens, 1994). In addition, cyberbullying and violence should also be evaluated. These are more difficult to assess but are a crucial factor in understanding a school's problem with violence.

Assessments need to be completed separately for each school level or building. There are three reasons for this. First, middle school students may be experiencing different types of violence form those which high school students experience. Studies have shown that younger students are frequently victimized by bullying behaviors, while older students may be more likely to be victimized by multiple and more severe types of violence. Therefore, developmental stages must be considered when conducting an evaluation. Second, the school building, although in the same district, may be located on different gang turf or in areas with varying substance abuse rates. Therefore, schools may have very different problems that need to be addressed. Third, each building has its own organizational culture or climate and this is a critical factor regarding school violence. The culture of the school and its implicit rules, roles, boundaries, etc. can either inhibit or promote bullying and violence. Also, it is important to be aware of the limitations of an evaluation. For instance, school surveys often do not account for students who choose not to come to school or are already suspended for delinquent behaviors (Farrell, Sullivan, Esposito, & Meyer, 2005).

Assessments for cyberviolence and cyberbullying supersede school buildings and districts. This form of bullying can bring humiliation to a nation-wide audience and be completely unnoticed by parents, teachers, and administrators. Assessment surveys should ask students about all forms, levels, and frequencies of this form of aggression.

Assessments need to be given to multiple individuals, including students, educators, parents, school social workers, school staff, local probation case managers, and local mental health workers. Collaborative processes are beneficial in that they raise consciousness and address the unique facets of a particular problem. That is, assessments serve to raise "school staff awareness about the nature, prevalence, and consequences of bullying" (Thakore et al., 2015). The goal is to clearly define objectives and create a method for measuring outcomes. Often, school administrators or personnel do not realize the severity of bullying or violence in the building until assessments are conducted and analyzed.

Whenever possible, standardized assessment instruments should be used. The availability of these tools is often rare or non-existent. Since there are often no system-wide standardized assessment instruments for schools to use to evaluate their systems and the level of violence exhibited in their schools, schools need to devise their own questionnaires or pay consultants to complete their assessments. Upon completion of the assessments, school administrators, as well as school social workers, can determine the combinations of interventions that will be appropriate for their schools and tailor specific interventions to their students, parents, and community's needs. Parents are encouraged to be active participants in remedying the issue of bullying in their child's school. This helps to unify the adult figures that children see around the school system into one task finding and effective intervention (Thakore et al., 2015).

School-Based Interventions

Schools are no longer what they used to be; instead of educating, teachers spend an inordinate amount of time and energy subduing altercations, resolving conflicts, and managing disruptive behavior. Instead of improving school programs, curriculum, and policies, a principal's time is often consumed with student discipline, weapon control, and handling gang conflicts. Because schools can no longer view the education of children as their only objective, schools seek to curtail violence in an effective and efficient manner.

Prior to the implementation of a prevention or intervention program, all school personnel should be trained to be aware and report on "warning signs or red flags" from students. These can include: changes in behaviors, increased isolation, acting out, fights, suicidal comments or ideations, odd, threatening, or suicidal posts on social media or in written work. In addition, processes need to be developed for personnel to report their concerns and for actions to be taken swiftly.

The following empirically based interventions have been found to be effective in school districts across the country. The programs discussed here are only a fraction of the programs that are available and used on a daily basis. School administrators who are interested in beginning such interventions should investigate multiple programs and curricula to find a match between their sociocultural and violence problems and the program which will best fit their needs.

Prevention

Stopping bullying and violence before it occurs is the main goal of prevention programs. Prevention programs should include students, parents, educators, school personnel, administrators, and community members. Interventions should incorporate skills training, violence policy and practice modifications, and school environment changes. Students, as well as personnel, and parents must be encouraged to report any signs of bullying or victimization, so that it may be dealt with immediately. There are apps which now can be used to report bullying. In other words, for prevention efforts to be successful, interventions must be employed at multiple levels of school functioning—not just at the individual level that simply tries to modify a person's behavior.

Pioneering programs that have been proven effective include: Second Step: A Violence Prevention Curriculum (Committee for Children, 1992) and the Violence Prevention Curriculum for Adolescents (Prothrow-Stith, 1987). The first curriculum is targeted for preschool through grade five students. It is designed to reduce impulsivity and aggressive behavior and increase social competence (Larson, 1994). The second curriculum (for adolescents) focuses on developing values against fighting, using alternative methods to resolve conflict, role playing, and using videotapes. The first curriculum has been found to be more effective than the latter, because it commences prevention interventions with children at an earlier age.

Despite the successes of these programs, prevention methods should be implemented at the system level. Again, the most effective prevention program will target as many levels as possible, with as many individuals as possible (Hahn et al., 2007). Although the generalizability of the Olweus Bullying Prevention Program has recently been disputed (Glew, Ming-Yu, Wayne, & Rivara, 2008; Vreeman & Carroll, 2007), these critics and other studies have suggested its layered approach is worth keeping (Molina, Bowie, Dulmus, & Sowers, 2004). Systemic prevention involves:

1. *Emergency drills.* Every school building should develop and practice emergency drills for violent crises (gunfire in the school building, gang altercation in the building, etc.). These drills should be practiced frequently to reduce hysteri-

cal behaviors and to prevent as many injuries as possible. Regular updates and in-service training should be held (Wheeler & Baron, 1994). School personnel should be prepared to deal with concerned parents along with students. Trump (2007) provides guidelines for schools to follow in the event of an actual emergency.

2. *Visitor screening.* Establish an effective visitor screening process to prevent unwanted or dangerous individuals from coming on the grounds. Only one entrance should be open for visitors and a sign-in process should be utilized. A security task force, either professional or made up of volunteers and school staff, could coordinate this and also patrol the school building (Stephens, 1994).

3. *Safe grounds.* Eliminate potentially dangerous environmental designs. Eliminate hiding places, increase lighting, and install more telephones and convex mirrors to improve the ability to survive. Increase supervision by staff at all times. Teachers should monitor the halls, and community should be used.

4. *Parents.* Involve parents in as many aspects of safety planning as possible. Recruit them as volunteers for special events, as hall monitors, or as safety task force members. Their involvement and support are crucial. Encourage them to supervise no violence at home as well as at the schools.

5. *School crime reporting.* Colleges and universities are required by law to collect and record campus crime data. Although K-12 schools are not mandated to do this, this procedure can provide information about persons, groups, times, and places that are related to violence and crime. School administrators can use this information to assess the overall violence in the school and to make adjustments as needed.

6. *School pride.* Every student should feel a sense of pride and ownership toward the school. Recruit students or have them organize groups or clubs to generate ideas and activities for violence reduction. Positive peer pressure can be effective. A strong school statement promoting positive social relationships and opposing bullying can be instrumental in modeling correct behaviors in students, victims, and bullies alike (Juvonen, 2005).

As previously mentioned, in-school violence interventions should be chosen based on the needs of the students and the issues present within each individual school. Multiple curricula, such as those discussed below, should be considered. Each curriculum may not address all of the problems of each school. Modifications need to be addressed at the system and individual levels.

Antibullying Intervention

P. K. Smith of Cambridge University suggests that "interventions must be inclusive and reshape the interactions and social experiences of bullies, victims, and peers" (Smith, 2004). This must be kept in mind when looking for a good fit between a school's violence level and an appropriate intervention. Besag (1989) has developed a complete curriculum for addressing the problem of bullying schools. This curriculum includes interventions for victims, bullies, and their parents. The curriculum focuses on a social learning approach, because bullying has been identified as a learned behavior. Changing aggressive behaviors and improving communication, social skills, and problem-solving skills are the main objectives. Victims are also part of the intervention. The focus for these children is empowerment. In other words, self-esteem improvement is emphasized by teaching social skills and communication skills. Positive role models are provided and new friendships are encouraged. Victims are taught how to stand up to bullies without fighting. Parents and bullies attend groups with their children so that they can reinforce these skills at home.

When improvements have been noted by both the victim and the bully, sessions including both children can be conducted to address the problem. Problem-solving, cooperation, and negotiation should be encouraged. Behavior modification plans for both the victim and the bully can also be utilized to reinforce and shape positive behavior.

The curriculum described here is very flexible in that it can be utilized by social workers at both the individual and group levels. Depending upon the seriousness and the extent of the problem with the school building, group interventions may be more efficient. This program can also be targeted to any age level and can work with the victim and the perpetrator individually or with both children if necessary.

Another promising intervention used for bullying was conducted by Oleweus (1991). This program encompassed parents, children, teachers by providing educational components about bullying. In addition, the program developed and helped enforce school rules regarding bullying and made efforts to protect and support victims (Kazdin, 1994). The influences at the micro level have been found to be the greatest strengths of the program.

Yet, another possible intervention employs multimedia to reduce bullying and victimization. The study was conducted among urban third graders. The authors reported a reduction in self-reported bullying and victimization. There was significant data to suggest that the multimedia may be positive option for this age group (McLaughlin, Laux, & Pescara-Kovach, 2006).

One researcher suggests that educators should be cautious not to attempt to utilize "quick fixes" as these may have unintended negative side effects. For example, zero tolerance policies may lack the ability to address the underlying issues at hand and may discourage the reporting of bullying. Mediation may also increase bullying and fail to address the fact that bullying is not always the result of a simple conflict (Casebeer, 2012).

Following the popularity of smartphones, several antibullying applications have become available, including Stop!t, Knowbullying, Bully Button, etc. Most are real-time apps. That allow a victim or bystander to electronically notify school personnel and receive help for bullying in the moment. Many schools are utilizing the apps. But there are also apps. That can be used by families and parents and some provide resources for help after the incident (Ye, Ferdinando, Seppanen, & Alasaarela, 2014).

Antiaggression Interventions

There are numerous interventions that target aggression. Several that have been empirically proven as effective in schools are discussed here. The first, the PATHS Promoting Alternative Thinking Strategies, is a classroom-based program which begins in elementary school. The curriculum teaches skills in five domains including: self-control, emotional understanding, positive self-esteem, relationships, and problem-solving skills. The main goals are to promote positive behavior and reduce aggression, delinquency, and criminal behaviors (blueprintsprograms.org).

Another curriculum, entitled Positive Youth development Program (Caplan et al., 1992) provides a 20-session curriculum to middle school students. Emphasis is placed on stress management, self-esteem, assertiveness, problem solving, health information, and social networks. These skills are considered to be critical for reducing and preventing aggression.

The Anger Coping curriculum is an 18-session program for fourth to sixth graders (Lochman, Lampron, Gemmer, & Harris, 1986). This intervention trains children in self-instruction, perspective taking, physiological cues to anger, social problem solving, and goal setting (Larson, 1994). This program uses role playing and videotaping and comes with a treatment manual that includes specific objectives and procedures for each session. The intervention has been used in school districts across the country.

The Positive Adolescents Choice Training (PACT) program, developed by Hammond (1991), specifically targets African American youth to reduce their disproportionate risk for becoming victims of perpetrators of violence (Kazdin, 1994). There are three major components that are taught over the 20-week sessions of this program: social skills training, anger management, and violence awareness education (Larson, 1994). Culturally sensitive videotapes are used to exhibit appropriate negotiation, problem solving, and communication techniques. Outcome studies have shown good success with this program.

The Peer Culture Development Program (National School Resource Network, 1980) was developed to enhance the leadership and interpersonal skills of youths. This program has been used in elementary and high schools to alter peer interaction patterns. The program attempts to reduce negative peer influences and student alienation, and to increase self-esteem, school interest, and the support of conventional rules. This program can be specifically used to help reduce the problem of gangs in schools. This intervention may reduce the recruitment rate of young children into gangs if these children are able to resist negative peer influences. Gang involvement will also be reduced if students feel a strong responsibility for them, have adequate self-esteem, and are positively involved in school. Schools facing a gang problem may wish to adapt this program into their curricula.

Sexual Orientation Education

School administrators and teachers have a constitutional obligation to teach all children. Part of this responsibility, which can significantly reduce violence in schools, involves educating children about differences and teaching children acceptance. Schools are often times faced with conflicts, including aggression toward students who are homosexual, bisexual, or transitioning. One of the reasons for this is that students often have very little understanding about the similarities and non-threatening nature of individuals of different sexual orientations. Consequently, stereotypes are often the only frame of reference that is relied upon. One of the most important interventions that a school can use to reduce violence against LGBTQ youth is an education that also includes parents and school personnel. Reinforcing non-judgment especially when done by school administrators on a systemic level is particularly effective in shaping attitudes of the respect and dignity of every human being. School policies and practices should be regularly reviewed to ensure that all students are protected from discrimination and violence.

Support groups for homosexual and bisexual youths may also be established within the school, and heterosexual youths may choose to attend some of these meetings to gain an understanding of the problems and discrimination that LGBTQ youths face on a daily basis (Sterzing, Gibbs, Gartner, & Goldbach, 2018). The safety needs of LGBTQ youths should be incorporated into school service planning. Likewise, schools should network with outside agencies, supports, and services that are located within the community (Sterzing et al., 2018).

Multicultural Interventions

Despite all of the attempts to facilitate multicultural understanding and acceptance, schools have made little improvement. Studies have noted that fewer minority students are graduating high school, obtaining higher education degrees, while most educators are Caucasian from Middle class communities (Stadler, 2001). Consequently, experts have repeatedly urged schools and agencies to develop multicultural violence prevention and intervention programs (Yung & Hammond, 1994). Intervention programming needs to be sensitive toward differing values, cultural mores, and beliefs that minority youths espouse. Intervention programs that are not sensitive will most likely have little effect on reducing school violence by or toward minority youths.

Training for non-minority youths and school personnel regarding multicultural issues is an important tool in the arsenal against school violence. Curricula in schools that consistently educate students about minority cultures to dispel common inaccurate beliefs and myths are worthy of consideration. Unfortunately, minorities have been the most likely to be victimized in schools and communities. Xenophobia and other misunderstandings have caused victimization. Until multicultural training is implemented in the schools, violence against minority youths is unlikely to be reduced.

Drug Abuse Intervention

As previously indicated, there is a clear drug/violence nexus in communities and schools (Dickinson, 2015), which makes it necessary for programming to address both. Schools can help lower the level of drug abuse by providing education and prevention curricula. These curricula should be started in the early elementary grades and continued through grade 12 for more effective outcomes. Curricula should be developmentally appropriate for each grade level and should include information about substances as well as the skills necessary to abstain from use (Wodarski & Feit, 1995). Youths who have been identified as having problems with substances will need more intensive treatment and should be referred to an outside agency that specialized in the use of addiction.

Our prevention program that has evinced positive results is the Teams-Games-Tournaments (TGT) Substance Abuse and Violence Prevention Program. Youth between ages 12 and 18 can be targeted for this program, which teaches knowledge about the substances and violence, in addition to coping and problem-solving skills. The curriculum is presented using games and tournaments so children have fun while they are learning critical skills and techniques. Modeling, role playing, and videotapes are also incorporated.

The Role of Teachers

Educating youth today is a completely different profession than it was a few decades ago. Teachers have been forced to incorporate social worker, police officer, and mediator into the job description. Less and less time is left for actual education. However, skills that are crucial for teachers are rarely taught to them in college. Instead, teachers are often thrown into positions with little training for successfully maintaining appropriate student behavior.

Schools in the process of implementing prevention or intervention programs need to take the time to train teachers. Teachers need to be skilled in behavior modification, conflict resolution, and negotiation. The Incredible Years-Teacher Classroom Management program has been noted as effective in training teachers to manage students effectively and also helps teachers learn how to connect and create positive relationships with children (Kirkhaug et al., 2016).

Multicultural training is essential, as is training regarding LGBTQ issues. Teachers also need training in self-defense, which should include de-escalating provocative students and physically defending themselves. A study completed in

Britain showed a positive link between a 1 year training course for teachers and a reduction of reported bullying. Teachers were able to gain a base of knowledge concerning ways to manage bullying behaviors in the classroom and then utilize them effectively (Salmivalli, Kaukiainen, & Voeten, 2005). Teachers have the right to be a safe in their work environments and to protect themselves from students who become aggressive with them.

Schools need to provide teachers with clear policies regarding violence, before violence becomes a problem within the school. Schools should not expect teachers to be security guards—their talents lie in educating and their time should be focused on that task. Therefore, if necessary, schools should hire professional security guards to handle physical altercations and weapon control.

Finally, students who are entering the field of education should be aware that other skills and duties besides educating youth will be required of them. They should be made aware that there may be some physical risk involved in becoming a teacher.

The Role of Parents

Parents also need skills training, and schools may be more accessible sites than local agencies to hold training classes. Groups of parents should be taught the same skills as teachers and students, with behavior modification and child management emphasized. The ability to recognize symptoms of drug and alcohol use in children should also be incorporated. Parents should be encouraged to reinforce the school's policies of no violence at home.

Research has found that family factors are correlated to a child's resiliency to bullying at school. Some of the family factors that increase resilience in bullied youth include maternal warmth, sibling warmth, and a positive atmosphere (Bowes, Maughan, Caspi, Moffitt, & Arseneault, 2010). It is crucially important for families to offer a supportive environment at home in order to decrease bullying behaviors.

Capable and willing parents should be recruited to teach these skills to parents. Other parents can take turns volunteering as hall monitors, dance chaperons, school grounds monitors, and bus aids. The more involved parents are, the more they will incorporate nonviolence into their home lives with their children. Hands-on, practical strategies taught in intervention programs are of critical importance to all persons who come into the school setting. "School-level interventions should aim at clarifying and communicating behavioral norms-that is, developing classroom and school-wide rules that prohibit bullying and promote adult modeling of respectful and non-violent behavior" (Thakore et al., 2015).

An effective program to reduce or prevent violence in the school requires a unified front by the adults working with students, including parents, teachers, school personnel, coaches, and school social workers. An adherence to the rules of removing pecking orders, codes of silence, and prejudice is crucial. All adults must work together with students to reduce school violence.

School Social Workers

School social workers have a responsibility to assess, design, implement, and evaluate programs for the prevention or reduction of violence within their schools. School social workers should serve as advocates for their students by requesting school administrators to have school wide assessments completed. Individuals should not wait until multiple acts of violence occur before they evaluate their schools. A study conducted by Astor, Behere, Fravil, and Wallace (1997) indicated that most school social workers and school personnel did not believe they had a violence problem and did not classify a violence problem until a severe lethal form of violence occurred. Unfortunately, school administrators or social workers who wait this long may have a large problem on their hands than they thought. It is recommended that all schools (elementary included) have a completed evaluation of their violence problems (type and level).

Once the results from an evaluation have been obtained, social workers should identify the types of interventions that are necessary for their school buildings. In addition, they should take lead roles in finding ready-made interventions or designing new ones. Practicing social workers also have the resources (or can obtain them) to implement programs. Basic skills, including problem solving, negotiation, and conflict resolution, are common interventions for students and adults who can meet with social workers. Therefore, social workers should be the ones to train school personnel, teachers, and parents. Afterward, interventions for the students can be implemented. Depending on the size of the school, social workers may need to recruit local agency social workers to help them with the large task of implementation of violence programs. Such programs should be incorporated into the curricula of the schools and all students should participate in them.

Schools have a unique opportunity to implement interventions more effectively than community agencies. The reasons for this are that they have a captive audience of students who cannot skip appointments, parents may have fewer transportation problems for school appointments, interventions can be implemented immediately when conflicts arise, and all parties can be included in interventions. The opportunity to reduce school violence should not be disregarded or underestimated.

Schools have an obligation to ensure the safety of their students and staff, as well as provide them with a positive learning environment. School social workers who have most, if not all, of the training and skills necessary to implement safety or violence prevention programs should serve to advocate for these programs in their schools. Although such programs still require refinement, they have been shown to be effective in curbing further violence in schools.

References

Albin, K. (2012). Bullies in a wired world: The impact of cyberspace victimization on adolescent mental health and the need for cyberbullying legislation in Ohio. *Journal of Law and Health, 25*, 155–190.

Antunes, M., & Ahlin, E. (2018). Minority and immigrant youth exposure to community violence: The differential effects of family management and peers. *Journal of Interpersonal Violence, 34*, 1–30.

Astor, R., Behere, W., Fravil, K., & Wallace, J. (1997). Perceptions of school violence as a problem and reports of violent events: A national survey of school social workers. *Social Work, 42*(1), 55–68.

Averdijk, M. (2011). Reciprocal effects of victimization and routine activities. *Journal of Quantitative Criminology, 27*(2), 125–149. https://doi.org/10.1007/s10940-010-9106-6

Banks, G., Hadenfeldt, K., Janoch, M., Manning, C., Ramos, K., & Patterson Silver Wolf, D. (2017). Gun violence and substance abuse. *Aggression and Violent Behavior, 34*, 113–116.

Batsche, G., & Knoff, H. (1994). Bullies and their victims: Understanding a pervasive problem in the schools. *School Psychology Review, 23*(2), 165–174.

Besag, V. (1989). *Bullies and victims in the schools: A guide to understanding and management.* Milton Keynes, England: Open University Press.

Bowes, L., Maughan, B., Caspi, A., Moffitt, T. E., & Arseneault, L. (2010). Families promote emotional and behavioural resilience to bullying: Evidence of an environmental effect. *Journal of Child Psychology & Psychiatry, 51*(7), 809–817.

Bright, R. M. (2005). It's just a grade 8 thing: Aggression in teenage girls. *Gender and Education, 17*(1), 93–101.

Booren, L. M., Handy, D. J., & Power, T. G. (2011). Examining perceptions of school safety strategies, school climate, and violence. *Youth violence and juvenile justice, 9*(2), 171–187.

Borum, R., Cornell, D. G., Modzeleski, W., & Jimerson, S. R. (2010). What can be done about school shootings? A review of the evidence. *Educational Researcher, 39*(1), 27–37.

Caplan, M., Weissberg, R., Grober, J., Sivo, P., Grady, K., & Jacoby, C. (1992). Social competence promotion with inner-city and suburban young adolescents: Effects on social adjustment and alcohol use. *Journal of Consulting and Clinical Psychology, 60*, 56–63.

Carson, D., & Esbensen, F. (2017). Gangs in school: Exploring the experiences of gang-involved youth. *Youth Violence and Juvenile Justice*, 1–21.

Casebeer, C. M. (2012). School bullying: Why quick fixes do not prevent school failure. *Preventing School Failure, 56*(3), 165–171.

Center to Prevent Handgun Violence. (1990). *Caught in the crossfire: A report on gun violence in our nation's schools.* Washington, DC: Author.

Centers for Disease Control and Prevention, National Center for Injury Prevention and Control. (2016, May 6). *National violent death reporting system.* Retrieved from http://www.cdc.gov/violenceprevention/nvdrs/

Committee for Children. (1992). *Second step: A violence prevention curriculum.* Seattle, WA: Author.

Currie, D. (2010). Survey finds widespread gangs, drug problems in U.S. schools. *Nation's Health, 40*(8), 7.

Department of Health and Human Services, Centers for Disease Control and Prevention. (2018). *Youth violence: Fact sheet.* Retrieved June 30, 2018, from http://www.cdc.gov/ncipc/factsheets/yvfacts.htm

Dickinson, T. (2015). Exploring the drugs/violence nexus among active offenders: Contributions from the St. Louis school. *Criminal Justice Review, 40*(1), 67–86. https://doi.org/10.1177/0734016814562422

Espelage, D., Merrin, G., & Hatchel, T. (2016). Peer victimization and dating violence among LGBTQ youth: The impact of school violence and crime on mental health outcomes. *Youth Violence and Juvenile Justice, 16*(2), 156–173.

Farrell, A. D., Sullivan, T. N., Esposito, L. E., & Meyer, A. L. (2005). A latent growth curve analysis of the structure of aggression, drug use, and delinquent behaviors and their interrelations over time in urban and rural adolescents. *Journal of Research on Adolescents, 15*(2), 179–204.

Furlong, M., & Morrison, G. (1994). Introduction to miniseries: School violence and safety in perspective. *School Psychology Review, 23*(2), 139–150.

Glew, G. M., Ming-Yu, F., Wayne, K., & Rivara, F. P. (2008). Bullying and school safety. *Journal of Pediatrics, 152*, 123–128.

Goldstein, A., Glick, B., Carthen, W., & Blancero, D. (1994). *The prosocial gang.* Newbury Park, CA: Sage.

Goldstein, A., & Soriano, F. (1994). Juvenile gangs. In L. Eron, J. Gentry, & P. Schlegel (Eds.), *Reason to hope: A psychosocial perspective on violence and youth.* Washington, DC: American Psychological Association.

Hahn, R., Fuqua-Whitley, D., Wethington, H., Lowy, J., Crosby, A., Fullilove, M., … Task Force on Community Preventive Services. (2007). Effectiveness of universal school-based programs to prevent violent and aggressive behavior a systematic review. *American Journal of Preventive Medicine, 33*(2), 114–129.

Hammond, R. (1991). *Dealing with anger: Givin' it. Takin' it. Workin' it out.* Champaign, IL: Research Press.

Hechinger, F. (1992). *Fateful choices: Healthy youth of the 21st century.* New York, NY: Carnegie Corporation of New York.

Hemenway, D., Vriniotis, M., Johnson, R. M., Miller, M., & Azrael, D. (2011). Gun carrying by high school students in Boston, MA: Does overestimation of peer gun carrying matter? *Journal of Adolescence, 34*(5), 997–1003.

Houbre, B., Tarquinio, C., & Thuillier, I. (2006). Bullying among students and its consequences on health. *European Journal of Psychology of Education, 21*(2), 183–208.

Jensen, G. (2000). Prohibition, alcohol, and murder: Untangling countervailing mechanisms. *Homicide Studies, 4*(1), 18–36.

Jiang, X., & Peguero, A. A. (2017). Immigrant generations and delinquency: Assessing the relative effects of family, school, and delinquent friends. *Race and Justice, 7*, 199–225.

Juvonen, J. (2005). Myths and facts about bullying in schools: Effective interventions depend upon debunking long-held misconceptions. *Behavioral Health Management*, 36–40.

Kazdin, A. (1994). Interventions for aggressive children. In L. Eron, J. Gentry, & P. Schlegel (Eds.), *Reason to hope: A psychosocial perspective on violence and youth.* Washington, DC: American Psychological Association.

Kirkhaug, B., Drugli, M. B., Handegard, B. H., Lyderson, S., Asheim, M., & Fossum, S. (2016). Does the incredible years teacher classroom management training programme have positive effects for young children exhibiting severe externalizing problems in school?: A quasi-experimental pre-post study. *Boston Medical Center Psychiatry, 16*(1), 362.

Kosciw, J. G., Greytak, E. A., Palmer, N. A., & Boesen, M. J. (2014). *The 2013 national school climate survey: The experiences of lesbian, gay, bisexual and transgender youth in our nation's schools.* New York, NY: GLSEN.

Larson, J. (1994). Violence prevention in the schools: A review of selected programs and procedures. *School Psychology Review, 23*(2), 151–164.

Lochman, J., Lampron, L., Gemmer, T., & Harris, S. (1986). Anger coping intervention with aggressive children: A guide to implementation in school settings. In P. Keller & S. Heyman (Eds.), *Innovations in clinical practice: A source book* (Vol. 6, pp. 339–356). Sarasota, FL: Professional Resources Exchange.

McLaughlin, L., Laux, J. M., & Pescara-Kovach, L. (2006). Using multimedia to reduce bullying and victimization in the third grade urban schools. *Professional School Counseling, 10*(2), 153–160.

Molina, I., Bowie, S. L., Dulmus, C. N., & Sowers, K. M. (2004). School-based violence prevention programs: A review of selected programs with empirical evidence. *Journal of Evidence-Based Social Work, 1*(2/3), 175–189.

Mongan, P., Hatcher, S., & Masche, T. (2009). Etiology of school shootings: Utilizing a purposive, non-impulsive model for social work. *Journal of Human Behavior in the Social Environment, 19*, 635–645.

National Center for Education Statistics. (2018). *Indicators of School Crime and Safety: 2018.* Retrieved June 11, 2018, from http://nces.ed.gov/programs/crimeindicators/crimeindicators2018/index.asp

National Gay and Lesbian Task Force Policy Institute. (2018). *National LGBTQ Taskforce: It's time to reevaluate the role of guns in America.* Washington, DC: Author.

National School resource Network. (1980). *Peer culture development.* (technical assistance bulletin 28). Washington, DC: National School Resource Network.

Oleweus, D. (1991). Bully/victim problems among school children: Basic facts and effects of a school-based intervention program. In D. J. Pepler & K. H. Rubin (Eds.), *The development and treatment of childhood aggression* (pp. 411–448). Hillsdale, NJ: Erlbaum.

Pilkington, N., & D'Augelli, A. (1995). Victimization of lesbian, gay, and bisexual youth in community settings. *Journal of Community Psychology, 23*, 34–56.

Pittaro, M. L. (2007). School violence and social control theory: An evaluation of the columbine massacre. *International Journal of Criminal Justice Sciences, 2*(1), 1–12.

Prothrow-Stith, D. (1987). *Violence prevention curriculum for adolescents.* Newton, MA: Education Development Center.

Richard, J. F., Schneider, B. H., & Mallet, P. (2011). Revisiting the whole-school approach to bullying: Really looking at the whole school. *School Psychology International, 33*(3), 263–284.

Saewyc, E. M., Skay, C. L., Pettingell, S. L., Reis, E. A., Bearinger, L., Resnick, M., … Combs, L. (2006). Hazards of stigma: The sexual and physical abuse of gay, lesbian, and bisexual adolescents in the United States and Canada. *Child Welfare, 85*(2), 195–213.

Salmivalli, C., Kaukiainen, A., & Voeten, M. (2005). Anti-bullying intervention: Implementation and outcome. *British Journal of Educational Psychology, 75*, 465–487.

Smith, P. K. (2004). *Bullying in schools: How successful can interventions be?* (Vol. 27(9), p. 334). Cambridge, England: Cambridge University Press.

Soriano, M., Soriano, F., & Jimenez, E. (1991). School violence among culturally diverse populations: Sociocultural and institutional considerations. *School Psychology Review, 23*(2), 216–235.

Stadler, P. (2001). Multicultural schools and monocultural teaching staff. *European Education, 33*(3), 40.

Stein, N. (1995). Sexual harassment in school: The public performance of gendered violence. *Harvard Educational Review, 65*(2), 145–162.

Stephens, R. (1994). School violence prevention and intervention strategies. *School Psychology Review, 23*(2), 204–219.

Sterzing, P., Gibbs, J., Gartner, R., & Goldbach, J. (2018). Bullying victimization trajectories for sexual minority adolescents: Stable victims, desisters, and late-onset victims. *Journal of Research on Adolescence, 28*(2), 368–378. https://doi.org/10.1111/jora.12336

Substance Abuse and Mental Health Services Administration. (2017). *Key substance use and mental health indicators in the United States: Results from the 2016 National Survey on Drug Use and Health* (HHS Publication No. SMA 17-5044, NSDUH Series H-52). Rockville, MD: Center for Behavioral Health Statistics and Quality, Substance Abuse and Mental Health Services Administration. Retrieved from https://www.samhsa.gov/data/

Swearer, S., Espelage, D., Vaillancourt, T., & Hymel, S. (2010). What can be done about school bullying? Linking research to educational practice. *Educational Researcher, 39*(1), 38–47.

Thakore, R. V., Apfeld, J. C., Johnson, R. K., Sathiyakumar, V., Jahangir, A. A., & Sethi, M. K. (2015). School-based violence prevention strategy: A pilot evaluation. *Journal of Injury and Violence Research, 7*(2), 45–53. https://doi.org/10.5249/jivr.v7i2.565

Thapa, A., Cohen, J., Guffey, S., & Higgins-D'Alessandro, A. (2013). A review of school climate research. *Review of Educational Research, 83*(3), 357–385.

Trump, K. S. (2007). A game plan. *American School Board Journal, 194*, 26–29.

U.S. Secret Service, National Threat Assessment Center. (2002). *Preventing school shootings: A summary of a U.S. Secret Service initiative report*. Washington, DC. Retrieved October 11, 2008, from http://www.ncjrs.gov/pdffiles1/jr000248.pdf

Vaughn, M. G., Perron, B. E., Abdon, A., Olate, R., Groom, R., & Wu, L. (2012). Correlates of handgun carrying among adolescents in the United States. *Journal of Interpersonal Violence, 27*(10), 2003–2021.

Vossekuil, B., Reddy, M., Fein, R., Borum, R., & Modzeleski, W. (2000). *USSS safe school initiative: An interim report on the prevention of targeted violence in schools*. Washington, DC: U.S. Secret Service, National Threat Assessment Center.

Vreeman, R. C., & Carroll, A. E. (2007). A systematic review of school-based interventions to prevent bullying. *Archives of Pediatrics & Adolescent Medicine, 161*, 78–88.

Wheeler, E. D., & Baron, S. A. (1994). *Violence in our schools, hospitals and public places: A prevention and management guide* (p. 284). Ventura, CA: Pathfinder Publishing. ISBN 0-934793-51-4.

Whitted, K. S., & Dupper, D. R. (2008). Do teachers bully students? Findings from a survey of students in an alternative education setting. *Education and Urban Society, 40*(3), 329–341.

Wike, T., & Fraser, M. (2009). School shootings: Making sense of the senseless. *Aggression and Violent Behavior, 14*, 162–169.

Wodarski, J., & Feit, M. (1995). *Adolescent substance abuse: An empirically-based group preventive health paradigm*. New York, NY: Haworth Press.

Wright, D. R., & Fitzpatrick, K. M. (2006). Violence and minority youth: The effects of risk and asset factors on fighting among African American children and adolescents. *Adolescence, 41*(162), 251–262.

Ye, L., Ferdinando, H., Seppanen, T., & Alasaarela, E. (2014). Physical violence detection for preventing school bullying. *Advances in Artificial Intelligence, 2014*. https://doi.org/10.1155/2014/740358

Yung, B., & Hammond, R. (1994). Native Americans. In L. Eron, J. Gentry, & P. Schlegel (Eds.), *Reason to hope: A psychosocial perspective on violence and youth*. Washington, DC: American Psychological Association.

Zhang, A., Musu-Gillette, L., & Oudekerk, B. A. (2016). *Indicators of school crime and safety: 2015 (NCES 2016-079/NCJ 249758)*. Washington, DC: National Center for Education Statistics, U.S. Department of Education, and Bureau of Justice Statistics, Office of Justice Programs, U.S. Department of Justice.

Chapter 5
Adolescent Sexuality

John S. Wodarski

Overview

One of the most pressing social problems confronting our society is the number of adolescents who are sexually active and who face the risk of the consequences of their sexual encounters. The recent trends are promising, as the alarming rise in teenage sexual activity and resulting pregnancies that occurred between the 1950s and the 1980s was followed by an equally dramatic decrease in these teenage tendencies between the late 1980s and present day (Guttmacher Institute, 2012; Santelli, Lindberg, Finer, & Singh, 2007). While these statistics show a vast improvement from previous decades, the USA still maintains much higher teenage pregnancy rates than most other developed countries (Guttmacher Institute, 2012). In the 1980s, the high incidence of teenage pregnancy was believed to be the result of a decrease in the average age of menses, combined with increasing sexual activity among adolescents (Chilman, 1979; Flick, 1986; Schinke, 1978). Moreover, approximately 50% of American adolescents do not use contraceptives the first time they have intercourse. The current decrease in teenage pregnancy is attributed to the corresponding decrease in sexual activity (responsible for 23% of the decrease) and to an increase in the proper use of one or more methods of contraception (responsible for 77% of the decrease) (Guttmacher Institute, 2012; Santelli et al., 2007). By age 15, 13% of teens have become sexually active; however, by age 19, this percentage increases to 70% (Guttmacher Institute, 2012). Another correlating factor to risky sexual behavior is that it may correlate with other risk behaviors, such as delinquency and drug use, to form a "risk behavior syndrome" (Clark, Brey, & Banter, 2003, p. 389). The risk behavior syndrome suggests multiple risks should be addressed together in prevention programs.

J. S. Wodarski (✉)
College of Social Work, University of Tennessee, Knoxville, TN, USA
e-mail: jwodarsk@utk.edu

© Springer Nature Switzerland AG 2019
J. S. Wodarski, L. M. Hopson (eds.), *Empirically Based Interventions Targeting Social Problems*, https://doi.org/10.1007/978-3-030-28487-9_5

Between 1950 and 1985, the nonmarital birthrate among adolescents younger than age 20 increased 300% for whites and 16% for blacks. It has been reported that from 1985 to 1990, increasing numbers of adolescents were becoming sexually active at younger ages, and the number of teenage mothers aged 13–15 rose by 26% (Rotheram-Borus, 1997, pp. 544–545). It was estimated in 1985 that roughly one million teenage girls became pregnant every year, resulting in 600,000 live births and 378,500 pregnancies terminated by abortion (Guttmacher Institute, 1985). It was estimated at that time that 84% of the pregnancies were intended. In 1988, figures increased when it was estimated that 11% of adolescents became pregnant. An estimated 4% had abortions. For 1988, the National Centers for Disease Control in Atlanta, Georgia, reported that 1,005,299 babies—or 26% of the US newborns—were born to unmarried women. In 1990, approximately 117 per 1000 teenage females became pregnant, and that number has steadily decreased to 68 per 1000 in 2008, which went against all expectations and predictions (Guttmacher Institute, 2012). Recidivism is an additional concern. It has been reported that 26% of the women who first gave birth at age 16 or younger gave birth a second time within 24 months (Story, 1987).

In addition to unintended teenage pregnancies, the rate of sexually transmitted infections (STIs) among sexually active teenagers is another area of concern. Despite the decreasing trends of teenage sexuality and teenage pregnancies, STIs are still producing alarming statistics, as approximately nine million new STIs are reported among teenagers every year (Guttmacher Institute, 2012). These rates are much higher than teenage STI rates being reported in most other developed countries, which are reminiscent of the pattern observed with teenage pregnancy rates (Kohler, Manhart, & Lafferty, 2008). Approximately 2.5 million adolescents have had sexually transmitted diseases, and 1 in 4 sexually active adolescents will have an STD before graduating high school (American Medical Association, 1991).

Adolescents who become pregnant are increasing risk for themselves and their babies for a bleak future marked by interrupted education, inadequate vocational training, poor work skills, economic dependency and poverty, large single-parent house-holds, and social isolation (Barth & Schinke, 1983). As Campbell (1968) commented, 90% of an adolescent's life script is written when she becomes a mother, and the story is often an unhappy one. Three out of four teenage mothers drop out of high school and only 1 in 50 finishes college. The cost to the teenage mother is high. Changes are increased that she and her baby will live in poverty. Moreover, the changes are great that the mother and baby will suffer ill health, as few pregnant teens obtain prenatal care.

The USA has a history of profound ambivalence toward human sexuality. This is nowhere more apparent than in our policies, regulations, and attitudes regarding the sexual behavior of children and adolescents (Ehrhardt, 1996, p. 1523). Adolescent pregnancy is increasingly commonplace today and poses many difficulties for both the individual involved and for society as a whole. Pregnant adolescents and their babies are at higher nutritional, health, social, and educational risk that the general population are in need of comprehensive, interdisciplinary care (McAnarney, 1985). For programs to successfully address this problem factors related to unintended pregnancies and consequences of teenagers' sexuality must be identified and understood. If one adopts a reality-based acceptance of teenage sexuality, the responsible public health policy ought to be to provide effective and comprehensive sex education that includes information on and access to contraceptive and sexually transmitted disease (STD)/human immunodeficiency virus (HIV) barrier methods to prevent pregnancy and sexually transmitted disease/HIV infection (Ehrhardt, 1996, pp. 1523–1524). This chapter provides a review of current literature on these factors and consequences. Relevant prevention strategies are examined to furnish the rationale for a more comprehensive practice model to prevent unsafe sexual practices, sexually transmitted disease, and teenage pregnancies.

The High Cost of Teenage Sexuality

Teenage Pregnancies Each teenage pregnancy translates into a significant cost to the taxpayer, which is a major cause for concern. In 1985, for example, teenage pregnancy cost each US taxpayer $16.65 in Aid to Families with Dependent Children, Medicaid, and food stamps (Guttmacher Institute, 1985). In another example, the city of Baltimore spent about $179,500,000 in 1987 on AFDC, Medicaid, and food stamps for families that were begun when the mother was a teenager. Had these births been delayed until the mother was at least 20 years old, Baltimore would have saved almost $72,000,000 in public outlays (Santelli, Rosenblatt, & Birn, 1990). The cost borne by Medicaid for a birth to a teenager age 14 or younger has been calculated as $3494; the cost for 15–17 year olds is $3224; and for 18–19 year olds, it is $2696, exclusive of pediatric care (Armstrong & Waszak, 1990). While the prevalence of teenage pregnancy has steadily declined since the late 1980s, the cost of this social problem to taxpayers continues to be of major concern. In 2008, taxpayers spent a total of $10.9 billion on costs related to teenage pregnancy, birth, and teenage motherhood. To present this statistic in another way, each child born to a teenage mother costs US taxpayers $1647 (The National Campaign, 2011).

The National Research Council estimates that for each year a first birth is delayed, the family income when the mother reaches age 27 is increased by $500. Thus, every year a first birth is delayed, the chances of a woman and her family having poverty-level income are reduced by about 22%. The Children's Defense Fund reports that women who first give birth as teens have about half the lifetime earnings of women who first give birth in their twenties (Armstrong & Pascale, 1990). Three major national surveys found the incidence of poverty among families begun by teen births to be 20%, 50%, and 60% greater than among families of mothers who gave birth to their first child at a later age (Furstenberg, Brooks-Gunn, & Morgan, 1987).

The Center for Population Options (CPO) determined that the federal government spent $21.6 billion in 1989 on families begun by teen mothers. This includes $10.4 billion for AFDC, $3.4 billion for food stamps, and $7.7 billion for Medicaid.

Based on the assumption that families begun by teen births comprise 53% of the welfare-recipient population, they consume 53% of the funding of these programs.

This represents the projected cost to the federal government over the subsequent 20 years of a family begun by a teen birth, again including only the three benefit programs. Reflected in the calculations are the observations that (a) approximately 1 in 3 teen mothers receives welfare, (b) the average length of time a woman who begins her family as a teen remains on welfare is 2.5 years, (c) the probability a teen mother will receive public assistance declines over her lifetime, and (d) the younger a women when she first gives birth, the more children she can be expected to have.

All considered, the CPO estimates that a family begun by a teenage mother in 1989 will cost taxpayers an average of $16,975 by the time that baby reaches age 20. This figure, however, is deceptively low because it represents an average across all first births to adolescent mothers, even though only one-third of families begun by a teen birth actually receive welfare. More informatively, the SPO projects that the government will spend an average of $50,925 over 20 years on each family begun in 1989 by a teen birth, who enrolled in public assistance. Presumably, the figure is averaged down by the families who drop out of the welfare system.

The CPO estimates that the families begun in 1989 by a teen birth will have cost the public treasure $6.4 billion by the year 2009.

Teenage Sexually Transmitted Disease More than two-thirds of adolescents with AIDS were infected through sexual contact with adults. The prevalence of HIV infection among adolescents is a source of concern. For some young adults, naivety is expressed about the HIV infection. Many believe that they are safe from the former through their selection of coital partners from among those they believe to be free of infection (Maticka-Tyndale, 1991, p. 63). Because it takes an estimated 5–10 years for the HIV infection to result in AIDS, many young adults who have AIDS contracted the virus as adolescents. Approximately 20% of people identified as having AIDS are between ages 20 and 29 (American Medical Association, 1991). In 2002, teen girls represented about half (51%) of HIV cases reported among 13–19 year olds (The Henry J. Kaiser Family Foundation, 2005, p. 2). It has been reported that in the USA, about 13% of those tested at Centers for Disease Control and Prevention anonymous test sites are adolescents (Centers for Disease Control and Prevention, 1992, pp. 219–228).

Adolescents continue to have the highest rates of STIs when compared to other age groups. In 2008, approximately 68,600 teenagers and young adults (ages 13–24) tested positively for HIV. In 2009, another 8300 teenagers and young adults were diagnosed with HIV (Center for Disease Control, 2012).

Contraceptive use has not kept up with adolescent coital activity. One significant reason for this may have to do with the development stage of the adolescent. The key to effective use of contraceptives may lie in a teen's cognitive ability to think abstractly—linking present behavior with future consequences, as well as recognizing the risks involved with unprotected sexual activity (Doctors, 1985). Many teens, especially younger ones, have not yet achieved this level of cognitive ability.

Current Expenditures AIDS is expensive. It is costly in terms of pain, suffering, and premature mortality, and in terms of fear, anxiety, and grief. It costs lovers their partners, parents with children, and children with parents. It is also costly in monetary terms. We spent about $10 billion on HIV-related activities in 1991. Federal government expenditures alone totaled $3.46 billion: $1.245 billion for research, $1.246 billion on medical care, $567 million for education and prevention, and $305 million in income support to AIDS victims (Office of Management and Budget, 1990). Federal expenditures on AIDS from 1982 to 1991 totaled almost $12 billion (National Center for Health Statistics, 1990; Office of Management and Budget, 1990). Since the federal government contributes approximately one-third of the total spent on AIDS, total spending during that time approaches $36 billion.

Hellinger estimates that the direct cost of AIDS will have been $5.8 billion in 1991, with the cost of treating an HIV-infected person averaging $5150 yearly and the cost of treating a patient with full-blown AIDS averaging $32,000 yearly.

Future Costs Forecasts of the future costs of AIDS vary. Foreman (1991) estimated total personal care costs to be $8.5 billion in 1991. They projected an additional $2.3 billion to be spent on personal care activity. Winkenwerder, Kessler, and Stolec (1989) estimated that federal spending on HIV-related illnesses reached $4.3 billion in 1992, and total national expenditures were estimated to be three times higher. Hellinger estimated the cumulative lifetime medical care expenses (in 1988 dollars) for all people diagnosed with AIDS to be $4.3 billion in 1990, $5.3 billion in 1991, $6.5 billion in 1992, and $7.8 billion in 1993. He additionally projected that expenditures for medical care alone to AIDS patients in 1994 would total $10.4 billion (Foreman, 1991). In spite of the armed forces' policy of discharging HIV-infected persons, the US General Accounting Office (US GAO) projects that AIDS will cost the US military and veterans' health care system $3 billion by the end of the 1990s (U.S. General Accounting Office, 1990).

Altogether, in 1989 alone, private insurers paid over $1 billion in AIDS-related health and life insurance claims, 71% more than in 1988 (Carrol, 1989).

The CDC estimated that over 500,000 persons in this country are HIV infected and do not know it (K. Golan, personal communication, August 1991). In 1990, 9% of deaths in the world were related to HIV/AIDS (Over, 1999, p. 219). The Henry J. Kaiser Family Foundation (2005) reported:

> The first cases of what would later become known as AIDS were reported in the United States in June of 1981…Since that time, more than 1.5 million people in the U.S. have been infected with HIV, including more than 500,000 who have already died. (p. 1)

Thus, HIV-related expenses are expected to continue to increase until some type of cure of solution is found. The government has a fundamental role to prevent the spread of HIV infection among those most likely to contract and spread the virus while protecting them from discrimination and stigmatization (Over, 1999, p. 222). Resulting from the former, the most vital aspect is that of information. Being educated properly would benefit those occupying the heterogeneous population.

Social Consequences of Teenage Sexuality

Adolescents who engage in sexual activity are most likely to have lower grades in school, lower expectations of achievement, and lower levels of parental control, and to lack strong religious beliefs. They are likely to see their parents and peers in conflict. Many adolescents' mothers have low self-esteem and are inclined to be passive and hold traditional stereotypical views of male–female roles (Lockhart & Wodarski, 1990).

There are even more detrimental consequences to repeat teenage pregnancies. Teenage mothers with more than one child are less likely to return to high school and graduate, and therefore find it more difficult to economically support their families. Therefore, the children of teenage mothers frequently do poorly in school and experience less support at home (Katz et al., 2011).

Assessment Measures

This section describes those measures that we have found helpful in evaluation of current interventions to reduce teenage pregnancy and sexually transmitted disease. We have chosen these measures based on the criteria of adequate reliability and ease of administration. A brief description of each is provided to assist professionals in determining whether to incorporate these assessment measures in evaluation.

Sex Knowledge

Sex Knowledge Test (Kirby, 1985) This inventory is a 34-item, multiple-choice scale. It includes the following areas: adolescent physical development, adolescent marriage, the probability of pregnancy, birth control, and sexually transmitted disease. The test was developed after literature and overall goals of sexuality education were examined. The test–retest reliability of the knowledge test was determined by administering the test to 58 adolescents on two occasions, 2 weeks apart, and then calculating the correlation coefficient between their scores on the first administration and their totals on the second administration. The reliability is 0.89.

Behavior Inventory (Kirby, 1985) Three aspects of behaviors were considered in developing the sex knowledge measures: the skills with which the behavior is completed, the comfort experienced during that behavior, and the frequency of that behavior. The Behavior Inventory measures these three aspects as demonstrated in:

1. Skills in taking responsibility for personal behavior.
2. Social decision-making skills.

3. Sexual decision making.
4. Communication skills.
5. Assessment skills.
6. Birth control assertiveness skills.
7. Comfort engaging in social activities.
8. Comfort talking about sex and birth control.
9. Comfort expressing concern and caring.
10. Comfort being assertive sexually.
11. Comfort having current sex life.
12. Comfort getting and using birth control.
13. Existence and frequency of sexual activity.
14. Frequency of use of birth control.
15. Frequency of communication about sex and birth control with parents.
16. Frequency of communication about sex and birth control with boyfriends or girlfriends.
17. Frequency of communication about sex and birth control with friends.

The questions that measure skills use a 5-point scale; the questions that measure comfort use 4-point Likert-type scales. The questions measuring sexual activity, use of birth control, and frequency of communication ask how many times during the previous month the respondent engaged in the specific activity.

Test–retest coefficients indicate that the items have a great range of reliability coefficients. The scale measuring skills ranges from poor (0.57) to excellent (0.88). Scales measuring comfort range from a low of 0.38 (comfort getting and using birth control) to a high of 0.70 (comfort having current sex life). The questions involving sexual activity have excellent reliability. The questions about whether respondents have ever had intercourse had a reliability of 1.00. The items measuring frequencies of communication have adequate, but not excellent, reliability (Kirby, 1985).

Attitude and Values Inventory (Kirby, 1985) This instrument includes 15 different scales, each consisting of 5-point Likert-type items measuring the following:

1. Clarity of long-term goals.
2. Clarity of personal sexual values.
3. Understanding of personal sexual values.
4. Understanding of emotional need.
5. Understanding of personal social behavior.
6. Understanding of personal sexual responses.
7. Attitudes toward various gender role behaviors.
8. Attitudes toward sexuality in life.
9. Attitudes toward the importance of birth control.
10. Attitudes toward premarital intercourse.
11. Attitudes toward the use of pressure and force in sexual activity.
12. Recognition of the importance of the family.
13. Self-esteem.
14. Satisfaction with personal sexuality.

15. Satisfaction with social relationships.

The reliabilities of the 15 different scales were determined in two different ways. First, the test–retest reliabilities were found by administering the questionnaire twice, at an interval of 2 weeks, to 51 participants in different programs, and then calculating the correlation coefficient between the first administration and the second administration of each scale. Second, the overall reliability of each scale was calculated by randomly selecting about 100 pretest and posttest questionnaires from each site, combining the questionnaires into a single file, and then calculating Cronbach's alpha for the items in each scale. Basically, using all of the measures of reliability, scales of the clarity of goals and values range from a coefficient of 0.54 to 0.90; scales addressing the understanding of needs, social behavior, and response range from 0.51 to 0.84; attitude scales range from 0.30 to 0.94; self-esteem scales range from 0.73 to 0.80; and satisfaction scales range from 0.64 to 0.88.

Youth HIV/AIDS Knowledge and Attitudes

Knowledge, Attitudes, Beliefs, and Practice (WHO, 1989) The Knowledge, Attitudes, Beliefs, and Practice (KABP) is a standardized survey instrument developed by the World Health Organization (WHO) for measuring AIDS-related knowledge, attitudes, beliefs, and practices of adolescents (World Health Organization, 1989). The instrument measures self-efficacy in avoiding pressure to have sex, in AIDS knowledge, and in attitudes and perceived social norms toward sexual intercourse. Behavior-specific questions elicit responses related to smoking, drug use, sexual intercourse, intention to engage in sexual intercourse in the next 3 months, and intention to use condoms when having sex (Seha, Klepp, & Ndeki, 1994).

Instructional Evaluation for Students (Kirby, 1985) This class evaluation contains two parts. The first part asks the respondents to rate numerous teaching skills of the instructor, characteristics of classroom interaction, and program structure and materials. The second part asks participants to assess as accurately as possible the current or future effects of the course. In particular, it asks how the course affected their:

1. Knowledge.
2. Understanding of personal behavior.
3. Clarity of values.
4. Attitudes toward birth control.
5. Communication about sexuality.
6. Communication with parents.
7. Probability of having sex.

Approaches to Prevention

Past Approaches to Prevention

Despite extensive documentation of early childbearing consequences, efforts to prevent or ameliorate teenage pregnancy have been ineffective (Schinke, 1997; Stout & Rivara, 1989). One reason for this failure appears to be the lack of a complete conceptual framework for understanding and preventing this growing social problem. An extensive literature review reveals that, rather than recognizing the factorial complexity of the phenomenon, most approaches to understanding and preventing teenage pregnancy can be characterized as either reductionistic models stressing a single underlying explanation or developmental models emphasizing a normal adolescent maturational process (Schinke & Gilchrist, 1977). The reductionistic approach explains teenage pregnancy as resulting from one problem condition or factor that leads to a single, straightforward assumption: Given easy, low-cost access to sex and contraceptive education and services, adolescents will be informed, responsible, and self-regulating in avoiding unplanned pregnancies. Prevention, as emphasized in traditional sex education, attempts to change attitudes by exposing adolescents to the unattractive consequences of their behaviors. This so-called scare tactic approach has not been effective in preventing teenage pregnancies (Dryfoos, 1983; Gilchrist, Schinke, & Blythe, 1979).

The search for a pathology that underlies teenage sexual activities has directed many efforts and has guided many of the reductionistic prevention programs. Researchers have looked for personality correlates of adolescents' vulnerability to having intercourse (Goldfarb et al., 1977), pregnancy risk (Rosen & Ager, 1981), and decision making about childbearing (Perlman, Klerman, & Kinard, 1981). Research has uncovered little reason to suspect that adolescents' sexual behavior is pathological (Gilchrist, 1981; Gilchrist & Schinke, 1983; Litt, Cuskey, & Rudd, 1980; Olson, 1980; Schinke, 1979). Nevertheless, a host of social service programs for teenagers has been based on the pathological orientation. Unfortunately, pathologically oriented sex education programs have had little or no effect on adolescents' sexual behavior (Kirby, 1980; Reid, 1982; Zelnik & Kim, 1982).

The developmentalists, in contrast, have strongly stressed the complexity of multiple interactional factors that influence adolescents' behavior (Jones & Bonte, 1990). They suggest that situational, social, interpersonal, and maturational factors may interact to lead adolescents into premarital sexual activities and can be factors that prevent adolescents from effectively applying their contraceptive knowledge and understanding (Cvetkovich & Grote, 1980; Sandberg & Jacobs, 1971). Cvetkovich and Grote (1980) further suggest that female adolescents may be placed at pregnancy risk "not by any form of pathology, moral or otherwise, but, by a unique convergence of factors which are 'normal' to the lives of many" (p. 2). Adolescence is a period of growth that demands mastery of critical developmental tasks, two of which are learning sexual functioning (Wagner, 1970) and the relational nature of sexual activities (McAlister, Perry, & Maccoby, 1979). Often times it is seen a deviant for a female to act upon her sexual desires due to the sexist constructions of society. To construct sexual desire as a normative feature of female adolescence, then, is to challenge psychology's covert but persistent collusion with a culture that alternately denies and denigrates girls' sexual feelings (Tolman, 2000, p. 70). McAlister et al. (1979) suggest that if prevention efforts are to be effective, their developers must consider factors that include the interpersonal aspects of risk taking, the social significance of many problem behaviors, and the role of peer pressure. In the Cvetkovich and Grote study (1980), females reported they became sexually active because they could not say no, because they wanted to please and satisfy their boyfriends, or because it seemed as though sexual activity was expected of them.

Current Prevention Strategies

Prevention programs may be classified into three general groups: sex education and information, contraceptive services, and the broadening of life options such as general education and employment during pregnancy and after childbirth (Dryfoos, 1983). Sex education is considered the primary prevention strategy of teenage pregnancy. In 1989, every state had a policy supporting HIV education, and two-thirds of states had policies supporting sexuality education. However, in 1990, a conservative backlash began that resulted in legal battles over sexuality education in more than 500 communities (Haffner, 1997). This resulted in the collision of whether there should be sexuality education in schools to what should be taught in such classes.

Sex education is one prevention strategy of teenage pregnancy that offers two major advantages: It can reach all young people before they become sexually active, and information can be provided to them at relatively low cost through the school, churches, and other delivery systems. In the past, sex education attempted to help adolescents understand the physical changes accompanying puberty, the biology of reproduction, and the responsibilities of family life. In an international study, researchers found that comprehensive sex education programs were significantly more successful in reducing teenage pregnancy when compared with no sex education and when compared with abstinence-only sex education programs. The comprehensive sex education programs were also more successful in reducing teenage sexual activity when compared to no sex education (Kohler et al., 2008).

Several studies aimed at HIV/AIDS prevention have incorporated skills-building elements with some notable successes. According to Auslander (1993), short-term, information-only interventions are ineffective in increasing HIV/AIDS-related knowledge and reducing high-risk activities. She suggests that, in addition to information, youth need to acquire skills to apply what they have learned when faced with situations that place them at risk. She states further that adolescents need to learn specific interpersonal skills to resist peer pressure to engage in unsafe sexual practices and take drugs, and they need skills to negotiate less risky activities with friends of partners. Auslander reviews three studies that suggest that HIV/AIDS prevention programs based on a cognitive-behavioral framework hold some promise. In the first, Rotheram-Borus and coworkers (Rotheram-Borus & Koopman, 1991) focused on improving knowledge and coping skills through video and art workshops, information about community resources, and reduction of the number of individual barriers to safer sex. The frequency of engaging in high-risk patterns of sexual behavior decreased as the number of intervention sessions increased. In the second study, Jemmott, Jemmott, and Fong (1992) provided inner-city Black male youths with a 5-h program designed to increase knowledge of STDs, reduce unsafe attitudes, and encourage problem solving related to risky sexual behavior through role playing, videotapes, games, and exercises. Their intervention resulted in greater knowledge, less risky attitudes, and less inclination to engage in risky behavior. Moreover, at 3-month follow-up, the adolescents were engaging in fewer occasions of sexual intercourse, had fewer sexual partners, used condoms more frequently, and engaged in anal intercourse less often than the adolescents in the control condition. Finally, Auslander (1993) compared a skills-training format (role plays, practice, demonstrations) to a discussion-only format to reduce HIV risk among adolescents who engage in delinquent activities. They found that the discussion group format was equally as effective as the skills-training group in imparting knowledge, changing attitudes, and increasing interpersonal skills to cope with HIV-risk situations.

The skills-training format, however, was more effective in changing the youths' intentions to engage in HIV-risk behaviors.

Another study that was conducted was by Hogben and Byrne in 1988. A five-step behavioral process was identified that aimed at effective contraception. Cognitive elements are engaged in the first and second steps, which concern gathering and processing information about contraception and acknowledging the likelihood of engaging in sexual intercourse (Hogben & Byrne, 1998, p. 63). Social learning variables related to modeling, expectancies, and reinforcement (direct or vicarious) are brought into play during the third and fourth steps, respectively, obtaining the contraceptive and communicating with a partner about contraception (Hogben & Byrne, 1998, p. 63). The fifth step is correct use of the contraceptive. The whole step-by-step process could easily be modeled in a behavioral social learning framework.

Most Americans today believe that sex education should address the complex problems of human sexuality that teenagers face. But a few people still believe that sex education, particularly when it covers methods of contraception, actually increases teenagers' sexual activity, causes an upswing in unintended pregnancies, and undermines the family unit (Kenney & Orr, 1984). Consequently, sex education remains controversial, despite the enormous diversity of nationwide program offerings. Many parents and teenagers believe, however, that sex education plays an important role in the prevention of unwanted teenage pregnancies (Bachman, Johnston, & O'Malley, 1980; Gallup Opinion Index, 1978).

There are some conflicting roles on whom, and how, is the appropriate individual to inform our adolescents of sexual behavior/information. From the former we know that adolescents are putting themselves at risk for HIV, pregnancy, and sexually transmitted diseases (STDs). We also know that the age that this occurs is getting younger and younger. Deciding on what messages to give students has proved to be a cause of conflict and polarization in many communities (Rea-Holloway, Blinn-Pike, & Berger, 2000, p. 246). These confusing messages range widely: Remain abstinent until emotionally and developmentally ready for sex; remain abstinent until marriage; remain abstinent, but be informed about contraception and disease prevention; and use that information to effectively protect against disease and unwanted pregnancy (Rea-Holloway et al., 2000, p. 246). The ascendant popularity of abstinence in sexuality education is closely linked to the discoveries of the alarming rates of unwanted pregnancy and STD transmission among adolescents (Bay-Cheng, 2001, p. 242). Resulting from this, in 1996 the federal government earmarked $50 million per year to support school-based abstinence curricula as part of welfare reform (Haskins & Bevan, 1997).

Another recent surge in funding for abstinence-only sex education demonstrates that this issue is an ongoing political controversy that will likely continue to change with the political climate (Dailard, 2006). However, the data shows that abstinence-only sex education programs were significantly less successful in reducing teenage pregnancy than were comprehensive sex education programs that taught teenagers about contraceptive use (Kohler et al., 2008). It has been shown that many teenagers who pledge to remain abstinent until marriage end up breaking their pledge and engaging in sexual activity before marriage, and the majority of those teenagers do not use contraceptives (Kohler et al., 2008).

Sex education rarely involves parents as primary sex educators of their children (McAnarney & Schreider, 1984). Research has revealed that fewer than 20% of parents tell their teenage children about intercourse, discuss birth control, or provide them with sex education literature (Schinke & Gilchrist, 1984). McAnarney and Schreider (1984) suggest several reasons for this: (a) Parents may not have adequate information to share, (b) parents may not know how to educate their child about sexuality, (c) parents may be uncomfortable with the subject, and (d) adolescents may be uncomfortable when parents assume the roles of sex educators, especially no discussion of the subject has occurred before puberty. Parents need to be prepared for their roles as sex educators before their children reach teenage years. Thus, an effective prevention program will include a parental component.

Very few sex education programs have been systematically evaluated (Kirby, 1985). With the exception of the aforementioned follow-up study by Jemmott et al. (1992), virtually no attempts have been made to conduct follow-up studies to ascertain the long-term effects of sex education on adolescents' knowledge, attitudes, and behavior. Evaluative studies of sex education have concluded that there was no evidence to support the belief that sex education would increase or decrease the sexual activities of teenagers (Kirby, Alter, & Scales, 1979; Stout & Rivara, 1989) or to support the claim that the decision to engage in sexual activities is influenced by sex education in school. However, females who are sexually active and had sex education that covered contraceptive methods appeared somewhat more likely to use contraceptives the first time they engaged in sexual intercourse. They also experience fewer pregnancies than sexually active females who did not have formal sex education (Zelnik & Kim, 1982). A need element of evaluative research of sex education programs is the study of long-term retention of knowledge.

The Comprehensive Parent, Peers, and School Prevention Model

Acknowledgment of a problem is the first step toward its resolution. Substantial research has been devoted to teenage pregnancy. Individuals who are associated with adolescents can demonstrate their concern about combating the problem of teenage pregnancy by developing prevention programs aimed at three groups: adolescents, parents, and schoolteachers and counselors. Another population of educators that should be introduced is physicians. So often it is forgotten that physicians represent an important member in schools or the family. In addition to meeting the health needs of students, faculty, and staff, they reinforce and provide credibility to health promotion messages (Taskforce of Pediatric AIDS, 1993, pp. 626–630). The combination of one-on-one interaction, and the confidentiality of the physician/patient relationship, can encourage frank and honest discussions (Taskforce of Pediatric AIDS, 1993, pp. 626–630). Physicians play an important role in reducing adolescents' sexual risks.

For effective pregnancy prevention training, information input and behavior change output must be considered. More important, training must address influential intervening variables, that is, cognitive and moral processed mediating the understanding and use of information in decision making. Thus, a comprehensive education program that gives teenagers, parents, and schoolteachers and counselors accurate sex education through a curriculum that is attractive, through social skills training in terms of assertiveness and problem solving, and through practice in applying this information in at-risk situations is needed.

In 1988, the Memphis City Schools developed and implemented the Family Life Curriculum, a knowledge- and skills-based sexuality education program designed for students from kindergarten through 12th grade with the stated purpose of reducing the high adolescent pregnancy rate (Oliver, Leeming, & Dwyer, 1998, pp. 143–147). This initiative was adopted in anticipation of the passage of a 1989 Tennessee state law mandating school-based sex education in counties with adolescent pregnancy rates exceeding 19.5 pregnancies per 1000 young women aged 15–17 (Oliver et al., 1998, pp. 143–147). After 5 years, the program was re-evaluated and it was found that the curriculum was only sporadically implemented. Thus, the program's effectiveness in reducing teenage pregnancy could not be properly assessed.

Notwithstanding, the report also called attention to the absence in the program of any initiatives to encourage parents' involvement with their children's sexuality education. While many school-based programs lack such a component, a small body of recent research suggests that the promotion of parental involvement may be an important component of school-based sexuality-education programs (Oliver et al., 1998, pp. 143–147). Therefore, the overall recommendation is that parents should engage in the sex education of their children.

More recent data shows that in 2006, US high schools were teaching curriculum related to issues of teenage sexuality, pregnancy, and STIs. The research shows that 76% of schools discussed the various risks related to teenage pregnancy, 58% taught a number of methods of contraceptive use, 38% specifically taught correct condom use, 87% taught abstinence as the most effective (but not the only) method to avoid pregnancy and STIs, 56% provided pregnancy prevention services, and 5% provided condoms at the school (Center for Disease Control, 2012).

Timing, Context, and Content

Research has indicated that if adolescents are to adopt the idea of pregnancy prevention, then sex education must be an integral part of their personal development and must begin before or during puberty (McAnarney & Schreider, 1984; Thornburg, 1981). In practice, most sex education curricula and programs have occurred too late in the developmental cycle (Blythe, Gilchrist, & Schinke, 1981; Gilchrist et al., 1979; Gilchrist & Schinke, 1983; Schinke, 1982; Schinke, Blythe, Gilchrist, & Burt, 1981). Auslander (1993) suggests that it is imperative that prevention programs address the social environments and culture of the contexts in which adolescents interact. This involves educating the staff, the foster parents, the biological parents, and all institutions in which adolescents will reside. She states further that, to maintain attitudinal and behavior change over time, realistic and culturally specific prevention practices need to be consistently reinforced among youth within their social environment. Coie et al. (1993, p. 1019) state that "the public schools offer a logical setting for broad-scale prevention interventions because 9 of 10 children in our society are found there." Moreover, they suggest that schools provide the greatest access to children who may be reliably identified as being at risk, while at the same time providing access to those who might be overlooked in the risk assessment protocols. DiClemente (1993) adds that "the school is only institution regularly attended by most young people, and virtually all youth attend schools before they initiate the behaviors that may place them at risk." The introduction of sex education prevention programs at the middle school level would be appropriate. This follows the suggestion by Doty and King (1985) that to have an impact on adolescent pregnancy rates and to circumvent our traditional practices of providing "too little, too late," sex education programs must begin to span preadolescence, early adolescence, and adolescence. Programs could be incorporated into health education courses or group discussions within local youth organizations associated with churches, as well as through other formal and informal community organizations (Doty & King, 1985).

Auslander (1993) reminds us that there is no one strategy that will be effective with all individuals. Rather, different strategies should be developed in response to the unique characteristics of the target population. She suggests that early prevention programs for youths who are not yet sexually active might be designed differently than those for youths who are sexually active, and interventions needed within schools would be different from those delivered in clinics.

Although it is often said that sex education programs should be values-free, Scales (1983) and McAnarney and Schreider (1984) have pointed out that sex education is not values-free. Each program and community, as well as the parents, will stress their beliefs, which are embodied in the program's goals (Scales, 1983). Therefore, the ideal program is grounded in a set of values. Students need not agree initially with these values, but they should be clearly stated so that they can make decisions based on a known standard. The following values will be incorporated into the prototypic sex education program:

1. Being a teen parent is not a good idea; it brings with it social, emotional, educational, financial, and medical consequences.
2. No one should be pressured into a sexual act against his or her will or principles.
3. Postponement of sexual intercourse should be strongly encouraged until adolescents have at least completed high school.
4. The double standards for males and females, which still exist in our society, are not to be condoned.
5. Having unprotected intercourse is like skydiving without a parachute—it is political, social, emotional, and financial suicide (Scales, 1983).

Peers

Prevention programs should assist adolescents in identifying and examining peer pressure and in exploring ways to make individual, deliberate decisions, especially since peers have a significant impact on each other's behaviors. According to DiClemente (1993), the use of peer educators as behavior change agents is perhaps the most underutilized to be understood by their classmates. Thus, we posit that sex education should be offered through a peer group experience. The former is posited due to a Choice Program that was completed by the Peer Education Program of Advocates for Youth. The program consisted of peer to peer instruction and interaction. The topic was "Condoms as They Relate to Pregnancy and STD Prevention" (Evans, 1999, p. 32). Related games were played, role plays, and informative discussions were held. The conclusion was that the Choice program was successful in instruction because the adolescents were met on the same level (i.e., by members of their peers). Peer learning structures should create a learning situation in which the performance of each group member furthers the attainment of overall group goals. This increases individual members' support for group performance, strengthens performance under a variety of similar circumstances, and further enhances the attainment of group goals. Group reward structures capitalize on peer influence and peer reinforcement. These are considered to be some of the most potent variables in the acquisition, alteration, and maintenance of prosocial norms among youths (Buckholdt & Wodarski, 1978). Peer programs that foster a sense of self-worth, awareness of one's own feelings, and assertiveness will help adolescents learn to act in their own interests, with a stronger sense of control over their own lives. Moreover, a prevention program must be aimed at males as well as females. Adolescent males are presently less aware of the risks of pregnancy, less informed about contraceptives, and less supportive of the use of contraceptives than are females, and they have the most to learn from a sex education program (Freeman, 1978).

Parent Component

Parents greatly influence their children's behavior. Next to those of peers, parental involvement and communication are most critical and should be strengthened to help adolescents become more responsible. Yoshikawa (1994) suggests that prevention interventions that combine comprehensive family support with early education may bring about long-term prevention through short-term protective effects on multiple risks. In a survey by Yankelovich, Skelly, and White (1979), 84% of the parings of teenagers said it was up to them to teach their children about sex-related topics, even though they supported sex education in public schools. Although parents want to be involved in educating their children about sex-related topics, they find it very difficult (Fox, 1980; Fox & Inazu, 1980). Parents need the skills to establish open communication with their children regarding sexual issues. The main thrust of the program with parents should be toward enhancing communication skills between parents and children, because lack of communication has been consistently shown to have an effect on teenage sexual activities (Cvetkovich & Grote, 1980; Fox & Inazu, 1980; McAnarney & Schreider, 1984). Focusing on increasing parents' skills in communicating, especially in the areas of values clarification and moral consciousness and the relational aspect of sexuality, as well as other sex-related topics, should be a major part of the program for the parental group of the prevention model. Parents, who are often less informed than their teenagers (Dryfoos, 1982a, 1982b), need to be involved in prevention programs in order to become more informed and comfortable with discussing sexual issues with their children. Parental involvement is a necessary element of any successful prevention model so that accurate and open communication, as well as the learning process, can be supported at home. Furthermore, fathers should be present with their sons and mothers with their daughters. Concluding, interactant communication styles (home, peer, professional, and multi-source) is a significant aspect that needs to be strengthened. It has been shown that adolescents who had interactant communication styles had greater birth control knowledge than those with a noninteractant learning style (Werner-Wilson, Fitzharris, & Morrissey, 2004, p. 63).

Summary

In order to alleviate the dilemma of teenagers having children, it is evident that the following points must be considered:

1. The timing of sex education is critical; sex education should occur in the middle school years.

2. Attractive curricula taught by qualified teachers are necessary.
3. Curricula should center particularly on gender roles, premarital sexual activity, contraception, abortion, AIDS, psychological issues (e.g., self-esteem and judgment), decision making, and problem solving. Moreover, curricula should include help-seeking strategies, life options, family relationships, and alternatives to pregnancy and parenting (Haslett, 1991; Herdt, 1989).
4. More research is needed on constitutional predisposition for risk taking and how such predisposition for risk taking and how such predispositions interact with the social contexts of adolescent development.
5. The incorporation of the peer group experience as a learning vehicle is necessary since peer norms influence sexual behavior (Benda & DiBlasio, 1991).
6. Sex education should involve the opportunity to practice appropriate behaviors for high-risk situations.
7. A final component of the comprehensive model should be the involvement of parents in the education of their children. One of the reasons that sex education has failed our youngsters is that educators have not employed enough foci to make it meaningful to them. The solution to the problem of pregnancy among teens requires an all-out effort by those societal forces capable of effecting change. Families, schools, peers, communities, businesses, and the media all possess powers to eradicate this social problem. The campaign cannot be waged from only one front, however; combined efforts are essential. The responsibility must be shared both for previous condoning of actions that have perpetuated the problem and for working toward mutual goals and solutions.

For better or worse, adolescence will occur as a vital aspect of human development. Although many parents, teachers, politicians, and adolescents themselves might prefer that sexuality were not involved in the process of moving from childhood to adulthood, it is. On a societal level, there is an obligation to provide safe passage for this transition (Tolman, Striepe, & Harmon, 2003, p. 4). How this happens depends on how adolescent sexual health is conceptualized. Conceptual models affect both the questions researchers ask and what society knows about adolescent sexuality (Tolman et al., 2003, p. 4).

References

American Medical Association. (1991). Adolescent health care: Use, costs and problems of access. In *Profiles of adolescent health* (Vol. 2). Chicago, IL: Author.

Armstrong, E., & Pascale, A. (1990). *Adolescent sexuality, pregnancy, and parenthood: The facts.* Washington, DC: Center for Population Options.

Armstrong, E., & Waszak, C. (1990). *Teenage pregnancy and too-early childbearing: Public costs, personal consequences.* Washington, DC: Center for Population Options.

Auslander, W. (1993). Challenges in HIV prevention among youth: Abuse survivors and participants in delinquent behavior. *Prevention Forum, 13*(4), 12–17.

Bachman, J. G., Johnston, L. D., & O'Malley, P. M. (1980). *Monitoring the future: Questionnaire responses from the nation's high school seniors, 1978.* Ann Arbor, MI: University of Michigan Institute for Social Research, Survey Research Center.

Barth, R. P., & Schinke, S. P. (1983). Coping with daily strain among pregnant and parenting adolescents. *Journal of Social Service Research, 7*(2), 51–63.

Bay-Cheng, L. Y. (2001). Sexed.com: Values and norms in web-based sexuality education. *Journal of Sex Research, 38*(3), 242.

Benda, B. B., & DiBlasio, F. A. (1991). Comparison of four theories of adolescent sexual exploration. *Deviant Behavior, 12*(3), 235–257.

Blythe, B. J., Gilchrist, L. D., & Schinke, S. P. (1981). Pregnancy-prevention groups for adolescents. *Social Work, 26*(6), 503–504.

Buckholdt, D., & Wodarski, J. S. (1978). The effects of different reinforcement systems on cooperative behavior exhibited by children in classroom contexts. *Journal of Research and Development in Education, 12*(1), 50–68.

Campbell, A. (1968). The role of family in the reduction of poverty. *Journal of Marriage and the Family, 30*(2), 236–246.

Carrol, W. (1989). *AIDS related claims survey: Claims paid in 1989*. Washington, DC: American Council of Life Insurance Association of America.

Center for Disease Control: National Center for HIV/AIDS, Viral Hepatitis, STD, and TB Prevention. (2012, June). *HIV testing among adolescents: What schools and education agencies can do*.

Centers for Disease Control and Prevention. (1992). Publicly funded HIV counseling and testing. *Patient Education Counsel, 19*, 219–228.

Chilman, C. S. (1979). *Adolescent sexuality in a changing American society: Social and psychological perspectives*. Washington, DC: U.S. Government Printing Office.

Clark, J. K., Brey, R. A., & Banter, A. E. (2003). Physicians as educators in adolescent sexuality education. *Journal of School Health, 73*(10), 389.

Coie, J. D., Watt, N. F., West, S. G., Hawkins, G., & David, J. (1993). The science of prevention: A conceptual framework and some directions for a national research program. *American Psychologist, 48*(10), 1013–1022.

Cvetkovich, G., & Grote, B. (1980). Psychological development and the social problems of teenage illegitimacy. In C. Chilman (Ed.), *Adolescent pregnancy and childbearing: Findings from research* (pp. 15–41; NIH Publication No. 81-2077). Washington, DC: Department of Health and Human Services.

Dailard, C. (2006). Legislating again arousal: The growing divide between federal policy and the teenage sexual behavior. *Guttmacher Policy Review, 9*(3), 12–16.

DiClemente, R. J. (1993). Preventing HIV/AIDS among adolescents: Schools as agents of behavior change. *Journal of the American Medical Association, 279*(6), 760–762.

Doctors, S. R. (1985). Premarital pregnancy and childbirth in adolescence: A psychological overview. In Z. DeFries, R. C. Friedman, & R. Corn (Eds.), *Sexuality: New perspectives* (pp. 45–70). Westport, CT: Greenwood Press.

Doty, M. B., & King, M. (1985). Pregnancy prevention: A private agency's program in public schools. *Social Work in Education, 7*(2), 90–99.

Dryfoos, J. G. (1982a). Contraceptive use, pregnancy intentions and pregnancy outcomes among U.S. women. *Family Planning Perspectives, 14*(2), 81–94.

Dryfoos, J. G. (1982b). The epidemiology of adolescent pregnancy: Incidence, outcomes, and interventions. In I. Stuart & C. Wells (Eds.), *Pregnancy in adolescence: Needs, problems, and management* (pp. 27–47). New York, NY: Van Nostrand Reinhold.

Dryfoos, J. G. (1983). *Review of interventions in the field of prevention of adolescent pregnancy*. Preliminary report to the Rockefeller Foundation [Monograph].

Ehrhardt, A. A. (1996). Editorial: Our view of adolescent sexuality-a focus on risk behavior with the development context. *American Journal of Public Health, 86*(11), 1523–1525.

Evans, K. J. (1999). Speaking each other's language on sexuality. *Social Policy, 30*(1), 32.

Flick, L. H. (1986). Paths to adolescent parenthood: Implications for prevention. *Public Health Report, 101*(2), 132–147.

Foreman, J. (1991, June). Care costs may nearly double by 1994. *Boston Globe*, p. 12.

Fox, G. L. (1980). The mother-adolescent daughter relationship as a sexual, socialization structure: A research review. *Family Relations, 29*(1), 21–80.

Fox, G. L., & Inazu, J. K. (1980). Patterns and outcomes of mother-daughter communication about sexuality. *Journal of Social Issues, 36*(1), 7–29.

Freeman, E. (1978). Abortion: Subjective attitudes and feelings. *Family Planning Perspectives, 10*(3), 150–155.

Furstenberg, F., Brooks-Gunn, J., & Morgan, S. (1987). Adolescent mothers and their children in later life. *Family Planning Perspectives, 19*(4), 142–151.

Gallup Opinion Index. (1978). *Report #156* (p. 28). Princeton, NJ: American Institute of Public Opinion.

Gilchrist, L. D. (1981). Group procedures for helping adolescents cope with sex. *Behavioral Group Therapy, 3*(1), 3–8.

Gilchrist, L. D., & Schinke, S. P. (1983). Counseling with adolescents about their sexuality. In C. S. Chilman (Ed.), *Adolescent sexuality in a changing American society* (pp. 230–249). New York, NY: Wiley.

Gilchrist, L. D., Schinke, S. P., & Blythe, B. J. (1979). Primary prevention services for children and youth. *Children and Youth Services Review, 1*(4), 379–391.

Goldfarb, J. L., Mumford, D. M., Schum, D. A., Smith, P. E., Flowers, C., & Schum, C. (1977). An attempt to detect "pregnancy susceptibility" in indigent adolescent girls. *Journal of Youth and Adolescence, 6*(2), 127–143.

Guttmacher Institute. (1985, March 11). *Report on adolescent pregnancy*. New York, NY: Author.

Guttmacher Institute. (2012). *Facts on American teens' sources of information about sex*. New York, NY: Author.

Haffner, D. (1997). Some progress: Some problems. In *Family life matters*. New Brunswick, NJ: Network for Family Life Education, University of New Jersey.

Haskins, R., & Bevan, C. S. (1997). Abstinence education under welfare reform. *Children and Youth Services Review, 19*, 465–484.

Haslett, D. C. (1991). *Sex education curricula for young teens: Implications for social work* (Unpublished dissertation). University of Illinois at Chicago.

The Henry J. Kaiser Family Foundation. (2005). The HIV/AIDS Epidemic in the United States. *HIV/AIDS Policy Fact Sheet*, 1–2.

Herdt, G. (Ed.). (1989). *Gay and lesbian youth*. New York, NY: Haworth Press.

Hogben, M., & Byrne, D. (1998). Using social learning theory to explain individual differences in human sexuality. *Journal of Sex Research, 35*(1), 63.

Jemmott, J. B., Jemmott, L. S., & Fong, G. T. (1992). Reduction in HIV risk-associated sexual behaviors among black male adolescents: Effects of an AIDS prevention intervention. *American Journal of Public Health, 82*, 372–377.

Jones, M. E., & Bonte, C. (1990). Conceptualizing community interventions in social service needs of pregnant adolescents. *Journal of Pediatric Care, 4*(4), 193–201.

Katz, K. S., Rodan, M., Milligan, R., Tan, S., Courtney, L., Gantz, M., … Subramanian, S. (2011). Efficacy of a randomized cell phone-based counseling intervention in postponing subsequent pregnancy among teen mothers. *Maternal and Child Health Journal, 15*, S42–S53.

Kenney, A. M., & Orr, M. T. (1984). Sex education: An overview of current programs, policies, and research. *Phi Delta Kappan, 65*(7), 491–496.

Kirby, D. (1980). The effects of school sex education programs: A review of the literature. *Journal of School Health, 50*(10), 559–563.

Kirby, D. (1985). Sexuality education: A more realistic view of its effects. *Journal of School Health, 55*(10), 421–424.

Kirby, D., Alter, J., & Scales, P. (1979, July). *An analysis of U.S. sex education programs and evaluation methods* (DHEW Publication No. CD-2021-79-DKFR). Washington, DC: U.S. Department of Health, Education, and Welfare.

Kohler, P. K., Manhart, L. E., & Lafferty, W. E. (2008). Abstinence-only and comprehensive sex education and the initiation of sexual activity and teen pregnancy. *Journal of Adolescent Health, 42*, 344–351.

Litt, I. F., Cuskey, W. R., & Rudd, S. (1980). Identifying adolescents at risk for noncompliance with contraceptive therapy. *Journal of Pediatrics, 96*(4), 742–745.

Lockhart, L., & Wodarski, J. (1990). Teenage pregnancy: Implications for social work practice. *Family Therapy, 17*(1), 30–47.

Maticka-Tyndale, E. (1991). Sexual scripts and AIDS prevention: Variations in adherence to safer-sex guidelines by heterosexual adolescents. *Journal of Sex Research, 28*(1), 63.

McAlister, A. L., Perry, C., & Maccoby, N. (1979). Adolescent smoking: Onset and prevention. *Pediatrics, 63*, 650–658.

McAnarney, E. R. (1985). Adolescent pregnancy and childbearing: New data, new challenges. *Pediatrics, 75*(5), 973–975.

McAnarney, E. R., & Schreider, C. (1984). *Identifying social and psychological antecedents of adolescent pregnancy*. New York, NY: William T. Grant Foundation.

The National Campaign to Prevent Teen and Unplanned Pregnancy. (2011). *Counting it up: The public costs of teen childbearing: Key data*. Washington, DC: The National Campaign to Prevent Teen and Unplanned Pregnancy.

National Center for Health Statistics. (1990). *Health: United States, 1989* (DHHS Publication No. [PHS] 90-1232). Hyattsville, MD: Author.

Office of Management and Budget. (1990). *Budget of the United States Government; fiscal year 1991*. Washington, DC: U.S. Government Printing Office.

Oliver, D. P., Leeming, F. C., & Dwyer, W. O. (1998). Studying parental involvement in school-based sex education: Lessons learned. *Family Planning Perspectives, 30*(3), 143–144.

Olson, L. (1980). Social and psychological correlates of pregnancy resolution among adolescent women: A review. *American Journal of Orthopsychiatry, 50*(3), 432–445.

Over, M. (1999). Confronting AIDS: A global economic perspective. *AIDS Patient Care and STDs, 13*(4), 219–228.

Perlman, S. B., Klerman, L. V., & Kinard, E. M. (1981). The use of socioeconomic data to predict teenage birth rates: An exploratory study in Massachusetts. *Public Health Reports, 96*(4), 335–341.

Rea-Holloway, M., Blinn-Pike, L., & Berger, T. (2000). Conducting adolescent sexuality research in schools: Lessons learned. *Family Planning Perspectives, 32*(5), 246.

Reid, D. (1982). School sex education and the causes of unintended teenage pregnancies: A review. *Health Education Journal, 41*(1), 4–11.

Rosen, R. H., & Ager, J. W. (1981). Self-concept and contraception: Pre-contraception decision making. *Population and Environment, 4*(1), 11–23.

Rotheram-Borus, M. J. (1997). Annotation: HIV prevention challenges-realistic strategies and early detection programs. *American Journal of Public Health, 87*(4), 544–545.

Rotheram-Borus, M. J., & Koopman, C. (1991). Sexual risk behavior, AIDS knowledge, and beliefs about AIDS among runaways. *American Journal of Public Health, 81*, 208–210.

Sandberg, E. C., & Jacobs, R. I. (1971). Psychology of the misuse and rejection of contraception. *American Journal of Obstetrics and Gynecology, 110*(2), 227–242.

Santelli, J., Rosenblatt, L., & Birn, A. E. (1990). Estimates of public cost for teenage childbearing in Baltimore city in FY 1987. *Maryland Medical Journal, 39*(5), 459–464.

Santelli, J. S., Lindberg, L. D., Finer, L. B., & Singh, S. (2007). Explaining recent declines in adolescent pregnancy in the United States: The contribution of abstinence and improved contraceptive use. *American Journal of Public Health, 97*(1), 150–156.

Scales, P. (1983). Adolescent sexuality and education: Principles, approaches, and resources. In C. S. Chilman (Ed.), *Adolescent sexuality in a changing American society* (pp. 207–229). New York, NY: Wiley.

Schinke, S. P. (1978). Teenage pregnancy: The need for multiple casework services. *Social Casework, 59*(7), 406–410.

Schinke, S. P. (1979). Research on adolescent health: Social work implications. In W. T. Hall & C. Y. Yong (Eds.), *Health and social needs of the adolescent: Professional responsibilities* (pp. 320–351). Pittsburgh, PA: University of Pittsburgh Graduate School of Public Health.

Schinke, S. P. (1982). School-based model for preventing teenage pregnancy. *Social Work in Education, 4*(2), 34–42.

Schinke, S. P. (1997). Preventing teenage pregnancy: Translating research knowledge. *Journal of Human Behavior in the Social Environment, 1*(1), 53–66.

Schinke, S. P., Blythe, B. J., Gilchrist, L. D., & Burt, G. A. (1981). Primary prevention of adolescent pregnancy. *Social Work with Groups, 4*(2), 121–135.

Schinke, S. P., & Gilchrist, L. D. (1977). Adolescent pregnancy: An interpersonal skill training approach to prevention. *Social Work in Health Care, 3*(2), 159–167.

Schinke, S. P., & Gilchrist, L. D. (1984). *Life skills counseling with adolescents.* Baltimore, MD: University Park Press.

Seha, A., Klepp, K., & Ndeki, S. (1994). Scale reliability and construct validity: A pilot study among primary school children in Northern Tanzania. *AIDS Education and Prevention, 6*(6), 524–534.

Story, M. (1987). Nutrition issues and adolescent pregnancy. *Contemporary nutrition, 12*(1), 1–2.

Stout, J. W., & Rivara, F. P. (1989). School and sex education: Does it work? *Pediatrics, 83*(3), 375–379.

Taskforce of Pediatric AIDS. (1993). Adolescents and human immunodeficiency virus infection: The role of the pediatrician in prevention and intervention. *Pediatrics, 92*(5), 626–630.

Thornburg, H. D. (1981). The amount of sex information learning obtained during early adolescence. *Journal of Early Adolescence, 1*(3), 171–183.

Tolman, D. L. (2000). Object lessons: Romance, violation, and female adolescent sexual desire. *Journal of Sex Education and Therapy, 25*(1), 70.

Tolman, D. L., Striepe, M. I., & Harmon, T. (2003). Gender matters: Constructing a model of adolescent sexual health. *Journal of Sex Research, 40*(1), 4.

U.S. General Accounting Office (1990). *Defense health care: Effects of AIDS in the military* (CAD/HRD-90-39). Washington, DC: Author.

Wagner, N. (1970). Adolescent sexual behavior. In E. Evans (Ed.), *Adolescents: Readings in behavior and development.* Hinsdale, IL: Dryden Press.

Werner-Wilson, R. J., Fitzharris, J. L., & Morrissey, K. M. (2004). Adolescent and parent perceptions of media influence on adolescent sexuality. *Adolescence, 39*(154), 63.

Winkenwerder, W., Kessler, A. R., & Stolec, R. M. (1989). Federal spending for illness caused by the human immunodeficiency virus. *New England Journal of Medicine, 320*(24), 1598–1603.

World Health Organization (1989). *Interview schedule for knowledge, attitudes, beliefs, and practices on AIDS of young people* (WHO/GPA/SBR). Geneva, Switzerland: Author.

Yankelovich, Skelly, and White, Inc. (1979). *The General Mills American family report, 1978-79.* Minneapolis, MN: General Mills.

Yoshikawa, H. (1994). Prevention as cumulative protection: Effects of early family support and education on chronic delinquency and its risks. *Psychological Bulletin, 115*(1), 28–54.

Zelnik, M., & Kim, Y. J. (1982). Sex education and its association with teenage sexual activity pregnancy, and contraceptive use. *Family Planning Perspectives, 14*(3), 117–126.

Chapter 6
Preventing HIV Infection in Adolescents

Charles W. Mueller, Robert Bidwell, Scott Okamoto, Eberhard Mann, and Sarah V. Curtis

Since its first appearance in 1981, acquired immunodeficiency syndrome (AIDS) has grown to have a profound impact on the world's adolescent and young adult population. According to a report from the 2010 United Nations Summit, HIV/AIDS is the leading cause of death for women aged 15–44 worldwide (United Nations [UN], 2010). Despite the fact that knowledge about the disease and how to prevent it has become more widespread, its prevalence continues to rise in many countries (World Health Organization [WHO], 2005).

AIDS is a disease caused by the human immunodeficiency virus (HIV). Some individuals express symptoms while many others do not. The Center for Disease Control (CDC) estimates that 20% of individuals infected with HIV are unaware of their infection (CDC, 2012). HIV is transmitted from one person to another through direct exchange of blood, semen, vaginal fluid, or breast milk. Once infected, an individual's immune system is invaded by the virus, and an active process of viral replication and immune cell destruction begins. Over time, often after many years, the immune system becomes compromised to a point where a person becomes vulnerable to repeated opportunistic infections affecting virtually any organ system. These infectious assaults, along with direct infection by HIV of the brain and other organs, can ultimately result in death. Research continues to yield treatments that improve the quality and length of life for those infected with HIV; however, since

C. W. Mueller (✉)
Department of Psychology, University of Hawai'i at Mānoa, Honolulu, HI, USA
e-mail: cmueller@hawaii.edu

R. Bidwell · E. Mann
Department of Pediatrics, University of Hawaii, Honolulu, HI, USA

S. Okamoto
School of Social Work, College of Health and Society, Hawai'i Pacific University, Honolulu, HI, USA

S. V. Curtis
College of Social Work, University of Tennessee, Knoxville, TN, USA

© Springer Nature Switzerland AG 2019   109
J. S. Wodarski, L. M. Hopson (eds.), *Empirically Based Interventions Targeting Social Problems*, https://doi.org/10.1007/978-3-030-28487-9_6

there remains no cure, prevention continues to be the only option for decreasing mortality resulting from AIDS.

The World Health Organization reports that adolescents and young adults (aged 15–24) accounted for 40% of new HIV infections in 2009 (WHO, 2011). Becoming infected with HIV is particularly devastating during adolescence. The stressors of coping with an HIV diagnosis can have a profound impact on an adolescent. Some of these stressors include being ostracized by peers, fear of the affects of HIV/AIDS, and familial conflict (Brown, Laurie, & Pao, 2000). The need for effective prevention programs for adolescents is imperative.

In July 2010, President Barack Obama released the *National HIV/AIDS Strategy for the United States*. The strategy discussed three primary goals: (1) reduce the number of people who become infected with HIV, (2) increase access to care and optimizing health outcomes for people living with HIV, and (3) reduce HIV-related health disparities (The White House Office of National AIDS Policy, 2010). Once individuals are aware of their HIV status, they can help prevent transmission. Increased federal funding for HIV prevention is related to an increase in the number of people who receive an HIV test and know their HIV status (Linas, Zheng, Losina, Walensky, & Freedberg, 2006). In 2012, the Center for Disease Control released a recommendation for infusing regular HIV testing into routine health care for adolescents (CDC, 2012). Incorporating HIV testing into routine health screening will help eliminate some of the negative stigma associated with HIV/AIDS. In 2011, the United Nations set a commitment to provide universal access to HIV prevention, treatment, care, and support by 2015. The time to act is now. What works for the reduction of HIV infections must be put into place to develop knowledge and skills that can save lives; the youth population is understandably targeted for this purpose.

Epidemiology

There are approximately 33.4 million people living with HIV/AIDS world-wide (UN, 2010). In the most vulnerable countries, less than 10% of those living with AIDS are even aware of their status. Currently in sub-Saharan Africa, 22.5 million people are living with HIV. This is two-thirds of all people with AIDS and of this number 59% are women (WHO, 2011). In Eastern Europe and Central Asia, the percentage of people living with HIV/AIDS has increased over 20% between the years of 2003 and 2005 (WHO, 2006). There are now over one million individuals living with the HIV infection in the U SA (CDC, 2012). Since the first cases of HIV/AIDS were seen in the USA nearly 30 years ago, over 575,000 Americans have lost their lives to AIDS (The White House Office of National AIDS Policy, 2010). Fortunately with the use of medications such as HAART (highly active antiretroviral therapy), the mortality and morbidity related to HIV/AIDS has experienced a reduced rate of increase (Weiss et al., 2006).

Within the USA, the youth population has seen an increasing number of infections. There were 4205 adolescents diagnosed with HIV in 2002 and by 2009, the number had doubled to 8300 new infections in adolescents aged 13–24 years (CDC, 2012). In addition, adolescents are the fastest growing portion of population newly diagnosed with HIV in the USA. Many adolescents may acquire the infection and are not diagnosed until later. The latency period for the HIV infection can be as long as 10 years (CDC, 2010). In 2008 the CDC estimated that of the 68,600 adolescents living with HIV, nearly 60% were unaware they were infected (CDC, 2012). Within the adolescent population in the USA, males tend to acquire the virus more often than females. White men who have sex with men (MSM) accounted for 61% of the new HIV diagnoses in 2009 (CDC, 2011). While gay and bisexual men continue to be the most affected population, the trend toward more transmissions occurring through heterosexual activity and intravenous drug use has occurred for several decades. Females most often acquire the disease through heterosexual activity (71%). Most startlingly in the U SA is the disproportionately large number of HIV/ AIDS infections found in African-Americans. In 2009, this race accounted for more than 44% of new HIV/AIDS cases. Minority races, women, and children are becoming more and more represented in those with the virus. Considering geographic data within the USA, urban areas contain large proportion of HIV infections; however, rural area infection rates are increasing. New York City houses 13.6% of the adolescents with HIV. Other epicenters in descending order are Houston, Los Angeles, Miami, Philadelphia, Washington, D.C., and Chicago.

There are certain groups of adolescents who are at particular risk for HIV infection such as gay and bisexual males, homeless and runaway adolescents, and other high risk homosexuals and intravenous drug users (Gallagher, Denning, Allen, Nakashima, & Sullivan, 2007). The number of studies related to prevention of HIV infections in these populations has increased in the past decade.

HIV-Related Knowledge and Risk Behavior

The vast majority of US high school students reports having received some form of HIV education, whereby, at the minimum, youth are told some basic biological facts, the major transmission routes, and ways to avoid infection. Many recent surveys have shown that most adolescents possess fairly accurate knowledge about the major aspects of HIV infection. They know that AIDS is caused by the HIV virus that is transmitted through unprotected hetero- and homosexual intercourse or use of shared needles with infected persons. They realize that HIV infection may take many years before causing symptoms of AIDS, and that it is incurable. Most teenagers have HIV/AIDS education in school. In 2011, 80% of the students in the national Youth Risk Behavior Survey reported that they had been taught about AIDS/HIV in school. In addition, programs have tried to reach parents and their adolescent children in their homes, whereas others have used social marketing and media approaches. When knowledge mistakes occur, youth tend to think that they can prevent transmission through washing, douching, or birth control pills. Another mistaken belief is that pre-ejaculatory fluid cannot transmit HIV. Some adolescents believe that cleanliness of a person may be an indicator as to whether or not one has HIV (Hoppe et al., 2004). Surveys from 40 other countries indicate that more than half of the young people have misconceptions about how HIV is transmitted.

According to the 2011 Youth Risk Behavior Survey, 52% of adolescents in high school in the USA are engaging in sexual intercourse and nearly half of those who were sexually active reported not using a condom during their last sexual intercourse. Adolescents have a variety of beliefs about sex and while some tend to engage in risky behaviors, others choose to avoid sex, use condoms if they do have sex, or remain monogamous (DiClemente & Crosby, 2006). The USA holds a relatively conservative view of educating adolescents on how to protect themselves from the risks of sexual activities. Many states receive funding from the federal government specifically allocated to teaching abstinence-until-marriage education to students. The issue with this is two-fold. First of all, this education is not inclusive of gay or bisexual individuals who disproportionately account for the majority of HIV infections. Secondly, this type of education is only focusing one protective factor. While abstinence is the only way to guarantee prevention of transmission, many adolescents are not remaining abstinent. Education.

For the last 10 years, the Centers for Disease Control and Prevention began to collaborate with local, state, and national educational and health agencies to develop HIV prevention programs for the youth. As of 2012, only 20 states mandate both sex and HIV education. Only 18 states mandate that information on condoms and contraception be included (Guttmacher, 2012). One issue with the education delivery system is that adolescents often label HIV/AIDS prevention programs as boring, and in one study the adolescents suggested that programs use peers (Hoppe et al., 2004). Most adults support STI/HIV education including topics like condoms and other forms of contraception. However, some communities wish to have the adolescents only taught to remain abstinent while concentrating on the failure rate of condoms. Evidence regarding the effectiveness of abstinence promotion strategies in changing young people's sexual risk behaviors is scarce. However, the US PEPFAR program that funds a large portion of HIV prevention in Africa requires that a third of these funds is allocated for promoting abstinence (Mantell et al., 2006). Still, in the most vulnerable places in Africa most all (90% or more) of the youth begin sexual activity in their teen years.

Mass media provide some preventive messages, and public and private community agencies have developed preventive services, often for specific groups of youth engaged in high risk behavior for HIV. However, the majority of sexually active teens, in spite of their knowledge about HIV and preventive behaviors, continue to engage in high risk sexual activities. Most adolescents who do use condoms do so inconsistently. A study by Drs. DiClemente, Crosby, and Wingood (2002) of adolescent females who reported 100% condom use for the duration of a study still acquired a sexually transmitted disease 17% of the time. Possible reasons for this phenomenon are an exaggeration of condom use, incorrect condom use, or not using condoms for the entirety of the time of penetration. In June 2000, four federal agencies convened at the Department of Health and Human Services to address the matter of the effectiveness of the condoms and found that they are in fact effective in preventing HIV transmission. While there is some evidence on positive behavior change, the rates of AIDS, sexually transmitted disease, and unprotected risky behaviors among adolescents are exceptionally high. Effective interventions must be developed to reduce risk behaviors using techniques shown to be beneficial.

Assessing HIV-Related Risk Behaviors

There is an emergence of the rapid behavioral risk assessment as well as rapid assessments in general. These types of assessments help to eliminate the lack of honesty which is evoked by having a face-to-face interview. They are also less time consuming and more financially viable (Gallagher et al., 2007). However, it should be noted that high risk populations like racial and ethnic minorities may have a distrust of assessments and the intervention program in general. This could be addressed by promoting their involvement in the program and connecting them to the changes that may result. Furthermore, some scientists criticize these types of assessments due to their limited samples of questions which could result in an inaccurate baseline of data and hence, inaccurate results. However the rapid assessments are beneficial if all primary data which the intervention targets are included (Trotter & Singer, 2005).

Conducting a valid assessment of adolescent HIV-related risk behaviors can be tricky. In one-on-one clinical settings, practitioners should be trained to conduct sensitive, straight-forward, and explicit interviews about sexuality and drug use. One useful strategy is to contextualize such questions into a much more complete psychosocial screening assessment. It is important to screen for risk and protective factors as well; adolescents without many protective factors should be the focus of an intervention more quickly (Bauman & Germann, 2005). Naturally, practitioners need to have adequately worked through their own comfort issues, especially as related to sexuality and substance use. Face-to-face interviews with adolescents are very prone to distortions especially when the practitioner is seen as untrustworthy or judgmental. In addition, the practitioner needs to be sure about how confidentiality is to be handled and must be ready to communicate this to the adolescent in a useful way.

When assessing clients on their risks for acquiring an STI, there are two main areas of focus—the individual-level and the ecological-level. When looking at the adolescent on an individual level, one must consider impulsivity, depression, self-efficacy with regard to choosing safer sex, barriers to condom usage, knowledge and risk perception as well as motivation to avoid contracting HIV/AIDS. There are several ecological factors as well: parental monitoring, communication level between adult and adolescent, peer and community norms, availability of services, gender, and power differentials (DiClemente & Crosby, 2006).

It is important to note that people in Africa (and in Botswana) do not have any more sexual partners on average than Americans and the average age of sexual debut is the same (Green, 2003). The latter is associated with a higher number of lifetime sexual partners which can also increase risk to HIV/AIDS (Green, 2003). However, there is a very high rate of AIDS in Botswana. Assessments at a broader community level identify factors related to these increased rates. Examples of factors affecting the people of Botswana are the lack of male circumcision, practice of dry sex, high consumption of alcohol, and high levels of stigma related to AIDS (Green, 2003). The main epidemiological factors that are likely to make Botswana more susceptible to HIV infections are the lack of male circumcision, high levels of casual sex, and prevalence of STDs rather than sex during menstruation or having dry sex (Green, 2003). This example is relevant as it addresses larger issues that can be targeted to change the direction of the epidemic. A community-based intervention will be discussed later in this chapter.

Most HIV prevention efforts have been conducted using small group interventions. Thus, individual face-to-face assessment interviews are not necessary or natural in many such prevention contexts. Indeed given the availability of national (and often local) data in adolescent risk behavior, many interventions are conducted without direct assessment of individual risk behavior. Local data about sexual behavior can often provide a more specific picture of the intervention group as long as the participants are relatively geographically homogenous. Together local and national data sources should point to the need for prevention and give a rough estimate of the sexual and substance use behaviors of the participants of any intervention.

While behavioral epidemiology provides a general description of the target population's risk behavior profile, it does not replace specific assessments of the actual youth who will be receiving the intervention. Most successful programs use paper-and-pencil questionnaires to assess the occurrence, frequency, and specific character of risk behaviors. Useful questionnaires are explicit (specifically identify types of sexual behavior, e.g., vaginal intercourse, anal intercourse, fellatio) and comprehensive (include all common sexual behaviors), specifically include options to indicate same-sex practices, include questions about the use of pregnancy and STI prevention practices, include similarly specific questions about substance use (including the use of needles for drug use and for tattooing and piercings), and indicate frequency or latency since last occurrence of behavior (e.g., "How often have you participated in each of the following sex practices in the past 30 days?"). Many successful programs also assess HIV-related risk reduction beliefs and skills (e.g., refusal skills) that are to be a focus of the intervention. Once an instrument has been selected or multiple measures combined or trimmed for use, a useful practice is to convene one or more of the focus groups of adolescents to review the instrument for length, comprehension, and suitability, and to suggest alternative wording for overly technical language (e.g., changing "fellatio" to "oral sex, that is putting your mouth on his penis and/or her vagina"). Specific assessment of risk behaviors can be used to fine-tune the prevention program (e.g., based on the percentage of participants who are sexually active but inconsistent users of condoms) and can serve as a pretest, thereby allowing for posttest and follow-up evaluations.

Effective Social Work Interventions

Preliminary Comments

Many clinic- and school-based adolescent HIV prevention studies that seem (or claim) to show positive intervention effects on risk behavior have major substantive and methodological limitations or both. As such, they often can just as easily be read as showing little or no effect. Problems relate to measurement, design, statistical analysis, and inferences from findings. Nevertheless, there are a limited number of reasonably solid empirical studies that measure behavior for some period of time after the intervention. From these studies, empirically based practice guidelines and conclusions can be derived.

Access to HIV/AIDS prevention services remains limited worldwide (The Henry J. Kaiser Family Foundation, 2012). In the USA, *the Center for Disease Control* is the nation's leading federal agency for *HIV prevention,* receiving nearly 90% of total *HIV prevention* funds. Federal *HIV prevention* funds independently correlate with increased *HIV* testing (Linas et al., 2006). Funding would seem to be a crucial factor in increasing testing in other countries as well.

One prevention method which has shown considerable promise is that related to male circumcision in countries such as those in Africa that have high prevalence of HIV/AIDS but low occurrence of male circumcision. On December 13, 2006, the National Institutes of Health (NIH) decided to allow subjects used as control subjects in a study to become part of the intervention (circumcision) for ethical reasons due to the apparent benefits observed in the study group. The study demonstrated at least a 50% reduction of HIV acquisition compared to the control group. If large-scale implementation of circumcision occurs in southern Africa, it can be expected to reduce new HIV infections by two million within the next 10 years (Sawires et al., 2007). Within the subsequent decade, 3.7 million HIV infections and 2.7 million deaths could be averted. Other prevention strategies known to reduce transmission rates such as the use of antiretroviral medications would further reduce new infections. In a cost-benefit analysis, implementing male circumcision would be in the best interest of these nations with high HIV/AIDS prevalence.

In the meantime, new approaches for HIV prevention in women are urgently needed. According to WHO, the number of women and girls infected with HIV has increased in every region of the world. Although condoms can provide a high level of protection (80–90%) against sexual transmission of HIV if used consistently and properly, many women are not in a position to persuade partners to use them. Sexual inequities cause a devastating problem for young woman. Women between the ages 15–24 years are three times more likely to have HIV than men in sub-Saharan Africa (WHO, 2011). The development of new technologies that put HIV prevention in the hands of women is therefore crucial. The use of a microbicide, a vaginally applied antimicrobial medication that can kill, block, or inactivate HIV, is one such technology. According to *The Lancet*, more than 60 microbicides were being researched for this purpose at the start of 2006. Female condoms, an HIV vaccine, and stigma reduction that would allow for sex partners to be more open about their HIV status would also assist in HIV/AIDS reduction. The anticipated loss of support from one's loved ones can be detrimental to the battle against this disease.

The fight is not just about those in a certain economic class, gender, or race. The productivity and well-being of entire nations hinge on a reduction of this epidemic. This disease also affects all kinds of people. This is not a closed society. There is no one who is immune. Prostitutes and drug addicts are just part of the picture. There are computer engineers, loving mothers, police officers, and neighbors with HIV/AIDS. Prevention through skills and education are most crucial when sexual activity and experimentation begin. Without implementation of effective programs in the crucial time of adolescence, this window of opportunity can be lost.

Characteristics of Effective Programs

HIV/AIDS prevention programs work best when they are intensive, comprehensive, and long term. The greatest positive effects occur when both treatment and prevention are emphasized. Programs that successfully influenced adolescent HIV risk behavior over time were of sufficient duration. Successful programs tended to have considerably longer interventions than those which did not influence risk behavior. The most common length of interventions included in the best-evidence interventions listed in a review by Lyles et al. in 2007 was between 9 and 18 h (Lyles et al., 2007). These interventions varied from 1 to 3 sessions to 6 or more sessions. Every long program did not and will not necessarily affect risk behavior, and many shorter programs seem to have beneficial effects on HIV-related knowledge and attitudes, if not risk behavior.

Education regarding other sexually transmitted infections is also important as the presence of symptoms known to be associated with them could prompt the person to go to a health provider. If the person has an STI, then there is a reasonable chance that he or she might be at risk of also having HIV/AIDS. Dissemination of information about STIs and their symptoms could foment the possibility of people finding out their HIV status. The clinics which provide such testing should provide youth friendly services while ensuring confidentiality. There should be an integration of the family planning services with the STI testing. It is also important that adolescents have access to testing by increasing the number of testing sites.

Nearly every successful program had clear, targeted goals and expectations concerning risk behavior. The most successful programs often targeted both abstinence and delay in initiation of intercourse along with safer sex precautions for those who are sexually active. Risk behaviors that should be the dependent measures in studies and interventions to reduce HIV infection include sexual abstinence rates, delay in initiation of sexual intercourse, various forms of sexual intercourse, unprotected sex, sexual intercourse with multiple partners, use of condoms during sexual intercourse, coercive sexual experiences, variations on these categories (e.g., use of condoms with spermicide or unprotected anal intercourse with multiple partners), and substance abuse and injection drug use.

Understandably, programs that are focused on actual risk behavior seem to have stronger behavioral impacts. This may be a truism, but is less obvious in historical context. When transmission routes for HIV and the attendant risks these posed for adolescents were first understood, schools were the major service-delivery organization to respond, probably because of their established history of struggling with health and sex education and their presence in the lives of most, though not all, youth. With hindsight, it seems almost preordained that the school systems would be best able to contribute to the educational component of HIV prevention. Along with public service announcements, media programs, and other community work, this (educational) need is being fairly well addressed. However, the standard educational system has often struggled with affecting behavioral change, particularly adolescent sexual behavior. As other professions (including social workers) have joined in the effort, state-of-the-art interventions, be they conducted in schools or elsewhere, have clearly evolved into programs with strong behavioral foci. As such, social work interventions with adolescents need to have strong behavioral components.

All successful programs incorporated some form of social learning principles. The majority of less successful programs did not do so or did so only in very indirect ways. A variety of social learning models have been used, including social inoculation theory, theory of reasoned action, cognitive-behavioral theories, problem-solving theory, behavioral skills theory, and more general social learning theory. Programs that actively and explicitly use a limited number of specific social learning principles in the planning and implementation of the intervention are most effective. This seems to go along with the need for clear goals and a clear plan on how to achieve those goals. Thus the point for the practitioner is two-fold. Use some specific form of the social learning theory to explicitly inform the development of the intervention, and plan and conduct an intervention using the fidelity to these ideas. There is no evidence that prevention based on alternative theoretical frameworks (e.g., self psychology, psychoanalysis, family dynamics, or didactic education) effectively reduces risk behavior over time.

Nearly all programs that influence risk behavior have strong skills-development component, usually toward the end of the intervention. Less successful programs are much less likely to include specific skills-development activities. Different successful programs identify somewhat different skills; however, common foci of skills include avoidance of risk situations, development of assertion and refusal skills, sexual-communication and negotiation skills, accurate assessment of benefits and risks of a particular behavior, and skills in the effective use of condoms. Most all included skills building and interpersonal skills development. Other beneficial interventions include the development of a plan to reduce risk taking behaviors while also recognizing the triggers for risky sex such as alcohol consumption. In addition, social groups were targeted in some of the evidence-based interventions. Any program that involves prevention will also make a clear statement that condoms are the most effective way for a sexually active person to prevent HIV transmission (WHO, 2004).

Successful programs tend to be conducted in small and medium sized peer groups. Successful programs use standard group techniques designed to facilitate participant rapport, to clarify values and explore beliefs, and to directly practice learned behaviors (e.g., active learning, sharing ideas, and role-playing). In summary, the use of small groups seems to increase the likelihood of successful risk reduction and probably encourages more effective use of rapport building, values clarification, norm development, and skills-based techniques. However, successful programs can be conducted in classroom-sized groups as long as other criteria are met.

Some successful programs take advantage of the naturally occurring social interactions of peers (Wodarski, Wodarski, & Parris, 2004). Unlike most programs that formed groups based on other criteria, the Teams-Games-Tournaments intervention identified teen cliques and used these cliques to form the intervention groups. This program has successfully been used to prevent adolescent substance abuse. Targeting substance abuse could help reduce risky behaviors that could lead to HIV infection (Griffin, Botwin, & Nichols, 2006), but this effective method that appeals to young people could also be used for HIV education. Given that teens in peer networks share many common behaviors including sexual activity, substance use, and other risk behaviors, such clique-based groupings may increase the impact or efficiency. There seems to be growing interest in the use of peers in HIV prevention education and their use is supported by the social network theory which states the great influence peers have on one another (Ozer, Weinstein, Maslach, & Siegel, 1997). The reasoning behind using an intervention that utilizes peers as facilitators and as members who interact in a group learning environment includes the following: peer group interaction may help promote a more cooperative stance and improved interpersonal skills, there may be a reduction in anxiety that may result from the differences (age, background, etc.) between an adult and the adolescents, other peers may provide more individualized feedback, and teaching another student may increase an adolescent's confidence and knowledge (Wodarski et al., 2004).

Many successful programs used highly trained and sufficiently motivated facilitators. Some of the best programs provided 20–40 or more hours of facilitator training. Less successful programs tended to spend less time on this training or made no mention of the extent of training. The best studies had trained observers check to ensure the facilitators delivered the agreed upon program. Many studies allowed for self-selection of facilitators. This may be an important lesson: There is little evidence that forcing someone to be a facilitator (e.g., school teacher chosen because she teaches a particular class) will lead to a quality program.

Many successful programs incorporate substantial local planning into the program development process. Such planning can include ethnographic inquiry (e.g., interviews and participant observations), pilot studies, and direct input from the youth and adults in the community. While such procedures likely lead to a more culturally sensitive and localized program, they pose at least two hazards to the social worker. First, they prevent the relatively easy, direct application of the packaged intervention program that proved to be successful elsewhere. Second, such procedures can lead program developers away from the very characteristics found in the empirically demonstrated programs. For example, some members of the community may not want any skills-development components. The development of the Diffusion of Effective Behavioral Interventions was funded by the Center for Disease Control's Division of HIV/AIDS Prevention. It has been funding community-based organizations for 20 years to promote such prevention programs to look at their efficacy and effectiveness. There have been many different programs created for a variety of populations to be more effective for each. In the best-evidence interventions, many target specific high risk populations with success.

Nearly all successful programs described strategies to actively connect with the adolescents and to explore values and norms about responsible behavior. Most programs utilize group exercises to establish rapport among the youth and with the facilitators. This rapport is then relied upon to explore beliefs about risk behaviors and perceptions about norms concerning those behaviors. Increased HIV risk occurs when either partner has some desire to have a child. This requires a specific type of intervention related to parenthood (DiClemente et al., 2002). In particular, programs targeted for disenfranchised youth need to pay particular attention to developing such rapport. Once accomplished, the remainder of the HIV prevention program can probably precede in similar fashion as those described herein. In many communities (but not all), early sexual risk behavior is correlated with other risk behaviors such as substance use, school failure, and status offenses (Zweig, Lindberg, & McGinley, 2001). Some comprehensive and well-planned HIV prevention programs targeted at such high risk youth have not successfully influenced their HIV risk-behavior.

Most successful programs work with similar aged peers in groups. Often groups are based upon grade in school. Programs have been successful with a variety of ages, ranging from 11.3 years old to 17.8 years old (overall mean age equal to 14.5). Successful programs have been conducted with same- and mixed-gender groups. Within the successful programs, there is no compelling evidence that boys or girls benefit more from HIV prevention programs. Similarly, there is no evidence that Caucasian, African-American, or Latino youth benefit more or less from such programs (although there remains little empirical research on other ethnic groups).

Very few studies have used booster sessions (individual or group interventions delivered sometime after the initial sessions). However, the impact of even the best HIV prevention programs often diminishes with time. One possible direction might focus on relapse prevention approaches borrowed from substance abuse intervention programs.

Successful programs can be conducted within or outside the school. Health clinics, shelters, jails, and community organizations like recreation centers have been the sites of successful programs. Very few programs have successfully integrated families into HIV prevention intervention. Programs that have attempted to do so report difficulties sustaining family involvement. One program was fairly successful involving families by using homework assignments that explicitly directed students to interview the parents about their own views about abstinence and birth control. The involvement of parents seems logical but it has not been a component of all

HIV/AIDS prevention groups. The increased involvement of parents seems to decrease the likelihood of the adolescents being involved in high risk behavior (Barnes, Hoffman, Welte, Farrell, & Dintcheff, 2006).

Designing and Implementing a Successful Program

Given the emerging evidence about effective HIV prevention for adolescents, a general set of guidelines can be proposed. While much more research in this area needs to be done, the following design and implementation steps are supported by the existing literature:

1. Develop a commitment to a sufficiently intense and long intervention program.
2. Conduct preliminary pilot and ethnographic work to better understand the local context of adolescent risk, community attitudes, youths' prior experiences with HIV and HIV education, and barriers that might interfere with the development of effective skill-based behaviors that will help youths avoid or minimize risk. Pay particular attention to various ethnic and cultural values related to sexuality and teen sexuality in particular.
3. Develop clear goals and objectives for the program. Be sure to keep a risk behavior focus. A sample goal might be to reduce HIV infection. Sample objectives could include some of the following: Increase adolescent abstinence, delay initiation of sexual intercourse, increase condom use, decrease sexual intercourse with multiple partners, decrease unprotected anal sex, decrease sexual exploitation, decrease injection drug use, or decrease needle sharing.
4. Identify a social learning theory model that fits your goals and objectives and your analysis of the context of risk behavior. Many successful interventions involve several different theories. Those theories found in such interventions include the social cognitive theory, social learning theory, the AIDS risk reduction model, information-motivation-behavior model, theory of gender and power, social inoculation, and cognitive-behavioral theories, and transtheoretical models that recognize the stages of change.
5. Identify and review available existing HIV prevention programs. Examine their suitability to your context and goals. Be specific about goals and behaviors to be targeted.
6. Develop (or modify) a program with explicit connections to the theoretical model(s) used and adjusted to the specific local context. Be sure that the planned program has sufficient focus on behaviors and the development of skills that modify risk behaviors.
7. Identify and train motivated facilitators in the program. Pilot test your program and solicit and incorporate facilitator and pilot participant feedback to fine-tune your intervention program.

8. Consider innovative additions (not yet empirically validated) such as creative family involvement, the use of booster sessions or relapse prevention techniques, or outreach to the particularly disenfranchised youth. However, do not let any such innovations or modifications take away from delivering a program that includes empirically demonstrated criteria for success.

9. Consider evaluation of your intervention. Focus your intervention and your evaluation on behavior. Remember there is still much that needs to be learned about adolescent prevention. You can become part of the effort.

10. Review your intervention plan. Be sure that the complete plan fits specifically with your goals and objectives. Be sure you have trained and motivated facilitators delivering a sufficiently long, yet clear and focused, program, informed by specific, identified social learning ideas, tailored to your target population, with strong activities designed to develop group rapport, clarify values, and teach and practice risk reduction behaviors.

11. Implement the program with integrity. Make note of variations from the plan. Upon completion, review and revise the plan as indicated.

Samples of Successful Programs

The following programs were accessed through the Center for Disease Control [CDC] and were described as three of the best-evidence interventions for HIV/AIDS prevention as of 2012.

The Becoming A Responsible Teen (BART) intervention is based on the social learning theory as well. This program is unique in that it addresses the needs of the individuals in the group such as informational and motivation and behavioral needs using the IMB risk reduction model. The intervention lasts 8 weeks with weekly sessions between 90 and 120 min. African-American youth were specifically targeted for this intervention during the study. In the first two, games and discussions are used for HIV/AIDS education, a video that targets the population are viewed, and discussions regarding values and pressures surrounding sex take place. The next four sessions involve skills building. Among the skills developed during the sessions are condom use, cognitive restructuring regarding beliefs that prevent use of condoms, assertiveness, and communication skills. Role-plays are used to promote this skill building. The seventh session includes a presentation from HIV-positive youth who discuss how being infected has affected them. This is followed by teaching behavioral self-management and problem solving for the remaining of the seventh session and into the eighth session. The last session also attempts to empower the participants to teach others what they learned. Use of incentives such as T-shirts, certificates, and small sums of money is encouraged to get participants to attend all sessions (CDC, 2007).

Focus on Youth (FOY) and Informed Parents and Children Together (ImPACT) target high risk African-American youth living in low income areas. This program targets skill building as does other programs; however, this program is composed of two parts as listed above. Focus on Kids is an intervention that uses games, discussions, and videos along with homework regarding HIV/AIDS related topics such as safe sex and substance abuse. When paired with the second component, more significant positive outcomes were observed. Informed Parents and Children Together involves educating parents on the need for monitoring and communicating with their children. This is followed by a role-play related to their child's sexual involvement and skill building regarding correct condom use. This program resulted in a significant reduction in sexual intercourse and unprotected sex as a result of a 3 year study done between the years of 1999 and 2002 in the Baltimore, Maryland area with over 800 youth (CDC, 2007).

Another best-evidence program is Be Proud! Be Responsible!. This intervention targets African-American male adolescents. This program uses techniques such as games, group discussions, role-playing, and videos to deliver factual knowledge about HIV/AIDS and risky behaviors. This intervention also aids participants in assessing their own risky behaviors and helps to clarify myths surrounding HIV/AIDS. Evaluation of this program revealed significant decreases in risky sexual behavior as well as a decrease in sexual partners when compared to the control group (CDC, 2007).

Community-based interventions as described by DiClemente et al. (2002) facilitate change through indirect and direct methods. The more commonly used direct methods are utilized in individual and small group programs whereby volunteers, counselors, and other outreach people educate and provide material to individuals. With the indirect methods specific to community interventions, the at-risk individuals do not have to come into direct contact with outreach people. These would include organizational or community policy changes that promote behavior change with regard to risk behaviors. Both methods should be implemented to create the greatest amount of change.

The core characteristics of a community intervention are as follows:

1. A comprehensive needs assessment for the community.

    This should be multidimensional with regard to ecological factors and also have data regarding HIV/AIDS morbidity and mortality rates.
2. Develop a theoretical framework to guide the development, implementation, and program evaluation.

    Models include those which attend to organizational, social, and educational factor and emphasize collaboration between communities and the governments that influence them.
3. Integrate behavioral change models.

    These usually include social learning models, social cognitive theory, the theory of reasoned action, the theory of planned behavior, and the transtheoretical model. Newer models include addressing risk and protective factors.
4. Use implementation models to guide intervention delivery.

    Two theoretical models include the social marketing theory which uses advertising techniques to promote a message about the HIV/AIDS epidemic and the diffusion of innovation theory which uses a process of increasing awareness of the issue. First the target audience must understand the intervention, foresee benefits to a behavior change, and make their decision and implement the change. Finally, there is confirmation of the benefits to the target group and hopefully to others in the community through this process.

5. Use diverse intervention modalities.

This is done to increase the potential of the intervention overall to target behavior change (DiClemente et al., 2002).

Unresolved Issues and Future Research Directions

While we were able to identify more and less successful HIV prevention programs, it is important to recognize that no single program was completely successful. Some programs seemed to have an impact on one aspect of risk behavior but not another. Indeed, there is a great need for improved, empirically demonstrated prevention methods. Even successful programs, which involve a considerable investment of time and energy, need to be improved, refined, and strengthened.

There is relatively little need for programs that are below the standards set forth here. We should be sure that existing delivery systems (e.g., schools, mass media) continue to provide important educational programs. However, we should not merely repeat the same messages to already knowledgeable youth. Instead, social workers (and others) who want to contribute to real reductions in HIV rates in youth and young adults should find ways to deliver high quality programs guided by what has been described here.

There remain many fruitful research areas in need of further exploration. The extent to which individual participant characteristics (gender, ethnicity, age, sexual orientation, prior sexual experiences, extent of related risk behaviors, personality characteristics, family dynamics, etc.), program characteristics (family involvement, booster sessions, use of natural peer groups, group sizes, use of peer counselors, etc.), and other ecological factors (poverty, opportunity for success, community quality of life, etc.) influence program success should continue to be examined.

Most importantly, the need for prevention is now. There is much to gain. Lives are at risk as well as an endless amount of money in the healthcare system trying to keep those with the disease alive. The amount for prevention is tiny compared to what there is to lose (Pinkerton & Holtgrave, 1998).

References

Barnes, G. M., Hoffman, J., Welte, J. W., Farrell, M. P., & Dintcheff, B. A. (2006). Adolescents' time use: Effects on substance use, delinquency, and sexual activity. *Journal of Youth Adolescence, 36*, 697–710.

Bauman, L. J., & Germann, S. (2005). Psychosocial impact of the HIV/AIDS epidemic on children and youth. In C. Levine, G. Foster, & J. Williamson (Eds.), *A generation at risk: The global impact of HIV/AIDS on orphans and vulnerable children* (pp. 93–133). New York, NY: Cambridge University Press.

Brown, L. K., Laurie, K. J., & Pao, M. (2000). Children and adolescents living with HIV and AIDS: A review. *Journal of Child Psychology and Psychiatry, 44*(1), 81–96.

Centers for Disease Control and Prevention. (2007). Compendium of evidence-based HIV prevention interventions. *HIV/AIDS Prevention Research Synthesis.* Retrieved from http://www.cdc.gov/hiv/topics/research/prs/subset-best-evidence-interventions.htm

Centers for Disease Control and Prevention. (2010). *Weekly morbidity and mortality reports.* Retrieved from http://www.cdc.gov/mmwr/pdf/wk/mm5924.pdf

Centers for Disease Control and Prevention. (2011). *Estimates of new HIV infections in the United States, 2006–2009.* Retrieved from http://www.cdc.gov/nchhstp/newsroom/docs/HIV-Infections-2006-2009.pdf

Centers for Disease Control and Prevention. (2012). *HIV testing among adolescents: What schools and education agencies can do.* Retrieved from http://www.cdc.gov/healthyyouth/sexualbehaviors/pdf/hivtesting_adolescents.pdf

DiClemente, R. J., & Crosby, R. A. (2006). Preventing HIV infections in adolescents: What works for uninfected teens. In M. E. Lyon & L. J. D'Angelo (Eds.), *Teenagers, HIV, and AIDS* (pp. 143–161). Westport, CT: Praeger Publishers.

DiClemente, R. J., Crosby, R. A., & Wingood, G. M. (2002). HIV prevention for adolescents: Identified gaps and emerging approaches. *Prospects, 32*(2), 135–153.

Gallagher, K. M., Denning, P. D., Allen, D. R., Nakashima, A. K., & Sullivan, P. S. (2007). Use of rapid behavioral assessments to determine the prevalence of HIV risk behaviors in high-risk populations. *Public Health Reports, 122*(1), 56–62.

Green, E. C. (2003). *Rethinking HIV prevention: Learning from successes in developing countries.* Westport, CT: Praeger Publishers.

Griffin, K. W., Botwin, G. J., & Nichols, T. R. (2006). Effects of a school-based drug abuse prevention program for adolescents on HIV risk behavior in young adulthood. *Prevention Science, 7*(1), 103–112.

Guttmacher Institute. (2012). *Facts on American teens' sources of information about sex.* Retrieved from http://www.guttmacher.org/pubs/FB-Teen-Sex-Ed.pdf

The Henry J. Kaiser Family Foundation. (2012). *The global HIV/AIDS epidemic* (HIV Policy Program Publication No. 3030-17). Retrieved from http://www.kff.org/hivaids/upload/3030-17.pdf

Hoppe, M. J., Graham, L., Wilsdon, A., Wells, E. A., Nahom, D., & Morrison, D. M. (2004). Teens speak out about HIV/AIDS: Focus group discussions about risk and decision-making. *Journal of Adolescent Health, 35*(4), 345–360.

Linas, B. P., Zheng, H., Losina, E., Walensky, R. P., & Freedberg, K. A. (2006). Assessing the impact of federal HIV prevention spending on HIV testing and awareness. *American Journal of Public Health, 96*(6), 1038–1043.

Lyles, C. M., Kay, L. S., Crepaz, N., Herbst, J. H., Passin, W. F., Kim, A. S., … Mullins, M. M. (2007). Best evidence interventions: Findings from a systematic review of HIV behavioral interventions for US populations at high risk, 2000-2004. *American Journal of Public Health, 97*(1), 133–143.

Mantell, J. E., Harrison, A., Hoffman, S., Smit, J. A., Stein, Z. A., & Exner, T. M. (2006). The *Mpondombili* project: Preventing HIV/AIDS and unintended pregnancy among rural South African school-going adolescents. *Reproductive Health Matters, 14*(28), 113–122.

Ozer, E. J., Weinstein, R. S., Maslach, C., & Siegel, D. (1997). Adolescent AIDS prevention in context: Impact of peer educator qualities and classroom environments on intervention efficacy. *American Journal of Community Psychology, 25*(3), 289–323.

Pinkerton, S. D., & Holtgrave, D. R. (1998). A method for evaluating the economic efficiency of HIV behavioral risk reduction interventions. *AIDS and Behavior, 2*(3), 189–201.

Sawires, S. R., Dworkin, S. L., Fiamma, A., Peacock, D., Szekeres, G., & Coates, T. J. (2007). Male circumcision and HIV/AIDS: Challenges and opportunities. *The Lancet, 369*(9562), 708–713.

Trotter, R. T., II, & Singer, M. (2005). Rapid assessment strategies for public health: Promises and problems. In E. J. Trickett & W. Pequegnat (Eds.), *Community interventions and AIDS* (pp. 130–152). New York, NY: Oxford University Press.

United Nations Department of Public Information. (2010). *Millennium development goals: Goal 6: Combat HIV/AIDS, malaria and other diseases.* Retrieved from http://www.un.org/millenniumgoals/pdf/MDG_FS_6_EN.pdf

Weiss, L., French, T., Waters, M., Netherland, J., Agins, B., & Finkelstein, R. (2006). Adherence to HAART: Perspectives from clients in treatment support programs. *Psychology, Health & Medicine, 11*(2), 155–170.

The White House Office of National AIDS Policy (2010). *National HIV/AIDS strategy for the United States.* Retrieved from http://www.whitehouse.gov/sites/default/files/uploads/NHAS.pdf

Wodarski, J. S., Wodarski, L. A., & Parris, H. N. (2004). Adolescent preventive health and teams-games-tournaments: A Research and Development paradigm entering its fourth decade. *Journal of Evidence-Based Social Work, 1*(1), 101–124.

World Health Organization. (2004). *HIV/AIDS and adolescents: Young people—a window of hope in the HIV/AIDS pandemic.* The Department of Child and Adolescent Development.

World Health Organization. (2005). *HIV infection rates decreasing in several countries but globally number of people living with AIDS continues to rise.* Geneva, Switzerland: Press Release.

World Health Organization. (2006). Young people and HIV: The evidence is clear-act now! Study identifies prevention interventions set to go. *Indian Journal of Medical Sciences, 60*(9), 394–397.

World Health Organization. (2011). *HIV in the WHO African region: Progress towards achieving universal access to priority health sector interventions.* Brazzaville, Republic of Congo: WHO Regional Office for Africa.

Zweig, J. M., Lindberg, L. D., & McGinley, K. A. (2001). Adolescent health risk profiles: The co-occurrence of health risks among females and males. *Journal of Youth and Adolescence, 30*, 707–728.

Chapter 7
Helping Families Affected by Substance Abuse: What Works and What Does Not

Jan Ligon

The consumption of illicit drugs worldwide continues to expand as does the world's supply of drugs. Opium production increased 65% from 2016 to 2017; cocaine reached the highest level of production ever in 2016, while the production of marijuana not only continues to expand, but the THC potency levels have also increased (World Drug Report, 2018). Of particular concern in the USA is the increase in opioid consumption and drug overdose deaths, which are now the leading cause of death for people under the age of 50. According to the National Safety Council (2018), "the odds of dying from an accidental opioid overdose are greater than dying in a motor vehicle crash."

Opioids, primarily synthetic opioids, accounted for over two-thirds of all drug overdose deaths in 2017 (CDC, 2018). From 1999–2017 more than 700,000 people died from a drug overdose (CDC, 2019). At the federal level, a strategy to address the opioid crisis is identified as "to improve access to prevention, treatment, and recovery support services to prevent the health, social, and economic consequences associated with opioid misuse and addiction, and to enable individuals to achieve long-term recovery" (USDHHS, 2018).

Effects on Families, Children, and Significant Others

For every person who has a substance abuse problem, there are numerous concerned significant others (CSOs) who are affected (Meyers, Roozen, & Smith, 2011). The number of CSOs (partners, parents, grandparents, children, siblings, co-workers, and others) far exceeds the number of people with a substance misuse problem. This

J. Ligon (✉)
School of Social Work, Andrew Young School of Policy Studies, Georgia State University, Atlanta, GA, USA
e-mail: jligon@gsu.edu

© Springer Nature Switzerland AG 2019   127
J. S. Wodarski, L. M. Hopson (eds.), *Empirically Based Interventions Targeting Social Problems*, https://doi.org/10.1007/978-3-030-28487-9_7

very large group of people has been referred to as the "silent majority" in addiction prevention, treatment, and recovery (Ligon, 2005). While the economic impact of drug abuse approaches \$100 billion annually in the USA (Rhyan, 2017), the personal and emotional impacts of drugs on children are profound (Normile, Hanlon, & Eichner, 2018) and include:

- Poor outcomes and costs associated with prenatal exposure to opioids,
- Accidental ingestion of opioids,
- Increased risk of removal from the home and placement in the foster care system,
- Increased risk of trauma and adverse childhood experiences (ACEs), which are linked to negative health consequences later in life.

The authors stress the importance of services and programs that address the needs of families and children who are affected by drug use and abuse. Gruber and Taylor (2006) note four compelling reasons for taking a family perspective on substance abuse: "(1) It occurs in families, (2) It harms families, (3) Families both participate in and can perpetuate active addiction, and (4) Families are a potential treatment and recovery resource (p. 3)."

While it is understandable that most of the research and scholarship focuses on those who have substance use problems, the literature is very limited in addressing best practices for engaging and helping families and significant others. Indeed, many of the established terms and approaches currently used with CSOs are not evidence-based. Conversely, programs and interventions that have evidence of helping are often not known to helping professionals and, therefore, not utilized.

What Does not Work: Terms and Approaches Lacking Evidence of Support for Effectiveness

The use of terms, models, and approaches that lack any evidence of being useful are replete in the helping professions. For example, "birth order" has been used to explain a wide range of differences based on birth position (oldest, middle, youngest, etc.). This continues despite studies reporting that birth order is not predictive of personality traits (Damian & Roberts, 2015). The authors go on to note that this evidence does not assure that birth order predictions will abate "because people are susceptible to weighing anecdotal information more heavily than data-driven findings (p. 14120)." Indeed there are also anecdotal, long-standing terms, lacking empirical support, that are used with families and significant others who are affected by drug use and abuse. The three most common, the trifecta of these terms, are family disease, family roles, and codependency.

Family Disease

The notion that addiction is a disease is well established and endorsed by such significant entities as the National Institute of Drug Abuse and the American Society of Addiction Medicine. The concept has segued over the years into the family aspect of addressing substance abuse and addiction. Families affected by drug use are often told that their condition is that of a "family disease." As stated by Roth (2010), "the patient who returns to a sick family would seem to be much more likely to relapse than one who returns to a family recovering together (p. 2)." However, the acceptance by families of this label is questionable.

Meurk et al. (2016) found that less than half of families studied defined addiction as a disease while most family members believed that addiction should be described as a symptom of other problems (71%) or as a dependency (64%). Similar findings were reported in a 2006 survey (ADTQ). As the disease definition has evolved to more specifically define addiction as a brain disease, only one-third of the families studied identified the term to explain addiction (Meurk et al., 2016). Indeed Barnett, Hall, Fry, Dikes-Frayne, and Carter (2017) studied service provider buy-in to addiction as a disease, noting "there is mixed evidence of support for the DMA (disease model of addiction) among drug and alcohol treatment providers" (p. 718).

As noted by the Centers for Substance Abuse Treatment (CSAT, 2004), conveying to CSOs that they are part of a family disease also employs a concept that has "limited controlled research evidence" but is nonetheless "influential in the treatment community as well as the general public" (CSAT, 2004, p. 8). It is therefore noteworthy that a family disease approach is still commonly used, despite research to support that most families do not believe it.

Family Roles

In 1981, author Sharon Wegscheider wrote, "in ten tears of working with alcoholic families, I have watched the same five basic roles played out in virtually every family. I have labeled them The *Enabler*, the *Hero*, the *Scapegoat*, the Lost Child, and the *Mascot* (Wegscheider, 1981, p. 84)." With the birth of these terms four decades ago, which were based solely on her personal observations, with the clients characterized in the pronoun "her," a simple Google search portrays the continued widespread use of these terms. The most commonly used of the five roles is "The Enabler," which minimizes the complexity of the effect of substance abuse on CSOs so that "efforts to change their behaviors in order to aid recovery may be sabotaged" (Schumm, Kahler, O'Farrell, Murphy, & Muchowski, 2014, p. 275).

Research by Vernig (2011) concluded that "their clinical utility does not win out over the problems inherent with this manner of classification" (p. 535). He goes on to conclude that "to better understand the dynamic and multifaceted roles that family members play in a home where a parent is dependent on alcohol, it is necessary to move away from a strict role theory and focus on not only the commonalities but the differences that come into play when family members cope with the myriad social, emotional, financial, and interpersonal consequences of alcohol dependence" (p. 541).

Codependency

For over three decades, codependency has flourished as a concept that has yielded a 25th anniversary edition of the book *Codependent No More* (Beattie, 1989), which is the #1 Best Seller in Amazon's "New Age Mysticism" category, a book in the "For Dummies" series (Lancer, 2015), and a website with an international conference (http://coda.org/). While the term's meaning varies greatly, CSAT (2004) defines "codependency as being overly concerned with the problems of another to the detriment of attending to one's own wants and needs" (p. 24). As noted by Knudson and Terrell, "codependency is not only a controversial topic concerning its diagnostic validity, but also shows controversy in its origins of development." (Knudson & Terrell, 2012, p. 256).

Despite the wide acceptance of codependency, the term, as with enabling, has been criticized for being disproportionally assigned to women (Anderson, 1994). CSAT (2004) further notes that "although the term codependent originally described spouses of those with alcohol abuse disorders, it has come to refer to any relative of a person with any type of behavior or psychological problem. The idea has been criticized for pathologizing caring functions, particularly those that have traditionally been part of a woman's role, such as empathy and self-sacrifice. Despite the term's common use, little scientific inquiry has focused on codependence. Systematic research is needed to establish the nature of codependency and why it might be important" (p. 24).

What Works: Terms and Approaches Having Evidence of Support for Effectiveness

While the details of evidence-based approaches exceed the scope of this chapter, there are well-established models with empirical support to be considered. These include CRAFT, the 5-Step Method, Behavioral Couples Therapy, the Nurturing Parenting Program, and Motivational Interviewing.

Community Reinforcement Approach and Family Therapy (CRAFT) is an evidence-based model that "focuses on enhancing the happiness of the CSO overall" (p. 385) by developing strategies and goals that support desired changes (Meyers et al., 2011). The authors note that the goals of CRAFT are to help families move their loved one toward treatment, reduce the loved one's alcohol and drug use, and to improve the life quality of CSOs.

5-Step Method

Developed in the UK, the 5-Step Method (Copello, Templeton, Orford, & Vellman, 2010) views CSOs as "ordinary people facing highly stressful circumstances" and goes on to note that there is "no room within the method to think of family members as part of the 'disease of addiction' or having responsibility for causing the addiction problem" (p. 88).

The authors note the five steps as follows: "1. listen, reassure and explore concerns, 2. provide relevant, specific and targeted information, 3. explore coping resources, 4. discuss emotional support, and 5. discuss and explore further needs. "It is a pragmatic and flexible approach that considers the impact of addiction upon family members to be a very stressful experience that can be improved by working systematically with family members, through a series of steps covering the key components of the model" (Copello et al., 2010, p. 98)".

Behavioral Couples Therapy

Behavioral Couples Therapy (Fals-Stewart, Lam, & Kelley, 2009) is an evidence-based program, easily modified for use with families, which employs a session-by-session manual used to develop improved communications and positive reinforcement skills that can be very helpful when there is a person with a substance abuse problem in the family.

Behavioral Couples Therapy "is a form of behavior therapy that incorporates both the partner and the individual seeking help for alcohol or other drugs. The goal of Behavioral Couples Therapy (BCT) is to improve the couple's relationship while building support for abstinence. This means increasing positive activities and improving communication between partners, with both acceptance and change, to facilitate success in recovery from alcohol and other drugs" (https://www.recovery-answers.org/resource/behavioral-couples-therapy/).

The Nurturing Parenting Program

The Nurturing Parenting Program (USDOJ, 2010) offers an array of well-established evidence-based interventions, including Families in Substance Abuse Treatment and Recovery, which is manualized and contains 17 sessions. The program is predicated on these assumptions: developing empathy, facilitating parent-child bonding and attachment; teaching parents appropriate expectations of children's growth and development to foster positive brain development and feelings of self-worth, trust, and security; employing discipline that promotes the dignity of children and adults; empowering adults and children to nurture themselves, others and their environment, including animals; promoting positive self-worth; and helping all family members develop a meaningful level of self-awareness and acceptance." (www.nuturingparenting.com)".

Motivational Interviewing (MI)

Introduced by Miller and Rollnick's seminal book four decades ago (Miller & Rollnick, 1991), Motivational Interviewing arguably transformed the way professionals work to help people make changes. The underpinnings of MI are "(a) expressing empathy, which serves many goals such as increasing rapport, helping clients feel understood, reducing the likelihood of resistance to change, and allowing clients to explore their inner thoughts and motivations; (b) developing discrepancy, which essentially means that clients argue, to themselves, reasons why they should change by seeing the gap between their values and their current problematic behaviors; (c) rolling with resistance, which means that clients' reluctance to make changes is respected, viewed as normal rather than pathological, and not furthered by defensive or aggressive counseling techniques; and (d) supporting clients' self-efficacy, which means that clients' confidence in their ability to change is acknowledged as critical to successful change efforts" (Lundahl, Kunz, Brownell, Tollefson, & Burke, 2010, p. 137).

A meta-analysis spanning 25 years of studies found that MI "works across a wide range of problem behaviors/types and is unlikely to harm clients. Compared to other active and specific treatments, MI was equally effective in our review and shorter in length" (Lundahl et al., 2010, p. 154). Although MI originally targeted substance abuse, the model has been widely used across healthcare settings, exercise and fitness, gambling problems, and in behavioral health (Schumacher & Madson 2015).

Conclusion

There are critical differences in the approach assumptions of the evidence-based group and those lacking empirical support that are summarized in this chapter. The latter group uses labels (family disease, codependency, family roles) whereas all of the evidence-based models do not. One might argue that in Motivational Interviewing, the stages of change (precontemplation, contemplation, etc.) are labels, but these are in place to guide the helper on what to do, based on that stage, and not to label the person seeking help. The terms lacking evidence employ a hierarchical approach involving an expert professional and the client or patient, where the evidence-based models avoid this and rely on being with and following the lead of the person seeking help. What is most concerning, however, is that the predominantly used terms and approaches lack any evidence of helping and actually may be harmful.

Moving helping professionals away from using historical, anecdotal, and unsupported approaches to those that are evidence-based is an ongoing challenge. This struggle is not unique to our fields. As noted by Shelton and Lee (2019) "in public health, a major gap exists between the evidence-based interventions (EBIs), practices, and policies shown to promote health and prevent disease ("what we know works and what is actually delivered in real-world settings ("what we do")" (p. S132)".

As stated by Rieckmann et al., "improving access to evidence-based, efficacious services is an immediate challenge" (Rieckmann, Abraham, Zwick, Rasplica, & McCarty, 2015, p. 1129). While there are many families affected by substance abuse that need support, the help and assistance provided must be scrutinized. It is important to move away from approaches that lack evidence of helping to those that have been found to be useful.

References

Anderson, S. (1994). A critical evaluation of the concept of codependency. *Social Work, 39*(6), 677–685.

Barnett, A., Hall, W., Fry, C. L., Dikes-Frayne, E., & Carter, A. (2017). Drug and alcohol treatment providers' views about the disease model of addiction and its impact on clinical practice: A systematic review. *Drug and Alcohol Review, 37*(6), 607–720.

Beattie, M. (1989). *Codependent no more: How to stop controlling others and start caring for yourself*. Center City, MN: Hazelden.

Center for Substance Abuse Treatment (CSAT). (2004, Revised 2015). *Substance abuse treatment and family therapy*. Treatment Improvement Protocol (TIP) Series, No. 39. HHS Publication No. (SMA) 15-4219. Rockville, MD: Substance Abuse and Mental Health Services Administration. Retrieved from http://adaiclearinghouse.org/downloads/TIP-39-Substance-Abuse-Treatment-and-Family-Therapy-55.pdf

Centers for Disease Control and Prevention, National Center for Injury Prevention and Control, Division of Unintentional Injury Prevention. (2018). *Drug overdose deaths*. Retrieved from https://www.cdc.gov/drugoverdose/

Centers for Disease Control and Prevention. (2019). *Drug overdose deaths among women aged 30–64 years in the United States, 1999–2017*. Retrieved from https://www.cdc.gov/mmwr/volumes/68/wr/mm6801a1.htm

Copello, A., Templeton, L., Orford, J., & Vellman, R. (2010). The 5-step method: Principles and practice. *Drugs: Education, Prevention, and Policy, 17*, 86–99.

Damian, R. I., & Roberts, B. W. (2015). Settling the debate on birth order and personality. *Proceedings of the National Academy of Sciences of the United States*. Retrieved from https://www.pnas.org/content/112/46/14119

Fals-Stewart, W., Lam, W., & Kelley, M. L. (2009). Learning sobriety together: Behavioural couples therapy for alcoholism and drug abuse therapy for alcoholism and drug abuse. *Journal of Family Therapy, 31*, 115–125.

Gruber, K. J., & Taylor, M. F. (2006). A family perspective for substance abuse: Implications from the literature. *Journal of Social Work Practice in the Addictions, 6*(1/2), 1–29.

Knudson, T. M., & Terrell, H. K. (2012). Codependency, perceived interparental conflict, and substance abuse in the family of origin. *The American Journal of Family Therapy, 40*, 245–257.

Lancer, G. (2015). *Codependency for dummies* (2nd ed.). Hoboken, NY: John Wiley and Sons.

Ligon, J. (2005). Families and significant others: The silent majority in addiction treatment and recovery. *NAADAC News, National Association for Addiction Professionals, 15*(4), 8.

Lundahl, B., Kunz, C., Brownell, C., Tollefson, D., & Burke, B. (2010). A meta-analysis of motivational interviewing: Twenty-five years of empirical studies. *Research on Social Work Practice, 20*(2), 137–160.

Meurk, C., Fraser, D., Weier, M., Lucke, J., Carter, A., & Hall, W. (2016). Assessing the place of neurobiological explanations in accounts of a family member's addiction. *Drug and Alcohol Review, 35*, 461–446.

Meyers, R. J., Roozen, H. G., & Smith, J. E. (2011). The community reinforcement approach: An update of the evidence. *Alcohol Research & Health, 33*(4), 380–388.

Miller, W. R., & Rollnick, S. (1991). *Motivational interviewing: Preparing people to change addictive behavior*. New York, NY: Guilford Press.

National Safety Council. (2018) *Preventable injury and fatality statistics, 2017*. Retrieved from https://injuryfacts.nsc.org/all-injuries/overview/

Normile, B., Hanlon, C., & Eichner, H. (2018). *State strategies to meet the needs of young children and families affected by the opioid crisis*. National Academy for Health Policy. Retrieved from https://nashp.org/wp-content/uploads/2018/09/Children-and-Opioid-Epidemic-1.pdf

Rhyan, C. (2017). *The potential societal benefit of eliminating opioid overdoses, deaths, and substance use disorders exceeds $95 billion per year*. Retrieved from https://altarum.org/about/news-and-events/economic-toll-of-opioid-crisis-in-u-s-exceeded-1-trillion-since-2001

Rieckmann, T., Abraham, A., Zwick, J., Rasplica, C., & McCarty, D. (2015). A longitudinal study of state strategies and policies to accelerate evidence-based practices in the context of systems transformation. *Health Services Research, 50*(4), 1125–1145.

Roth, J. D. (2010). Addiction as a family disease. *Journal of Groups in Addiction & Recovery, 5*, 1–3.

Schumacher, J., & Madson, M. B. (2015). *Fundamentals of motivational interviewing: Tips and strategies for addressing common clinical challenges*. New York, NY: Oxford University Press.

Schumm, J. A., Kahler, C. W., O'Farrell, T. J., Murphy, M. M., & Muchowski, P. (2014). A randomized clinical trial of behavioral couples therapy versus individually based treatment for women with alcohol dependence. *Journal of Consulting and Clinical Psychology, 82*(6), 993–1004.

Shelton, R. C., & Lee, M. (2019). Sustaining evidence-based interventions and policies: Recent innovations and future directions in implementation science. *American Journal of Public Health, 109*(S2), S132–S134.

U.S. Department of Health and Human Services. (2018). *Strategy to combat opioid abuse, misuse, and overdose*. Retrieved from https://www.hhs.gov/opioids/sites/default/files/2018-09/opioid-fivepoint-strategy-20180917-508compliant.pdf

U.S. Department of Justice (USDOJ). (2010). *The nurturing parenting program*. Washington, DC: Office of Justice Programs, Office of Juvenile Justice and Delinquency Prevention.

Vernig, P. K. (2011). Family roles in homes with alcohol-dependent parents: An evidence-based review. *Substance Use and Misuse, 46*, 535–542.

Wegscheider, S. (1981). *Another chance: Hope & health for the alcoholic family*. Palo Alto, CA: Science and Behavior Books.

World Drug Report. (2018). United National Office on Drugs and Crime. Retrieved from https://www.unodc.org/wdr2018/

Internet Resources

5-Step Method. Retrieved from http://www.drugs.ie/features/feature/family_intervention_the_5_step_method

Addiction and the Family International Network (AFINet). Retrieved from http://www.afinetwork.info/

Community Reinforcement Approach and Family Therapy (CRAFT). Retrieved from https://www.robertjmeyersphd.com/craft.html

Motivational Interviewing. Retrieved from https://motivationalinterviewing.org/

Nurturing Parenting Program. Retrieved from https://www.nurturingparenting.com/

Chapter 8
Crime

Lisa A. Rapp and John S. Wodarski

Overview

Unless we begin to care for offenders, and extend them a humanity (whether we believe that they deserve it or not) that is founded on nonviolence principles, we will continue to perpetuate the very violence and behavior that drives our current fears about offenders and victimization (Lutze, 2006, p. 395).

No one wants to be victimized by crime and those who are (or whose relatives or friends are) want the offender to be held accountable and to never re-offend. The challenge is to balance two needs. On the one hand, there is the need to hold offenders accountable and to promote public safety. On the other hand, there is the need to prevent and rehabilitate offenders so that they can become constructive members of society.

This is more than a corrections challenge; it is a reflection of our humanity, of our country's commitment to the values of social justice and safety. This challenge must be understood and viewed in an ecological framework. No one person acts without affecting and being affected by others. So, we must look not only at the functionality of (potential) offenders, but also at the functionality of their families, neighborhoods, communities, institutions, and culture. We must realize that most of those incarcerated eventually return to society. Should we allow them to return as better criminals, as people without the skills to integrate constructively into society or should we work toward rehabilitation and a positive, productive future? When people become offenders, we should do all that we can both to hold them accountable and to rehabilitate them so that they might return safely to society. Yes, there will

L. A. Rapp (✉)
School of Educational Social Services, Saint Leo University, St. Leo, FL, USA
e-mail: Lisa.Rapp-McCall@saintleo.edu

J. S. Wodarski
College of Social Work, University of Tennessee, Knoxville, TN, USA

© Springer Nature Switzerland AG 2019
J. S. Wodarski, L. M. Hopson (eds.), *Empirically Based Interventions Targeting Social Problems*, https://doi.org/10.1007/978-3-030-28487-9_8

always be a few who cannot be returned, but this fact does not justify a get tough philosophy that arguably perpetuates fear, violence, and inhumanity and overflows our prisons.

A Few Statistics

The Federal Bureau of Investigation's Uniform Crime Reporting Program (UCR), which captures 94% of the US population, found that in 2016 citizens experienced 5.7 million violent victimizations or 21.1 victimizations per 1000 persons. Likewise, there were approximately 15.9 million property victimizations or 119.4 victimizations per 1000 households (Bureau of Justice Statistics, 2016). However, it should be noted that fewer than half of all violent victimizations are reported to the police.

There are estimated to have been 10.6 million arrests in the USA in 2016. These include the 29 offenses tracked and exclude traffic violations (Federal Bureau of Investigation, 2016). For violent crimes, there were 515,151 arrests and for property crimes, there were 1,353,283 arrests in 2016 (Federal Bureau of Investigation, 2016). Other arrests included drug abuse violations, fraud, driving under the influence, etc.

Violent crime rates did not differ significantly by gender or race but they did differ by age. For instance, persons ages 12–34 had higher rates of violent victimization than persons ages 35 or older. Victimization rates also varied by income bracket (highest for persons in households earning less than $25,000 each year) and marital status (highest for persons who were separated) (Bureau of Justice Statistics, 2016).

Looking at several kinds of crime committed in 2016, there were over 6000 incidents of hate crime and over 1000 incidents of Human Trafficking reported. However, both of these forms of crime are vastly underreported (Federal Bureau of Investigation, 2016).

There were 1,707,350 incidents of family and intimate partner violence, according to the BJS (2016). This includes current and former partners, making a rate of 6.3 per 1000. In 2016, there were 676,000 children victimized by abuse or neglect resulting in a national rate of 9.1 per 1000 (U.S. Department of Health and Human Services, 2018).

Substance abuse is implicated in this relative-as-perpetrator category of crime, as it is in many other kinds of crime. In a study conducted by the Arrestee Drug Abuse Monitoring Program, 60% of arrestees tested positive for one or more drugs at the time of arrest (Office of National Drug Control Policy, 2011). In 2002, perpetrators of violent crimes were believed by their victims to have been drinking in approximately one million instances. In the same year, approximately 75% of spousal victims of crime said that the perpetrator was under the influence of alcohol (Bureau of Justice Statistics, 2007a).

The costs of crime include those which are tangible and hence calculable monetarily, such costs being related to property loss, medical expenses, public safety programs, private security strategies. Much more difficult to calculate are the intangible costs, such as the pain and suffering caused by the criminal events, as well as the subsequent diminishment of the quality of life for victims and their families (Shapiro, 1999).

Looking at tangible costs, these are considerable. Crime costs as much as $15 billion in economic losses for victims and $179 billion in assorted government expenditures in 2007 (from McCollister). In 2003, nearly half of the billions that victims received went to medical expenses while 12% went to mental health counseling (National Center for Victims of Crime, 2004). Considering the costs of domestic or intimate partner violence alone, the Centers for Disease Control and Prevention [CDCP] determined that the 2003 health-related costs stemming from physical assault, rape, homicide, and stalking were at least $5.8 billion annually (Centers for Disease Control and Prevention, 2003). The UCR also found that in 2010, the tangible costs of property crimes other than arson were approximately $16.21 billion (Federal Bureau of Investigation, 2011). A single serious violent crime could cost up to $17 million (DeLisi et al., 2010).

There are many other costs as well, such as the costs to keep the U S corrections system going. In 2001, this was estimated to be in excess of $38 billion (National Center for Victims of Crime, 2004). In 2000, the national budget for reduction of drug use alone was 9.936.6 million, with an anticipated request for fiscal year 2007 being 12,655.8 million (Bureau of Justice Statistics, 2007b). This is just part of the annual cost of alcohol abuse, at about $150 million, and drug abuse, at about $96 million (McDonald & Finn, 2000).

Juveniles

Juveniles have contributed significantly and tragically to criminal and especially violent, conduct in our country. Significantly, "violent crime is for the most part a young man's activity," referring to those 25 years old and younger (McDonald & Finn, 2000, p. 38). Looking at 2009 juvenile arrests, for example, youth (those under 18 years of age) accounted for nearly one in ten of those arrested for murder. One out of ten arrested for abuse of drugs was a juvenile. Nearly one out of five arrested for weapon related crime, theft of a motor vehicle, robbery, burglary, and larceny-theft was a juvenile (Puzzanchera, Adams, & Kang, 2012).

Yet we must not overestimate the part juveniles do play in criminal activity. Krisberg and Wolf assert that juvenile crime is one of the social issues most vulnerable to mischaracterization by the media. "More children are killed by their parents or guardians than by other youth. Virtually no one guesses that teenagers are more often the victims of crime than any other age group" (Krisberg & Wolf, 2005, p. 67).

Still, there is serious juvenile crime. The changing character of juvenile crime, the increasing push to try juveniles in adult court, and the struggle to understand the factors that contribute to juvenile crime will be discussed at length below. For the moment, it is simply critical to point out the need to understand the etiology of juvenile crime since most adult criminals committed their first crime as a minor

(Moffitt, 1993). The good news is that there is promising research on and demonstrations of effective societal responses that balance punishment with rehabilitation, which will also be examined later.

Minorities

Minority groups, especially African-Americans, have been increasingly over-represented as perpetrators and victims of crime and violence. In the 1970s, 1980s, and 1990s, federal and state criminal codes were revamped with mandatory sentences, sentence enhancements, and other initiatives designed in part to reduce racial disparity in incarceration (Schlesinger, 2011). Instead, the opposite has happened. Racial and ethnic minorities now account for 60% of people in prison (Bureau of Justice Statistics, 2011), much of which can be accounted for a rise in Hispanics prosecuted from immigration offenses (U.S. Sentencing Commission, 2004). By 2010, black non-Hispanic males had an imprisonment rate seven times greater than white non-Hispanic males (Bureau of Justice Statistics, 2011). This rate stands out because blacks and Hispanics make up only 28.9% of our country's adult population (U.S. Census Bureau, 2012).

African-Americans are sentenced not only more frequently, but also more severely. Today's laws call for stiffer penalties for traits and behaviors black are more likely to have like living in public housing or owning a firearm (Schlesinger, 2011). The gap has only widened since the federal Sentencing Reform Act became effective in 1988. Previously, average sentence length for blacks and whites was nearly identical. By 2001, the average sentence for whites was nearly 40 months but nearly 70 for blacks (U.S. Sentencing Commission, 2004). This disparity in the minority composition of America's imprisoned extends to juvenile offenders, with 40% of the juveniles arrested annually being African-American (Redding & Mrozoski, 2005).

African-Americans are also disproportionately represented as victims of violence. For this group of Americans, 27 people per 1000 are victimized by violent crime, whereas for Whites, the rate is 20 per 1000. According to the FBI's UCR statistics, African-Americans constituted about half of all murder victims in 2010, despite that fact the group's minority status (Federal Bureau of Investigation, 2011).

These statistics may give the impression that African-Americans are to blame for crime and violence. However, studies have indicated that there is nothing inherent about the African-American culture that provokes violent crime like homicide (Loeber & Farrington, 2011). Instead, community characteristics, which include unemployment, family disruption, poor educational systems, and economic deprivation, are the factors that increase crime and violence (Pearson, 1994; Roscoe & Morton, 1994) and minority groups are disproportionately represented in these types of communities.

Women

In absolute numbers, there are far fewer women than men arrested and incarcerated. Approximately 1 out of 4 people arrested are women (Federal Bureau of Investigation, 2012). Yet, between 1977 and 2007, the number of incarcerated women increased 832%, which is twice the rate increase for men (Goodwin, 2015). The USA currently incarcerates one-third of the World's female inmates (Goodwin, 2015).

This drastic rise is connected with the war on drugs. Women's drug use has not increased in the last 30 years, only their incarceration rates. Many women who become criminals share common risk factors: (1) living in poverty and having insufficient social support, (2) having been victimized, frequently as children, by physical and sexual abuse, (3) suffering from serious mental and physical health issues, including substance abuse, and (4) being mothers, typically single (Greene & Pranis, 2004; Holtfreter, Reisig, & Morash, 2004; Hyman, Garcia, & Sinha, 2006). The children of incarcerated women are arguably the most devastated, their lives even more destabilized and unpredictable than they were when their mothers were caring for them. As Greene and Pranis conclude, "Incarcerating women does not solve the problems that underlie their involvement in the criminal system. Their imprisonment creates enormous turmoil and suffering for their children" (Greene & Pranis, 2004, Conclusion, para 3).

Minority Women

Minority women are especially vulnerable to incarceration as a result of the war on drugs, even though their offenses are minor compared with the drug related offenses of the men. Once arrested, these women do not have the information more serious drug offenders to use to plea bargain down their sentences. Also, the Federal sentencing guidelines curtail judges' discretion in sentencing these women. According to Goodwin (2015), one in 113 Caucasian women will be imprisoned, compared to 1 in 45 Latinas and 1 in 18 African-American women.

Trends in Crime

From the 1930s until the 1960s, there was a downward trend in crime in the USA. However, in the 1960s, according to a report prepared by McDonald and Finn in 2000 for the National Institute of Justice [NIJ], there was a significant turnaround. There was an increase in crimes reported to the police, police arrests, prosecutions, convictions, incarcerations, and supervision (probation and parole). Concomitantly, there were increasingly severe laws passed and more financial resources expended at local, state, and federal levels of government. One dynamic stands out—the rise in the use of illegal drugs and of crimes committed, especially as a part of the burgeoning cocaine trade, and made more violent by the ready access to firearms. The NIJ report also notes that alcohol abuse was a large contributory factor in the commission of violent crimes (McDonald & Finn, 2000).

Statistics for homicide, as a "bellwether crime," are revealing. In the early 1930s, the homicide rates peaked at 9.7 per 100,000 people and then declined until the middle of the 1960s. At this time, the rate rose strikingly for two decades until it reached 10.2 per 100,000 in 1980. Notably, however, the rate began to decrease, reaching 6.8 per 100,000 in 1997. Due to victim failure and/or reluctance to report crimes to the police, trends for other crimes were not available until 1973, with the establishment of the National Crime Victimization Survey. This survey shows that since 1973, the violent crime rates have for the most part also decreased (McDonald & Finn, 2000).

According to the NIJ report, however, within this general trend there are buried troubling observations. After 1970, the probability of a 15–24-year-old person killing or being killed rose significantly. This connects with the rising drug trade, along with the availability of guns. The perpetrators and victims were mostly male. Furthermore, they were more likely to be African-Americans, who were 7 times more likely to be killed than were Whites and 8 times more likely to kill than were Whites. This trend did begin to change in 1994, although it is still high among young people. The same tendency occurred for other types of violent crime, with the rates for the 15–24 year olds having risen faster than for older (or younger) perpetrators (McDonald & Finn, 2000).

Despite a slight uptick in homicides in the early 2000s (Centers for Disease Control and Prevention, 2005), violent crime has continued to trend downward (Federal Bureau of Investigation, 2011). In 2010, violent crime was down 6% from 2009, 13.2% from 2012, and 13.4% from 2001.

Fear of Crime

Post 9–11 United States seems to be a more fearful place than it was prior to the devastating terrorist attack on what many Americans take to be this country's values of freedom, democracy, and respect for the individual. Yet, Americans are also very fearful of homegrown criminal violence and infractions. In order to address fear of any kind, one must know the facts about the sources of the fear—the crimes, their context, their victims, and especially their perpetrators. Pulling the facts together may sound easy. Yet, with a social problem as complex as crime in this multifaceted society, such gathering of fact is exceedingly difficult. Add to this, shocking media images and political rhetoric and one gets a distorted picture of this deep, burdensome and costly social issue (Gilliam & Iyengar, 2000).

Part of the picture is graphically real and vividly true. For example, citizens are presented terrible pictures of the Columbine children running from the deadly shots fired by sniper-classmates and the horror of the shootings at Virginia Tech has been immortalized in posed pictures of the perpetrator himself. Yet, Cornell (2005) points out, "[p]ublic perception of school violence can be skewed by a few highly publicized, extreme cases, leading authorities to adopt dubious zero tolerance policies or to pursue questionably practices such as profiling" (Cornell, 2005, p. 62). In other words, public perception and attitudes about crime are more a reflection of general concerns about crime or society than direct experiences with crime itself (Lereventz, 2012).

To take another familiar example, the beautiful faces of children tragically abducted by child molesters lurking in the neighborhood or by the school playground are urgently scattered across the visual media. This example will be discussed in greater detail to highlight the danger of not getting the facts about crime right—a false sense of security that the societal response is targeted appropriately and being carried out effectively. One of the distortions here comes from how the media, aided by political pronouncements, has inordinately narrowed public attention to one kind of child molestation danger, the so-called stranger danger. That is, the fear of the unknown assailant who could be anywhere, ready to groom, and then attack innocent, unsuspecting children. However, as Levenson and D'Amora point out, such dangerous strangers constitute approximately 7% of those victimizing children. On the other hand, family members are the perpetrators in 39% of the cases and non-family members known to the victim make up another 59%. Unfortunately, in response to public fear, politicians have responded quickly, but arguably without the sufficient but necessary measured, objective attention to such evidence.

The media has also fanned the flames of fear by its choice of which instances of sexual abuse to cover and of how to shape the coverage. Since Jacob Wetterling was abducted and disappeared in 1989, there have been a number of young children whose abduction and murder have been followed closely and passionately in the media. Because of this, "extraordinary media attention, the publicity of such events creates a sense of alarm and urgency among citizens." However, the media has created in the citizenry the impression that such instances of child abduction, abuse, and murder are common and increasing in frequency. In fact, there are studies showing that this kind of sexual abuse of children is declining rather than rising (Levenson & D'Amora, 2006). More significantly, this kind of incident is exceedingly rare. Levenson points out that according to the National Center for Missing and Exploited Children, there are 100 such cases annually in the USA. She then compares this statistic with the National Highway Traffic Safety's Administration's 2004 report that 500 children less than 15 year of age were killed by drunk drivers in a year's time, as well as the Child Welfare League of American's finding that in 2002, 1121 children died due to physical neglect or abuse suffered at the hands of their parents or caregivers. This is to say, five times as many children are killed by drunken drivers and 11 times as many are abused or neglected by those caring for them.

This is not to diminish the utter tragedy of the abduction/murder cases, but rather to point out that the public's emotional response to these relative few cases may prompt legislation to be written for a very narrow sets of circumstances, leaving children in danger in many other kinds of situations. Ironically and tragically, most of the people from whom children need protection are in their families and among their acquaintances, who have either not yet offended or not yet been caught. This dimension of threat becomes invisible, as it were, through the distorted lenses of media and, subsequently, behind much of the current sexual predator legislation. How one understands the threat of crime must be based in sound evidence if Americans are to meet effectively the very real threat of child sexual abuse. If the entire target in not sight, then the "remedies" will at best fall short.

So, if one may generalize from this example, it is imperative that when one attempts to examine the array of criminal activity against which society must mount effective responses consonant with the values of freedom, democracy, and the value of the individual, one must get the facts straight to the best of one's ability.

That said, unfortunately fear can be impervious to fact. Insofar as fear drives legislation and decreases public willingness to invest seriously stretched public funds in innovation interventions, fear can defeat effective, positive societal responses to crime. The NIJ report cites a set of surveys conducted in 12 cities indicating that despite the recent decline in the number of those victimized by crime, people are no less fearful (McDonald & Finn, 2000). In 1992, crime was the top problem identified, as had never previously occurred in public opinion polls. In October of 2006, the attitude was a bit better than it was in the early 1990s. Yet, after the spell of optimism at the turn of the century, public opinion is again "fairly pessimistic," and this despite the fact that again federal crime statistics are at "modern lows" (Saad, 2006, p. 1).

One of the most divisive issues in the public discourse breaks around access to firearms and (any) controlling regulations. This is another place where it is essential to have the pertinent facts on the relationship between guns and violence as well as the (in)effectiveness of various policies governing their use, manufacture, and sale (National Research Council of the Nation Academies, 2005).

In 1998, guns were used in a variety of violent crimes. First, 65% of reported murders were committed with a gun (McDonald & Finn, 2000). This is consistent with 2005 numbers, where 55% of the murders were committed with a handgun, while 16% used another type of gun (Bureau of Justice Statistics, 2007a). Other crimes wherein guns were utilized include 38% of the robberies and 19% of the aggravated assaults. It is very likely that the prevalence of private gun ownership plays a significant role in these statistics. For instance, in 1994 firearms were owned by 44 million people in this country (McDonald & Finn, 2000).

Certain highly publicized crimes, albeit rare events, have heightened public fear. Examples include school and college shootings and specific high-impact terrorists attacks (McDonald & Finn, 2000). Many individuals have an increased concern for their own safety, which may be reflected in increased ownership of guns and in the strong beliefs in the right of individuals to own and bear arms.

Philosophical Trends in Societal Response to Crime

From early in the 1900s until the 1970s, judges had significant discretion in sentencing, including the use of indeterminate sentencing. The theory informing this policy was that the goal of probation, incarceration, and parole was rehabilitation of the offender (McDonald & Finn, 2000). This was especially true for juvenile offenders, who have their own juvenile court system. Here, the state has seen itself, according to the doctrine of parens patriae, as the beneficent parent who was correcting the path of the wayward youth. The young person was seen as only partly responsible for his (or, much less often, her) crime due to parental neglect and poverty. Furthermore, it was believed that these young persons were capable of being reshaped into a law abiding person (Redding, Sevin Goldstein, & Heilbrun, 2005). Sentencing discretion, then, allowed judges to tailor the punishment to the particularities of the offense and the perpetrator, a "quasi-clinical task" (McDonald & Finn, 2000, p. 33). This view of punishment could also be called, "enlightened instrumentalism," in that the punishment was aimed at addressing "pathological conditions lurking behind their criminal behavior" (Reidy, 2007, p. 159).

However, this policy gave way in the 1980s and 1990s to a get tough approach once rehabilitation was believed not to work for either adults or juveniles. This belief was significantly bolstered by Martinson's well-known and extensively cited 1974 examination of evaluations of criminal and juvenile programs (Martinson, 1974). These new policies, mandated in law, have been guided by four strategies: (1) mandatory incarceration for certain kinds of offenses (such as the sale of drugs or use of guns), (2) the reduction of judges' discretion for certain kinds of offenders (repeat offenders), (3) the ending of indeterminate sentencing, and (4) the inception of "intermediate sanctions," as a balance to the increased use of incarceration (McDonald & Finn, 2000, p. 33). These changes embodied the shift in attitude from helpful (wanting to rehabilitate the offender) to a harsher attitude. One indicator of this change is the public attitude about the death penalty, going from 38% approval in 1965 to 75% approval in 1997 (McDonald & Finn, 2000). This illustrates the shift to the retributivist belief that punishment is innately good from the belief that it is an instrumental good (Reidy, 2007).

The consequences of get tough policies are numerous, not all of which have benefited society. Take, for example, the Three Strikes law as it played out in California. As the Justice Policy Institute [JPI] explained, the fear of crime hit a high point in 1994 when California responded by enacting the Three Strikes law. Whereas most of the 23 states that also enacted this kind of law did not use it much, having fewer than 400 Three Strikes prisoners each, California had 4322 such prisoners. Yet, there were unintended and unforeseen consequences as this policy put people in prison from 25years to life for nonviolent crimes such as shoplifting a $2 item or forging a check under $100. It is noteworthy that states without Three Strikes laws subsequently saw a greater decrease in violent crime, including murders, than did Three Strikes states. With respect to incarceration rates between 1993 and 2002, California had a 17.7% increase, whereas the non-Three Strikes state of New York had a 5.7% decrease. The Three Strikes law has cost states millions of dollars that could be better spent on education and other ways to handle nonviolent criminals (Russell, 2004).

Corrections Today

Incarceration rates have declined for the past 9 years by approximately 18% (Bureau of Justice Statistics, 2016). Correctional supervision still stands at a little over 6.6 million adults (Bureau of Justice Statistics, 2016) or 1 in 38 adults. Almost 2.2 million of these offenders were in prison or jail, with just under five million on probation or parole (Bureau of Justice Statistics, 2016). Human Rights Watch cites these numbers as evidence of this country's "appalling addiction to incarceration" (Fellner, 2006, para 1). Human Rights Watch asks why, with the general decline in the rate of crime in this country, has the prison population rate kept climbing? This is a staggering number of adults who could be working, paying taxes, and taking care of their families.

The treatment of juvenile offenders continues to be cause for debate, as many approaches have failed. Although the Juvenile court began as a means to rehabilitate juveniles and their families, retributive justice, replaced this philosophy during the 1990s, when juvenile offending was increasing. Beginning in 1992, the practice was built into the laws of 45 states (Austin, Johnson, & Gregoriou, 2000, p. iii). In 1997, the number of juveniles placed in crowded adult prisons was estimated to have been 13,876 young people (no estimate available for those in the jails) (Austin et al., 2000, p. x).

Perhaps we need to step outside this narrowly framed debate. It may be persuasively argued, instead, that juveniles are neither merely young people in need of therapy and beneficence to set them straight nor simply criminals in need of a get-tough approach to punishment (Redding et al., 2005; Scott, 2000). This characterization of the problem is a false dilemma and far too simplistic. A third option is a balanced approach, which would be better in that it would hold the young person accountable along with recognizing the value of multifaceted rehabilitation efforts.

It is also necessary to see that what Byrne calls the surveillance versus treatment debate forms around the assumption that the proper focus of societal concern with crime is the individual offender. Yet this is misguided. We need to take an ecological approach, realizing that offending happens in the context of family, peers, neighborhood, community, and country (Byrne & Taxman, 2006). For example, when juvenile gun violence was escalating, it might well have been because of the increased availability of handguns rather than the development of some kind of "superpredator" (Redding et al., 2005, p. 5). Then too, it makes no sense to punish an offender and then release him or her back into a toxic social environment, expecting him or her to simply go straight without help from society. All contextual elements need societal attention.

Summary

Our current correctional system is overburdened and overwhelmed. As Greene and Pranis of Justice Strategies observe,

"Over the final quarter of the 20th century, U.S. criminal justice policies underwent a period of politicization and harsh transformation. Draconian sentencing laws and get-tough correction led to an unprecedented increase in jail and prison populations, driving the United States' rate of incarceration head and shoulders above that of other developed nations" (Greene & Pranis, 2004, Introduction, para 4).

This was the result of the general belief by politicians and the public that nothing was working with regard to reforming criminals. Rehabilitation was forgotten and both juveniles and adults were placed at risk for abuse within the correctional system and for recidivism after their release from the prison or jail. However, the conclusion that "nothing works" was a simplistic conclusion to what we now know is a complex dynamic. Punishment by itself is largely ineffective. Moreover, traditional criminal measures are short sighted since most of those incarcerated are released back into society, with no life or work skills. Without evidence-based, widespread rehabilitative efforts, those released will pose a renewed threat to public safety. Furthermore, as imprisonment can teach prisoners how to be better criminals if no rehabilitative measures are consistently and effectively provided, those released may pose a greater threat than they posed prior to incarceration. Finally, the cost of incarceration is simply too expensive, taking much needing financial resources away from, for example, investing in education and prevention. University of Oregon's president, Dave Frohnmayer, has starkly observed that in the past two decades, its state's prison-related spending has skyrocketed. As a result, for K-12 students in 2005, $6492 was spent per child and $4497 per university student in 2006. This contrasts with $24,648 spent per person incarcerated in 2005 (Caylor, 2007). We can do much better.

Assessments of Risk Factors, Placement, and Needs

Most adult criminals began their offending patterns as children, frequently at an early age. Approximately 8% of juvenile offenders whose offending is serious, violent, and chronic tend to be multiple-problem youth who exhibit behavioral and other problems in early childhood, with an early onset of criminality perhaps the most robust predictor (Office of Juvenile Justice and Delinquency Prevention, 2001).

In fact, it is a relatively small number of juvenile offenders, 8–10%, who commit from 60 to 80% of the serious and violent crimes and who do not mature out of their criminal behaviors (Krisberg & Wolf, 2005; Redding et al., 2005). Fortunately, many so-called life-course persistent offenders can be picked out from those who cease criminal behavior as they leave adolescence (Moffitt, 1993, p. 674; Redding et al., 2005). Those who become career offenders tend to (1) begin at a young age,

(2) frequently engage in criminal behavior during adolescence, (3) specialize in a particular type of crime, (4) commit serious offenses, and (5) and demonstrate "offense escalation" (Redding et al., 2005, p. 14; Moffitt, 1993). This distinction between kinds of juvenile offender allows society to shape its response most effectively through carefully and evidence-based policies and laws. "Media sensationalism and public sentiment as measured by opinion polls must not be the driving force behind reform" (Redding et al., 2005, p. 14). Despite this evidence, support among policy makers for a punitive approach to juvenile offenders remains (Endrass, 2012).

It is critical to identify this subgroup of serious offenders so that corrections efforts are focused more intensely on these high-risk offenders. It is actually counterproductive to mix high and low risk offenders together. The low risk offenders learn the antisocial behaviors of the high-risk offenders who have become their peers. Also, such association with high-risk offenders interrupts the prosocial peer relationships that are helping the low risk offenders stay low risk. Furthermore, more intense supervision often results in more violations, which pushes the low risk offender toward a higher risk category (Lowenkamp, Latessa, & Holsinger, 2006; Lurigio, 2005).

It is essential to note that many male juveniles exhibit some delinquent behavior, usually nonviolent. However, most of these young people grow out of their antisocial behavior without formal intervention. In fact, in many cases, punishment backfires, slowing down maturation out of delinquent behavior and even increasing the likelihood of career criminality (Krisberg & Wolf, 2005; Redding et al., 2005; Scott, 2000).

Risk and Protective Factors

In order to intervene effectively to reduce crime and violence among juveniles and adults, comprehensive assessments should be completed which identify both the risk factors associated with criminal behavior and the protective factors that mitigate criminal behavior. Here risk is defined as "external or internal influences or conditions that are associate with or predicative of a negative outcome (such as delinquency or antisocial behavior)" (DeMatteo & Marczyk, 2005, pp. 20–21). Similarly, a protective factor is defined as "external or internal influences or conditions that decrease the likelihood of a negative outcome or enhance the likelihood of a positive outcome" (DeMatteo & Marczyk, 2005, p. 21).

In assessing risk factors, it is also useful to distinguish between static and dynamic factors. Static risk factors are those that cannot be changed, such as the gender or age of the offender and the age of the commission of the first crime. These factors are useful for prediction purposes. Dynamic risk factors, by contrast, are those which can be modified, such as substance abuse, certain mental illnesses, access to guns, and participation in gangs. Interventions should be aimed at eliminating or mitigating dynamic risk factors.

Risk and protective factors can be categorized according to an ecological approach, which recognizes that "an individual functions within a complex and interrelated network of contexts that exert an independent influence on risk level" (DeMatteo & Marczyk, 2005, pp. 22), an approach with does not pathologize the individual.

The following is a brief outline of risk and protective factors in the categories of individual, the family, the school-related, peer-related, and the environment (neighborhood, community).

Individual Risk Factors It should be noted that how a behavior is evaluated depends on the developmental level of the actor; some acts common and appropriate to very young people may not be appropriate for a more mature adolescent. Also, risk factors at this level typically operate in connection with factors at the other levels (categories) to be described.

1. Early disruptive, antisocial, aggressive behaviors (Farrington, Loeber, & Berg, 2012; Hawkins et al., 2000; Hawkins, Lishner, Jenson, & Catalano, 1987; Krisberg & Wolf, 2005; Rapp & Wodarski, 1997).
2. Impulsivity, risk-taking, low IQ, restlessness, concentration difficulties (DeMatteo & Marczyk, 2005; Hawkins et al., 1987; Krisberg & Wolf, 2005; Loeber, Farrington, Stouthamer-Loeber, Moffitt, & Caspi, 1998).
3. Association with negative peers (Elliott, Huizinga, & Ageton, 1985).
4. Alcohol and drug use, considered by many to be the strongest dynamic risk (Bushman & Cooper, 1990; DeMatteo & Marczyk, 2005; Elliott et al., 1985).
5. Drug dealing (DeMatteo & Marczyk, 2005; Farrington et al., 2012).
6. Mental health problems (Sevin Goldstein, Olubadewo, Redding, & Lexcen, 2005; Tate & Redding, 2005).

Individual Protective Factors
1. Intelligence and education (DeMatteo & Marczyk, 2005; Kandel et al., 1998).
2. Attitude that antisocial behavior is totally unacceptable (DeMatteo & Marczyk, 2005; Department of Health and Human Services, 2001).

Family Risk Factors
1. Family management problems, including inadequate or insufficient parenting and supervision (DeMatteo & Marczyk, 2005; Hawkins et al., 2000; Krisberg & Wolf, 2005; Kumpfer & Alvarado, 2003; Rapp & Wodarski, 1997; Yoshikawa, 1994).
2. Family conflict, hostility, and aggression; child abuse, child neglect (DeMatteo & Marczyk, 2005; Farrington, 1991; Hawkins, Catalano, & Miller, 1992; Krisberg & Wolf, 2005).
3. Parental attitudes favorable to crime and violence, parental criminality (DeMatteo & Marczyk, 2005; Hawkins et al., 1987; Rapp & Wodarski, 1997).
4. Family use of secrecy and deception (Krisberg & Wolf, 2005).
5. Family poverty (Krisberg & Wolf, 2005).

Family Protective Factors

1. Positive family influence (DeMatteo & Marczyk, 2005; Kumpfer & Alvarado, 2003).
2. Warmth and strength of familial relationships (DeMatteo & Marczyk, 2005; Melton, Petrila, Poythress, & Slobogin, 1997).
3. Good parental supervision; clear rules and values (DeMatteo & Marczyk, 2005).
4. One or more strong relationships with an adult (DeMatteo & Marczyk, 2005; Hawkins et al., 2000).

School Risk Factors

1. Poor academic performance, dropping out of school, and low level of commitment to school (DeMatteo & Marczyk, 2005; Hawkins et al., 2000; Krisberg & Wolf, 2005; Rapp & Wodarski, 1997; Yoshikawa, 1994).
2. Early antisocial behavior in school (Farrington, 1991; Hawkins et al., 2000).

School Protective Factors

1. Educational commitment and success (DeMatteo & Marczyk, 2005; Department of Health and Human Services, 2001).
2. Involvement in extracurricular activities (DeMatteo & Marczyk, 2005).

Peer-Related Risk Factors

1. Negative peer relationships, frequently considered the most significant risk factor (DeMatteo & Marczyk, 2005; Krisberg & Wolf, 2005).
2. Gang membership (DeMatteo & Marczyk, 2005; Department of Health and Human Services, 2001; Krisberg & Wolf, 2005).

Peer-Related Protective Factors

1. Association with Prosocial Peers, although this Is Debated (DeMatteo & Marczyk, 2005)

Environment/Neighborhood/Community Risk Factors

1. Economically deprived areas with high levels of unemployment (DeMatteo & Marczyk, 2005; Hawkins et al., 2000; Krisberg & Wolf, 2005).
2. Getting public assistance (Loeber et al., 1998).
3. Disorganized neighborhoods with high levels of crime and violence and low levels of supervision (DeMatteo & Marczyk, 2005; Yoshikawa, 1994).
4. Availability of firearms (Rapp & Wodarski, 1997; Reiss & Roth, 1993).
5. Media portrayals of violence (DeMatteo & Marczyk, 2005; Donnerstein, Slaby, & Eron, 1994).

Environment/Neighborhood/Community Protective Factors

1. Availability of structured activities, well-managed classrooms/schools (DeMatteo & Marczyk, 2005).
2. Good community structure and sense of belonging (DeMatteo & Marczyk, 2005).

Not all individuals who engage in crime and violence will have the same risk factors. Certain risk factors will be stronger for some individuals than for others. Risk factors having varying potency depend upon the developmental age and stage. Nevertheless, risk factors have been found to increase the possibility of crime and delinquency, as well as of other problem behaviors. Consequently, risk factors should be assessed carefully for each individual. Clearly, the more risk factors an individual has, the more likely he or she will be of evincing criminal and violent behaviors. As well, protective factors will vary from individual to individual, requiring careful, individualized assessments. Enhancing protective factors should be an integral part of individual and societal prevention and early intervention efforts.

Assessments and Classification

Risk assessment and classification refer to the process of evaluating offenders' current needs regarding treatment and their likelihood of re-offending. This amounts to assessing the offenders' risks to themselves and to the public. The ascertained level of risk is then translated into the appropriate and recommended level of supervision or intervention for the offender. These assessments use to be informal, highly discretionary, and inconsistent (Wiebush, Baird, Krisberg, & Onek, 1995). Often, these procedures were criticized as inequitable, erroneous, and unreliable.

We are currently in the fourth wave of reform for the Juvenile Justice system (Grisso, 2017). This reform is based on our knowledge of the timeline for brain development (National Research Council of the Nation Academies, 2005) and prior studies which found incarceration causes harmful effects and escalates offending (Petrosino, Turpin-Petrosino, & Guckenburg, 2010). A main tenet of the reform has been to accurately identify youths who pose, low, moderate, or high risk and match them to the appropriate level of care (Andrews & Bonta, 2017). Structured risk and need assessment tools have been developed and tested for implementation (Monahan & Skeem, 2014).

In order for the correctional system to utilize the following alternative interventions, a clear, standardized assessment system must be in place. Interventions must match needs of and risks posed by the offenders. Offenders who are provided inappropriate interventions, no matter how innovative, will likely fail.

Interventions

As discussed in the first section of this chapter, society's response to the problem of serious crime and violence has been inconsistent. Mass incarceration is extraordinarily expensive and counter-productive. So efforts have turned to developing and utilizing a continuum of care (Vincent & Perrault, 2018). This continuum of care moves beyond traditional choices and would be able to match offenders with the level of treatment that would best meet their needs. The following is a brief introduction to some of these alternative approaches.

It is best to avoid harm, thus the best approach to crime is prevention. Preventive programs include community policing and after school programs. For those who have already committed offenses, there are alternative approaches to traditional incarceration such as "intermediate sanctions." These sanctions "enhance surveillance or provide more effective interventions for offenders who would not have gone to prison in their absence" (McDonald & Finn, 2000, p. 33). Such intermediate sanctions include day reporting centers and "therapeutic diversions," which combine sanctions and therapy like drug courts and mental health courts (Goetz & Mitchell, 2006).

For those incarcerated, an alternative to punishment alone is rehabilitative programs that both reduce the tendency of those incarcerated simply to learn how to become a better, more dangerous criminal and reduce the recidivism rate, once prisoners are released. We could also conceptualize such rehabilitation programs as preventive interventions for re-offending. Rehabilitation programs include General Equivalency Diploma (GED) programs, life skills, sex offender treatment, and drug treatment. For these programs to be maximally effective, it is critical that we have transitional programs for those about to re-enter society. Such transitional programs include therapeutic communities (for drug offenders) and prison-to-work programs.

Prevention Programs

The creation and implementation of innovative ideas have been encouraged in an attempt to reduce crime and violence. Prevention programs have been placed at the forefront in an effort to deter juveniles and young adults from becoming involved with crime.

Community Policing

In the 1980s, law enforcement administrators and academics used police research to generate the concept of community policing in order to improve their efficacy (McDonald & Finn, 2000). This policing approach does not address specific problems faced by law enforcement; rather, it calls for an all-encompassing change in the way police perform their duties. Community policing strategies vary depending on the needs and responses of the communities involved, although there are certain basic principles common to all community policing efforts. Essentially, community policing involves collaboration between the police and the community to identify and solve community problems. In addition, it encourages police–citizen interaction and a focus on prevention and problem solving (Police Foundation, 2015).

The traditional, centralized, large police stations have isolated police officers from the communities they serve. In addition, the use of patrol cars versus foot patrol has also added to this perceived distance of police from the citizens they serve. This isolation has tended to hamper crime-fighting efforts. It is often the citizens who have the most information about the crimes occurring in their communities. Without strong ties to the community, police do not have access to this important information and citizen assistance. Community policing offers a way for the police and the community to work together to resolve the serious problems that are ongoing within the community (Police Foundation, 2015).

The two core components of community policing are community partnership and problem solving. These components address specific citizen concerns and provide more attentive police service. Plans to reduce crime or problems in the area are devised by citizens and police officers and are implemented by both.

Research has indicated that community policing has been effective in reducing crime (Police Foundation, 2015). Officers who patrol by horse, bicycle, segue, or foot, etc. are able to connect with citizens, attend to minor problems before they escalate, and/or identify potential problems and remedy the issue.

Community policing is a prevention idea that can be tailored to meet each community's specific problems and needs. Community policing is not the answer to all problems and it may not be amenable to all communities. However, the concept provides a logical, comprehensive, preventive approach to police service delivery that relies on empirically based studies (Carter, 1995).

In and After-School Programs

Tremendous progress has been made regarding our development and implementation of prevention programs for youth. The vast majority of these evidence-based programs are delivered in and after school. Blueprints for Healthy Youth Development (https://cspv.colorado.edu/blueprints/) provide a clearinghouse and rating system for prevention programs aimed at reducing offending, violence, and enhancing positive healthy development of youth and families.

Effective programs can be found for all age levels and offending levels and can be implemented in schools or communities by using the extensive guidelines and manuals provided by the developers. The rating system provides clear information on the level of effectiveness of the program for the designated problems and youth.

The programs differ in their prevention goals, for instance, some focus on life skills, social skills, academic skills, drug resistance skills, etc. Some are intended for all youth within an age range, while others target only at-risk youth. Many can be administered by parents, school personnel, or trained volunteers, and all have been evaluated and proven to be effective. Additionally, some programs encourage parents to receive interventions and some work with teachers and school administrators to modify school policies, procedures, and learning environments.

The clearinghouse and rating system has provided an extremely beneficial service to policy makers, counselors, schools, and anyone interested in investing time and money toward prevention of crime and violence.

Therapeutic Diversion

Drug Courts

The first drug court appeared in Miami in 1989 as an alternative response to incarceration for substance abusers who had been arrested. It was at this time that crack cocaine was a serious problem and courts were quickly overwhelmed with felony drug cases and prisons were overfilled. Incarceration itself did nothing to address the underlying problem of addiction; many offenders were in and out of the criminal justice system multiple times, severely taxing the system (Bureau of Justice Assistance, 2003). The drug court tries to rectify this by combining the supervisory and sanctioning roles of the courts with the therapeutic role of treatment. The goal of this kind of court is to help substance abusers both move into and maintain recovery and stop their criminal behavior, which reduces the strain on the courts and prisons.

A number of innovative drug courts have reported success in reducing the levels of drug abuse, incarceration, and criminal recidivism among drug offenders. Drug courts also reduce costs for the Criminal Justice system and assist individuals in receiving the treatment they need (National Institute of Justice, 2018). The courts hear the cases of nonviolent drug offenders and are run by a group including judges, social workers, treatment providers, prosecutors, defense attorneys, and citizens. They work directly with the offender and together they decide on the type of rehabilitation program required. Offenders who are mandated to treatment are usually expected to begin that day. This process takes extensive coordination and team effort with community treatment programs (National Institute of Justice, 2018).

A key component of the drug court program is coordinated comprehensive supervision. Most offenders who volunteer to attend the drug court do so to beat incarceration. However, these programs are tightly supervised and maintained. Drug testing, immediate notice of any treatment failures, and routine progress reports are utilized to keep track of offenders. For those offenders who require more intensive services, transfers to residential treatment centers are available. Drug courts usually follow offenders over a longer period of time, and aftercare is considered a must. Drug court rehabilitations usually also include educational opportunities, employment training and placement, and housing and health assistance (Tauber, 1994).

Thus, the substance abusing offender is motivated, on the one hand, by the threat of jail or prison and, on the other hand, by the promise that if he or she successfully completes the program, he or she may have one or a combination of the following considerations: charges dismissed, reduced, or set aside; given a lesser penalty (Office of National Drug Court Policy, n.d.; Fox & Huddleston, 2003; National Institute of Justice, 2006a).

Overall, the benefits of the drug court program include a reduction of the cost per defendant, added capacity to incarcerate the most serious offenders, a reduction in police overtime and other witness costs, a reduction in grand jury and indictment costs, a lower percentage of those relying on public assistance, and a reduction of medical and social service costs (Office of Justice Programs, 1996).

In an effort to increase the benefits of this kind of court, researchers are examining in detail how drug courts are working, paying attention to dynamics such as "how target populations and participant attributes affect program outcomes, the judge's role in the success of drug court participants, treatment issues, drug court interventions for juveniles, and cost-benefit analyses of drug courts" (National Institute of Justice, 2006b). As of 2015, there are over 3000 operating drug courts in the USA (National Institute of Justice, 2018).

Mental Health Court and Mental Health Services

As a result of factors such as inadequate social safety nets, inadequate access to mental health treatment, and stigmas associated with mental illness, people suffering from mental illness are all too often unfairly and inhumanely arrested and incarcerated. The probability of a mentally ill person being arrested is nearly twice that of a non-mentally ill person. The mentally ill person is less likely to get bail and more likely to receive a harsher sentence than a non-mentally ill person. It is estimated that 64% of jails, 56% of prisons, and 45% of federal prisons contain individuals who suffer from mental illness (James & Glaze, 2006). The typical offense is nonviolent. Unfortunately, few receive their medications, much less treatment. What is more, once such persons have a criminal record, they are even less likely to obtain needed mental health treatment and have increased difficulty finding employment and housing (Judge David L. Bazelon Center for Mental Health Law, 2004).

Mental Health Courts are a relatively new alternative response to incarceration for people with criminal charges (usually nonviolent) who also suffer from mental illness alone or mental illness along with substance abuse (Bureau of Justice Assistance, 2012). They were based on the drug court formats. Whereas there were 25–30 such courts in 2004, the number exceeded 150 by 2006, and is now more than 240 (Bureau of Justice Assistance, 2012). The goals are (1) to decrease the likelihood of incarceration or recidivism that contribute to the escalation of mental illness and criminal behavior by (2) stepping into the legal process to get the arrested person appropriate mental health treatment, as well as connecting them with other needed resources, (3) monitor progress, (4) ensure voluntary, and informed consent is used. This kind of therapeutic court has two justifying beliefs: (1) the public is better protected by helping the mentally ill, hence reducing recidivism, and (2) criminal punishment is both ineffective and immoral (Judge David L. Bazelon Center for Mental Health Law, 2004). Initial studies have found support for these courts as effective in improving the functioning and reducing substance use (Bureau of Justice Assistance, 2012).

Intermediate-Level Sanctions

Intermediate-level sanctions were designed to offer less punishment and more ser-vices for those who do not need intensive supervision or punishment. The philoso-phy is to offer the least restrictive environment to every offender. Not only does this reduce cost, but it has also been empirically supported in generating the most effica-cious outcome such as reduction in recidivism and increase in employment (Cochran, Mears, & Bales, 2014).

Day Reporting Centers

An intermediate-level sanction created in the 1970s in Great Britain and utilized from the 1990s and currently is the Day Reporting Center (DRC) (Pennsylvania Department of Corrections, 2003), which can be described as a highly structured program utilizing supervision, sanctions, and services (Diggs & Pieper, 1994) for offenders. This program is intended to help reduce prison and jail overcrowding and to assist in community reintegration. Thus, DRCs are community-based corrections programs serving those who are probationers or parolees (Pennsylvania Department of Corrections, 2003). Offenders required to attend a DRC live at home and report daily and in person to the center. They are expected to keep detailed itinerary notes on their daily travels, destinations, cohorts, and purposes. Offenders also call into their respective DRC several times a day. In addition, DRC staff contact offenders to verify their whereabouts and to monitor them. Drug testing and counseling are mandatory components of the program (Diggs & Pieper, 1994; Pennsylvania Department of Corrections, 2003). Offenders are also able to continue with their employment and educational goals.

Day reporting centers can be adapted to diverse populations, although violent offenders are not usually included. DRCs have been used as halfway-in and halfway-out steps. For instance, offenders who are in violation of their parole or probation may be placed in day reporting programs, or offenders who are released early from jail or prison may be placed in these programs prior to parole. The centers have also been used to monitor arrested individuals prior to trial.

Unfortunately, there have been mixed results for DRCs in that some studies have indicated reduced re-arrest rates, while other studies indicated an increase in new arrests for participants. A main obstacle for these sanctions has been completion rates, as offenders have not successfully complied with their sanctions or completed all of their mandatory services (Boyle, Ragusa-Salerno, Lanterman, & Marcus, 2013).

One suggestion is to utilize more advanced dynamic and static risk assessment instruments to correctly assess which offenders would most likely be successful in a DRC program (Cohen, Lowenkamp, & VanBenschoten, 2016). These community-based programs are worth further evaluation as they may offer potential supports in a less restrictive, costly environment than traditional incarceration to particular offenders.

Substance Abuse Treatment during Community Supervision

Community supervision of offenders often involves monitoring offenders through meetings and telephone contact and by assisting with employment or education. One critical component that has often been left out of this supervision has been substance abuse treatment. Research has indicated that treatment for substance-abusing offenders can be effective in reducing and eliminating drug use and in reducing recidivism (Sung, Mahoney, & Mellow, 2011). Yet, only in the last few decades has mandatory substance abuse counseling emerged as a part of community supervision and unfortunately is often the first program to be cut to reduce budgets. For example, in Florida, drug offender probation was intensive, utilizing individually tailored treatments plans in combination with surveillance strategies, such as drug testing (Florida Department of Corrections, 1999). Substance abuse treatment was a critical component of supervision for offenders, however in May, 2018, these programs were eliminated to manage the State's budget deficit and offenders were no longer offered substance abuse treatment. Ironically, this short-sighted strategy will actually increase the cost of corrections as many of those offenders will be re-arrested (Farrington, 2018).

Researchers have suggested that to be effective, offenders' needs must be accurately assessed and matched to the correct type of drug abuse program. This program should also be considered a mandatory part of the offenders' community supervision. In other words, consequences should be included if the offender does not attend and participate appropriately in treatment (Sung et al., 2011). Research has also indicated that these programs need to focus on long-term recovery with a high level of support for offenders.

Some offenders may require more intensive treatment, especially those with co-occurring disorders, such as mental health and substance abuse problems. These individuals require more complex and comprehensive treatment and support like integrated dual disorders treatment (IDDT) or cognitive-behavioral treatment (CBT) (Peters, Young, Rojas, & Gorey, 2017). These specialized forms of evidence-based programs combined with intermediate sanctions have been shown to be effective in reducing substance use and recidivism (Peters et al., 2017).

If we intend to utilize community supervision or intermediate sanctions as methods for reducing prison populations, costs, and recidivism, then we need to deliver comprehensive programs to offenders to meet their differing needs.

Programs During Incarceration

Due to overcrowding and understaffing and the soaring costs of prisons and jails, as well as punitive attitudes toward prisoners, many institutions have not provided treatment and services for the rehabilitation of inmates. New initiatives have been started with a focus on rehabilitating and preparing inmates for community living. These programs provide expanded services for inmates as they prepare to return to the community.

Education, Life Skills, and Parenting Programs

In a 1993 US Department of Education survey of prisoners, it was found that 70% of inmates were not functionally literate. Programs addressing this deficit were first federally funded in 1992 (U.S. Department of Education, 1994) and many prisons provide GED classes for offenders. However, these classes are now being expanded to better meet the needs of inmates, especially once they are released. Life skills programs were first funded in 1993 to enhance the chances of offenders released back into society to succeed rather than re-offend. Skills taught include communication skills, financial management, interpersonal skills, as well as stress and anger management. Also, employability and job search skills are taught, including resume writing and interview skills. Computer skills are also being taught to increase inmates' employability. Some inmate programs further include specific vocational training and actual part-time employment in the community (Brewster, 2015). Maryland's Prison to Work program is one such program which believes that such employment development efforts will increase the job options and success rates of released prisoners, thus reducing recidivism (Bailey, n.d.).

Other non-conventional programs have also been added in recent years to further these outcomes. For instance, many prisons also have Community College courses and arts programs. These programs assist offenders in learning additional skills which can be beneficial upon release. Many have utilized their newly acquired art skills to find employment (Brewster, 2015).

Hoffmann, Byrd, and Kightlinger (2010) estimate that there are just under two million children whose parent or parents are incarcerated. Data suggests that incarcerated parents often struggle with accurate knowledge of child development, parenting skills, and discipline practices for their children, they also lose connection and communication with their children while incarcerated. This poses a serious problem for their release and the expectation that they will just assume these responsibilities upon return to their families. Consequently, programs have been initiated to educate and support offenders' parenting skills. Many programs work first with the inmate and then slowly integrate children into the programming to increase bonding, improve communication, and assist inmates in practicing their parenting skills in "real-time" with their children. Studies have found an increase in empathy and bonding between parent and child, an increased knowledge of appropriate disciplinary tactics, and enhanced knowledge of child development. Likewise, children have shown reduction in sadness and improvements in academic achievement and behaviors (Hoffmann et al., 2010). These programs often face many barriers such as transportation of children, movement of inmates, and funding, however they offer future potential worth investigating.

Drug Treatment during Incarceration

One of the few appreciated facts about crime is that offenders are disproportionately substance abusers, ranging from 60 to 85%, in contrast with approximately 40% of this country's population having used drugs (National Institute of Justice, 1996; Office of National Drug Control Policy, 2001). Research studies have indicated that correctional drug treatment programs can have a substantial effect on the behavior of chronic drug-abusing offenders (National Institute of Justice, 1996).

Similar to services in the community, drug abuse treatment should match the needs of the inmate. Group versus individual treatment should also be chosen based on individual inmate needs. Studies have shown that improvements can still be made even when the inmate is mandated to treatment inside the institution. Consequently, some institutions are beginning to mandate treatment to reduce drug abuse and criminal acts after release (National Institute of Justice, 1996).

Aftercare or Re-Entry

Aftercare or re-entry programs are designed to assist newly released offenders with their transition back into the community. These community-based programs are similar to the already described intermediate sanctions; however, they focus on transitioning into and adjusting to society. This can be an especially difficult process when offenders have been imprisoned for many years and for young people who went into prison before developing the necessary life and employability skills (Barak & Stebbins, 2017). Most correctional systems have placed little emphasis on this part of correctional supervision, often believing their job is over when the inmate walks out the door. But after years of neglect, aftercare or re-entry programming is starting to become strongly emphasized.

The goals of aftercare include interventions that directly target the offender's needs. These usually include community-based treatment, continuity of care, employment, housing, and case management (Barak & Stebbins, 2017). Aftercare and re-entry programs attempt to help offenders adapt to and thrive in their communities, however they have often been criticized as strategies which are too little and too late. Although these programs tend to be fairly intensive and lengthier than regular parole, with over 500,000 inmates released each year, caseloads and programs are overtaxed. James (2015) noted that there were over five million ex-offenders in Aftercare programs in 2015.

Therapeutic Communities

A therapeutic community (TC) is a form of aftercare which embodies a continuity of care model to help inmates with a history of substance abuse transition back into the community to maximize their chances of successful reintegration and productivity (Jason, Olson, & Harvey, 2015). TCs vary by treatment philosophy, length of stays, staff qualifications, and services. However, there has been consistent evidence indicating that these residences and programs reduce recidivism and substance use (Inciardi, Martin, & Butzin, 2003).

Oxford Houses (OH) are another variation on a TC. These recovery homes are self-run, abstinence-only residences which do not include professional staff. Residents live together in a single-family home with democratic governing. They support one another in sobriety and lawfulness and network together as a family. Empirical evidence shows these recovery homes to be more effective than others and they can now be located on SAMHSA's National Registry of Evidence Based Programs and Practices (SAMHSA, 2013) In addition, Jason, Olson, & Harvey (2015) found residents in these homes had a higher continuous sobriety rate and more days of paid employment than residents in TCs. In addition, there was a dose effect, in that all residents showed greater improvement with longer stays in both types of programs.

Conclusion

We began and we will end with the acknowledgement that no one wants to be victimized by crime. Victims, along with their relatives and friends, understandably want offenders to be held accountable. Yet, if we let personal and media driven fear distort the clarity and depth of our understanding of the incidence, nature, and complex etiology of crime and thus prompt ineffective policy, we will all lose. We will simply see many prisoners released into society, angry, with better criminal skills, and ready to re-offend. This will make our society more dangerous and exacerbate fear.

To avoid this unnecessary outcome, we must increase research and programming to reduce societal, institutional, community, family, and personal stressors in individual lives rather than being content to myopically pathologize and punish offenders. In this way, we will be more likely to achieve a balance between offender accountability and public safety, on the one hand, and the extension of humanity and treatment to offenders, on the other. We must begin with prevention, such as community learning centers. This is a much more efficient use of stressed public monies and facilities than building more prisons. We must expand research so as to determine the best interventions to use as alternatives to prison. We must also devise effective treatment and educational programs for those within prison, so that once they are ready for release, they will already have some good rehabilitation under their belts. Finally, and critically, we must provide continuity of care programs post-release. Without this, few such people will be able to meet the severe reintegration challenges. At every point along the way, we must engage in risk assessment and match the response to the individual's needs. In this way, we will all move forward.

References

Andrews, D. A., & Bonta, J. (2017). *The psychology of criminal conduct* (6th ed.). Abingdon, Oxon: Taylor & Francis.

Austin, J., Johnson, K. D., & Gregoriou, M. (2000). *Juveniles in adult prisons and jails: A national assessment (NCJ 182503)*. Bureau of Justice Assistance. Retrieved March 25, 2007, from http://www.ncjrs.gov/pdffiles1/bja/182503.pdf

Bailey, D. (n.d.) *Prison to work project for the Maryland Department of Education.* Retrieved March 26, 2007, from http://www.ceanational.org/pr2wrk.htm

Barak, A., & Stebbins, A. (2017). Re-entry as performance: Reflections from institution x. *Critical Social Policy, 37*(2), 287–309. https://doi.org/10.1177/0261018316676732

Boyle, D. J., Ragusa-Salerno, L. M., Lanterman, J. L., & Marcus, A. F. (2013). An evaluation of day reporting Centers for parolees. *Criminology & Public Policy, 12*(1), 119–143. https://doi.org/10.1111/1745-9133.12010

Brewster, L. (2015). Prison fine arts and community college programs: A partnership to advance Inmates' life skills. *New Directions for Community Colleges, 2015*(170), 89–99. https://doi.org/10.1002/cc.20147

Bureau of Justice Assistance. (2003). *Juvenile drug courts: Strategies in practice.* Retrieved March 24, 2007, from http://www.ncjrs.gov/pdffiles1/bja/197866.pdf

Bureau of Justice Assistance. (2012). *Criminal justice interventions for offenders with mental illness: Evaluation of mental health courts in Bronx and Brooklyn, New York.* Retrieved August 24, 2018, from https://www.ncjrs.gov/pdffiles1/nij/grants/238264.pdf

Bureau of Justice Statistics. (2011). *Prisoners, 2010 (revised).* Retrieved from http://bjs.ojp.usdoj.gov/index.cfm?ty=pbdetail&iid=2230

Bureau of Justice Statistics. (2007a). *Crime characteristics.* Retrieved January 31, 2007, from http://ojp.usdoj.gov/bjs/cvict_c.htm

Bureau of Justice Statistics. (2007b). *Drug control budget.* Retrieved February 14, 2007, from http://www.ojp.usdoj.gov/bjs/dcf/dcb.htm

Bureau of Justice Statistics. (2016). *Correctional Populations in the United States, 2016.* Retrieved August 22, 2018, from https://www.bjs.gov/index.cfm?ty=pbdetail&iid=6226

Bushman, B., & Cooper, H. (1990). Effects of alcohol on human aggression: An integrative research review. *Psychological Bulletin, 107,* 341–354.

Byrne, J. M., & Taxman, F. S. (2006). Crime control strategies and community change – Reframing the surveillance vs. treatment debate. *Federal Probation, 70*(1), 3–12.

Carter, D. (1995). Community policing and D.a.R.E.: A practitioner's perspective. A Bulletin, 1-19.

Caylor, B. (2007). *University of Oregon president: "It's cellblocks or classrooms."* Retrieved March 26, 2007, from http://safetyandjustice.org/info/or/story/1008

Centers for Disease Control and Prevention. (2003). *Costs of intimate partner violence against women in the United States.* Atlanta, GA: U.S. Department of Health and Human Services.

Centers for Disease Control and Prevention. (2005). Homicide and suicide rates—National violent death reporting system, six states, 2003. In MMWR Weekly, 45 (15), 377–380. Retrieved February 13, 2007, from http://www.cdc.gov/MMWR/preview/mmwrhtml/mm5415al.htm

Cochran, J., Mears, D., & Bales, W. (2014). Assessing the effectiveness of correctional sanctions. *Journal of Quantitative Criminology, 30*(2), 317–347. https://doi.org/10.1007/s10940-013-9205-2

Cohen, T. H., Lowenkamp, C. T., & VanBenschoten, S. W. (2016). Does Change in Risk Matter? *Criminology & Public Policy, 15*(2), 263–296. https://doi.org/10.1111/1745-9133.12190

Cornell, D. G. (2005). School violence. In R. E. Redding, N. E. Sevin Goldstein, & K. Heilbrun (Eds.), *Juvenile delinquency: Prevention, assessment, and intervention* (pp. 45–66). New York: Oxford University Press.

DeMatteo, D., & Marczyk, G. (2005). Risk factors, protective factors, and the prevention of antisocial behavior among juveniles. In R. E. Redding, N. E. Sevin Goldstein, & K. Heilbrun (Eds.), *Juvenile delinquency: Prevention, assessment, and intervention* (pp. 19–44). New York: Oxford University Press.

DeLisi, M., Koloski, A., Sween, M., Hachmeister, E., Moore, M., & Drury, A. (2010). Murder by numbers: Monetary costs imposed by a sample of homicide offenders. *The Journal of Psychiatry & Psychology, 21,* 501–513.

Department of Health and Human Services. (2001). *Youth violence: A report of the surgeon general.* Rockville, MD: Author.

Diggs, D., & Pieper, S. (1994). Using day reporting centers as an alternative to jail. *Federal Probation, 58*(1), 9–12.

Donnerstein, E., Slaby, R., & Eron, L. (1994). The mass media and youth aggression. In L. Eron, J. Gentry, & P. Schlegel (Eds.), *Reason to hope: A psychosocial perspective on violence and youth*. Washington, DC: American Psychological Association.

Elliott, D., Huizinga, D., & Ageton, S. (1985). *Explaining delinquency and drug use*. Beverly Hills, CA: Sage.

Endrass, J. (2012). The efficacy of deterrent and punitive measures. *International Journal of Offender Therapy and Comparative Criminology, 56*(3), 335–337.

Farrington, B. (2018). Florida prisons cutting programs to offset $50m shortfall. *Orlando Sentinel*. Retrieved August 26, 2018 from http://www.orlandosentinel.com/news/breaking-news/os-florida-prison-cuts- 20180502-story.html

Farrington, D. (1991). Childhood aggression and adult violence. In D. Pepler & K. Rubin (Eds.), *The development and treatment of childhood aggression* (pp. 5–29). Hillsdale, NJ: Erlbaum.

Farrington, D., Loeber, R., & Berg, M. T. (2012). Young men who kill: A prospective longitudinal study from childhood. *Homicide Studies, 16*(2), 99–128.

Federal Bureau of Investigation. (2011). *Crime in the United States, 2010*. Retrieved May 14, 2012, from http://www.fbi.gov/about-us/cjis/ucr/crime-in-the-u.s/2010/crime-in-the-u.s.-2010

Federal Bureau of Investigation. (2012). *Crime in the United States, 2012*. Retrieved August, 22, 2018, from https://ucr.fbi.gov/crime-in-the-u.s/2012/crime-in-the-u.s.-2012/tables/42tabledata decoverviewpdf/table_42_arrests_by_sex_2012.xls

Federal Bureau of Investigation. (2016). *2016 Crime in the United States*. Retrieved August 22, 2018, from https://ucr.fbi.gov/crime-in-the-u.s/2016/crime-in-the-u.s.-2016/topic-pages/offenses-known-to-law-enforcement

Fellner, J. (2006). US addiction to incarceration puts 2.3 million in prison. *Human Rights Watch*. Retrieved March 25, 2007, from http://hrw.org/english/docs/2006/12/01/usdom14728_txt.htm

Florida Department of Corrections. (1999). *Community supervision: Overview of community corrections*. Retrieved March 26, 2007, from http://www.dc.state.fl.us/pub/annual/9899/stats/stat_cs.html

Fox, C., & Huddleston, W. (2003, May) Drug courts in the U.S. *Issues in Democracy*. Retrieved March 24, 2007, from http://usinfo.state.gov/journals/itdhr/0503/ijde/fox.htm

Goetz, B., & Mitchell, R. E. (2006). Pre-arrest/booking drug control strategies: Diversion to treatment, harm reduction and police involvement. *Contemporary Drug Problems, 33*, 473–520.

Gilliam, F. D., & Iyengar, S. (2000). Prime suspects: The influence of local television news on the viewing public. *American Journal of Political Science, 44*(3), 560–573.

Goodwin, M. (2015). Invisible women: Mass incarceration's forgotten casualties. *Texas Law Review, 94*(2), 353–386.

Greene, J. & Pranis, K. (2004). *Hard hit: The growth in the imprisonment of women, 1977–2004*. Institute on Women & Criminal Justice. Retrieved March 2, 2007, from http://www.wpaonline.org/institute/hardhit/index.htm

Grisso, T. (2017). *Policy brief: Assuring the future of developmental reform in juvenile justice: Recommendations of the fourth wave forecasting project*. Retrieved August 24, 2018, from http://www.nysap.us/Products.html#FourthWave

Hawkins, J., Catalano, R., & Miller, J. (1992). Risk and protective factors for alcohol and other drug problems in adolescence and early adulthood: Implications for substance abuse prevention. *Psychological Bulletin, 112*, 64–105.

Hawkins, J. D., Herrenkohl, T. I., Farrington, D. P., Brewer, D., Catalano, R. F., Harachi, T. W., et al. (2000). Predictors of youth violence. *Juvenile Justice Bulletin*. Washington, DC: U.S. Department of Justice, Office of Justice Programs, Office of Juvenile Justice and Delinquency Prevention.

Hawkins, J., Lishner, D., Jenson, J., & Catalano, R. (1987). Delinquents and drugs: What the evidence suggests about prevention and treatment programming. In B. S. Brown & A. R. Mills (Eds.), *Youth at high risk for substance abuse* (pp. 81–131). Rockville, MD: U.S. Department of Health and Human Services.

Hoffmann, H., Byrd, A., & Kightlinger, A. (2010). Prison programs and services for incarcerated parents and their underage children: Results from a national survey of correctional facilities. *The Prison Journal, 90*(4), 397–416.

Holtfreter, K., Reisig, M. D., & Morash, M. (2004). Poverty, state capital, and recidivism among women offenders. *Criminology & Public Policy, 3*(2), 185–120.

Hyman, S. M., Garcia, M., & Sinha, R. (2006). Gender specific associations between types of childhood maltreatment and the onset, escalation and severity of substance use in cocaine dependent adults. *The American Journal of Drug and Alcohol Abuse, 32*, 655–664.

Inciardi, J., Martin, S., & Butzin, C. (2003). Five-year outcomes of therapeutic community treatment of drug-involved offenders after release from prison. *Crime & Delinquency, 49*, 1–20.

James, D. J., & Glaze, L. E. (2006). *Mental health problems of prison and jail inmates.* Washington, DC: U.S. Department of Justice Office of Justice Programs, Bureau of Justice Statistics.

James N. (2015) Offender reentry: Correctional statistics, reintegration into the community, and recidivism. *Congressional Research Service.* Retrieved August 10, 2018, from https://fas.org/sgp/crs/misc/RL34287.pdf

Jason, L. A., Olson, B. D., & Harvey, R. (2015). Evaluating alternative aftercare models for ex-offenders. *Journal of Drug Issues, 45*(1), 53–68.

Judge David L. Bazelon Center for Mental Health Law. (2004). *The role of mental health courts in system reform.* Retrieved January 31, 2007, from http://www.bazelon.org/issues/criminalization/publications/mentalhealthco urts/index.htm

Kandel, E., Mednick, S. A., Kirkegaard-Sorenson, L., Hutchings, B., Knop, J., Rosenberg, R., et al. (1998). I.Q. as a protective factor for subjects as high risk for antisocial behavior. *Journal of Consulting and Clinical Psychology, 56*, 24–226.

Krisberg, B., & Wolf, A. M. (2005). Juvenile offending. In R. E. Redding, N. E. Sevin Goldstein, & K. Heilbrun (Eds.), *Juvenile delinquency: Prevention, assessment, and intervention* (pp. 67–84). New York: Oxford University Press.

Kumpfer, K. L., & Alvarado, R. (2003). Family-strengthening approaches for the prevention of youth problem behaviors. *American Psychologist, 58*, 457–465.

Levenson, J.S., & D'Amora, D.A. (2006). Social policies designed to prevent sexual violence: The emperor's new clothes? *Criminal Justice Policy Review.*

Lereventz, A. (2012). Narratives of crimes and criminals: How places socially construct the crime problem. *Sociological Forum, 27*(2), 348–371.

Loeber, R., & Farrington, D. P. (2011). *Young homicide offenders and victims: Risk factors, prediction, and prevention from childhood.* New York: Springer.

Loeber, R., Farrington, D. P., Stouthamer-Loeber, M., Moffitt, T. E., & Caspi, A. (1998). The development of male offending: Key findings from the first decade of the Pittsburgh youth study. *Studies on Crime and Crime Prevention, 7*, 141–171.

Lowenkamp, C. T., Latessa, E. J., & Holsinger, A. M. (2006). The risk principle in action: What have we learned from 13,676 offenders and 97 correctional programs? *Crime Delinquency, 52*, 77–93.

Lurigio, A. J. (2005). Editorial introduction: Taking stock of community corrections programs. *Criminology and Public Policy, 4*(2), 259–261.

Lutze, F. E. (2006). Boot camp prisons and corrections policy: Moving from militarism to an ethic of care. *Criminology and Public Policy, 5*(2), 389–400.

Martinson, R. (1974). What works? Questions and answers about prison reform. *The Public Interest, 35*, 22–54.

McDonald, D., & Finn, P. (2000, January 31). *Crime and justice trends in the United States during the past three decades.* Cambridge, MA: Abt Associates.

Melton, G. B., Petrila, J., Poythress, N. G., & Slobogin, C. (1997). *Psychological evaluations for the courts: A handbook for mental health professional and lawyers* (2nd ed.). New York: The Guilford Press.

Moffitt, T. E. (1993). Adolescence-limited and life-course-persistent antisocial behavior: A developmental taxonomy. *Psychological Review, 100*, 674–701.

Monahan, J., & Skeem, J. (2014). The evolution of violence risk assessment. *CNS Spectrums, 19*(5), 419–424. https://doi.org/10.1017/S1092852914000145

National Center for Victims of Crime. (2004). *Cost of crime.* Retrieved March 24, 2007, from http://www.ncvc.org/ncvc/main.aspx?dbName =DocumentViewer&DocumentID=38710

National Institute of Justice. (1996). *Drug and crime facts 1994 (publication no. NCJ 154043)*. Washington, DC: Author.

National Institute of Justice. (2006a). *Drug courts: The second decade*. Retrieved March 24, 2007 from http://www.ncjrs.gov/pdffiles1/nij/211081.pdf

National Institute of Justice. (2006b). *Drug courts: The second decade (summary)*. Retrieved March 24, 2007, from http://www.ojp.usdoj.gov/nij/pubs-sum/211081.htm

National Institute of Justice. (2018). *Drug courts*. Retrieved August 24, 2018 from https://www.nij.gov/topics/courts/drug-courts/Pages/welcome.aspx

National Research Council of the Nation Academies. (2005). *Firearms and violence: A critical review*. Washington, DC: The National Academies Press.

Office of Justice Programs. (1996). *Summary assessment*. Washington, DC: Drug Resource Center, American University.

Office of Juvenile Justice and Delinquency Prevention. (2001). *The 8% Solution*. OJJDP fact sheet. Retrieved August 24, 2018, from https://www.ncjrs.gov/pdffiles1/ojjdp/fs200139.pdf

Office of National Drug Control Policy. (2011). *Arrestee Drug Abuse Monitoring Program II: Annual report*. Retrieved from http://www.whitehouse.gov/ondcp/arrestee-drug-abuse-monitoring-program

Office of National Drug Control Policy. (2001). *Drug treatment in the criminal justice system*. Retrieved March 26, 2007, from http://www.whitehousedrugpolicy.gov/publications/pdf/944-6.pdf

Office of National Drug Court Policy. (n.d.). *Drug courts*. Retrieved March 24, 2007, from http://www.whitehousedrugpolicy.gov/enforce/drugcourt.html

Pearson, D. (1994). The black man: Health issues and implications for clinical practice. *Journal of Black Studies, 25*(1), 81–98.

Pennsylvania Department of Corrections. (2003). *Day reporting centers*. Retrieved March 26, 2007, from http://www.cor.state.pa.us/state/lib/stats/DAY_Reporting_Centers.pdf

Peters, R., Young, M., Rojas, E., & Gorey, C. (2017). Evidence-based treatment and supervision practices for co-occurring mental and substance use disorders in the criminal justice system. *The American Journal of Drug and Alcohol Abuse, 43*(4), 475–488. https://doi.org/10.1080/00952990.2017.1303838

Petrosino, A., Turpin-Petrosino, C., & Guckenburg, S. (2010). Formal system processing of juveniles: Effects on delinquency. *Campbell Systematic Reviews, 2010*(1), 1–88. https://doi.org/10.4073/csr.2010.1

Police Foundation. (2015). *Community policing*. Retrieved August 24, 2018, from https://www.policefoundation.org/projects/community-policing/

Puzzanchera, C., Adams, B., & Kang, W. (2012). *Easy access to FBI arrest statistics 1994–2009*. Retrieved from http://www.ojjdp.gov/ojstatbb/ezaucr/.

Rapp, L., & Wodarski, J. (1997). Juvenile violence: Its high risk factors, current interventions and implications for social work practice. *Journal of Applied Social Sciences*.

Redding, R. E., & Mrozoski, B. (2005). Adjudicatory and dispositional decision making in juvenile justice. In R. E. Redding, N. E. Sevin Goldstein, & K. Heilbrun (Eds.), *Juvenile delinquency: Prevention, assessment, and intervention* (pp. 232–256). New York: Oxford University Press.

Redding, R. E., Sevin Goldstein, N. E., & Heilbrun, K. (Eds.) (2005). Juvenile delinquency: Past and present. In *Juvenile delinquency: Prevention, assessment, and intervention* (pp. 3–18). New York: Oxford University Press.

Reidy, D. A. (2007). *On the philosophy of law*. Belmont, CA: Thomson Wadsworth.

Reiss, A., & Roth, J. (Eds.). (1993). *Understanding and preventing violence*. Washington, DC: National Academy Press.

Roscoe, M., & Morton, R. (1994). *Disproportionate minority confinement*. Washington, DC: Office of Juvenile Justice and Delinquency Prevention.

Russell, M. (2004). *A decade later, most states barely use '3 Strikes' (press release)*. Justice policy institute. Retrieved January 31, 2007, from http://www.justicepolicy.org/print_article.php?&id=451

Saad, L. (2006, October 19). *Worry about crime remains at last year's elevated levels much more pessimistic about crime trends than 5 years ago.* Retrieved March 18, 2007, from http://www.galluppoll.com/content/?ci=25078&pg=1

Schlesinger, T. (2011). The failure of race neutral policies: How mandatory terms and sentencing enhancements contribute to mass racialized incarceration. *Crime & Delinquency, 57*(1), 56–81.

Scott, E. S. (2000). The legal construction of adolescence. *Hofstra Law Review, 29,* 547–598.

Sevin Goldstein, N. E., Olubadewo, O., Redding, R. E., & Lexcen, F. J. (2005). Mental health disorders: The neglected risk factor in juvenile delinquency. In R. E. Redding, N. E. Sevin Goldstein, & K. Heilbrun (Eds.), *Juvenile delinquency: Prevention, assessment, and intervention* (pp. 85–110). New York: Oxford University Press.

Shapiro, E. (1999). *Cost of crime: A review of the research studies (information brief).* St. Paul, MN: Minnesota House of Representatives Research Department.

Sung, H., Mahoney, A., & Mellow, J. (2011). Substance abuse treatment gap among adult parolees: Prevalence, correlates, and barriers. *Criminal Justice Review, 36*(1), 40–57.

SAMHSA. (2013). National Registry of Evidence-Based Programs and Practices.

Tauber, J. (1994). Drug courts: Treating drug-using offenders through sanction incentives. *Corrections Today, 56*(1), 28–35.

Tate, D. C., & Redding, R. E. (2005). Mental health and rehabilitative services: System reforms and innovative approaches. In R. E. Redding, N. E. Sevin Goldstein, & K. Heilbrun (Eds.), *Juvenile delinquency: Prevention, assessment, and intervention* (pp. 45–66). New York: Oxford University Press.

U.S. Census Bureau. (2012). *State and county quickfacts.* Retrieved from http://quickfacts.census.gov/qfd/states/00000.html

U.S. Department of Education. (1994). *Adult education—Functional literacy and life skills program for state and local prisoners.* Retrieved March 26, 2007, from http://www.ed.gov/pubs/Biennial/416.html

U.S. Department of Health & Human Services, Administration for Children and Families, Administration on Children, Youth and Families, Children's Bureau. (2018). Child maltreatment 2016. Retrieved from https://www.acf.hhs.gov/cb/research-data-technology/statistics-research/child-maltreatment

U.S. Sentencing Commission. (2004). *Fifteen years of guidelines sentencing: An assessment of how well the criminal justice system is achieving the goals of sentencing reform.* Retrieved from http://www.ussc.gov/Research/Research_Projects/Miscellaneous/15_Year_Study/index.cfm

Vincent, G. & R. Perrault, (2018). *Risk Assessment and Behavioral Health Screening (RABS) project final technical report.* Retrieved August 24, 2018, from https://www.ncjrs.gov/pdffiles1/ojjdp/grants/251912.pdf

Wiebush, R., Baird, C., Krisberg, B., & Onek, D. (1995). Risk assessment and classification for serious, violent, and chronic juvenile offenders. In J. Howell, B. Krisberg, J. Hawkins, & J. Wilson (Eds.), *Serious, violent, & chronic juvenile offenders.* Thousand Oaks, CA: Sage.

Yoshikawa, H. (1994). Prevention as cumulative protection: Effects of early family support and education on chronic delinquency and its risks. *Psychological Bulletin, 115,* 28–54.

Chapter 9
Homelessness

Shanae Shaw and Namkee Choi

One of our most serious social problems is the deterioration of housing and other living conditions in central cities and the resulting homelessness. The number of the homelessness is a matter of dispute between governments and advocates for the homeless due to inconsistent definitions, methodologies, and samples studied (Kondratas, 1991; Mihaly, 1991; Morrison, 1989; Newman, 2001; Tsemberis, McHugo, Williams, Hanrahan, & Stefancic, 2007). The exact number may not be in the millions, as estimated by homeless advocates, but most parties agree that it is at least in the hundreds of thousands, excluding the rising number of individuals and families living doubled up with friends or relatives (Dyrness, Spoto, & Thompson, 2003). Other homeless persons can be found living in cars and abandoned buildings (Fertig & Reingold, 2008). For homeless families, demographic data indicate that poor families, headed up mostly minority, young, single mothers with children, occupy an increasing share of the rank and file of the homeless (Grim, Gultekin, & Brush, 2015). A major cause of homelessness is poverty. Families make up approximately one-third of all homeless and are the fastest-growing group of homeless (Henry, Watt, Rosenthal, Shivji, & Abt Associates, 2017; National Coalition for the Homeless, 2007). Children are estimated to make up between one-third and one-half of the members of homeless families (Henry et al., 2017; Mihaly, 1991). Most studies of the homeless indicate that the number of homeless families and extremely poor families with children who are precariously housed and thus at risk of homelessness is also increasing.

The cost of human suffering due to homelessness is manifested in tens of thousands of poor individuals, families, and children sleeping in temporary shelters or living doubled up with equally poor relatives or friends. Homeless children exhibit

S. Shaw (✉)
School of Social Work, University of Alabama, Tuscaloosa, AL, USA
e-mail: sklogan@crimson.ua.edu

N. Choi
Steve Hicks School of Social Work, The University of Texas at Austin, Austin, TX, USA

© Springer Nature Switzerland AG 2019
J. S. Wodarski, L. M. Hopson (eds.), *Empirically Based Interventions Targeting Social Problems*, https://doi.org/10.1007/978-3-030-28487-9_9

a host of academic, physical, and psychological problems that interfere with their proper development (Bassuk & Rosenberg, 1990; *Homelessness: A solvable problem*, 2007; National Alliance to End Homelessness, 2000; Rafferty, 1995; Schanzer, Dominguez, Shrout, & Canton, 2007; Thompson, Zittel-Palamara, & Maccio, 2004). Insecurity, instability, and uncertainty about the next meal and bed undoubtedly cause enormous stress and anguish and overwhelm adults and children alike. Homeless and near-homeless individuals and families who move from one dangerous neighborhood to another in deteriorating central cities are also susceptible to crime and violence on the city streets. The overall physical health of children and adults alike living the shelters can lead to health problems such as respiratory and intestinal infections (*Homelessness: A solvable problem*, 2007; Schanzer et al., 2007).

In 1987 the federal government initiated efforts to tackled the increasing rate of homelessness with the passage of the Stewart B. McKinney Homeless Assistance Act to provide funding to Housing and Urban Development (Office of Policy Development and Research, 1995). In the decades following the passing of the McKinney Act, several programs were established during the following decades to provide services to homeless individuals. These programs ranged from shelter and rapid rehousing services to longer-term shelter solutions such as The National Alliances to End Homelessness A Plan Not a Dream: How to End Homelessness in Ten Years initiated in 2000 (Berg, 2015). Despite these efforts approximately 553,742 remain homeless (National Alliance to End Homelessness, 2017).

While poverty is a key contributor to homelessness, it is also important to consider the role that natural disasters may play in the occurrence of homelessness as well. Natural disasters have the potential to cause spikes in homelessness in the impacted region. For instance, Hurricane Katrina had a major effect on the number of homeless families. Sard and Rice (2005) reports that "in October of 2005, about 60,000 people still were living in mass shelters, while about 435,000 people remained in hotels or motels. These figures do not include tens of thousands of families that are living doubled up with friends or relatives or in other accommodations that will not be adequate for the longer term" (Sard and Rice 2005).

Social workers have been diligently researching the causes and effects of homelessness and assisting the homeless not only to blunt the negative effects of homelessness on a daily basis, but to find permanent housing for them. Given the severity of the problem of homelessness and the underlying structural issues, however, social work interventions for the homeless need to be geared to effect more systemic changes to prevent homelessness among poor individuals and families. This chapter includes, first a review of homelessness, including its causes, its effects, and the status of policies and programs that have been designed to address it. This section is followed by recommendations to increase social work advocacy for affordable low-income housing and supportive services for individuals and families who are homeless or at risk of becoming so.

The Causes of Homelessness

Prior to the mid-1970s, a majority of the homeless were single, older males with substance (mostly alcohol) abuse and physical or mental health problems who lived in urban, skid-row neighborhoods and were rarely seen by the general public (Rossi, 1994). Most of those homeless men were not literally shelterless but lived in single-room-occupancy hotels or found beds in cheap accommodations (Rossi, 1994). Since the mid-1970s, however, homeless persons, both men and women, who were literally shelterless, became more numerous and visible on our city streets. Moreover, in the 1980s and into the 1990s, increasing numbers of poor families with children became homeless, and temporary homeless shelters serving both single adults and families have proliferated. The current population of homeless, single adults, like their earlier counterparts, has much higher rates of mental illness, substance abuse, and jail or prison history than the domiciled population (Foster & Hagan, 2007; Gowan, 2002; Urbanoski et al., 2018; US Conference of Mayors, 2006). These disabilities may have been primary, and at least precipitating, factors causing these individuals' homelessness, as was the case of their counterparts in the 1950s and 1960s. Compared to their domiciled counterparts, the mostly single, minority-group women who head homeless families also have higher incidences of psychiatric hospitalizations prior to having become homeless, but the rates are in the single digits. Homeless mothers are also more likely than domiciled poor mothers to have abused drugs. Thus, mothers' drug abuse may have made poor families more vulnerable to homelessness (Baum & Burnes, 1993; Jencks, 1994; North, Eyrich, Pollio, & Spitznagel, 2004). But most studies show that family homelessness in the 1980s and the 1990s was primarily attributable to the increased number of poor people, especially poor, single-female-headed families and to the lack of affordable low-income housing units rather than to individual or behavioral deficits (DeAngelis, 1994; Johnson & Kreuger, 1989; Leonard, Dolbeare, & Lazere, 1989; McChesney, 1990; Rossi, 1989; Shinn & Gillespie, 1994; Timmer, Eitzen, & Talley, 1994). The same reasons are attributed to today's causes of homelessness (Brock, 2007). These two factors—the increase in the number of poor people, especially poor, minority, single female-headed families, and the declining stock of affordable low-income housing units—are intertwined with the declining economic base and the deepening of racial segregation in many cities. Unless these structural barriers to improved living and housing conditions are dealt with, the plight of the homeless may not be alleviated. In sum, in terms of numbers, sociodemographic characteristics, and reasons for homelessness, today's homeless population is quite different from that of the 1950s and 1960s.

Poverty, Lack of Affordable Low-Income Housing, and Rent Burdens

The rising problem of poverty has become worse during the latest recession. In the years between 2007 and 2010, the number of "extremely low income renters," or those making less than 30% of the area median income, increased by 900,000 (Bravve, Bolton, Couch, & Crowley, 2012). The poverty rate grew from 12.5% in 2005 to 15.1% in 2012, resulting in a 52-year high of 46 million American people in poverty. The highest rates of poverty were found among Blacks (27.4%) and Hispanics (26.6%) while non-Hispanic Whites experienced poverty at a far lower rate of 9.9% (U.S. Census Bureau, 2011). This is reflected in unemployment numbers from the U.S. Bureau of Labor Statistics, Blacks experienced unemployment at 14.4% rate in June 2012 (Bureau of Labor Statistics, 2012), a number consistent with trends since the 70s (Fox, 2012). Of the 38.2 million poor persons in 2005, children living with a female householder accounted for 13.6 million, as compared to 9.1 million in 1993. The US Census Bureau reported that in 2005 15.6% of families with children under 18 were below the poverty level, while 37.7% of female-headed households with children under 18 years old were below the poverty level (U.S. Bureau of the Census, 2005).

The problem is not only the increased number of poor, single mothers with children but also the erosion of incomes and worsening poverty among this group over the years. For example, the average incomes of the poorest 20% of single mothers with children were at 33% of the poverty level in 1973 and 1979, but they were at 26% and 25% in 1983 and 1989, respectively. The average poor, female-headed family with children was surviving at only about half the poverty level in 1991 (Shinn & Gillespie, 1994). These millions of poor, female-headed families with children, together with increasing numbers of other poor families and individuals, are evidence that even the benefits of the robust economy in the mid- to late-1980s did not trickle down to those in the bottom economic strata. Not much has changed since the 1980s:

> The nation has been losing affordable rental housing for more than 30 years. This is the housing stock that is affordable, at 30 percent of income, to the third of renter households with incomes of $16,000 or less. From 1993 to 2003, the inventory of these units-with inflation-adjusted rents of $400 or less, including utilities---plunged by 1.2 million. With such drastic losses to upgrading, abandonment, or demolition, the shortage of rentals affordable and available to low-income households was a dismal 5.4 million (Joint Center for Housing Studies, 2006).

To poor people, decent and affordable housing is an elusive goal that they cannot afford to achieve. Poor homeowners are likely to have a hard time paying their mortgages. But, through economic booms and busts, poor renters are likely to have an even tougher time trying to bear increasing rent burdens. That is, despite stagnant income among renter households, gross rents increased continuously for the past two decades. According to the State of the Nation's Housing report by the Joint Center for Housing Studies of Harvard University (1995), the median income of renter households, from 1970 to 1994, fell by 16% to $15,814 annually, while gross rents increased more than 11% to $403 monthly. Moreover, the largest rent increases were for units at the low end of the market. As a result, in 1990 some 43% (5.4 million) of all low-income renters (with incomes of $10,000 or less) paid more than half of their income for rent. A 2012 National Low Income Housing coalition report compared the "housing wage" (or full-time hourly wage needed to afford decent housing while spending no more than 30% of income on housing) to the average hourly wage for renters in a given area. The study found that in 86% of US counties, the "housing wage" exceeds the average hourly wage earned by renters and that the amount affordable housing is decreasing (Bravve et al., 2012).

Much of the rent hike is due to the fact that housing programs have been cut back since the 1980s, squeezing subsidized and low-cost (monthly rent of $300 or less) unsubsidized housing units, despite increasing numbers of poor renters. For example, net new federal commitments to provide assisted (or subsidized) housing averaged less than 100,000 units in the period from 1988 to 1993, down from 300,000 to 400,000 units in the late 1970s (Joint Center for Housing Studies, 1995). In most major cities, the waiting lists for Section 8 housing subsidy and public housing units stretch for years. The number of low-cost unsubsidized rental units has also declined below 1974 levels, which is inevitable given that, between 1973 and 1983 alone, the country permanently lost some 4.5 million affordable rental units through demolition or structural conversion to higher-priced housing (U.S. House of Representatives, 1990).

The mismatch between the decreasing supply of affordable low-income rental housing units and the increasing demand for these units, attributable to the increasing numbers of poor households and the erosion of real incomes among such households, has been proven in many studies to be the primary cause of homelessness in many cities (McChesney, 1990; Ringheim, 1993; Shinn & Gillespie, 1994). In Ringheim's study (1993) of Houston between 1976 and 1983, rent increased far in excess of inflation, while renter incomes stagnated, a pattern that explained increasing vulnerability to homelessness among extremely poor minority-group (especially Black) households with children, even amid massive vacancies in rental housing units. An analysis of 482 New York City families who were newly homeless showed that nearly half of them (43%) had been primary tenants in their own living quarters in the year prior to the shelter request and that 47% of the primary tenants had left their residences due to eviction or rent problems (Weitzman, Knickman, & Shinn, 1990).

Because of the tight low-income rental market, the failure rates of rental-assistance vouchers or certificates (the number of households failing to find affordable housing even with a voucher or certificate) reached 50–60% in big cities (U.S. House of Representatives, 1990). In spite of some preventive measures in the 1990 Cranston-Gonzalez National Affordable Housing Act (PL 101-625), tens of thousands of subsidized rental housing stocks will be lost as the federal contract with private developers runs out in coming years. Thus, in the absence of major public policy changes regarding low-income housing, the housing afford ability crisis and the gross human suffering we have seen in the plight of the homeless will continue to affect tens of thousands of poor families with children.

The statistics are staggering as we enter into the new millennium. According to Harvard's Joint Center for Housing Studies, 2006 press release:

- Between 2001 and 2004, the number of households spending more than half of their income on housing increased by nearly 2 million-up 14%-to 15.8 million.
- Even working families face problems, with 49% of working poor (working at least half the year with incomes up to poverty levels) and 17% of near poor working families (poverty to twice the poverty level) spending more than half of their income on housing.
- Families in the bottom expenditure quartile with children that allocate more than half of their spending to housing have only an average of $400 left to spend on all other items. As a result, they spend only two-thirds as much on food and half as much on clothing as those with low housing outlays (spending less than 30% on housing).
- The supply of rental housing affordable to households with incomes of $16,000 or less—who account for a quarter of all renters—fell by 13% in inflation-adjusted terms between 1993 and 2003. And a significant portion of the remaining affordable rental stock is in financial distress, with 12% of owners of properties with average rents of $400 and under reporting negative net operating income in 2001 (Joint Center for Housing Studies, 2006).

Poor, single mothers who lack education and job skills often depend on public assistance as a major income source. But the real dollar value of Aid to Families with Dependent Children (AFDC) has declined almost by half since the mid-1970s. The increasing rent burden borne by these poor, single mothers on welfare indicates that affordability problems are disproportionately visited upon them and that these problems may be especially severe in situations where they have compounding physical or mental health problems or both to deal with. A comparison between homeless families and a representative sample of low-income family households in St. Louis city and county found that homeless families are significantly younger, never married, female-headed families of color. Housed and homeless families are not significantly different in number of children or in the educational level of the household head, but housed families are larger and have higher incomes, suggesting the presence of another adult earner (Johnson, McChesney, Rocha, & Butterfield, 1995). The extremely poor households headed by young, single females dependent on insufficient welfare benefits and the vagaries of the welfare bureaucracy or on low-paying, unstable jobs as their primary or sole source of income can be easily thrown into homelessness out of already precarious housing situations. As one single, homeless mother put it: "I am in a job and I spend $15 too much and my apartment is gone" (Choi & Doueck, 1996).

Urban Decline and Spatial Isolation of Poor Blacks

Increasing numbers of young, Black, single-female-headed households along with the concentration of poverty and the crisis of housing affordability among Black families are the logical consequences of the social and economic marginalization of central cities and the spatial segregation of poor Blacks in dilapidated inner-city neighborhoods where the tax base, quality of the public schools, and availability of social services are all declining. The level of homelessness in the Black community reflects these disparities. One out of every 141 individuals within a Black family experienced homelessness in 2010, seven times the amount of homelessness among White families (Institute for Children, Poverty and Homelessness, 2012).

As Wilson (1987) has so powerfully illustrated, the deindustrialization that took away well-paying manufacturing and other low-skilled jobs from cities, combined with the outmigration of middle-class Blacks and Whites to the suburbs, has left poor Blacks concentrated in central cities with few jobs and services. Over the past few decades, the demand for poorly educated labor has declined markedly and the demand for labor with a higher level of education (e.g., high-tech information-processing white-collar jobs) has increased substantially. Because of their poor education, poor Blacks in central cities have not been able to gain access to these well-paying jobs (Kasarda, 1989; Wilson, 1987). Even minimum-wage jobs that do not require much education have not been easily accessible to poor, urban Blacks, who seldom have private means of transportation, because most, if not all, of these jobs have moved to suburbs. Ultimately, Blacks are disproportionately poor and even more disproportionately homeless (Hanks, Solomon, & Weller, 2018; National Alliance to End Homelessness, 2016; Susser, Moore, & Link, 1993).

Wilson showed that increased joblessness among young Black males over the past decades was positively correlated with the increased numbers of single female-headed families, because the high rate of joblessness means that the availability of potential marriage partners who can afford raising a family has declined. At the same time that the number of employment opportunities available to males with lower skill levels was declining, the ages of sexual maturity and the initiation of sexual activity dropped considerably over the past few decades, thus exposing more young women to the risk of early pregnancy (Rossi, 1994). Also, poor educational preparation and long-term poverty often breed attitudes of fatalism, powerlessness, and hopelessness among these young men and women. On top of these attitudes, the reality of their dim prospects for the future is not a good incentive for young men and women to postpone sexual activities and childbearing (Joint Economic Committee, 1992).

Massey, Gross, and Shibuya (1994) confirmed that industrial changes and outmigration of the nonpoor to suburbs were indeed responsible for the residential segregation of poor Blacks in central cities in the early 1970s. But Massey et al. also showed that, in later years, racial discrimination in housing markets was a more powerful force that isolated Blacks economically and socially and contributed to the concentration of poverty in Black neighborhoods. That is, because of racial discrimination, both nonpoor and poor Blacks moving out of a poor Black neighborhood had a much higher probability of moving into another poor Black neighborhood than into a nonpoor neighborhood, Black or White. Poor Blacks, especially, tend to gravitate from one poor Black neighborhood to another, without much possibility of leaving these economically depressed and dilapidated areas. So the vicious cycle of joblessness, single parenthood, poverty, and welfare dependency continues. In the absence of any spatial and economic policies that would systematically reduce the social and economic deprivation of poor, urban Blacks, their plight has been worsening.

Concentration of poverty also implies a simultaneous concentration of crime, violence, family disruption, and educational failure (Massey et al., 1994). The disappearance of businesses—as sources of legitimate economic activities—has stimulated the influx of drugs and criminal activities (see Wacquant & Wilson, 1989). As these extremely harsh and disadvantaged neighborhood conditions are not conducive to maintaining even a minimal level of housing quality, they put much of the rental stock now occupied by low-income households at risk of loss. Although poor renters may pay a high share of their income for rent, their payments are generally insufficient to properly maintain old units (Joint Center for Housing Studies, 1995). Because of this problem as well as the falling property values that accompany escalating violence and worsening economic situations in the neighborhood, owners of rental units in poor neighborhoods often disinvest in the properties and foreclose or abandon units (Timmer et al., 1994). It is an irony that boarded-up houses and abandoned buildings have become increasingly common fixtures of central city landscapes at a time when increasing numbers of poor families are looking for shelter.

Because investment in the upkeep of rental units is often inadequate, poor families in central cities often live in substandard units. One study shows that substandard housing and landlords' refusal to fix the problems were cited as the primary reason for homelessness by as many as one-fifth of the sample homeless families (Choi & Doueck, 1996). Apparently, the physical dilapidation of some units reached a point that threatened the daily survival of these families. Children were bitten by bugs and became sick in unheated apartment buildings. Moreover, the drug-related violence, and crime that ravage poor, inner-city neighborhoods often drive families with children out to homelessness. In Choi and Doueck's study, 10% of the sample families attributed their homelessness directly to such life-threatening violence and crime in their neighborhoods, but most of the families who lived in cities also mentioned it as a contributing factor. Interviews with 100 homeless women with children staying in shelters in Richmond, Virginia, also identified excessive use of drugs and vandalism in the neighborhood as a reason for homelessness (Khanna, Singh, Nemil, Best, & Ellis, 1992). Because of the crushing effects of poverty, rent burdens, physical inadequacy of housing, and dangerous neighborhoods, many families in central cities are at risk of becoming homeless even if they are not currently so.

Unlike unattached, homeless adults, homeless families seldom spend nights on the streets. Upon becoming homeless, many families double up with relatives or friends until they have overstayed their welcome, and then they go to family shelters. There most of them are assisted in finding housing. But lack of a private vehicle, limited welfare grants and earnings, and racial discrimination in housing markets usually send these families back to the same depressed, poor Black neighborhoods from which they came and in which they are likely to go through a revolving door of homelessness (see Choi & Doueck, 1996; Grant, Gracy, Goldsmith, Shapiro, & Redlener, 2013).

Mental Illness, Drug Abuse, and Domestic Violence

As mentioned, homeless mothers are more likely to have had a history of hospitalization for mental illness than are poor, housed mothers, but the rate is far lower than for those homeless individuals, both men and women, unaccompanied by children. A study of 677 New York City mothers who requested shelter and 495 poor, housed mothers showed that only 4% of the former as compared to 0.8% of the latter had ever experienced mental hospitalization (Weitzman, Knickman, & Shinn, 1992). Studies based on probability or nonprobability samples of homeless, sheltered mothers in different locations (Bassuk & Rosenberg, 1988; Burt & Cohen, 1989; Folsom et al., 2005) may show rates of psychiatric hospitalizations or prevalence of mental illness a little higher than found by Weitzman et al.'s study.

If there were enough affordable housing, mental illness of a mother or father alone would not force families onto streets or into shelters. Few studies of homeless families attribute homelessness directly to the mother's preexisting mental disorder. It appears that mothers with severe mental illness lose custody of their children because of their inability to take care of them before they become homeless. Mothers accompanied by children are thus not likely to become homeless solely or primarily because of

mental disorder. But because of the shortage of affordable low-income housing and the resulting competition among the poor for it, mentally ill people are more likely to lose out in the competition and be vulnerable to homelessness than are poor people who do not have such a disability.

A very serious problem with the mental health of homeless mothers and children is that their homeless experiences are likely to not only exacerbate existing disorders but also cause all sorts of emotional distresses, notably depression and anxiety, which may interfere with normal daily functioning. Without adequate supportive services, many homeless families may thus have a tougher time coping with homelessness as well as impaired mental and emotional status. Affordable and appropriate housing should be viewed as a necessary component of mental health care (Moxham, 2012).

With respect to substance abuse, most studies with comparison groups reported drug abuse two to eight times higher among homeless than among housed mothers, with the prevalence rates among homeless mothers fluctuating between 8 and 50% (see McChesney, 1995). The wide range may be due to the fact that most studies of homeless families are based on those staying in temporary shelters, some of which do not admit mothers with substance abuse problems. Unlike psychiatric disorders, drug abuse may have led some families to homelessness, because the habit eats up money that would otherwise be available for paying rent. Even when a substance abuse problem was caused by the family's friends or relatives, who shared housing with the family, the family's risk of homelessness was elevated (Weitzman et al., 1992). In Choi and Doueck (1996), equal proportions of homeless mothers reported their own substance abuse and that of roommates, husbands or partners, or other relatives as the primary reason for homelessness.

Many poor mothers who have lived most of their lives in poor, inner-city neighborhoods are easy prey to the rampant crack epidemics in them. Even those who resisted were at high risk for being in a relationship with a substance abuser. In a study of 80 homeless mothers in Massachusetts shelters, more than 40% of the women reported that their most recent boyfriend or spouse was a substance abuser (Bassuk, 1992). When the man's alcohol or drug abuse problem spirals out of control, the woman usually leaves the relationship to avoid the physical abuse that usually accompanies a substance abuse problem. These women may double up with friends or relatives for a while, eventually ending up in homeless shelters. Women with strong social supports are at a decreased risk of becoming homeless (Anderson & Rayens, 2004; Goodman, Saxe, & Harvey, 1991). But homeless mothers often lack the social support that others can rely upon in times of hardship: Either their parents are dead, their parents and siblings do not live in the same geographic area, or they are estranged from their parents and siblings (Bassuk, 1990). Even parents or siblings who are willing to help are often in no position to do so, due to their own poverty and overcrowding (Choi & Doueck, 1996; Rossi, 1994).

Many studies report that homeless mothers are significantly more likely to have been abused as both child and adult than housed poor mothers (see Long, 2015; McChesney, 1995), although one study found no such difference (Goodman et al., 1991). As to the role of domestic violence in precipitating homelessness among poor women, there are also different assessments. Bassuk's (1992) and Weitzman et al.'s (1992) studies report that despite high incidence of past victimization among homeless mothers, domestic violence only infrequently precipitated the current episode of homelessness. On the other hand, other studies (Hagen, 1987; Zorza, 1991) reported that domestic violence is a leading cause of homelessness among women with children. These different assessments may be due to the fact that some studies included but others excluded battered-women's shelters (National Coalition for Homelessness, 2006). Studies that did not include battered-women's shelters may have resulted in an undercount of battered women who became homeless (Steinbock, 1995).

Minority women and women living in poverty are at especially high risk of victimization by violence because they experience much higher rates of frequent, uncontrollable, and threatening life events than the general population (Browne, 1993; Schanzer et al., 2007). Urban decline, joblessness, poverty, drug and alcohol problems, and frequent family disruptions inevitably expose residents of most, if not all, ghettos to violence by strangers as well as by family members and friends.

For poor, minority mothers who lack economic independence and are virtually imprisoned by their environment, "opportunities for improvement of living conditions or escape from threatening situations may be severely limited, and the level of protective resources is typically low" (Browne, 1993, p. 371). Thus, although domestic violence may be a direct cause of homelessness for many families, the relationship between domestic violence, poverty, and urban decline must not be forgotten (Paranjape, Heron, & Kaslow, 2006).

The Effects of Homelessness

The Effects of Homelessness on Families

Food, shelter, and clothing are basic human rights and necessities for a bare minimum standard of living. Deprivation of one or more of these basic necessities disrupts normal physical and emotional functioning. For a family, the loss of a shelter can cause especially serious problems, because it more often than not entails hunger and a lack of clothing at the same time. Loss of a home means a loss of most of the family's other belongings. The feeling of uprootedness, grief for a lost home, and the lack of the sense of security provided by having one's own home may also engender depression and anxiety even among the most resilient, impairing their ability to function normally. Once they become homeless, families face enormous difficulties in conducting their daily lives as usual. In fact, it is downright impossible to have an orderly life at a welfare hotel without cooking facilities but with illicit drug traffic or at a temporary shelter where families are required to take their meager belongings and leave during the day (because shelter staff are volunteers who have daytime jobs). Lack of privacy and rules that need to be followed in congregate living environments can be nerve-racking for both parents and children. A study done to identify women's perceptions of their relationship with their children in a shelter environment revealed that most women feel a loss of being able to discipline their children as they were unable to provide them with the "basic needs for shelter, food, safety, and emotional nurturance" (Lindsey, 1998; Torquati, 2016). The physical experience of a whole family's being compacted in a small space can be stifling and literally create breathing problems among both adults and children (Kozol, 1988; Schanzer et al., 2007). Increased levels of enteric infections like "Giardia, Salmonella, and Shigella" have also been found (Bass, Brennan, Mehta, & Kodzis, 1990). Wood, Valdez, Hayashi, and Shen (1990) suggest these infections are spread through the use of food handling, through oral means, such as the sharing of water fountains, and the sharing of community restrooms. Of preschoolers participating in Head Start programs, it was also found that homeless children showed significantly more problem behaviors, including symptoms of depression, social withdrawal, and schizoid behavior than did housed children. Moreover, homeless children generally perceived themselves as less cognitively, socially, and physically competent and as being less well accepted by their mothers than did housed children. Teachers also rated homeless children less cognitively competent than housed children, but rated the two groups similarly on peer relations and physical competence (DiBiase & Waddell, 1995; Yu, North, LaVesser, Osborne, & Spitznagel, 2008).

Studies comparing school-age, homeless children and their poor, housed peers show mixed results. Ziesemer, Marcoux, and Marwell's (1994) study reported that previously homeless children were similar to low-income, mobile children in academic performance, adaptive functioning, and problem behaviors, although both groups had substantially more problems than the norm. Academically, almost two-thirds of both groups were below the grade level. Rescorla, Parker, and Stolley (1991) reported that homeless, school-age children scored significantly lower than their poor, housed peers in vocabulary, but that the two groups did not differ significantly in their block design and reading scores, although the latter scored somewhat higher. The homeless children were not significantly different from the poor, housed children in behavior problems. Zima, Wells, and Freeman's (1994) study of 169 homeless, school-age children in Los Angeles and Whitman, Accardo, Boyert, and Kendagor's (1990) study of homeless children in a St. Louis shelter also found that their language and reading skills were severely delayed.

The dislocation of children from their communities and their subsequent bouncing between shelters often require them to transfer into new schools (Rafferty, 1995). Children also skip school for lack of transportation to a new school, lack of proper school clothing (especially in areas with harsh winters), lack of immunization records, and bureaucratic problems that delay the transfer of school records or even lose them entirely (Dupper & Halter, 1994; Rafferty, 1995). Despite the initial 1990 federal mandate to remove the residency requirement in the best interest of homeless children, some states continued to impose the requirement in a manner that bars homeless children from attending their schools of origin or new schools in areas where the children are currently living (Rafferty, 1995). Recently, a 2015 reauthorization of the McKinney-Vento Homeless Assistance Act, attempts to guarantee educational rights for children experiencing homelessness by enacting Every Student Succeeds Act (National Center for Homeless Education, 2017; U.S. Department of Education, 2016). Homelessness has been conceptualized as a trauma in and of itself (Goodman et al., 1991). Add that to the multiple developmental and health problems that predate their homelessness, and it is clear that these children are too often put at a serious academic disadvantage by having their education interrupted by such obstacles. Thus, it is not unexpected that a majority of school-age homeless, previously homeless, and poor mobile children must repeat grades or are failing or producing below-average work, despite the fact that most homeless youth do want to graduate from high school and attend college (Tierney, Gupton, & Hallett, 2008). Considering the fact that homeless children have gone through negative life changes including the major loss of a home and separation from loved ones, friends, and familiar environment, it is not surprising that the majority of them suffer from severe anxiety and depression, as measured by the Children's Manifest Anxiety Scale and the Children's Depression Inventory (Bassuk & Rosenberg, 1990; Bassuk & Rubin, 1987; Wagner & Menke, 1991; Zima et al., 1994). These disadvantages may even begin before birth as women who gave birth within a year of being homeless receive lower levels of prenatal and postnatal care (Doskoch, 2011; Richards, Merrill, & Baksh, 2011). In Bassuk and Rubin's (1987) study, a majority of school-age, homeless children said that they think about killing themselves, but they would not. The acute stress associated with being homeless also contributes to depression among children. Nevertheless, only a minority of children had ever received psychiatric evaluation, to say nothing of treatment, because of their parents' lack of awareness of the children's problems and their lack of access to community mental health clinics (Zima et al., 1994).

Given these multiple barriers to proper cognitive and emotional development, homeless children face a severely compromised future (Harpaz-Rotem, Rosenheck, & Desai, 2006). Lack of protective environment and the resulting sense of insecurity and loss of feelings of self-control and self-efficacy can lead to states of passivity and learned helplessness, especially as the chaos and environmental insults persist over time (Donahue & Tuber, 1995). Most homeless children are not able to stave off the trauma of living in overcrowded emergency shelters or violence-ridden welfare hotels, and "visions of academic achievement or career aspirations tend to get overshadowed by the harsh realities they face daily" (Donahue & Tuber, 1995, p. 251). Thus, the primary victims of homelessness are innocent children, who are crushed, physically and emotionally, by the weight of the trauma of homelessness and are unable to transcend the negative environment.

Policies and Programs

Policy Responses

In 1987, triggered by widespread homelessness, the Stewart B. McKinney Homeless Assistance Act (PL 100-77) was passed with broad bipartisan support. Unfortunately, it has not addressed the fundamental problems of the low-income housing market. Instead of encouraging construction and rehabilitation of low-income housing units, opening them to homeless and other low-income people, the McKinney Act provides funds for emergency shelters, transitional housing, and temporary services for the homeless. This law is a notable example of federal policies and programs that continue to treat homelessness and the problems it brings as emergencies. The McKinney Act was expressly designed to be only a first, emergency response to homelessness and to meet the "critically urgent" needs of the nation's homeless (U.S. House of Representatives, 1993). These emergency-relief efforts no doubt alleviate suffering of the homeless, but they also tend to be "ad hoc, stopgap policies dealing, for the most part, only with manifestations of the problems" and to divert resources from long-term and fundamental solutions (Lipsky & Smith, 1989, p. 6). The federal homeless-assistance policies are also fraught with the inflexibility of the government's regulations governing the Emergency Assistance (EA) portion of the AFDC program. That is, funds from the EA program are restricted to housing families only in temporary shelters for a limited period. It is an irony that a family evicted for nonpayment of rent will be housed in a shelter for over $3000 a month, when the same amount could keep them in their apartment for more than a year (Dugger, 1993; Messinger, 1993).

The 1990 Cranston-Gonzalez National Affordable Housing Act revised the McKinney Act to make it more responsive to state and local situations. The core of the 1990 Act is the Housing Opportunity Partnerships (HOP) program, which mandates states and localities to build a long-term investment partnership with the private sector and to develop a strategy to expand the supply of affordable housing with preference to rehabilitation of substandard stock. Another aspect of the act, HOPE initiatives, would help low-income families buy public housing and other foreclosed property owned by HUD, provide supportive services to voucher recipients, provide rental assistance and supportive services for homeless persons with disabilities, and so on (U.S. Senate, 1990). Despite its good intention and plan, however, the level of appropriation under the act has been far short of what is needed to increase low-income housing stocks, to prevent homelessness, and to help homeless families obtain permanent housing. Lack of federal dollars and initiatives also translates into lack of state-sponsored programs aimed at prevention of homelessness. The curtailment of various social service budgets and the resulting budget shortfalls, as well as a general lack of political will, explain the lack of state programs for prevention of homelessness (Johnson & Hambrick, 1993).

Under President Bill Clinton, the Interagency Council on the Homeless, which had been created by Title II of the McKinney Act, was charged with developing federal strategies to break the cycle of homelessness. The council proposed a continuum-of-care (CoC) approach, which was borrowed from the mental health field. The CoC system seeks to provide services to homeless individuals in three different service arenas: emergency shelter programs, transitional housing, and permanent supportive housing (Wong, Park, & Nemon, 2006). Under this approach, a local board, with financial support from the U.S. Department of Housing and Urban Development (HUD), provides a set of services ranging from shelters and mental health and substance abuse services to permanent housing and strategies to prevent homelessness (Johnson & Cnaan, 1995; U.S. Department of Housing and Urban Development [HUD], 1994). But in 1994, the council was defunded and made part of the White House Domestic Council, and, starting with fiscal year 1995, the programs were funded from HUD's operations budget (Hombs, 1994).

Another important federal funding source for homeless assistance is the Federal Emergency Management Agency (FEMA). FEMA's Emergency Food and Shelter (EFS) Program funds the purchase of food, consumable supplies essential to the operation of shelters and mass-feeding facilities, per diem sheltering cost, small equipment, the limited leasing of capital equipment, utility and rent or mortgage assistance to people on the verge of becoming homeless, first month's rent to help families and individuals move out of shelters or other precarious circumstances and into a stable environment, emergency lodging, and minor rehabilitation of shelter facilities (Hombs, 1994). As illustrated by its title, EFS is specifically designed for emergency needs for food and shelter.

In the 2000s, policies affecting the homeless situation have continued to evolve, in attempt to meet the needs of the countries homeless population. Despite efforts to progress it is also essential to note homeless based policies that are not linked to housing, shelter, or food services. The National Coalition for the Homeless stated in an August 2005 publication:

> An unfortunate trend in cities around the country over the past 25 years has been to turn to the criminal justice system to respond to people living in public spaces. This trend includes measures that target homeless persons by making it illegal to perform life-sustaining activi-ties in public. These measures prohibit activities such as sleeping/camping, eating, sitting, and begging in public spaces, usually including criminal penalties for violation of these laws (National Coalition for the Homeless, 2005).

In recent years, it has become a criminal act to sleep, sit, or store belongings in public spaces in many cities where people are forced to live in public spaces. There is selective enforcement of these laws, such as loitering or open container laws, against the homeless (National Coalition for the Homeless, 2005).

> As criminalization measures move people away from services, make it more difficult for people to move out of homelessness, and cost more due to incarceration and law enforce-ment costs than more constructive approaches, cities would be wise to seek constructive alternatives to criminalization. When cities work with homeless persons and advocates toward solutions to homelessness, instead of punishing those who are homeless or poor, everyone can benefit (National Coalition for the Homeless, 2005).

The Affordable Care Act, championed by President Barack Obama and passed by Congress in 2010, offers hope for some needed changes. This Act offers providers and policy makers a chance to ease the fragmentation within behavioral health ser-vices (Mechanic, 2012). According to Mechanic, "the act allows providers to better coordinate Medicaid behavior services with social service and housing programs that seek to prevent and manage homelessness among people with serious mental illnesses" (Mechanic, 2012, p. 377). While this policy does not offer housing or food service, it paves the way for homeless individuals to access health care services through the expansion of Medicaid to eligible people earning less than 133% of the Federal Poverty level (United States Interagency Council on Homelessness, 2014). Medical and mental health services are significant within the homeless population considering the prevalence chronic illnesses and serious mental health disorders within this group (Schanzer et al., 2007). Approximately 20% of homeless individu-als reported having at least one serious mental illness (National Coalition for Homeless, 2009; Substance Abuse and Mental Health Services Administation, 2011).

Shelters, Transitional Housing, and Safe Havens

The most notable program that has sprung out in response to the increasing numbers of homeless families since the mid-1980s was the opening of an extensive number of shelters and housing services. Emergency Shelters and Transitional Housing are two methods of shelter and housing services often available to homeless individuals.

A 2017 point-in-time report suggests that Transitional housing services were used by a vast majority (65%) of homeless individuals (National Alliance to End Homelessness, 2017). While permanent housing is often the goal for many homeless individuals and families, emergency shelters are often the point of entry to access these services (Brown et al., 2017). Shelters often operate on a first-come-first-serve basis and normally have limited requirements to get in. In 2017 there were approximately 277,537 shelter beds available. Of this number 48% were designated for adult only households while 50% targeted people in homeless families and 1% of beds were for children only (Henry et al., 2017).

Shelters help homeless families by providing a roof over the heads of thousands who might otherwise be sleeping on the streets. As mentioned, however, shelters are not fundamental or long-term solutions to homelessness, because they do not add permanent housing units or improve conditions in our cities, and they may in fact divert money from housing construction and rehabilitation and from other social services and financial assistance for the poor (Ferlauto, 1991). Moreover, shelter-based programs create unintended yet severe problems: Helping sheltered families tends to give them benefits that similarly situated poor families who do not enter or are denied a homeless shelter do not get (Berlin & McAllister, 1994). Housing service that sheltered families receive gives them a competitive edge over other poor families not served by a shelter. The flourishing of shelters also hides these poor families from the public by warehousing them and may help foster the perception that individual deficits rather than structural factors are responsible for their homelessness. Last but not least, congregating in one place families that have severe economic and other related problems creates an environment that is detrimental to the proper development of children. As discussed earlier, homeless children suffered before they became homeless and these helpless children deserve a better life than being warehoused in unsanitary, noisy, and unstable shelter environments (National Coalition for the Homeless, 2006). A report from the U.S. Conference of Mayors (2011) reveals large numbers of individuals and families with children are also being turned away from shelters due to the lack of vacancies, so for many, the use of shelters are not available.

While normally for a limited time period, transitional housing services are used to provide a longer-term solution to homelessness than shelters. These services can be used to cover the 24 months of housing. In a national report documenting bed availability in transitional housing there were a reported 120,249 beds available in transitional housing and approximately 49% of beds were for adult only homeless, 49% were designated for homeless individuals and families, and less than 1% of beds were for homeless children only (Henry et al., 2017). This form of housing helps homeless individuals transition from unstable housing situations by providing additional services including employment maintenance, financial management, health maintenance, and activities of daily living (Aguinaldo et al., 2016).

Similar to transitional housing, safe haven services also provide services to homeless individual experiencing mental illness. There are approximately 1600 beds available in these locations all of which are available to individual homeless adults (Henry et al., 2017). Serving as refuge for individuals experiencing mental health issues, safe haven provides shelter services in addition to various supportive services to address the specific needs of the subpopulation (Housing and Urban Development).

Rapid Rehousing and Permanent Supportive Housing

Many communities respond to homelessness in their areas through a process referred to as rapid rehousing. Rapid rehousing is used to assist families to quickly exit the state of homelessness and secure permanent housing (United States Interagency Council on Homelessness, 2018). In 2009 the Homelessness Prevention and Rapid Rehousing Program was established through the American Recovery and Reinvestment Act. This program operated for 3 years until funding was discontinued in 2012 after contributing to services for an estimated 1.4 million people (National Alliance to End Homelessness, 2014). Also established in 2009, the Homeless Emergency Assistance and Rapid Transition to Housing (HEARTH) Act, reauthorizing the McKinney Vento Act by enacting various service changes and outlined updates to homeless definitions, the CoC programs, and the Emergency Solutions Grant Program (HUD Exchange).

Permanent Supportive Housing implements a comprehensive approach to ending homelessness. Permanent Housing services provide approximately 353,800 beds each year (Henry et al., 2017). The term "Housing First" is often associated with permanent supportive housing and several communities have adopted this concept in their local efforts to combat the homelessness. These programs "combine permanent community-based housing with support services that assist chronically homeless individuals to sustain their housing and work toward a community-based recovery and reintegration" (Kertesz & Johnson, 2017). Perhaps the most unique aspect of the Housing first movement is it is straying from the traditional linear approach of that emphasizes progressing homeless people through a series of treatment services prior moving on to more permanent housing options (Johnsen & Teixeira, 2010). Several studies have found that Housing First based interventions to be more effective than linear approaches to homelessness (Goering et al., 2014).

Social Work Interventions

Previous research on homelessness, especially in mental health disciplines, has focused on personal deficits and pathologies, resulting in the medicalization of this devastating social problem and contributing to the depoliticizing of the problem (Snow, Anderson, & Koegel, 1994). Recently, however, with the increasing involvement of social workers and other social scientists with homeless families, their economic predicament has been highlighted and the need for macro intervention has been emphasized: As illustrated earlier, the primary cause of family homelessness is poverty and the lack of affordable housing units, not personal pathology of family members. Some families, of course, have mental and behavioral problems that precipitate their homelessness. Thus, supportive services are needed for the homeless, but homelessness cannot be prevented or eliminated without enough housing for the poor. Homeless families need permanent housing, and they should be able to afford it. Provision of permanent housing and the families' ability to afford such housing is also directly related to the revitalization of central cities and improved economic opportunities for poor minority groups in this society.

Although social workers are aware of these structural causes of homelessness, their involvement in dealing with day-to-day grievances and the devastating effects of homelessness on families often leave no time for dealing with structural issues. But social work practitioners and scholars need to go beyond emergency-based interventions with homeless families to advocacy and lobbying that would affect structural changes. In this section, I recommend social work interventions in the following areas to deal with structural problems as well as the enormous negative physical health, mental health, and educational effects of homelessness on families and children.

Shinn (1997) explains that member of society view homelessness as either a "state or trait" and that programs are enacted based on one view or the other. Regardless of how homelessness is viewed, Shinn (1997) believes the best way to approach this problem is through prevention.

Expansion of Low-Income Housing Subsidies

A follow-up study of formerly homeless families in St. Louis showed that families who received a Section 8 placement were much less likely to become homeless again than those who did not (Stretch & Kreuger, 1992). Long waiting lists for Section 8 vouchers or certificates in most cities must be dealt with to prevent homelessness and to place homeless families in permanent housing as soon as possible. Rental- or mortgage-assistance programs for those who face a temporary financial crisis have also proven effective in preventing homelessness in Virginia (Johnson & Hambrick, 1993). In locations where the failure rate of Section 8 vouchers or certificates is high, a rental-assistance program similar to that in Virginia can be adopted.

Increased Funding for the CDBG and Restoration of Funding for Section 8 Substantial Rehabilitation and New Construction Programs

The federal government must restore its financial sponsoring of physical redevelopment and rehabilitation, designating funds to flow to areas most adversely affected by urban decline. A recent study conducted in Worcester, Massachusetts revealed that one of the protective factors for preventing homelessness included the receipt of "cash assistance for housing subsidy (Bassuk et al., 1997). Private and public partnership in building subsidized housing must be vigorously pursued.

Improved Programs to Preserve Existing Low-Income Housing Municipal governments must adopt and enforce better property maintenance codes and take over abandoned property before disrepair becomes blight. State and city housing rehabilitation programs must also be targeted toward upkeep of existing low- or moderate-income rental properties with appropriate restrictions to prevent market upgrading (Schwartz, Bartelt, Ferlauto, Hoffman, & Listokin, 1992).

The Stuart B. McKinney Homeless Assistance Act for Permanent Housing

Nunez (2001) promotes the idea that shelters should be viewed as "homes where people become employable and continue their education," and that doing this will prevent permanent homelessness. The focus of the McKinney Act on emergency shelters, transitional housing, and temporary services for the homeless must be replaced with that on short- and long-term rental subsidy for permanent housing, rehabilitation of abandoned buildings and houses, and enforcement of building codes in rental units in poor neighborhoods. That is, the funding under the act must be used to prevent homelessness rather than to supply emergency housing and services for the homeless. With the new preventive focus, the funding could then be used to assist those at risk of becoming homeless, reducing the pain and suffering of many poor families and saving taxpayers money.

Grassroots Organizations for Permanent Housing

Grassroots organizations modeled after Habitat for Humanity must be used to increase homeowners hip among poor tenants by mobilizing them to rehabilitate abandoned or foreclosed units and by providing them with technical and legal assistance for property acquisition. The McKinney Act and HUD must subsidize such rehabilitation and homesteading programs.

More Efficient Management of Public Housing Projects

Due to concentration of poverty, many high-rise public housing projects in large metropolitan areas are characterized by austere living conditions and infested with drug-related violence and crime. Moreover, because of flagrant mismanagement by local housing authorities, some large cities have vacancy rates over 30% and many others have vacancy rates over 20%, while waiting lists run to years (Hinds, 1993). As evidenced by efficiently run public housing projects, however, the negative living conditions and mismanagement are not inherent weaknesses of public housing programs. Well-planned and -managed public housing projects can provide the most stable low-income housing. Construction of low-rise public housing projects scattered in mixed-income neighborhoods must follow the demolition of standalone high-rise projects in poor, isolated Black neighborhoods. HUD must enforce more stringent adherence to regulations by local public housing authorities.

Creation of Employment Opportunities for Inner-City Residents

When asked about how they were able to get out of homelessness, formerly homeless families said they had been helped most by an increase in income, the support of family and friends, and access to affordable housing (Dornbusch, 1993). Increase in income is most likely to come with employment. Creation of well-paying jobs and improvement of the employability of inner-city residents through skills-upgrading programs must be top priorities of urban policy. If a realistic hope of employment exists, people will be far more motivated to seek education and training (Fainstein & Fainstein, 1995). Low-wage workers who are not currently eligible for job-training programs directed at the unemployed or welfare recipients must be given opportunities to upgrade their skills.

Improvement of Placeability

The improvement of employability must be accompanied by improvement of placeability, which refers to "the perceived attractiveness of an applicant to an employer" (Wodarski, 1995, p. 3). The long-term unemployed or those who have not had substantial work history may need to brush up their job-seeking and interview skills to be able to identify and link with job openings and to increase employers' willingness to hire them. Once they land jobs, they may need to improve work performance skills and on-the-job social skills to increase their chances of keeping the jobs. Social workers need to provide the homeless and those at risk of becoming homeless with the comprehensive employment preparation and training in these job-related skills through a job club (see Wodarski, 1995).

Child Care and Transportation Services

Especially for single mothers, lack of child care is a major barrier to employment. Subsidized child care programs must be available for all those who need them. Parents who work in low-wage jobs often need child care services that offer extended or flexible hours, because work hours for many jobs stretch beyond the conventional nine-to-five schedule. Sick-child care services are also needed for parents with young children, especially when the parents are struggling with their new jobs. Frequent absence from work because of a sick child may lead to low productivity and dismissal. Children from poor families and deteriorating urban areas also need preschool or after-school programs that would stimulate their intellectual and developmental growth.

Availability and cost of transportation are frequently deciding factors in whether an individual can engage in an effective job search and take a job that is suitable for him or her. Because many cities have inadequate, poorly funded, and fragmented public transport systems, a significant number of potential workers from inner-city neighborhoods have been unable to avail themselves to jobs in the suburbs. Others have been forced to leave employment due to the cost and time involved in commuting. Without transportation, many homeless people also have a hard time finding housing and managing other aspects of their daily lives. A solution may be vouchers or transport coupons in cities with well-developed public transit systems. In other cities, if a major expansion of public transportation systems is too costly, a public-and-private-partnership venture such as Wisconsin's Job-Ride program, which transports low-income Milwaukee residents to suburban jobs (Nelson, 1993), needs to be developed. Also, zoning and financial incentives can be offered to regional and urban developers who can then cluster or plan to integrate public transport corridors with their developmental models (see Lowe, 1995).

Welfare Benefits, Earnings, and Health Care

To ensure the long-term economic independence of poor families currently receiving public assistance, they must be allowed to keep a higher proportion of their earnings and maintain their health benefits for a longer period before the public programs. Although schools cannot correct the damage done by poverty and unstable housing, they can be a sanctuary for many children by providing continuity in at least one important aspect of their lives. Homeless children should feel welcome at school, and greater sensitivity from school personnel toward them will go a long way to ease their pain.

Social workers, in cooperation with school counselors, may also need to develop school-based interventions for students that enhance understanding, tolerance, and respect for persons with diverse personal and financial backgrounds. Social workers can also provide in-service training for faculty and staff to increase their awareness of the specific academic and emotional needs of homeless children and to discuss appropriate interventions to promote these children's academic achievement and personal growth. For best results, an interprofessional case management system for homeless and precariously housed school-age children needs to be established. The case management team can comprise a case manager-social worker stationed at a designated social service agency, a school counselor, a school nurse, shelter staff, and volunteers who would provide tutoring, group activities, and transportation.

The case manager would identify homeless and precariously housed children, facilitate case management team meetings to establish and coordinate a system of needs assessment, service planning, and delivery of services such as referrals to health clinics and counseling, and monitor the effectiveness of services. The case management team would also advocate and make arrangements for specific services that are necessary for children's academic progress. In addition, Huntington, Buckner, and Bassuk (2008) suggest that interventions for children should include interventions for families since the well-being of a child can be determined by the levels of emotional distress felt by the mother.

Technology

As a result of several technological advancements, technology in many ways has become essential to navigating our society. This impact can be observed in the mobile phone use in our society. While many people primarily use mobile phones to communicate with friends and family, the capabilities of this device have expanded exponentially throughout the past decade. Currently, mobile phones can be utilized to assist with a range of tasks extending from simple communication to employment opportunities, health maintenance, locating of housing opportunities. Considering the common need for employment, healthcare maintenance, and housing services, it is essential for homeless individuals to have access to some form of mobile phone and/or internet service. A study of one individual family showed that the use of technology such as email and internet can be beneficial in helping to keep families off the streets (Jones & Crook, 2001). Because of this Jones and Crook (2001) advocate this technology is provided to families by all homelessness programs.

In an attempt to combat technological deficits in poorer communities the Federal Communications Commission established the Lifeline Support for Affordable Communications program in 1985. This program provides phone service discounts to qualifying low-income consumers (Federal Communication Commission, 2017). The program has grown since its establishment providing phone services to more than ten million Americans in 2017 (Universal Service Administrative Company, 2017). While it is difficult to determine exactly what percentage of consumers were homeless, studies show that cell phone ownership among homeless individuals is not uncommon in certain area. For example, using a sample of 421 homeless adults, one study reports that 94% of participants owned a cellphone (Rhoades, Wenzel, Rice, Winetrobe, & Henwood, 2017).

Social work practitioners working with homeless individuals must acknowledge the impact of technology in our society. This can be done by ensuring that clients have access to technology services through phone or internet use. Social workers can assist by helping clients navigate through the process of obtaining a mobile phone or by providing clients with instructions for accessing the local internet services such as those offered by public libraries. In doing this, practitioners must also equip clients with the knowledge and skillset to not only maintain their access to technology but also provide resources that demonstrate to clients how to efficiently operate these devices.

Summary

Despite the implementation of several policies to tackle homelessness over the past several decades, hundreds of thousands of people continue to experience homelessness throughout the USA. While the exact number of homeless individuals is matter of debate due to varying definitions, research suggests that poverty is a major contributor to homelessness and that homeless families are one of the fastest-growing homeless groups. In addition to poverty, lack of affordable housing, rent burdens, urban decline, isolation, mental illness, drug abuse, and domestic violence are possible contributors to individual and family homelessness. While homelessness impacts both the individual and family unit in a direct manner, there are also additional effects of homelessness especially for homeless families with children. Several studies suggest differences in cognitive capacity of homeless children when compared to their housed counterparts.

1987 marked an essential moment in homeless policy development. During that year the Stewart B. McKinney Homeless Assistance Act was passed making it the federal government's first formal response to homelessness. While several reauthorizations of this act have been implemented throughout the past several decades, the primary goal remains which is to provide services the homeless population through housing and other vocational and treatment aids. Currently through the Continuum of Care Initiative homeless individuals have the opportunity to receive a series of shelter services including emergency shelter, transitional housing, and permanent supportive housing. These three forms of shelter provide over 700,000 beds each year. Rapid rehousing is also a newer concept that emphasizes a housing first model of which studies have shown is a more effective approach than traditional linear approaches.

Social workers play a key role in assisting homeless individuals in accessing appropriate services. Primarily social workers must strive to extend services beyond emergency shelters and into a more permanent solution for clients. Social workers assist clients with the completion of housing applications in addition to employment preparation and training and, in many cases, financial management. School social workers play a vital role in providing school-based intervention services. Because they are often the first to be called upon to help families with children cope with special needs and the daily crises that result from homelessness, social workers have witnessed the suffering of these families. In addition to the daily practice that aims at finding housing and improving the physical and mental health of each family on a micro-scale, social workers must engage in macro-scale interventions with larger systems. Social workers must advocate, lobby, and take political and legislative actions to call for structural changes that would help prevent homelessness.

References

Aguinaldo, J., Ahluwailia, A., Hambly, K., Koornstra, J., Rankin, B., & Roesslein, K. (2016). Needs and supports in transitional housing for people living with HIV/AIDS in Ontario Canada. *Journal of Social Service Research, 42*(3), 352–362.

Anderson, D. G., & Rayens, M. K. (2004, January 5). Factors influencing homelessness in women. Public health nursing.

Bass, J. L., Brennan, P., Mehta, K. A., & Kodzis, S. (1990). Pediatric problems in a suburban shelter for homeless families. *Pediatrics, 85*, 33–38.

Bassuk, E. L. (1990). Who are the homeless families? Characteristics of sheltered mothers and children. *Community Mental Health Journal, 26*(5), 425–434.

Bassuk, E. L. (1992). Women and children without shelter: The characteristics of homeless families. In M. J. Robertson & M. Greenblatt (Eds.), *Homelessness: A national perspective* (pp. 257–264). New York, NY: Plenum Press.

Bassuk, E. L., Buckner, J. C., Weinreb, L. F., Browne, A., Bassuk, S. S., Dawson, R., & Perloff, N. (1997). Homelessness in female-headed families: Childhood and adult risk and protective factors. *American Journal of Public Health, 87*(2), 241–248.

Bassuk, E. L., & Rosenberg, L. (1988). Why does family homelessness occur? A case control study. *American Journal of Public Health, 78*, 783–788.

Bassuk, E. L., & Rosenberg, L. (1990). Psychosocial characteristics of homeless children and children with homes. *Pediatrics, 85*(3), 257–261.

Bassuk, E. L., & Rubin, L. (1987). Homeless children: A neglected population. *American Journal of Orthopsychiatry, 57*(2), 279–286.

Baum, A. S., & Burnes, D. W. (1993). *A nation in denial: The truth about homelessness*. Boulder, CO: Westview.

Berg, S. (2015). *Ten-year plans to end homelessness*. National Low Income Housing Coalition. Retrieved from http://nlihc.org/sites/default/files/Sec7.08_Ten-Year-Plan_2015.pdf

Berlin, G., & McAllister, W. (1994). Homeless family shelters and family homelessness. *American Behavioral Scientist, 37*(3), 422–434.

Bravve, E., Bolton, M., Couch, L., & Crowley, S. (2012). *Out of reach 2012*. Washington, DC: National Low Income Housing Coalition.

Brock, E. (2007, February). Cities respond to call to end homelessness. *American City & County, 122*(2).

Brown, M., Mihelicova, M., Lyons, J., DeFonzo, J., Torello, S., Carrion, A., & Ponce, A. (2017). Waiting for shelter: Perspectives on a homeless shelter's procedures. *Journal of Community Psychology, 45*.

Browne, A. (1993). Family violence and homelessness: The relevance of trauma histories in the lives of homeless women. *American Journal of Orthopsychiatry, 63*(3), 370–383.

Bureau of Labor Statistics. (2012). *The unemployment situation June 2012*. Retrieved from http://www.bls.gov/news.release/empsit.nr0.htm/

Burt, M. R., & Cohen, B. E. (1989). Differences among homeless single women, women with children, and single men. *Social Problems, 36*, 508–524.

Choi, N. G., & Doueck, H. J. (1996, February). *Homeless families with children: Barriers to finding decent housing*. Paper presented at the 42nd annual program meeting of the Council on Social Work Education, Washington, DC.

DeAngelis, T. (1994). Homeless families: Stark reality of the '90s. *The American Psychological Association Monitor, 25*(4), 1–39.

DiBiase, R., & Waddell, S. (1995). Some effects of homelessness on the psychological functioning of preschoolers. *Journal of Abnormal Child Psychology, 23*, 783–792.

Donahue, P. J., & Tuber, S. B. (1995). The impact of homelessness on children's level of aspiration. *Bulletin of the Menninger Clinic, 59*, 249–255.

Dornbusch, S. M. (1993). Some political implications of the Stanford studies of homeless families. In S. Matteo (Ed.), *American women in the nineties* (pp. 153–172). Boston, MA: Northeastern University Press.

Doskoch, P. P. (2011). Homelessness in year before delivery linked to reduced levels of prenatal and postnatal care. *Perspectives on Sexual and Reproductive Health, 43*(4), 266–267.

Dugger, C. W. (1993, July 26). Homeless shelters drain money from housing, experts say. *The New York Times.*

Dupper, D. R., & Halter, A. P. (1994). Barriers in educating children from homeless shelters: Perspectives of school and shelter staff. *Social Work in Education, 16*(1), 39–45.

Dyrness, G. R., Spoto, P., & Thompson, M. (2003). *Crisis on the streets: Homeless women and children in Los Angeles.* Los Angeles, CA: University of Southern California Center for Religion and Civic Culture.

Eisenberg, E., & Keil, J. (2000). Growth, construction, and housing prices. *Housing Economics, 48*(9), 1056–5140.

Fainstein, S. S., & Fainstein, N. (1995). A proposal for urban policy in the 1990s. *Urban Affairs Review, 30*(5), 630–634.

Federal Communication Commission. (2017, September). *Lifeline support for affordable communication.* Federal Communication Commission. Retrieved from https://www.fcc.gov/consumers/guides/lifeline-support-affordable-communications

Ferlauto, R. C. (1991, Summer). A new approach to low-income housing. *Public Welfare*, 30–35.

Fertig, A. R., & Reingold, D. A. (2008). Homelessness among at-risk families with children in twenty American cities. *Social Service Review, 82*(3), 485–510.

Folsom, D. P., Hawthorne, W., Lindamer, L., Gilmer, T., Bailey, A., Golshan, S., … Jeste, D. V. (2005). Prevalence and risk factors for homelessness and utilization of mental health services among 10,340 patients with serious mental illness in a large public mental health system. *American Journal of Psychiatry, 162*, 370–376.

Foster, H., & Hagan, J. (2007). Incarceration and intergenerational exclusion. *Social Problems, 54*, 399–433.

Fox, E. J. (2012, July 6). African-American jobless rate surges. *CNN.* Retrieved from http://money.cnn.com/2012/07/06/news/economy/black-unemployment-rate/index.htm

Goering, P., Veldhuizen, S., Watson, A., Adair, C., Kopp, B., Latimer, E., … Powell, G. (2014). National final report. *Cross-Site At Home/Chez Soi Project.* Mental Health Commission of Canada. Retrieved from https://www.mentalhealthcommission.ca/sites/default/files/mhcc_at_home_report_national_cross-site_eng_2_0.pdf

Goodman, L., Saxe, L., & Harvey, M. (1991). Homelessness as psychological trauma: Broadening perspectives. *American Psychologist, 46*, 1219–1225.

Goodman, L. A. (1991a). The relationship between social support and family homelessness: A comparison study of homeless and housed mothers. *Journal of Community Psychology, 19*, 321–332.

Goodman, L. A. (1991b). The prevalence of abuse among homeless and housed poor mothers: A comparison study. *American Journal of Orthopsychiatry, 61*(4), 489–500.

Gowan, T. (2002). The nexus: Homelessness and incarceration in two American cities. *Ethnography, 3*, 500–534.

Grant, R., Gracy, D., Goldsmith, G., Shapiro, A., & Redlener, I. (2013). Twenty Five Years of Child and Family Homelessness: Where Are We Now? *American Journal of Public Health, 103*(S2).

Grim, E. C., Glutekin, L. E., & Brush, B. L. (2015). Do Policies Aimed Toward the Homeless Help Families? The Detroit Experience. *Journal of Policy Practice*, 1–3.

Hagen, J. L. (1987). Gender and homelessness. *Social Work, 32*, 312–316.

Hanks, A., Solomon, D., & Weller, C. (2018, February 21). Systematic inequality. Retrieved from center for american progress: https://www.americanprogress.org/issues/race/reports/2018/02/21/447051/systematic-inequality/

Harpaz-Rotem, I., Rosenheck, R. A., & Desai, R. (2006, October). The mental health of children exposed to maternal mental illness and homelessness. *Community Mental Health Journal, 42*(5), 437–448.

Henry, M., Watt, R., Rosenthal, L., Shivji, A., & Abt Associates. (2017). *The 2017 Annual Homeless Assessment Report (AHAR) to Congress*. Washington, DC: Office of Community Planning Development, The U.S. Department of Housing and Urban Development, Abt Associates.

Hinds, M. D. (1993, June 9). With help of federal rescue effort Philadelphia Housing Agency falters. *The New York Times*.

Hombs, M. E. (1994). *American homelessness: A reference handbook* (2nd ed.). Santa Barbara, CA: ABC-CLIO.

Homelessness: A solvable problem. (2007, March 5). America.

Housing and Urban Development. (n.d.). *Safe Haven*. HUD Exchange. Retrieved from https://www.hudexchange.info/resources/documents/SafeHavens.pdf

Huntington, N., Buckner, J. C., & Bassuk, E. L. (2008). Adaptation in homeless children: An empirical examination using cluster analysis. *American Behavioral Scientist, 51*(6), 737–755.

Institute for Children, Poverty, & Homelessness. (2012). *Intergenerational disparities experienced by homeless black families*. New York, NY.

Jencks, C. (1994). *The homeless*. Cambridge, MA: Harvard University Press.

Johnsen, S., & Teixeira, L. (2010). *Staircases, elevators and cycles of change: Housing first and other housing models for homeless people with complex support needs*. Retrieved from https://www.crisis.org.uk/media/20498/staircases_elevators_and_cycles_of_change_es2010.pdf

Johnson, A. K., & Cnaan, R. A. (1995). Social work practice with homeless persons: State of the art. *Research on Social Work Practice, 5*(3), 340–382.

Johnson, A. K., & Kreuger, L. W. (1989). Toward a better understanding of homeless women. *Social Work, 34*, 537–540.

Johnson, A. K., McChesney, K. Y., Rocha, C. J., & Butterfield, W. H. (1995). Demographic differences between sheltered homeless families and housed poor families: Implications for policy and practice. *Journal of Sociology and Social Welfare, 22*(4), 5–22.

Johnson, G. T., & Hambrick, R. S. (1993). Preventing homelessness: Virginia's homeless intervention program. *Journal of Urban Affairs, 15*(6), 473–489.

Joint Center for Housing Studies. (1995). *The state of the nation's housing 1995*. Cambridge, MA: Harvard University Press.

Joint Center for Housing Studies. (2006). *The state of the nation's housing 2006*. Cambridge, MA: Harvard University Press.

Joint Economic Committee. (1992). *Teenage pregnancy: The economic and social cost* (Hearing before the Subcommittee on Education and Health of the 102nd Congress of the United States). Washington, DC: U.S. Government Printing Office.

Jones, J. M., & Crook, W. P. (2001). Homelessness and the social welfare system: The briar patch revisited. *Journal of Family Social Work, 6*(3), 35–51.

Kasarda, J. D. (1989). Urban industrial transition and the underclass. *Annals of the American Academy of Political and Social Science, 501*, 26–47.

Kertesz, S., & Johnson, G. (2017). Housing first: Lessons from the United States and challenges for Australia. *Australian Economic Review, 50*(2), 220–228.

Khanna, M., Singh, N. N., Nemil, M., Best, A., & Ellis, C. R. (1992). Homeless women and their families: Characteristics, life circumstances, and needs. *Journal of Child and Family Studies, 1*(2), 155–165.

Kondratas, A. (1991). Ending homelessness: Policy challenges. *American Psychologist, 46*(1), 1226–1231.

Kozol, J. (1988). *Rachel and her children: Homeless, families in America*. New York, NY: Crown.

Leonard, P. A., Dolbeare, C. N., & Lazere, E. B. (1989). *A place to call home. The crisis in housing for the poor*. Washington, DC: Center on Budget and Policy Priorities and Low Income Housing Information Service.

Lindsey, E. W. (1998). The impact of homelessness and shelter life on family relationships. *Family Relations, 47*(3), 243–252.

Lipsky, M., & Smith, S. R. (1989). When social problems are treated as emergencies. *Social Service Review, 63*, 5–25.

Long, S. M. (2015). Navigating homelessness and navigating abuse: How homeless mothers find transitional housing while managing intimate partner violence. *Journal of Community Psychology, 43*(8):1019–1035.

Lowe, M. (1995). Out of the car, into the future. In R. L. Kemp (Ed.), *America's cities: Problems and prospects* (pp. 51–58). Brookfield, VT: Ashgate.

Massey, D. S. (1994). America's apartheid and the urban underclass. *Social Service Review, 68*, 471–487.

Massey, D. S., Gross, A. B., & Shibuya, K. (1994). Migration, segregation, and the geographic concentration of poverty. *American Sociological Review, 59*, 425–445.

McChesney, K. Y. (1990). Family homelessness: A systemic problem. *Journal of Social Issues, 46*(4), 191–205.

McChesney, K. Y. (1995). A review of the empirical literature on contemporary urban homeless families. *Social Service Review, 69*, 429–460.

Mechanic, D. (2012). Seizing opportunities under the Affordable Care Act for transforming the mental and behavioral health system. *Health Affairs, 31*(2), 376–382.

Messinger, R. W. (1993, August 7). Out of hotels, into homes. *The New York Times.*

Mihaly, L. (1991). Beyond numbers: Homeless families with children. In H. Kryder-Coe, L. M. Salmon, & J. M. Molnar (Eds.), *Homeless children and youth: A new American dilemma* (pp. 11–32). New Brunswick, NJ: Transaction.

Morrison, K. (1989). Correlations between definitions of the homeless mentally ill population. *Hospital and Community Psychiatry, 40*(9), 952–954.

Moxham, L. (2012). Affordable and appropriate housing: A necessary component of mental health care. *Australian Nursing Journal, 20*(1), 37.

National Alliance to End Homelessness. (2000). A plan: Not a dream; how to end homelessness in ten years. Retrieved from https://b.3cdn.net/naeh/b970364c18809d1e0c_aum6bnzb4.pdf

National Alliance to End Homelessness. (2014, February 14). *Resources.* National Alliance to End Homelessness. Retrieved from https://endhomelessness.org/resource/core-components-of-rrh/

National Alliance to End Homelessness. (2016). *Racial inequality.* National Alliance to End Homelessness. Retrieved from https://endhomelessness.org/homelessness-in-america/what-causes-homelessness/inequality/

National Alliance to End Homelessness. (2017). *State of homelessness.* National Alliance to End Homelessness. Retrieved from https://endhomelessness.org/homelessness-in-america/homelessness-statistics/state-of-homelessness-report/

National Coalition for the Homeless. (2005, August). *A dream denied: The criminalization of homelessness in U.S. cities.* National Coalition for the Homeless.

National Coalition for the Homeless. (2006, June). *NCH fact sheet #12.* National Coalition for Homeless.

Nelson, T. M. (1993). Wisconsin picks up the tab. *Planning, 59*(12), 18–19.

Newman, S. J. (2001). Housing attributes and serious mental illness: Implications for research and practice. *Psychiatric Services, 52*(10), 1309–1370.

Nunez, R. (2001). Family homelessness in New York City: A case study. *Political Science Quarterly, 116*(3), 367–379.

National Center for Homeless Education. (2017, August). Enrolling children and youth experiencing homelessness in school. Retrieved from National Center for Homeless Education: https://nche.ed.gov/downloads/briefs/enrollment.pdf

National Coalition for Homeless. (2009, July). Mental illness and homelessness. Retrieved from National Coalition for Homeless: https://www.nationalhomeless.org/factsheets/Mental_Illness.pdf

National Coalition for the Homeless. (2007). Homeless Families with Children. Retrieved from National Coalition for Homeless: http://www.nationalhomeless.org/publications/facts/families.pdf

North, C. S., Eyrich, K. M., Pollio, D. E., & Spitznagel, E. L. (2004, January). Are rates of psychiatric disorders in the homeless population changing? *American Journal of Public Health, 94*(1), 103–108.

Office of Policy Development and Research. (1995, December 12). *Stewart B. McKinney Homeless Programs*. Office of Policy Development and Research. Retrieved from https://www.huduser.gov/portal/publications/homeless/mckin/intro.html

Paranjape, A., Heron, S., & Kaslow, N. J. (2006). Utilization of services by abused, low-income African-American women. *Journal of General Internal Medicine, 21*(2), 189–192.

Rafferty, Y. (1995). The legal rights and educational problems of homeless children and youth. *Educational Evaluation and Policy Analysis, 17*(1), 39–61.

Rescorla, L., Parker, R., & Stolley, P. (1991). Ability, achievement, and adjustment in homeless children. *American Journal of Orthopsychiatry, 61*(2), 210–220.

Rhoades, H., Wenzel, S., Rice, E., Winetrobe, H., & Henwood, B. (2017). No digital divide? Technology use among homeless adults. *Journal of Social Distress and the Homeless, 26*(1), 73–77.

Richards, R., Merrill, R. M., & Baksh, L. (2011). Health behaviors and infant health outcomes in homeless pregnant women in the United States. *Pediatrics, 128*(3), 438–446.

Ringheim, K. (1993). Investigating the structural determinants of homelessness: The case of Houston. *Urban Affairs Quarterly, 28*(4), 617–640.

Rosenheclc, R., Bassuk, E., & Solomon, A, (2001). *Special populations of homeless Americans.* Retrieved April 1, 2007, from www.aspe.hhs.gov/progsys/homeless/symposium/2-Spclpop.htm

Rossi, P. H. (1989). *Down and out in America: The origins of homelessness.* Chicago, IL: University of Chicago Press.

Rossi, P. H. (1994). Troubling families: Family homelessness in America. *American Behavioral Scientist, 37*(3), 342–395.

Sard, B., & Rice, D. (2005). Changes needed in Katrina transitional housing plan to meet families needs. *Center on Budget and Policy Priorities.* Retrieved November 15, 2008, from http://www.cbpp.org/10-13-05hous.pdf

Schanzer, B., Dominguez, B., Shrout, P. E., & Canton, C. L. M. (2007). Homelessness, health status, and health care use. Research and practice. *American Journal of Public Health, 97*(3), 464–469.

Schwartz, D. C., Bartelt, D. W., Ferlauto, R., Hoffman, D. N., & Listokin, D. (1992). A new urban housing policy for the 1990s. *Journal of Urban Affairs, 14*(314), 239–262.

Shinn, M. (1997). Family homelessness: State or trait? *American Journal of Community Psychology, 25*(6), 755–769.

Shinn, M., & Gillespie, C. (1994). The roles of housing and poverty in the origins of homelessness. *American Behavioral Scientist, 37*(4), 505–521.

Snow, D. A., Anderson, L., & Koegel, P. (1994). Distorting tendencies in research on the homeless. *American Behavioral Scientist, 37*(4), 461–475.

Steinbock, M. R. (1995). Homeless female-headed families: Relationships at risk. In S. M. H. Hanson, M. L. Heims, D. J. Julian, & M. B. Sussman (Eds.), *Single parent families: Diversity, myths and realities* (pp. 143–159). Binghamton, NY: Haworth Press.

Stretch, J., & Kreuger, L. W. (1992). Five-year cohort study of homeless families: A joint policy research venture. *Journal of Sociology and Social Welfare, 19*(4), 73–88.

Substance Abuse and Mental Health Services Administation. (2011, July). Current Statistics on the Prevalence and Characteristics of People Experiencing Homelessness in the United States. Retrieved from SAMHSA: https://www.samhsa.gov/sites/default/files/programs_campaigns/homelessness_programs_resources/hrc-factsheet-current-statistics-prevalence-characteristics-homelessness.pdf

Susser, E., Moore, R., & Link, B. (1993). Risk factors for homelessness. *Epidemiologic Reviews, 15*, 546–556.

Thompson, S. J., Zittel-Palamara, K. M., & Maccio, E. M. (2004). Runaway youth utilizing crisis shelter services: Predictors of presenting problems. *Child & Youth Care Forum, 33*, 387–403.

Tierney, W. G., Gupton, J. T., & Hallett, R. E. (2008). *Transition to adulthood for homeless adolescents*. Los Angeles, CA: Center for Higher Education Policy Analysis.

Timmer, D. A., Eitzen, D. S., & Talley, K. D. (1994). *Paths to homelessness. Extreme poverty and the urban housing crisis*. Boulder, CO: Westview.

Torquati, J. C. (2016). Personal and social resources as predictors of parenting in homeless families. *Journal of Family Issues, 23*(4):463–485

Tsemberis, S., McHugo, G., Williams, V., Hanrahan, P., & Stefancic, A. (2007). Measuring homelessness and residential stability: The residential time-line follow-back inventory. *Journal of Community Psychology, 35*(1), 29–42.

U.S Bureau of the Census, American Fact Finder. (2005). *Poverty status in the past 12 months of families: 2005* (2005 American Community Survey, S1702). Washington, DC: U.S. Government Printing Office.

U.S. Census Bureau. (2011). *Income, poverty, and health insurance coverage in the United States: 2011*. Washington, DC: U.S. Government Printing Office.

U.S. Conference of Mayors. (2006). *A status report on hunger and homelessness in America's cities: 2006*. Washington, DC: Author.

U.S. Conference of Mayors. (2011). *A status report on hunger and homelessness in America's cities: 2006*. Washington, DC: Author.

U.S. Department of Housing and Urban Development. (1994). *Priority; Home!: The federal plan to break the cycle of homelessness (HUD-1454-CPD U)*. Washington, DC: Author.

U.S. Department of Education. (2016, July 27). Education for Homeless Children and Youths Program Non-Regulatory Guidance. Retrieved from https://www2.ed.gov/policy/elsec/leg/essa/160240ehcyguidance072716.pdf

U.S. House of Representatives. (1990). *Public housing and section 8 programs* (Hearing before the Subcommittee on Housing and Community Development of the Committee on Banking, Finance and Urban Affairs (Serial No. 101-91)). Washington, DC: U.S. Government Printing Office.

U.S. House of Representatives. (1993). *Need for permanent housing for the homeless* (Hearing before the Subcommittee on Housing and Community Development of the Committee on Banking, Finance and Urban Affairs (Serial No. 10.3-21)). Washington, DC: U.S. Government Printing Office.

U.S. Senate. (1990). *Cranston-Gonzalez National Affordable Housing Act (P.L. 101-625; Senate Report No. 101-316)*. Washington, DC: U.S. Government Printing Office.

United States Interagency Council on Homelessness. (2014). *The Affordable Care Act's role in preventing homelessness*. United States Interagency Council on Homelessness. Retrieved from https://www.usich.gov/resources/uploads/asset_library/ACA_Homelessness_Fact_Sheet.pdf

United States Interagency Council on Homelessness. (2018, August 15). *Rapid re-housing*. United States Interagency Council on Homelessness. Retrieved from https://www.usich.gov/solutions/housing/rapid-re-housing/

Universal Service Administrative Company. (2017). *Lifeline participation*. Universal Service Administrative Company. Retrieved from https://www.usac.org/li/about/process-overview/stats/participation.aspx

Urbanoski, K., Veldhuizen, S., Krausz, M., Schutz, C., Somers, J. M., Kirst, M., Fleury, M-J., Stergiopoulos, V., Patterson, M., Strehlau, V., Goering, P. (2018). Effects of comorbid substance use disorders on outcomes in a Housing First intervention for homeless people with mental illness. *Addiction, 113*(1), 137–145.

Wacquant, L. J., & Wilson, W. J. (1989). The cost of racial and class exclusion in the inner city. *Annals of the American Academy of Political and Social Science, 501*, 8–25.

Wagner, J., & Menke, E. (1991). The depression of homeless children: A focus for nursing intervention. *Issues in Comprehensive Pediatric Nursing, 14*, 17–29.

Weinreb, L., & Rossi, P. H. (1995). The American homeless family shelter "system". *Social Service Review, 69*, 86–107.

Weitzman, B. A., Knickman, J. R., & Shinn, M. (1990). Pathways to homelessness among New York City families. *Journal of Social Issues, 46*(4), 125–140.

Weitzman, B. C., Knickman, J. R., & Shinn, M. (1992). Predictors of shelter use among low-income families: Psychiatric history, substance abuse, and victimization. *American Journal of Public Health, 82*(11), 1547–1550.

Whitman, B. Y., Accardo, P., Boyert, M., & Kendagor, R. (1990). Homelessness and cognitive performance in children: A possible link. *Social Work, 35*(6), 516–519.

Wilson, W. J. (1987). *The truly disadvantaged*. Chicago, IL: University of Chicago Press.

Wodarski, J. S. (1995). Employment interventions with adolescents. *Directions in Child & Adolescent Therapy, 2*(4), 3–15.

Wood, D. L., Valdez, B., Hayashi, T., & Shen, A. (1990). Health of homeless children and housed, poor children. *Pediatrics, 86*, 858–866.

Wong, Y.-L., Park, J. M., & Nemon, H. (2006, January). Homeless service delivery in the context of continuum of care. *Administration in Social Work, 30*(1).

Yu, M., North, C. S., LaVesser, P. D., Osborne, V. A., & Spitznagel, E. (2008, February). A comparison study of psychiatric and behavior disorders and cognitive ability among homeless and housed children. *Community Mental Health Journal, 44*(1).

Zedlewski, S., Clark, S., Meier, E., & Watson, K. (1996). *Potential effects of congressional welfare legislation on family income*. Washington, DC: Urban Institute.

Ziesemer, C., Marcoux, L., & Marwell, B. E. (1994). Homeless children: Are they different from other low-income children? *Social Work, 39*(6), 658–668.

Zima, B. T., Wells, K. B., & Freeman, H. E. (1994). Emotional and behavioral problems and severe academic delays among sheltered homeless children in Los Angeles County. *American Journal of Public Health, 84*, 260–264.

Zorza, J. (1991). Woman battering: A major cause of homelessness. *Clearinghouse Review, 25*, 421–429.

Chapter 10
Unemployment

Anna Celeste Burke

Introduction

Operational Definitions

Unemployment refers to the inability to gain entry into the labor market or to the "involuntary withdrawal from the workforce due to plant closures, layoffs, or other types of dismissals" (Leana & Feldman, 1991, p. 65). Since the mid-1970s, the US economy has undergone dramatic changes, contributing to intermittent high unemployment rates and large numbers of workers confronted with job loss. Between 1981 and 1988 alone, estimates are that 10.8 million US workers experienced unemployment (Fraze, 1988). Following the so called "Great Recession," unemployment reached 10% in October, 2010. In July 2012, the Bureau of Labor Statistics found that 12.8 million people were unemployed. Despite the current low unemployment rates, slower growth, rapid technological change, and dramatic demographic shifts are forecast for the foreseeable future meaning many individuals will continue to face unemployment (U.S. Department of Labor [U.S. DOL], 1996; Fernald & Li, 2019). Since the 1980s and 1990s it has also became increasingly difficult for young people to negotiate the transition from school to work (Mann, Miller, & Baum, 1995; Sum, Fogg, & Taggert, 1988). This is particularly true for young people with little education or training, but even those with college degrees find job acquisition more challenging given rapid changes in the labor market and inadequate information about the nature of skills in demand (Sum et al., 1988; WIAC, 2017.

A. C. Burke (✉)
The Ohio State University, Columbus, OH, USA

© Springer Nature Switzerland AG 2019
J. S. Wodarski, L. M. Hopson (eds.), *Empirically Based Interventions Targeting Social Problems*, https://doi.org/10.1007/978-3-030-28487-9_10

Extent and Costs of Unemployment

Figures provided by the US government indicate that even though rates are low more than 6 million individuals are currently unemployed (Bureau of Labor Statistics, 2019). Of those who are currently unemployed, twenty percent are regarded as "long-term unemployed," having been without a job for 27 weeks or more. The official government-produced measure of unemployment known as the U-3 rate, or simply U3, measures the number of people who are jobless but actively seeking employment and does not include all jobless workers.

Those who are not actively looking for work or who are unable to work because of a physical or emotional disability may be excluded, as may be those who are working part-time or who have retired prematurely because they could not find full-time work. It has been estimated that the actual number of unemployed is much higher than that indicated by official figures (Tal, Moran, Rooth, & Bendick, 2009). In fact, if discouraged workers, marginally attached workers, and workers with part-time jobs who'd prefer to be working full time are included, the number of people facing problems in the labor market is double thar reported in official unemployment statistics (cf. Bureau of Labor Statistics, 2019).

In addition, many unemployed workers are not eligible for unemployment insurance (UI) benefits. In October 2008, only 32% of unemployed people received UI benefits (Bureau of Labor Statistics, 2008). To qualify for UI benefits, a worker must be ready and willing to work, unemployed, registered to work at the local employment service, and have worked in covered employment during a base eligibility period. State-funded benefits provide a maximum of 26 weeks while an extended federal benefit program (for states above a specific unemployment threshold) may provide an additional 13 weeks of UI benefits (Karger & Stoesz, 2006).

Estimates are that two out of three workers will experience unemployment at some point in their lifetimes (U.S. DOL, 1996). The likelihood of experiencing unemployment is greater for minority groups, women, immigrants, youth, and persons with disabilities. For instance, the October 2008 unemployment rate was 8.8% for Hispanics and 11.1% for Blacks (Bureau of Labor Statistics, 2008). Moreover, members of these groups have more difficulty finding work when unemployed (Kates et al., 1990; Leana & Feldman, 1991, Snyder & Nowak, 1984).

On average, workers entering the labor force since the mid-1970s can expect to change jobs more times than those who entered the labor force the three preceding decades. In recent years many jobs have emerged in the most highly competitive and least stable sectors of the economy. Small businesses have created a majority of new jobs in the USA for the last decade or so, but have a failure rate of about 50%. Since a majority of these jobs offer low wages and few benefits, workers have few resources to fall back on during transitions from one job to another. Workers in more well-established sectors of the economy are also more likely than their predecessors to have career patterns marked by lateral moves and reversals that require workers to reestablish themselves in existing careers or retool for entirely new ones.

Because work is so central to well-being in contemporary society, unemployment is a major source of concern. Since work provides access to material resources, economic deprivation is a major consequence of unemployment (Jacobsen, 1987). As the century ends, individuals without work will find it increasingly difficult to rely on the so-called safety net to meet even their most basic needs for food, shelter, and health care. Reductions in income subsidy, food stamps, Medicaid, and housing programs raise the stakes for getting and keeping a job.

Work also meets various social, psychological, and emotional needs for individuals. For many adults it is a primary source of identity, status, and legitimacy. The inability to establish a significant attachment to the labor market early on greatly limits future earnings and increases the likelihood of subsequent episodes of unemployment (Halli & Rao, 2013). Moreover, youth who want to work and are unable to do so are at increased risk for psychological distress, a deteriorating self-image, loss of commitment to conventional lifestyles, and antisocial attitudes and behaviors (Daly & Delaney, 2013).

There have been numerous studies targeting the effects of job loss on well-being, including cross-sectional studies, longitudinal studies, and studies that follow individuals throughout job loss periods. At any age, job loss has been associated with a wide variety of negative physical and mental health consequences such as increased cardiovascular disease, hypertension, negative mood, hopelessness, depression, and anxiety (Dooley & Catalano, 1988; Kates et al., 1990; Kinicki & Latack, 1990; Paul & Moser, 2009; Wanberg, 2012; Winefield, Tiggemann, & Winefield, 1990, 1991). A loss of one's job is detrimental to an individual's well-being, which is not solely related to the loss of income and financial stability (Ervasti & Venetoklis, 2010). Losing one's job can be traumatic event and individuals may experience symptoms common to victims of rape, incest, disease, and crime. These symptoms include shock, confusion, helplessness, fear, and depression (Guindon & Smith, 2002). Unemployment has been found to be associated with a decrease in psychological well-being, a decrease in physical well-being, a worse economic situation, and for couples, an increased likelihood to get divorced (Strom, 2003). The impact of job loss on couples can be profound: one partner often passes stress to the other partner, changing the quality of their relationship and increasing the likelihood for depression (Howe, Levy, & Caplan, 2004). Unemployment decreases family cohesion and increases the chances of spousal abuse, child abuse, and other harsh punishments (Curadi, Todd, Duke, & Ames, 2009; Joel Wong, Uhm, & Li, 2012). Other studies have found similar results. Gallo, Bradley, Sigel, and Kasl (2000) determined physical well-being by report in symptoms and medical indices and found that unemployment has been associated with a diminished physical functioning. Waters and Moore (2001) conducted a qualitative study measuring the coping-efforts and psychological health of 200 unemployed participants and 128 employed participants. Regression analysis indicated that unemployed individuals had significantly higher levels of depression and lower levels of self-esteem. According to Sersic's (2006) study, older and less educated persons as well as people experiencing more obvious work deprivation and less social support experience more negative psychological effects. In Paul and Moser research in 2009, they found the people who were largely impacted were men, blue-colored workers who were experiencing long-term unemployment. Those living in countries without strong unemployment protection faced a larger negative impact on their mental health.

Additionally, Murphy and Athanasou (1999) used a meta-analytical approach to study the effects of reemployment on mental health and found that mental health is likely to increase upon reemployment. Murray, Gien, and Solberg (2003) studied the mental health of 112 employed women and 112 unemployed women in the context of a massive layoff and found that the unemployed women experienced higher levels of distress. The authors indicated that although employment also proved stressful, it acted as a protective factor for good mental health.

Efforts to put a dollar amount on costs of unemployment typically include estimates of lost productivity, reduced consumption, and additional subsidy provided by taxpayers for unemployment compensation and other benefits for the unemployed. Needless to say, any such estimate runs into billions of dollars quickly. One recent study found that countries with higher unemployment rates had higher rates of depression hospitalizations as unemployment appeared to be risk factor for hospitalization. These high cost hospitalizations add to the overall social costs for the unemployed (Fortney et al., 2007). A 1% rise in unemployment, for example, has been estimated to add $55 billion to the federal deficit. Given the range of health, social, and psychological problems associated with unemployment, such dollar estimates fall far short of representing the full impact of unemployment on individuals, their families, and the larger community.

Relevance of Social Work's Involvement

Although unemployment can have a devastating impact on individuals and their families, a number can mitigate these negative effects. Reemployment appears to result in a reduction of negative symptoms and a return to previous levels of well-being (Paul & Moser, 2009; Turner, Kessler, & House, 1991). Demographic characteristics; developmental needs; previous physical and mental health history; and personal, social, and financial resources all interact with specific employment-related issues to determine the impact of the unemployment experience. Those who are seeking jobs for the first time, for example, may have very different needs from those who lose jobs after working for many years.

Furthermore, circumstances tend to worsen significantly for the jobless as the period of unemployment lengthens (Blustein, Kozan, & Connors-Kellgren, 2013). According to Langens and Mose's (2006) cross-sectional study of 119 unemployed participants, persons with longer periods of unemployment had less productive coping methods and more somatic complaints.

Social workers have a vital role to play in facilitating entry and reentry by workers into the labor market. The broad-based approach to client assessment typical of a "person-in-environment" or ecological model is well-suited to assessing the needs of the unemployed. Traditional social work practice that combines a commitment to instrumental concerns with skillful use of clinical counseling techniques can have substantial benefits for unemployed clients and their family members. A major challenge for social workers, however, is to become more adept at identifying employment-related problems and more deliberate and effective in dealing with these matters. Further development of occupational or industrial social work as a field of practice is one way to involve more social workers in employment-related concerns. The scope of change in the labor market and the rapid transformation of social service systems in the USA means, however, that social workers in many practice settings must develop expertise with employment-related problems. Clients receiving services in a variety of systems are likely to be confronted with unemployment even if it is not the presenting problem or their primary reason for seeking services. Current trends in welfare reform that link benefits to work are already involving social workers more directly in the tasks of helping clients prepare, choose, find, and retain employment.

Assessment Methods

A variety of specialized tools have been developed for assessing work-related attitudes, skills, and abilities. In addition, however, given the potential for unemployment to impact on health, psychological well-being, and marital and family relations, it is important to assess clients in these domains as well. Client narratives are one way an assessment could take place as the client tells their story (Russell, 2011). There are also many standardized instruments that can be administered and scored by hand or by computer exist to assess clients in these areas. In addition, local adult education providers at high schools and community colleges and counselors in public and private employment agencies offer thorough assessment of education and vocational preparation.

Work History

Assessment with unemployed clients begins with a work history. At a minimum, a work history should include educational background and preparation for employment, work experience including the type and extent of previous employment, reasons for termination from prior position(s), and nature and extent of recent efforts to secure employment. A work history, especially in the context of a broader social history, can help specify the nature and extent of employment-related problems and put them in perspective. It provides the first opportunity to scope out client strengths, resources, and deficits, and may indicate that a preexisting or coexisting health, mental health, or substance abuse problem is standing in the way of a client's efforts to get and keep a job. A work history is the place to ascertain whether an episode of unemployment is an isolated event or part of a pattern of repeated terminations. It may also point to a specific deficit that a client needs to address, such as a language barrier, illiteracy, tardiness, or excessive absence.

The work history suffers from the same limitations associated with any self-report source. Corroborating information from a partner or some other family member, from employers or other referral sources, and from responses to standardized instruments is, of course, useful in developing clarity about employment issues. The work history is not a substitute for a structured clinical interview or psychiatric evaluation. Examination of mental health status or referral for psychiatric evaluation may be indicated by findings obtained from work history or from responses to standardized instruments used to assess psychological well-being.

Education, Vocational Preparation, and Unemployment-Related Activities

Hundreds of instrument exist to assess educational level and preparation from employment. These include tools for measuring achievement, aptitude, interest, and values and for matching client profiles to specific occupations and jobs. *Career Success: Tools for the 21st Century* (Griffin, McGaw, & Care, 2012) is one compendium of such resources. Compendiums identify instruments, describe their specific uses, and, in many cases, cite published articles that review their psychometric properties and prior use. Tools vary not only in the specific areas they measure, but in their suitability for various age and grade levels or special populations, the format used to collect information, the number of items and length of time needed to collect information, the costs associated with the purchase and scoring instruments, and so on. Comparative information about nine computer-assisted career guidance (CACG) systems is also available (Sampson et al., 1990; Sampson & Reardon, 1990). Computerized systems save staff time and can involve clients more directly in vocational assessment.

The most critical issue during assessment is to get a clear sense of educational level and to identify deficits in basic skills. The inability to read, write, or carry out math calculations is a handicap in the current labor market. Even low-wage, entry-level jobs often require literacy skills, in contrast to entry-level jobs in previous decades that relied primarily on physical attributes of strength, stamina, or dexterity. Poor literacy skills may impact on the job acquisition process by making it impossible for a client to read job postings or fill out applications.

Grade attainment in school is not an adequate measure of basic educational achievement. Numerous tests are available, however, to gauge achievement. Those most commonly used by program participants in the Job Training Partnership Act include the Test of Adult Basic Education (TABE), the California Achievement Test (CAT), the Wide Range Achievement Test (WRAT), and the Adult Basic Learning Examination (ABLE). These instruments are used not only to appraise basic skills but to sort and assign individuals to appropriate programs, to diagnose or establish where learning should begin, to benchmark progress, and as posttests to measure gain from program participation (National Commission for Employment Policy, 1988). Many other tests exist to assess aptitude and interest. Further evaluation in these areas is recommended for clients who need help choosing an occupation or changing careers.

One recent study, Gowan and Nassar-McMillan (2001), used a Job Loss Questionnaire to assess people's past experiences concerning their job loss. Not only did the questionnaire examine education and vocational training of participants, but researchers also examined whether participants in the study had participated in self-awareness training (such as career assessments or one-on-one counseling) and action-oriented programs (like job search workshops). Results were coded so that researchers could use the results of the questionnaire to understand general trends in unemployment attitudes and experiences. In addition, one study found that when unemployed individuals engage in solution-oriented coping strategies, levels of depression decrease (Waters & Moore, 2001).

Work Attitudes and Values

Individuals vary in the value they place on work and their commitment to the employment role. Commitment to employment appears to be higher for married men with dependent children than for others (Jackson, 1994; Warr & Jackson, 1984). Persons who place greater value on work than on other roles are at greater risk for health and mental health problems during episodes of unemployment (Bartell & Bartell, 1985; Kasl & Cobb, 1979; Walsh & Jackson, 1995; Warr & Parry, 1982). A higher level of commitment to the work role is associated with greater motivation to find a job (Leana & Feldman, 1991), but may increase vulnerability to negative consequences from setbacks or delays in obtaining employment. Commitment to paid employment can be assessed with an eight-item measure developed by Rowley and Feather (1987).

Health and Mental Health Status

For many, the unemployment experience is "an emotional roller coaster, characterized by loss, grief… a sense of inadequacy, depression, lowered self-esteem, increased stress, social isolation, an increased tendency toward minor psychiatric illness, erratic mood shifts, and a progressive loss of optimism about finding unemployment" (Fergusson, McLeod, & Horwood, 2014). General psychological distress or untreated symptoms of a substance abuse or mental health problem can greatly inhibit an individual's capacity to deal with unemployment. Similarly, poor physical health is an obvious impediment to employment. Ideally, a psychological disorder, medical condition, or physical or psychological limitation should be identified and evaluated during the assessment process.

Job loss has been associated with increased risk for a variety of debilitating and even life-threatening disorders such as hypertension, stroke, and heart disease (Brenner, 2016; Ruhm, 2016). Assessment of health status is vital and can be best accomplished with a physical exam. A thorough physical exam is warranted if the client has not had an exam within 6 months, symptomatic, or has a personal or family history of cardiovascular problems. Specific attention should be paid to blood pressure and immunological and cardiovascular risk factors such as serum cortisol and cholesterol levels (Ametz et al., 1991). Other chronic health problems should be monitored closely as well since the stress of unemployment can exacerbate symptoms or disrupt management of chronic disorders such as diabetes (Kates et al., 1990). Checklists of ailments, somatic complaints, and measures of subjective health may also be used to assess and monitor health status.

Dozens of instruments exist to measure mental health and psychological well-being. Tools for measuring self-efficacy (Sherer et al., 1982), self-control (Rosenbaum, 1980), and self-esteem (Rosenberg, 1965) have all been widely used with unemployed and other types of clients. Low self-esteem is associated with mental health and substance abuse problems. More important, however, low self-esteem is associated with mental health, self-efficacy, or self-control may inhibit clients from taking actions needed to deal with unemployment. The Mental Health Inventory (Viet & Ware, 1983) assesses general mental health (32 items) and cognitive impairment (6 items). The SCL-90-R is a self-report symptom checklist that includes subscales for depression, anxiety, and somatization as well as other major psychiatric disorders. This instrument has been widely used with both clinical and non-clinical populations. Norms and clinical cut points have been established for men and women and other subgroups (Derogatis, 1994). This tool is useful for monitoring mental health in non-clinical populations and can also be used as a screening device to identify individuals in need of referral for further psychiatric evaluation. A reduced set of 53 items referred to as the Brief Symptom Inventory (BSI) is also available for assessing mental health. Similarly, subscales for somatization, anxiety, and depression can be used independently for screening and to monitor change in symptom levels over time. Specific inventories developed by Beck and associates can be used to gauge hopelessness (Beck, Ward, Mendelsen, Mock, & Erbaugh, 1961). Tools for assessing alcohol and drug involvement include Michigan Alcoholism Screening Test (MAST; Selzer, 1971), Index of Alcohol Involvement (IAI; MacNeil, 1991), and the McMullin Addiction Thought (MAT) Scale (McMullin & Gehlaar, 1990).

McKee-Ryan, Song, Wanberg, and Kinicki (2005) used theoretical models to conduct and organize a literature review of unemployment literature. Based on the inventory gathered from the study, they found that the General Health Questionnaire (Goldberg, 1978), the Beck Depression Inventory (Beck & Beck, 1972), the Center for Epidemiological Studies-Depression Scale (Randolph, 1977), the Hopkins Symptoms Checklist (Derogatis, Lipmann, Rickles, Uhlenhuth, & Covi, 1974), the Manifest Anxiety Scale (Taylor, 1953), the State-Trait Anxiety Inventory

(Spielberger, Gorsuch, & Lushene, 1970), the Life Satisfaction Scale (Quinn & Shepard, 1974), the Present Life Satisfaction Scale (Warr, 1978), and the Quality of Life Delighted-Terrible Scale (Andrews & Withey, 1976) were used to assess psychological well-being.

In addition, US government figures indicate that the number of older workers participating in the workforce will increase by 49.3% over the next decade. By 2012, there will be 31,026,000 workers age 55 and older, accounting for 19.1% of the total workforce. To assist unemployed older workers, employment counselors may have to help individuals manage grief and loss of previous positions and assess for physical and mental factors as they relate to occupational safety. Employment counselors should use a holistic approach when working with older people and consider needs as well as personal and social resources (Kirk & Belovics, 2005).

Financial Strain

Financial strain adds to the risk of negative health and mental health problems for unemployed individuals and their family members and can interfere with planning and decision-making about prospects for retraining or reemployment. In fact, financial strain has been identified as the single most damaging consequences of unemployment (Crowe & Butterworth, 2016). A recent study used data from the Survey of Income and Program Participation and found that unemployed women were more likely not to receive needed medical care and also to be without telephone service. Lack of food resources, inadequate dental care, and inability to pay for housing increased more than 60% for unemployed women in the survey (Lovell & Oh, 2005). An assessment of financial resources ought to identify immediate financial problems confronting clients provides a basis for making realistic decisions about options to pursue further education or training or to seek reemployment, identify areas in which clients can make adjustments in expenditures or pursue other strategies to maintain a reasonable standard of living, and establish the length of time a household can maintain financial stability during a period of unemployment. A second wage earner, unemployment insurance, substantial savings, or assets that can be easily liquidated (e.g., stocks, bonds) are variables that can cushion the impact of job loss. How much an individual is bothered by or concerned about finances may not always be related to the actual availability of resources. Subjective financial strain can be measured using an instrument such as the eight-item Financial Concerns Scale (Mallinckrodt & Fretz, 1988; Russell, Holmstrom, & Clare, 2015).

Family and Partner Relationships

The dynamic of partner and family relations may shift dramatically with changes in employment status. Even couples and families with considerable resources are likely to experience increased financial strain as a result of job loss. In addition to financial strain, a change in employment status of one family member may radically alter roles, patterns of communication, and relationships. A variety of strategies exist to assess family distress, family functioning, and the quality of the partner of spouse relationship. The Dyadic Adjustment Scale (DAS), for example, is a 32-item instrument developed to assess the overall quality of dyadic relationships (Spanier, 1976; Spanier, Lewis, & Cole, 1975). Subscales on this instrument measure dyadic consensus, cohesion, and affection expression and satisfaction, and are widely used to measure the quality of relationships between partners (McGonagle, Kessler, & Schilling, 1992; Stein, Bush, Ross, & Ward, 1992).

The Family Assessment Device (FAD) uses a 60-item questionnaire to evaluate family functioning in relation to six dimensions: problem solving, communication, roles, affective responsiveness, affective involvement, and behavior control. Items included in this instrument also provide information about general family functioning (Epstein, Baldwin, & Bishop, 1983). The Family Crisis Oriented Personal Evaluation Scale (FCOPES) is a 3D-item instrument designed to assess family strategies for dealing with problems such as unemployment (McCubbin & Thompson, 1991). The Family Hardiness Index (FHI) serves a similar purpose, providing information about capacity of the family to deal with the stresses of such major life events (McCubbin & Thompson, 1991).

Effective Social Work Interventions

A protocol for assessment and intervention with unemployed clients encompasses more or less distinct phases or processes involving engagement and stabilization, goal setting and action planning, and implementation and termination. Follow-up is also advisable with individuals who have experienced employment-related difficulties. Although evidence suggest many individuals recover quickly from the negative effects of unemployment, other studies indicate increased risk for health and mental health problems 2–3 years following an episode of unemployment (Ametz et al., 1991; Brenner, 1987; Moser et al., 1984).

Engagement and Stabilization

Engagement and stabilization actually begin during assessment, particularly if the same service provider is involved in both assessment and intervention. During this phase, primary tasks for the provider include efforts to establish rapport and convey empathy, overcome denial or debilitating negative thoughts and feelings, and resolve crises and achieve as much stability for clients as possible. Moderate self-disclosure by the service provider about his or her own experiences with unemployment and expressions of confidence about the ability to help other deal with these issues appear to heighten credibility and aid in rapport building (Caplan, Vinokur, Price, &

van Ryn, 1989; Janis, 1981; Meichenbaum, 1985). Researchers have found that the focus on engagement is different when working with people who have been unemployed short term compared to long term. For those who are facing long-term unemployment social workers need to help them find focus and create realistic goals. Those who have been unemployed in the short-term phases benefit from assistance in preventing premature disengagement in services (Korner, Reitzle, & Silbereisen, 2012).

Hayhoe (2006) proposed that the Stages of Grief and Loss Model can be used to understand the psychological well-being of clients experiencing job loss. People drift through the stages of the model fluidly, and clients can experience multiple stages simultaneously. The first stage is known as "shock/denial" in which individuals are usually unwilling to talk about their unemployment. In this stage, often clients pretend that the job loss is not happening to them. They usually feel numb, often feel as though they want to escape, and are fixated on the question, "Why." To help clients in this stage, the social worker should teach members of the clients social network, particularly family members, to be empathetic listeners (working on listening skills). People in this stage are not ready to actively change what has happened to them, so the best response to shock and denial is to be supportive and available.

The next stage is disorganization when the numbness wears off and people experience what Boss (1988) characterized as "boundary ambiguity," being "physically present but emotionally unavailable" (Hayhoe, 2006, p. 65). Clients in this stage go through the motions of job searching and rethinking their life courses but take forever to get resources, act confused and inconsistent, and feel out of touch. Social workers should explain to family members that even though the client is physically going through the motions that may be needed, they are not emotionally ready to act. It is important to teach families to help out with the everyday decisions at home, and social workers must find resources to help the family get by.

Next comes the volatile emotions stage which includes feelings of bitterness, hurt, resentment, hostility, and frustration, so social workers should listen to clients in this stage vent and be supportive while helping family members cope with the range of emotions.

Guilt is the next stage usually experienced, and clients fixate generally on the "if only…" and "what ifs." It is important to tell clients that they made good decisions in the past. The following stage is loss and loneliness, which is usually accompanied by the guilt stage. This is the most painful stage, when clients feel a loss of identity, career, and friends. They often feel sad, lonely, and depressed. Help clients deal with depression, and always check for suicidal ideation during this stage.

The final two stages are relief and recovery in which clients begin to see positive outcomes for their futures and start to take real actions. To help clients, start working on problem solving skills, find retraining opportunities, and assist in job searching.

Although responses to unemployment vary greatly, denial or an "initial vacation period" is common for many individuals early in the job loss experience (Borgen, Hatch, & Amundson, 1990). Denial can delay decision-making and action, potentially extending the period of unemployment. Such a delay is disadvantageous because of unemployed workers typically have fewer resources and less support as the period of unemployment lengthens (Sales, 1995). Clients overwhelmed by anger, guilt, and shame about their unemployed status may also be paralyzed into inaction.

Denial and self-blame can be countered by engaging clients in conversation about their unemployment experiences. Allowing clients to vent anger and express other negative sentiments may be helpful (Eitel, 2014).

Normalizing the unemployment experience by informing clients about the integral nature of unemployment to work in a dynamic economy can reduce stigma and provide relief to clients. "Plant closing, economic recessions, technological advanced, global competition, new styles of work, and changing social relationships can all lead to a loss of jobs" (Kate et al., 1990, p. 5). Acknowledging the presence of such conditions and the challenges they pose for workers can counter client misattributions about the causes of unemployment. Clients should also be reassured that there are strategies and skills they can use to improve their prospects in the labor market, shifting their focus toward action to overcome their unemployed status. Success in this regard is likely to be prediction discovering and correcting distorted cognitions and punitive self-talk, while helping clients identify and take responsibility for deficits they possess in employment-related knowledge, skill, motivation, or behavior.

Crisis resolution is central to stabilization of the client and client-family system. It is essential in this early period to identify and resolve crises provoked or uncovered by the unemployment experience. This is the point at which to deal with health, substance abuse, or mental health problems revealed during assessment, which can interfere with the client's ability to pursue employment-related goals. Problems related to family conflict and domestic violence should also be addressed, as should any legal or financial crises.

Case management skills, involving brokering and coordination of services, and advocacy on behalf of clients can contribute to rapport building and stabilization. Service providers should ensure that unemployed individuals make full use of benefits and supports available to them such as unemployment compensation, extended health coverage from employer-paid or union-sponsored health benefit programs, or other public benefits such as food stamps, cash assistance, or public health insurance. Referral for financial planning or debt counseling may also be appropriate at this stage, particularly if financial matters have reached a crisis point. Individuals who have received lump-sum severance payer who have had retirement savings refunded to them at termination should also be encouraged to seek financial counseling.

Case management is also useful for coordinating care and making sure that client needs are met as they change over time. This is particularly important for clients who need multiple services or in cases for which sequencing of services is warranted. Making appropriate referrals for specialized services that can help clients achieve employment-related goals is an integral function of case management. Such efforts are effective, however, only if clients follow through and are able to obtain the referred benefit or service. Advocacy may be particularly important to avoid delays in the receipt of services or to challenge the denial of benefits to clients.

Unemployed clients may be reluctant to confront an agency account a delay out of fear that they will not get the services they need, or they may not understand the process for grieving a decision made by an agency to deny them benefits. Advocacy for unemployed clients may also include referral for legal assistance if a client appears to have been the victim of wrongful termination or some other form of malfeasance or discrimination in the labor market. Overall, stabilization is a critical part of the intervention process. Taris (2002) found that lower scores on mental distress tests increase the likelihood that individuals will become reemployed.

Goal Setting and Action Planning

During the goal-setting and action-planning phase, clients must make decisions about to deal with their current joblessness. The primary decision unemployed clients face is whether to seek employment. The vast majority of unemployed individuals will opt to find work. In today's rapidly changing labor market, however, workers are increasingly likely to be confronted by the need to upgrade existing skills or to retool before seeking reemployment (Ling & O'Brien, 2013; Mindzak, 2016). Renewed emphasis on work as an adjunct or alternative to welfare and disability benefits means many more long-term unemployed or disadvantaged workers may be seeking assistance with employment-related decisions. Many of these individuals may lack basic educational or vocational skills and can often benefit by choosing to improve language and literacy skills, and by acquiring more specialized technical or vocational skills before seeking employment. This is especially true, however, if training in basic education leads to a year or more of postsecondary education (U.S. DOL, 1995).

A still small, but growing, number of persons may seek self-employment or withdrawal from the labor market as an alternative to retraining or job seeking. Individuals who decide not to pursue employment will need very different services and supports from those who want to find work. Moreover, those who want to try their hand at starting a new business face a very different set of challenged from those who opt for early retirement or who qualify for long-term disability.

It is important that findings from the assessment process be used to carefully evaluate the practicality of making the decision to pursue some goal other than finding a job. Bezanson (2004) advocates following a solution-focused therapy model whereby the employment counselor focuses on the client's strengths and facilitates empowerment of the individual. This model stresses active listening, summarizing, asking open questions, and amplifying "solution talk." In addition, this method advocates holistic goal setting, taking into account work, leisure, relationships, finances, future education, and retraining. Although decisions are rarely irreversible, there are real limits to resources and their use can constrain subsequent decision-making. Early retirement typically involves more adjustment than may be obvious. Clients may find it difficult to be realistic about their ability to make ends meet on the reduced income that typically accompanies retirement. Moreover, older workers often encounter more difficulty finding new employment, and an extended absence may make matters worse. The pursuit of additional education and training and the start-up of a new business both require substantial investment of time, money, and personal resources. A great deal of risk is associated with the start-up of small businesses. Most fail, often because of unrealistic planning and inadequate resources. New businesses cannot be counted on as a source of income for individuals and their families for 5 years after they are established. Add to this 6 months or more of planning and it becomes clear that self-employment is not an immediate alternative to reemployment.

Once a choice has been made, clients need to develop an action plan. An individualized service plan (ISP) or some other similar device should be used to set out the terms of agreement between client and provider about the specific plan of action to be used to achieve employment-related goals. This action plan should set out goals, specific measurable objectives associated with client goals and the activities intended to achieve objectives and strategies for measuring progress toward objectives. It should also specify terms and conditions surrounding termination and, ideally, should include plans for recontact or follow-up at agreed-upon times.

Implementation Phase

Effective intervention efforts must blend knowledge acquisition and skill building specific to the vocational needs of clients, with supportive counseling and opportunities to reinforce cognitive and behavioral changes that will make it possible for unemployed clients to realize their goals. Convincing evidence indicates that extended periods without work create more problems for workers and their families (Feather, 2012). Notwithstanding earlier precautions about helping clients carefully evaluate the feasibility of choosing not to search for work, every effort should be made to move clients toward action in as short a time as possible.

Individual Intervention

Job Search Assistance A variety of well-established techniques exist that can help clients find employment quickly and without a reduction in the quality of the jobs obtained (Johnson & Wegmann, 1982). Supportive networks assist job seekers in reestablishing their motivation even before they are ready to seek jobs. It also reduces the isolation and helps individuals fight against the feelings of inadequacy (Russell, 2011). Indeed, some evidence suggests that job search assistance training can increase placement rates, decrease the length of time needed to find a job, and result in higher quality employment as indicated by hours worked per week, earnings, and wage rate (Caplan et al., 1989; Vinokur et al., 1991). In any case, effective job search assistance involves a short-term, highly focuses set of activities aimed at helping workers find and get jobs. These activities can best be conceptualized as a set of planned behaviors (Russell et al., 2015) learned and carried out in the context of directive behavioral counseling. Counseling should be focused on teaching clients search behaviors in a safe, positive setting where they can learn and practice such skills.

Counseling about search behavior is rooted in helping clients develop a fundamental understanding about the concept of a labor market as a structure in which workers are queued, sorted, and selected for entry into various job openings. Distinctions are drawn between the primary and secondary sectors of the labor market and between the formal labor market and informal or hidden labor market. Primary sector jobs tend to be located in larger, more well-established firms and offer better salaries and benefits and more opportunity for advancement, but they comprise a smaller proportion of available openings and generally carry more entry requirements than those in the secondary sector. Moreover, many jobs in both the primary and secondary sectors are never posted publicly. The concept of the so-called hidden labor market is used to represent the notion that positions are constantly being created by turnover or job growth, but most are filled before ever reaching newspaper ads or employment agency listings. Specific information about the local labor market, including areas of the economy that are shrinking and growing, is also useful to clients looking for work.

A variety of props, scripts, and practice or rehearsal opportunities are important to improving job acquisition skills. The resume is a standard prop used in the implementation of a search strategy. Resume preparation should stress identification and representation of behaviorally specific attributes that clients bring to the workplace, rather than listing vague, positive characteristics. Skill inventories can be used to help clients list marketable skills they have acquired, not only from previous employment but from hobbies and community activities. Examining the skills clients have acquired may extend the range or type of position a client is qualified to pursue. In addition to a well-written resume, portfolios containing cover letters, reference letters, and thank-you letters to send to potential employers following an interview can all be used to bolster job acquisition efforts. Similarly, a standard application form, complete with well-thought-out answers to tough questions, can be included in such a portfolio and can serve as a model for completing applications on site. As technology is increasing, individuals are going to need help utilizing the internet and the computer as part of their job strategy (Wanberg, 2012).

Direct contact of employers is a key strategy for penetrating the hidden labor market and increasing the pool of possible job opportunities. Rather than waiting for jobs to be posted, clients should be encouraged to identify and contact establishments that might have positions appropriate to their interests and qualifications. Telephone book yellow pages and employer listings obtained from the chamber of commerce are common resources clients can use for this purpose. Once identified, employers should be contacted with inquiries about current or anticipated openings and the application process. Scripts are often useful guides for clients making telephone contact with potential employers (Johnson & Wegmann, 1982).

Clients may also use direct contact with employers to set up information interviews. During an information interview a client should not ask for a job. Instead, information interviews enable clients to learn more about the business or industry and gain greater clarity about the kind of setting in which they want to work. They also expand client networks and can result in referrals or recommendations for jobs in similar establishments. Employers have, on occasion, been known to create positions for clients when suitably impressed during information interviews or to offer them positions later. Such interviews are also typically less stressful than job interviews and can, at the very least, offer clients the opportunity to practice interviewing skills under low-risk circumstances (Johnson & Wegmann, 1982).

Direct contact of employers is only one of the ways in which clients can generate job leads. One of the most interesting and consistent findings from surveys of workers is the large number who report that friends, family members, or acquaintances helped them find the jobs they hold (Jones & Azrin, 1973; Sillikar, 1993). Typically, two out of three workers indicated they found their jobs through leads from friends, family members, or acquaintances. Formal sources, such as newspaper want ads or employment agency postings, were much less common sources of job referrals (Murphy & King, 1996). Thus, a network orientation to job finding has become an increasingly important part of job search assistance counseling. This means increasing the ability and willingness of clients to approach friends, relatives, and acquaintances with inquiries about job leads. Formulating and practicing such requests is an important precursor to actually using this strategy.

Self-presentation and interviewing skills are critical job search behaviors. Role playing and videotaping are commonly used strategies for providing clients with opportunities to practice and get feedback about their performance. This sort of rehearsal can be particularly important in preparing clients who are anxious about the interview situation. Videotaping can help clients review their performance to search for elements of their self-presentation, such as a nervous gesture, lack of eye contact, or a seemingly evasive or incongruent response, which might be interpreted as a danger signal by an employer (Cheramie, Fuller, Simmering, Marler, & Cox, 2014).

Danger signals, also sometimes referred to as *marginal utility signals*, are behaviors and background or status characteristics that employers regard as reducing the utility (i.e., the value) or increasing the risk of hiring a particular applicant. Role playing can help clients anticipate and respond to employer concerns about the so-called marginal utility signals such as age, a gap in work history, termination from a previous job, or an identifiable disability (Johnson & Wegmann, 1982). Both younger and older workers will find it to their advantage to practice making positive statements about their age. For example, older workers can be counseled to emphasize that they bring maturity, dependability, depth of knowledge, sound judgment, and experience to the job. Young workers can tout the value of their enthusiasm, energy, flexibility, and openness to new ideas since they come to the workplace with few preconceptions. Together the client and service provider should identify and rehearse the best way to explain extended periods of unemployment or previous terminations, particularly when related to such sensitive matters as an accusation, arrest, or conviction for a criminal offense. Clients who are comfortable, forthright, and willing to take the initiative with their intentions "to learn from past mistakes" can make positive impressions on employers. This sort of rehearsal may also be particularly important to differently abled clients who must convey their willingness and ability to be productive employers, but must also speak frankly about accommodation needs. A recent study by Thompson and Dickey (1994) revealed that few individuals with disabilities felt they knew how to communicate with employers about these matters.

Supervised search is a core feature of effective job search assistance. Supervised search involves supporting and monitoring client involvement in search-related behavior once the core behaviors have been specified and acquired. Both the learning of job search-related behaviors and the motivation to put them into practice can be enhanced through consistent use of positive reinforcement, including verbal encouragement and acknowledgement, for attempted behaviors. A number of studies highlight the importance of search-related effort to job search success. Individuals who find jobs more quickly tend to engage in more job search-related behaviors indicated by the number of job leads generated, applications filed, and interviews completed (Cheramie et al., 2014).

Supervised search also involves helping clients track the number and type of search efforts they make. Clients should be advised to keep a weekly count of direct contacts with employers; information interviews completed; requests made of relatives, friends, and acquaintances for job leads; new job leads generated; resumes sent out; applications filed; job interviews obtained; contacts with employment agencies; and reviews of newspaper want ads. Weekly totals can be tabulated or graphed to provide counselor and client with a clear message of effort.

In addition, supervised search can provide clients with the opportunity to debrief and reflect on search efforts, honing their search skills while receiving reinforcement and support. Overcoming setbacks has been demonstrated to have positive benefits for a variety of planned change activities (Janis, 1981; Meichenbaum, 1985). One of the consequences of trying harder may be that clients actually increase the amount of rejection they experience. Persistence in the face of such rejection is a key to eventual success in the labor market. Learning to cope with search-related setbacks involves anticipating situations in which a setback is likely to occur (e.g., a rejection from an employer after making an application or going to a job interview). Clients should be encouraged to generate alternatives to a dysfunctional response to setbacks such as reducing search efforts or failing to follow through on subsequent interviews. Alternatives might include seeking out support from a family member or friend or choosing among predetermined rewards that acknowledge the effort rather than the outcome. Clients should be positively reinforced for their efforts to anticipate, plan for, and cope with setbacks.

In addition to ongoing support and encouragement, clients may need a variety of material supports to carry out a job search (Oliveira, 2016). Discussion between provider and client should occur, early on, about access to key search resources such as telephone, word processing, copying, postage, transportation to interviews, and a reliable system for retrieving messages. Service providers need to be explicit about the kinds of assistance they can offer clients and they need to be sure that clients have plans for how to get the other material supports they need.

Setting aside a designated space in the home to better organize and support the search effort is advisable. This strategy can also help reinforce the notion that searching for a job is a structured activity, requiring a full-time commitment until employment is obtained. Public employment agencies may offer some resources to unemployed clients who use their services. Libraries and adult education centers often offer low-cost access to word processors and copiers. An answering machine is a lower cost alternative for receiving messages than an answering service. Clients without access to an automobile will need special assistance in getting to interviews. Public transportation requires that clients allow more time to arrive punctually at an interview site and that they take care when scheduling more than one interview in a day. Renting or borrowing a car may be an alternative for some clients.

One of the great advantages of individualized intervention is the ability to tailor strategies to specific clients. Obviously, clients who come into counseling with well-written, recently revised resumes will not need to revise them again. Individualized intervention can also focus on unique client concerns that might inhibit or impede job search activity, such as anxiety related to the job interview. In some cases clients may benefit from developing additional skills related to problem solving, stress management, assertiveness, anger, and conflict management. Job search assistance is most effective, however, when focused on providing clients with training in specific search-related information and behaviors and motivating them to take action as quickly as possible. Several sessions held in close succession for a week or two to develop job search competencies are preferable to the more traditional model of weekly counseling sessions. Once the client has entered the supervised search stage, weekly sessions should be sufficient to monitor and maintain client progress.

Job Coaching Job coaching typically involves providing a broader range of assistance to unemployed individuals. For the job coach, intervention activities may encompass all aspects of employment: choosing, finding, getting, and keeping a job. Job coaches may also play a more active role in the job acquisition process, acting more like job developers by contacting employers on behalf of clients or encouraging an employer to create a position for a particular client. This aspect of job coaching requires service providers to acquire extensive knowledge of the local labor market and close ties to employers.

Job coaching is often integral to the success of supported employment for clients with a history of chronic unemployment, substance abuse, or mental illness. Supported employment may involve some employer accommodation to special needs of clients, but typically relies on coaches to monitor and support client performance in the workplace. The Work Personality Profile (WPP) is an instrument designed to measure basic work habits and work-related behaviors in employment settings (Bolton & Roessler, 1986). Situational assessments can yield a realistic sample of the individual's responses to a wide variety of stimuli relevant to task performance and interpersonal relationship demands on the job. Job coaches work with clients to handle issues as diverse as notification of an employer about an absence or tardiness, management of conflicts between clients and coworkers or supervisors, and resolution of problems with child care or transportation.

Mentoring Mentors are sometimes used to do many of the same things that job between a client and a coworker or community volunteer rather than a paid, professional coach. A number of communities have formed mentoring programs to support and encourage individuals interested in changing careers or starting their own businesses. Social workers can make referrals on behalf of unemployed clients to such programs if they already exist in the community or can attempt to set up such a relationship on a more informal basis. This relationship can be especially helpful for individuals with disabilities who are even more likely to face unemployment (Bellman, Burgstahler, & Ladner, 2014). The local chamber of commerce and service organizations such as Kiwanis can provide assistance in finding mentors or can be encouraged to start such a program if none exists in the community.

Self-Employment Assistance The Small Business Administration often sponsors workshops on start-up and operation of small businesses for aspiring entrepreneurs, many targeted at women and members of ethnic minorities. Self-employment assistance programs have been provided in some communities. These programs increased the percentage of unemployed individuals who actually started their own businesses, among those who expressed such an intention (Weaver & Weaver, 2016). Such activities also provide opportunities for networking and mentoring. Mentoring and networking are important because of the technical expertise and social support provided, but they can also facilitate acquisition of financial resources to start a new business.

Vocational Education and Career Counseling Vocational and career counseling are integral to achieving objectives related to remediation, retooling, or upgrading job-related skills. Clients who have chosen to pursue education or training as an alternative to employment will require guidance and support as they sort through the maze of options, paperwork, and deadlines associated with their participation. Such activities may be particularly challenging for an individual who may still be reeling from job loss or who has been out of school for some time.

Vocational counseling can provide clients with greater clarity about their aptitudes and interests; information about training requirements for specific occupations or jobs; eligibility and admission criteria for various programs; availability of financial assistance during the education or training period; estimates of the commitment (e.g., time, money, effort) required to participate in one program or another; and information about logistics such as scheduling, child care, or transportation. Unless service providers are familiar with the range of services available to clients, referral to a local adult education program, community college, or vocational rehabilitation specialist is the best way to provide clients with the technical information and assistance they need.

Apart from acquiring technical information about education and training options, clients may need supportive counseling to manage stress, stay motivated, and overcome anxiety about their capacity to perform in classroom settings. Individual counseling can be used as a supplement to classroom activities to help clients learn how to organize learning into smaller, more manageable steps, attaching recognition, and reward to their accomplishments. Individualized intervention can also be used to focus on building specific skills that can enhance realization of education and training objectives such as time management, studying, and test taking.

Gowan and Nassar-McMillan (2001) found that women were less likely than men to attend job search workshops and action-oriented programs, but both genders were equally likely to attend self-awareness programs. Also, older individuals were more likely to attend job trainings than younger individuals. Thus, social workers must understand differences in demographic groups' patterns for seeking help in dealing with unemployment.

Adjusting to Retirement or Disability The decision not to return to work has profound repercussions for most clients. A great deal of support may be required in order to adjust to an abrupt transition from worker to nonworker. Those who lose jobs permanently due to illness or injury will likely need ongoing help adjusting to changes in their lives imposed by their conditions. Researchers have found that from 10 to 50% of individuals in western countries have been forced into early retirement. With the inability to choose retirement the adjustment period is more difficult to endure (Van Solinge & Henkens, 2008). Anticipating and developing strategies to compensate for losses associated with leaving the work role will be a central focus of individual intervention for clients who decide not to work. Strategies will typically include developing alternative sources of social support, self-esteem, and structure. Part-time work or volunteer activities can greatly ease the transition and guard against social isolation and withdrawal. One type of intervention that could be helpful, particularly for workers that will not seek reemployment, is for a social worker or therapist to assist the unemployed person begin creative writing project to explore the negative feelings associated with job loss (Soper & Von Bergen, 2001).

Group Intervention

Group interventions for the unemployed are a mainstay of traditional approaches to intervention with this population. Almost any intervention activity that can be delivered to an individual client can be delivered in a group context. Traditionally, group interventions have been primarily didactic in nature, focusing on knowledge building, cognitive skills development, or both. Increasingly, however, groups have gained recognition as important sources of socialization and support for unemployed clients (Milner, Krnjacki, Butterworth, & LaMontagne, 2016).

Job Clubs and Support Groups Although job search assistance skills can be taught in the context of individual counseling, such training more commonly occurs in a group. The group context provides more opportunities for members to practice skill building and acts as a source of additional social support and contacts that can generate job leads (Sillikar, 1993). Job search assistance programs that combine targeted search behavior training with small group interactions have been phenomenally successful in helping clients find work (Azrin, Flores, & Kaplan, 1975; Jones & Azrin, 1973; Murphy & King, 1996; Rife & Belcher, 1994; Stidham & Remley, 1992; U.S. DOL, 1995).

Job clubs and similar groups, including both time-limited and open-ended groups, have demonstrated their value as a basis for providing mutual support as well as job search assistance training. Social support has been identified as an important mediator of the negative effects associated with stressful life events, including unemployment (Caplan et al., 1989; Kates et al., 1990). The group has been found to maximize the motivation of individuals and provides a safe environment for learning. Researchers also found that the group was an added support when individuals experienced setbacks, often a barrier to job searches (Vuori, Price, Mutanen, & Malmberg-Heimonen, 2008). Unfortunately, since socialization and support are often tied to employment and employment-centered networks, job loss can result in diminished support at a point when such support is most needed. Mutual support from job search assistance groups may include instrumental support such as carpooling or exchange of child care. These groups can also provide clients with companionship, encouragement, and acknowledgment for success in performing search-related behaviors. Contact with others experiencing unemployment can assist in reducing stigma and other negative feelings associated with unemployment (Ho, Shih, Walters, & Pittinsky, 2011).

Job search assistance training programs and support groups also provide clients with many of the material resources needed to develop search materials and carry out search activities. These include phone banks, word processors, copiers, stationery, and postage stamps. Many programs have offered clients stipends or assistance with the costs of transportation to the training site or to potential employers. These groups also offer unemployed clients a structured setting in which to learn and carry out search activities, and provide staff to consult about issues that come up during the supervised search period.

Recruitment strategy is a major consideration for providers of job search assistance training in groups. A variety of strategies may be required in order to reach unemployed workers, including media announcements, referrals from local human service agencies, public employment services, unions, and businesses. Drop-off can be expected in the numbers of individuals who are eligible to participate, express interest in participating, and actually join the group. It is not unreasonable to recruit two or three times the number of clients intended to join the group.

Vocational Education and Job-Training Programs Classroom training is a mainstay of intervention for clients interested in additional education or training. Such programs run the gamut from remedial education in basic language and literacy skills and preparation for the General Equivalency Diploma (GED) to include more specialized vocational training for specific jobs or occupations and postsecondary education leading to a 2-year or 4-year degree. Basic education focuses on literacy training in the three R's and may supplement classroom teaching with computer-assisted programs that enable unemployed persons to pursue more individualized learning objectives. These programs have succeeded in raising reading levels, improving writing ability and math skills, and preparing individuals to pass the test earning them the GED. Unfortunately, by themselves, such programs have demonstrated little ability to improve job prospects, benefits, or earnings among the unemployed (U.S. DOL, 1995). Unless they are closely linked to local employers, short-term (3–6 months) vocational training programs seem not to improve employment outcomes.

Long-term job training and postsecondary education, on the other hand, significantly improve the life chances of the unemployed. More extensive and costly training programs such as the Job Corps have been demonstrated to improve rates, earnings, and employment retention and reduce the likelihood of problems with the law (Allan & Steffensmeier, 1989; U.S. DOL, 2000). Even greater benefits accrue to those who earn 2-year <4-year degrees. The gap in earnings between workers with high school diplomas and bachelor's degrees widened dramatically in the 1980s (U.S. DOL, 1995). Postsecondary education increases earnings 6–12% for every year acquired and, even without obtaining a degree, results in better employment outcomes. It is advisable to help clients place participation in short-term, basic education or job-training programs within this broader context. The greatest benefit of basic education and acquisition of the GED is the fact that it increases the likelihood that an individual will pursue postsecondary education.

Marital and Family Intervention

A primary aim of marital and family counseling or psychoeducation with one or more families ought to be to foster open communication at all stages during client assessment and intervention. Family roles and relationships may be significantly disrupted by changes in the employment status of a family member (Broman, Hamilton, & Hoffman, 1990). Ideally, the spouse or partner, and other family members of unemployed clients, should be carefully evaluated and other members of the family ought to receive services as needed. Special attention should be paid to a family member who has developed somatic symptoms, who exhibits a sudden change of mood or behavior, or who develops specific problems at home, work, or school.

Psychoeducation for unemployed clients, their partners, and their families can be important to maintaining the integrity and stability of the client system. Such services provide information to family members about the psychosocial impact of job loss on the unemployed member and possible repercussions for family interactions.

Psychoeducation can increase awareness among family members about when to seek help for additional family members who show signs of increased distress and about the kinds of services and supports available to them. Such efforts should also be used to activate support for the unemployed client. Family members can show support by becoming involved in the important decisions that clients have to make about their employment-related options, and can offer tangible and intangible support to the unemployed clients once they have developed an action plan. Clients engaged in job search, for example, can benefit from partners and family members who understand that looking for a job is a full-time job, countering misplaced expectations that the unemployed client is free to assume additional household duties or child care responsibility.

Group sessions for families can serve many of the same functions that support groups offer to unemployed clients. These include opportunities to interact with others sharing similar feelings and experiences, potentially reducing the stigma and other negative feelings experienced by families when one of their members loses a job. Support groups can counter tendencies for some families to experience increased isolation from the loss of work-related social relationships. In addition, family support groups can foster mutual support, increasing tangible supports through carpooling, child care exchange, and so on.

Marital and family counseling can also be used to identify and resolve problems that develop over the course of the unemployment episode or elude detection during the assessment process. Marital and family counseling should encourage flexibility and adaptability among families and should help them to develop and maintain a positive outlook while the unemployed client is making strides toward realizing employment-related goals. Families may need particular help in this regard when the period of unemployment is extensive (i.e., greater than 6 months), the unemployed member takes a lower status or lower paying job, or the unemployed member decides to withdraw from the labor force. Skill-oriented counseling can also be used to teach partners and family members better ways to communicate with one another or to manage conflict provoked by unemployment. Such skills can benefit families during the period of unemployment and can also be of value to the family well after employment issues have been resolved. It is also advisable to involve partners and family members in termination and follow-up activities.

Termination and Follow-Up

The termination process can add clarity to accomplishments and bring closure to the unemployment experience and the intervention process. Both individuals and their family members should be encouraged to reflect on and summarize positive outcomes, highlighting *j* successes and acknowledging contributions of partners and family members. A number of job clubs and other training programs have adopted more formal termination activities, often with a ceremonial or celebratory character, to mark transitions for clients when they finish training, launch a new business, or find a job. Of course, milestones like completing a training program, earning the GED, and finding a job need to be acknowledged even if they do not coincide with termination. Moreover, termination with clients adjusting to disability or retirement may have less obvious markers or milestones of progress, but warrants a similar congratulatory response.

Many programs have developed alumni groups and sponsor reunions as opportunities to follow up with individuals. Plans for follow-up should be revisited at termination and should be aimed at ensuring adequate opportunity to evaluate the need for further intervention. This may be particularly important for the downward status mover, that is, an individual who finds new employment, but in a much less prestigious or lucrative position (West, Nicholson, & Rees, 1990). In addition, follow-up allows for further evaluation of the effectiveness of intervention efforts. Both termination and follow-up are appropriate points to readminister tools used to assess clients and their families.

Community Prevention and Intervention Efforts

Supporting Employment Transitions Communities have a variety of options to support workers and their families while they are unemployed. Perhaps the single most important factor is maintaining the financial integrity of unemployed individuals and their families during a period of unemployment. Unemployment insurance is a primary mechanism for providing workers with financial support during job transitions, although only one or two out of every three workers are eligible for unemployment insurance. Unemployment compensation provides coverage for a maximum of 6 months, although many states have provisions for supplemental coverage (U.S. DOL, 1996). Twenty-six weeks may not be long enough in particularly hard hit areas or during periods when unemployment rates reach into the double digits. Legislative language that automatically triggers extended benefits when unemployment reaches a preset target has been proposed as an efficient strategy for dealing with compensation under such conditions.

Individual development accounts (IDAs) have been identified as a means for encouraging workers to upgrade their skills or retool so they remain employable in a constantly changing labor market. Like individual retirement accounts (IRAs), IDAs are proposed as tax-free savings accounts set up by workers for further education or training. Proposals have also been made to change the rules associated with IRAs to allow their use for similar purposes.

Gaps and discontinuities in health care coverage are also a major source of concern in most communities. In the United States, most health care coverage is tied to employment, and …, job loss typically means the loss of health care coverage. This is particularly problematic given the fact that unemployment poses increased health and mental health risks for workers and their families. Moreover, the Clinton administration took action intended to guarantee that insurance companies cover so-called preexisting conditions when workers move from one job to another. The fear of being denied coverage for such conditions has prevented many workers from leaving a job for a better position.

Community Planning Initiatives   Better community planning can contribute to lower unemployment and to better support for those who become unemployed. Most communities suffer from insufficient integration of economic development, workforce development, and human services planning. Discontinuities between job training and vocational education programs and opportunities in the local labor market greatly limit the usefulness of education and training programs, and make job placement much more difficult (U.S. DOL, 1995). One-stop service centers have been promoted as a way to develop a seamless, client-driven system, providing a single point of entry for assistance with employment-related problems (Downs, 1991). Such centers have been proposed as one way to better integrate and coordinate support for education and training programs with health and human services, bridging the gap between social services and human resources development and economic planning.

References

Allan, E. A., & Steffensmeier, D. J. (1989). Youth, underemployment, and property crime: Differential effects of job availability and job quality on juvenile and young adult arrest rates. *American Sociological Review 54*(1), 107.

Ametz, B. B., Brenner, S. O., Levi, L., Hjelm, R., Petterson, I., Wasserman, J., ... Vigas, M. (1991). Neuroendocrine and immuno-logic effects of unemployment and job insecurity. *Psychotherapy and Psychosomatics, 55*, 76–80.

Andrews, F. M., & Withey, S. B. (1976). *Social indicators of well-being: American's perceptions of life quality*. New York, NY: Plenum Press.

Azrin, N., Flores, T., & Kaplan, S. (1975). Job finding club: A group assisted program for obtaining employment. *Behavior Research and Therapy, 13*, 17–22.

Bartell, M., & Bartell, R. (1985). An integrative perspective on the psychological response of women and men to unemployment. *Journal of Economic Psychology, 6*, 27–49.

Beck, A. T., & Beck, R. W. (1972). Screening depressed patients in family practice: A rapid technique. *Postgraduate Medicine, 52*, 81–85.

Beck, A. T., Ward, C. H., Mendelsen, M., Mock, J., & Erbaugh, J. (1961). An inventory for measuring depression. *Archives of General Psychiatry, 4*, 561–571.

Bellman, S., Burgstahler, S., & Ladner, R. (2014). Work-based learning experiences help students with disabilities transition to careers: A case study of University of Washington projects. *Work, 48*(3), 399–405.

Bezanson, B. J. (2004). The application of solution-focused work in employment counseling. *Journal of Employment Counseling, 41*(4), 183–191.

Blustein, D. L., Kozan, S., & Connors-Kellgren, A. (2013). Unemployment and underemployment: A narrative analysis about loss. *Journal of Vocational Behavior, 82*(3), 256–265.

Bolton, B., & Roessler, R. (1986). *Manual for the work personality profile*. Fayetteville, AR: University of Arkansas, Arkansas Research and Training Center in Vocational Rehabilitation.

Borgen, W. A., Hatch, W. E., & Amundson, N. E. (1990). The experience of unemployment for university graduates: An exploratory study. *Journal of Employment Counseling, 27*, 104–112.

Boss, P. (1988). *Family stress management*. Newbury Park, CA: Sage.

Brenner, M. H. (2016). Duration of unemployment and self-perceived health in Europe. *SPH Faculty Publications, 2*.

Brenner, S. (1987). Economic change, alcohol consumption and heart disease mortality in nine industrialized countries. *Social Science & Medicine, 25*, 119–132.

Broman, C. L., Hamilton, V. L., & Hoffman, W. S. (1990). Unemployment and its effects on families: Evidence from a plant closing study. *American Journal of Community Psychology, 18*, 643–659.

Bureau of Labor Statistics. (2008). *Employment situation summary for October, 2008*. Washington, DC: U.S. Department of Labor. Retrieved November 17, 2008, from http://www.bls.gov/news.release/empsit.nr0.htm

Bureau of Labor Statistics. (2012). *Employment situation summary for July, 2012*. Washington, DC: U.S. Department of Labor. Retrieved August 16, 2012, from http://www.bls.gov/news.release/empsit.nr0.htm

Bureau of Labor Statistics. (2019). *Employment situation summary for August 2019 Table A-15*. Washington, DC: U.S. Department of Labor. Retrieved September 27, 2019 from https://www.bls.gov/news.release/empsit.t15.htm

Caplan, R. D., Vinokur, A. D., Price, R. H., & van Ryn, M. (1989). Job seeking, reemployment, and mental health: A randomized field experiment in coping with job loss. *Journal of Applied Psychology, 74*(5), 759–769.

Cheramie, R., Fuller, B., Simmering, M. J., Marler, L. E., & Cox, S. S. (2014). Improving career development in students by developing job analysis skills. *Journal of Learning in Higher Education, 10*(2), 49–54.

Challenges and Opportunities in Workforce and Labor Market Information. *Workforce Information Advisory Council Informational Report released July, 2017*. https://www.doleta.gov/wioa/wiac/docs/2016_WIAC_Informational_Report_(full).pdf

Crowe, L., & Butterworth, P. (2016). The role of financial hardship, mastery and social support in the association between employment status and depression: Results from an Australian longitudinal cohort study. *BMJ Open, 6*(5), e009834.

Curadi, C. B., Todd, M., Duke, M., & Ames, G. (2009). Problem drinking, unemployment, and intimate partner violence among a sample of construction industry workers and their partners. *Journal of Family Violence, 24*, 63–74.

Daly, M., & Delaney, L. (2013). The scarring effect of unemployment throughout adulthood on psychological distress at age 50: Estimates controlling for early adulthood distress and childhood psychological factors. *Social Science & Medicine, 80*, 19–23.

Derogatis, L. R. (1994). *SCL-90-R: Administration, scoring, and procedures manual*. Minneapolis, MN: National Computer Systems.

Derogatis, L. R., Lipmann, R. S., Rickles, K., Uhlenhuth, E. H., & Covi, L. (1974). The Hopkins Symptom Checklist (HSCL): A measure of primary symptom dimensions. *Psychological Measurements in Psychopharmacology, 7*, 79–110.

Dooley, D., & Catalano, R. (1988). Recent research on the psychological effects of unemployment. *Journal of Social Issues, 44*, 1–12.

Downs, S. (1991). *Streamlining and integrating human resource development services for adults*. Washington, DC: National Governors' Association.

Eitel, K. M. (2014). *A phenomenological study of how individuals experience reemployment after being laid off* (Doctoral dissertation). Saint Mary's University of Minnesota, Winona, MN.

Epstein, N. B., Baldwin, L. M., & Bishop, D. S. (1983). The McMaster family assessment device. *Journal of Marital and Family Therapy, 9*, 171–180.

Ervasti, H., & Venetoklis, T. (2010). Unemployment and subjective well-being: An empirical test of deprivation theory incentive paradigm and financial strain approach. *Acta Sociologica, 53*, 119–139.

Feather, N. T. (2012). *The psychological impact of unemployment*. New York, NY: Springer Science & Business Media.

Fergusson, D. M., McLeod, G. F., & Horwood, L. J. (2014). Unemployment and psychosocial outcomes to age 30: A fixed-effects regression analysis. *Australian & New Zealand Journal of Psychiatry, 48*(8), 735–742.

Fernald, J., & Li, H. (2019). "Is slow still the new normal for GDP growth?". *FRBSF Economic Letter, 17*.

Fortney, J., Rushton, G., Wood, S., Zhang, L., Xu, S., Dong, F., & Rost, K. (2007). Community-level risk factors for depression hospitalizations. *Administration and Policy in Mental Health and Mental Health Services Research, 34*, 343–352.

Fraze, J. (1988). Displaced workers: Oakies of the 80's. *Personnel Administrator, 33*, 42–51.

Gallo, W., Bradley, E., Sigel, M., & Kasl, S. (2000). Health effects of involuntary job loss among older workers. *Journals of Gerontology, 55*, 131–140.

Goldberg, D. P. (1978). *Manual of the general health questionnaire*. Windsor, England: NFER NELSON.

Gowan, M. A., & Nassar-McMillan, S. C. (2001). Examination of individual differences in participation in outplacement program activities after a job loss. *Journal of Employment Counseling, 38*, 185–196.

Griffin, P., McGaw, B., & Care, E. (2012). *Assessment and teaching of 21st century skills* (p. 36). Dordrecht, The Netherlands: Springer.

Guindon, M. H., & Smith, B. (2002). Emotional barriers to successful reemployment: Implications for counselors. *Journal of Employment Counseling, 39*, 73–82.

Halli, S. S., & Rao, K. V. (2013). *Advanced techniques of population analysis*. New York, NY: Springer Science & Business Media.

Hayhoe, C. R. (2006). Helping families in transition due to unemployment. *Journal of Human Behavior in the Social Environment, 13*, 63–73.

Ho, G. C., Shih, M., Walters, D. J., & Pittinsky, T. L. (2011). *The stigma of unemployment: When joblessness leads to being jobless*. Los Angeles, CA: University of California.

Howe, G., Levy, M., & Caplan, R. (2004). Depressive symptoms in couples: Common stressors, stress transmission, or relationship disruption. *Journal of Family Psychology, 18*, 639–650.

Jackson, P. R. (1994). Influences on commitment to employment and commitment to work. In A. Bryson & S. McKay (Eds.), *Is it worth working? Factors affecting labour supply* (pp. 110–121). London, England: Policy Studies Institute.

Jacobsen, D. (1987). Models of stress and meanings of unemployment: Reactions to job loss among technical professionals. *Social Science & Medicine, 24*, 13–21.

Janis, I. L. (Ed.). (1981). *Counseling on personal decisions: Theory and research on short term helping relationships*. New Haven, CT: Yale University Press.

Joel Wong, Y., Uhm, S. Y., & Li, P. (2012). Asian Americans' family cohesion and suicide ideation: Moderating and mediating effects. *American Journal of Orthopsychiatry, 82*(3), 309.

Johnson, M., & Wegmann, R. (1982). *Job search training for youth*. Salt Lake City, UT: Olympus.

Jones, R., & Azrin, N. (1973). An experimental application of a social reinforcement approach to the problem of job finding. *Journal of Applied Behavior Analysis, 6*, 345–353.

Karger, H. J., & Stoesz, D. (2006). *American social welfare policy: A pluralist approach*. Boston, MA: Pearson Education.

Kasl, S., & Cobb, S. (1979). Some mental health consequences of plant closings and job loss. In L. Ferman & J. Gordus (Eds.), *Mental health and the economy* (pp. 255–299). Kalamazoo, MI: Upjohn Institute for Employment Research.

Kates, N., Greiff, B. S., & Hagen, D. Q. (1990). The clinical practice series, No. 12. The psychosocial impact of job loss. Arlington, VA, US: American Psychiatric Association.

Kinicki, A. J., & Latack, J. C. (1990). Explication of the construct of coping with involuntary job loss. *Journal of Vocational Behavior, 36*, 339–360.

Kirk, J. J., & Belovics, R. (2005). Recommendations and resources for counseling older workers. *Journal of Employment Counseling, 42*, 50–59.

Korner, A., Reitzle, M., & Silbereisen, R. K. (2012). Work-related demands and life satisfaction: The effects of engagement and disengagement among employed and long-term unemployed people. *Journal of Vocational Behavior, 80*, 187–196.

Langens, T. A., & Mose, E. (2006). Coping with unemployment: Relationships between duration of unemployment, coping styles, and subjective well-being. *Journal of Applied Biobehavioral Research, 11*(3–4), 189–208.

Leana, C. R., & Feldman, D. C. (1991). Gender differences in responses to unemployment. *Journal of Vocational Behavior, 38*(1), 65–77.

Ling, T. J., & O'Brien, K. M. (2013). Connecting the forgotten half: The school-to-work transition of noncollege-bound youth. *Journal of Career Development, 40*(4), 347–367.

Lovell, V., & Oh, G. (2005). Women's job loss and material hardship. *Journal of Women, Politics & Policy, 27*(3/4), 169–183.

MacNeil, G. (1991). A short-form scale to measure alcohol abuse. *Research on Social Work Practice, 1*, 68–75.

Mallinckrodt, B., & Fretz, B. R. (1988). Social support and the impact of job loss on older professionals. *Journal of Counseling Psychology, 35*, 281–286.

Mann, A. R., Miller, D. A., & Baum, M. (1995). Coming of age in hard times. *Journal of Health & Social Policy, 6*(3), 41–57.

McCubbin, H. L., & Thompson, A. I. (Eds.). (1991). *Family assessment inventories for research and practice*. Madison, WI: University of Wisconsin.

McGonagle, K. A., Kessler, R. C., & Schilling, E. A. (1992). The frequency of marital disagreements in a community sample. *Journal of Social and Personal Relationships, 9*, 507–524.

McKee-Ryan, F. M., Song, Z., Wanberg, C., & Kinicki, A. J. (2005). Psychological and physical well-being during unemployment. *Journal of Applied Psychology, 90*(1), 53–76.

McMullin, R. E., & Gehlaar, M. (1990). *Thinking and drinking: An expose of drinkers' distorted beliefs*. Wheelers Hill, VIC: Marlin Publications.

Meichenbaum, D. (1985). *Stress inoculation training: A clinical guidebook*. New York, NY: Pergamon Press.

Milner, A., Krnjacki, L., Butterworth, P., & LaMontagne, A. D. (2016). The role of social support in protecting mental health when employed and unemployed: A longitudinal fixed-effects analysis using 12 annual waves of the HILDA cohort. *Social Science & Medicine, 153*, 20–26.

Mindzak, M. W. (2016). *Exploring the working-lives of unemployed and underemployed teachers in Ontario* (Doctoral dissertation). The University of Western Ontario, London, ON.

Moser, K. A., Fox, A. J., & Jones, D. R. (1984). Unemployment and mortality in the opcs longitudinal study. *The Lancet 324*(8415), 1324–1329.

Murphy, G. C., & Athanasou, J. A. (1999). The effect of unemployment on mental health. *Journal of Occupational and Organizational Psychology, 72*, 83–99.

Murphy, G. C., & King, N. J. (1996). Australian data supporting validity claims of Axrin's Job Club program to reduce unemployment. *The Behavior Therapist, 79*(7), 104–106.

Murray, C. L., Gien, L., & Solberg, S. M. (2003). A comparison of the mental health of employed and unemployed women in the context of a massive layoff. *Women & Health, 37*(2), 55–72.

National Commission for Employment Policy. (1988). *Survey of basic skills remediation practices in the JTPA youth programs* (Unpublished document).

Oliveira, B. L. C. N. D. (2016). *Psycap and amotivation to search for a job: the role of need frustration and family support* (Doctoral dissertation). Universidade NOVA de Lisboa, Lisbon, Portugal.

Paul, K. I., & Moser, K. (2009). Unemployment impairs mental health: Meta-analyses. *Journal of Vocational Behavior, 74*, 264–282.

Quinn, R. P., & Shepard, L. J. (1974). *The 1972-73 quality of employment survey: Descriptive statistics, with comparison data from the 1969-70 survey of working conditions*. Ann Arbor, MI: University of Michigan, Institute for Social Research.

Randolph, L. (1977). The CES-D Scale: A self-report depression scale for research in the general population. *Applied Psychological Measurement, 1*, 385–401.

Rife, J., & Belcher, J. (1994). Assisting unemployed older workers become re-employed: An experimental evaluation. *Research on Social Work Practice, 4*, 3–13.

Rosenbaum, M. (1980). A schedule for assessing self-control behaviors: Preliminary findings. *Behavior Therapy, 11*, 109–121.

Rosenberg, M. (1965). *Society and the adolescent self-image*. Princeton, NJ: Princeton University Press.

Rowley, K. M., & Feather, N. T. (1987). The impact of unemployment in relation to age and length of unemployment. *Journal of Occupational Psychology, 60*, 323–332.

Ruhm, C. J. (2016). Health effects of economic crises. *Health Economics, 25*(S2), 6–24.

Russell, J., Holmstrom, A. J., & Clare, D. D. (2015). The differential impact of social support types in promoting new entrant job search self-efficacy and behavior. *Communication Research Reports, 32*(2), 170–179.

Russell, J. C. (2011). The use of narratives to contextualize the experiences and needs of unemployed, underemployed, and displaced workers. *Journal of Employment Counseling, 48*, 50–62.

Sales, E. (1995). Surviving unemployment: Economic resources and job loss. *Social Work, 40*(4), 483–491.

Sampson, J. P., Jr., & Reardon, R. C. (1990). Evaluating computer-assisted career guidance systems: Synthesis and implications. *Journal of Career Development, 17*, 143–149.

Sampson, J. P., Jr., Reardon, R. C., Humphreys, J. K., Peterson, G. W., Evans, M. A., & Dombrowski, D. (1990). A differential feature-cost analysis of nine computer assisted career guidance systems (3rd ed.). *Journal of Career Development, 17*, 81–112.

Selzer, M. L. (1971). The Michigan Alcoholism Screening Test: The quest for a new diagnostic instrument. *American Journal of Psychiatry, 127*, 89–94.

Sersic, D. M. (2006). When does unemployment imply impaired psychological health? The mediating role of psychological deprivation and social support. *Review of Psychology, 13*(1), 43–50.

Sherer, M., Maddox, J. E., Mercandante, B., Prentice-Dunn, S., Jacobs, B., & Rogers, R. W. (1982). The Self-Efficacy Scale: Construction and validation. *Psychological Reports, 51*, 663–671.

Sillikar, S. A. (1993). The role of social contacts in the successful job search. *Journal of Employment Counseling, 30*(1), 25–34.

Snyder, K., & Nowak, T. C. (1984). Job loss and demoralization: Do women fare better than men? *International Journal of Mental Health, 13*, 92–106.

Soper, B., & Von Bergen, C. W. (2001). Employment counseling and life stressors: Coping through expressive writing. *Journal of Employment Counseling, 38*, 150–160.

Spanier, S. (1976). Measuring dyadic adjustment: New scales for assessing the quality of marriage and similar dyads. *Journal of Marriage and the Family, 38*, 15–28.

Spanier, S., Lewis, R. A., & Cole, C. A. (1975). Marital adjustment over the family life cycle. *Journal of Marriage and the Family, 37*, 275–362.

Spielberger, C. D., Gorsuch, R. L., & Lushene, R. E. (1970). *Manual for state-trait anxiety inventory*. Palo Alto, CA: Consulting Psychologists Press.

Stein, C. H., Bush, E. G., Ross, R. R., & Ward, M. (1992). Married couples in relation to marital satisfaction and individual well-being. *Journal of Social and Personal Relationships, 9*, 365–383.

Stidham, H., & Remley, T. (1992). Job club methodology applied to a workforce setting. *Journal of Employment Counseling, 29*, 69–76.

Strom, S. (2003). Unemployment and families: A review of research. *Social Service Review, 77*, 399–430.

Sum, A., Fogg, N., & Taggert, R. (1988). *Withered dreams: The decline in the economic fortunes of young, non-college educated male adults and their families* (report to the William T. Grant Foundation Commission on Family, Work, and Citizenship). New York, NY: William T. Grant Foundation.

Tal, A., Moran, G., Rooth, D. O., & Bendick, M., Jr. (2009). Using situation testing to document employment discrimination against persons with psychiatric disabilities. *Employee Relations Law Journal, 35*(3), 40.

Taris, T. W. (2002). Unemployment and mental health: A longitudinal perspective. *International Journal of Stress Management, 9*, 43–57.

Taylor, J. (1953). A personality scale of manifest anxiety. *Journal of Abnormal and Social Psychology, 48*, 285–290.

Thompson, A. R., & Dickey, K. D. (1994). Self-perceived job search skills of college students with disabilities. *Rehabilitation Counseling Bulletin, 37*(4), 358–370.

Turner, J. B., Kessler, R. C., & House, J. S. (1991). Factors facilitating adjustment to unemployment: Implications for intervention. *American Journal of Community Psychology 19*(4), 521–542.

U.S. Department of Labor. (1995). *What's working (and what's not).* Washington, DC: U.S. Department of Labor, Office of the Chief Economist.

U.S. Department of Labor. (1996). *Labor force statistics from the current population survey* [online]. Bureau of Labor Statistics Homepage, cpsinfo@bls.gov.

U.S. Department of Labor. (2000). *Job Corps, AmeriCorps, and Peace Corps: An overview.* Retrieved from https://www.bls.gov/careeroutlook/2000/Fall/art03.pdf

U.S. Department of Labor. (2006). Employment status of the civilian noninstitutional population, 1940 to date. *Household Data Annual Averages.* Retrieved March 11, 2007, from www.dol.gov

Van Solinge, H., & Henkens, K. (2008). Adjustment to and satisfaction with retirement: Two of a kind? *Psychology and Aging, 23*(2), 422–434.

Viet, C. T., & Ware, I. E. (1983). The structure of psychological distress and well-being in general populations. *Journal of Consulting and Clinical Psychology, SI*, 730–742.

Vinokur, A. R., Michelle, G., & Edward, P. R. (1991). Long-Term Follow-Up and Benefit-Cost Analysis of the Jobs Program: A Preventive Intervention for the Unemployed. *The Journal of applied psychology, 76*, 213–9. https://doi.org/10.1037/0021-9010.76.2.213.

Vuori, J., Price, R. H., Mutanen, P., & Malmberg-Heimonen, I. (2008). Effective group training techniques in job-search training. *Journal of Occupational Health Psychology, 10*(3), 261–275.

Walsh, S., & Jackson, P. R. (1995). Partner support and gender: Contexts for coping with job loss. *Journal of Occupational and Organizational Psychology 68(3)*, 253–268.

Wanberg, C. R. (2012). The individual experience of unemployment. *Annual Review of Psychology, 63*, 369–396.

Warr, P. B. (1978). A study of psychological well-being. *British Journal of Psychology, 69*, 112–121.

Warr, P. B., & Jackson, P. R. (1984). Men without jobs: Some correlates of age and length of unemployment. *Journal of Occupational Psychology, 57*, 77–85.

Warr, P. B., & Parry, G. (1982). Paid employment and women's psychological well-being. *Psychological Bulletin, 91*, 498–516.

Waters, L. E., & Moore, K. A. (2001). Coping with economic deprivation during unemployment. *Journal of Economic Psychology, 22*, 461–482.

Weaver, R. L., & Weaver, R. L. (2016). Social enterprise self-employment programs: A two-dimensional human capital investment strategy. *Social Enterprise Journal, 12*(1), 4–20.

West, M., Nicholson, N., & Rees, A. (1990). The outcome of downward managerial mobility. *Journal of Organizational Behavior, 11*, 119–134.

Winefield, A. H., Tiggemann, M., & Winefield, H. R. (1990). Factors moderating the psychological impact of unemployment at different ages. *Personality and Individual Differences, 11*(1), 45–52.

Winefield, A. H., Tiggemann, M., & Winefield, H. R. (1991). The psychological impact of unemployment and unsatisfactory employment in young men and women: Longitudinal and cross-sectional data. *British Journal of Psychology, 82*(4), 473–486.

Chapter 11
Marital Conflict, Intimate Partner Violence, and Family Preservation

M. E. Betsy Garrison and Sarah V. Curtis

This chapter examines the empirical literature concerning family preservation. In this chapter, the term *family preservation* is being used in the nominal sense to answer the question, What do we know about keeping families together? Our definition of preservation does not include governmental legislation, such as the Family Preservation Act, or interventions specific to Intensive Family Preservation Services (For more information about either of these two topics, the reader is directed toward Banks and Scott (2016) and Lin and Lee (2016)).

When discussing families, the supposition must be made that not only do a multitude of problems exist in family life, but these problems interrelate. While, hypothetically, the problems of families may be separated, in reality, family problems are not distinct. Rarely, if ever, does family intervention involve the diagnosis, treatment, or both of a single, unrelated symptom, problem, or disorder. Often, for effective and long-term intervention, problems must be treated on multiple levels with a variety of therapeutic strategies.

Due to this multiplicity and interrelatedness, every chapter of this handbook has relevance to family preservation. So as not to duplicate the other chapters, however, we intentionally focus on family problems and disorders not explicitly discussed elsewhere in the book. Thus, we discuss marital conflict in terms of not only how couple members are affected, but also how family life impacts the health and well-being of the children. We do not address specific problems, such as chemical dependency, juvenile delinquency, and eating disorders, even though these problems affect family preservation, and we discuss family violence strictly in terms of domestic or spousal abuse, rather than child abuse, sibling abuse, or elder abuse, even though these problems, obviously, affect family preservation.

M. E. B. Garrison (✉)
School of Human Environmental Sciences, University of Arkansas, Fayetteville, AR, USA
e-mail: megarris@uark.edu

S. V. Curtis
College of Social Work, University of Tennessee, Knoxville, TN, USA

© Springer Nature Switzerland AG 2019   227
J. S. Wodarski, L. M. Hopson (eds.), *Empirically Based Interventions Targeting Social Problems*, https://doi.org/10.1007/978-3-030-28487-9_11

Marital Conflict

Definition

This chapter's discussion of marital conflict includes research on various stages of troubled marriages to the extent that couples have sought help, have been referred to various social service agencies, or were solicited to participate in studies that provided some type of assessment, psychoeducation, or intervention. The terms *marital discord*, *marital distress*, and *marital dissatisfaction* are used interchangeably in this body of literature and are included in our discussion of marital conflict.

Prevalence, Incidence, and Costs

Presumably, all marriages involve some degree of marital conflict, given that life is inherently stressful and that all relationships involve some degree of dissension. According to the National Survey of Family Growth, 48% of marriages will end in divorce before the 20th anniversary (CDC, 2010). The majority of these cases will involve at least one child under the age of 18 (Ganong, Coleman, Markham, & Rothrauff, 2011).

For several years now, marital conflict has been identified as a risk factor for health and mental problems and a major disruption in the workplace (Snyder, Heyman, & Haynes, 2005). Choi and Marks (2008) suggest that separation and divorce have strong negative consequences for the mental and physical health of both spouses. Lower marital quality has been linked to high levels of depression and a lower quality of life (Choi & Marks, 2008). Researchers compared the hypothetical cost of marital therapy, divorce therapy, and medical service usage, using secondary data from empirical studies. Results indicate that marital therapy is mainly paid by the government and it is less costly than divorce therapy and medical service usage (Caldwell, Woolley, & Caldwell, 2007).

Social Work Involvement

Riggio (2004) and Cui and Fincham (2010) stated that marital conflict and divorce are associated with multiple family problems that negatively affect the well-being of family members. The authors state their belief that the "reduction of marital conflict and the prevention of divorce should represent high priorities for modern families" (p. 462). Marital and family therapy is caught up in the current health care revolution and demands to demonstrate the effectiveness and cost-effectiveness of their interventions are being made (Moore & Crane, 2014). Researchers demonstrated that couples' marital happiness increased significantly following participation in cognitive behavioral group marital therapy. However, the program had a differential effect on the improvement of self-perceived problem-solving abilities depending on the initial problem-solving ability levels (Bélanger, Laporte, Sabourin, & Wright, 2015).

These demands present a challenge to family social workers to keep investigating and implementing interventions that meet the therapeutic needs of the growing number of people who are affected by marital conflict, divorce, and remarriage. Family social workers need to continue the struggle to balance their own Code of Ethics from the National Association of Social Workers (NASW) and standards of practice with the demands of the health care system for therapeutic and cost-effective interventions. Bagarozzi suggests that "social workers become advocates for the American family in this era of managed care" (Bagarozzi, 1995, p. 101).

Assessment Methods

In an article by Boughner, Hayes, Bubenzer, and West (1994), marital and family therapists reported that the two most commonly used assessments for all types of marital and family therapy were the Minnesota Multiphasic Personality Inventory-2 (MMPI-2) and the Myers-Briggs Type Indicator (MBTI). These instruments are typically given to individual members of the marital couple and interpreted separately. Information is provided by the publishers of these instruments on how couple profiles may be derived from the individual scores. Please refer to the article mentioned above for further information. Three other instruments commonly used to assess marital and family issues were reviewed that are more systemic in nature and measure relational rather than individual personality issues. These instruments are described in the following sections.

Dyadic Adjustment Scale (DAS) The DAS, developed by Spanier (1976, 1989), is a 32-item self-report assessment that measures the marital adjustment of couples with a total score and scores on four subscales: dyadic consensus, dyadic satisfaction, dyadic cohesion, and affectional expression. Busby, Christensen, Crane, and Larson (1995) shortened the DAS to 14 items to create the Revised Dyadic Adjustment Scale. The DAS is one of the most used measures of relationship adjustment and has been repeatedly affirmed through reliability and validity testing (South, Krueger, & Iacono, 2009). South et al. (2009) recently tested the DAS for invariance across gender. The study established invariance across gender which added to the validity of the DAS. Because of the invariance across gender, one can conclude that differences between men and women can be attributed to actual differences in relationship adjustment instead of arising from flaws in the instrument (p. 626). Ward, Lundberg, Zabriskie, and Berrett (2009) also confirmed the validity of the RDAS through comparing it with the Satisfaction with Married Life Scale. The instrument's manual is available from Western Psychological Services.

Recent studies used the DAS in combination with several other instruments to: (a) examine the role of collaboration in late-midlife and older couples' psychological well-being during times of illness (Schindler, Berg, Butler, Fortenberry, & Wiebe, 2010), (b) examine the role of the spouse/partner relationship in mediating quality of life for the couple (Morgan, 2008), (c) assess traditional versus integrative behavioral couple therapy for significantly and chronically distressed married couples (Christensen et al., 2004), and (d) improve relationships by evaluating the mechanisms of change in couple therapy (Doss, Thum, Sevier, & Atkins, 2005).

Marital Satisfaction Inventory (MSI) The MSI, developed by Snyder, Wills, and Keiser (1981), consists of 280 true-false, self-report items of 11 scales: conventionalization (social desirability), global distress, affective communication, problem-solving communication, time together, disagreements about finances, sexual dissatisfaction, role orientation, family history of distress, dissatisfaction with children, and conflict over children. Balderrama-Durbin, Snyder, and Balsis (2015) and Lou, Lin, Chen, Balderrama-Durbin, and Snyder (2016) affirm the reliability and validity of the MSI. The Marital Satisfaction Inventory was revised in 2008 by Herrington, Mitchell, Castellani, Joseph, Snyder, and Gleaves (Herrington et al., 2008). The revised version distinguishes between overt conflict and emotional distance, which the original measure did not accomplish. MSI instruments and manual are available from Multi-Health Systems, Inc.

Recent studies used the MSI in combination with other instruments: (a) in a validation study of the MSI with gay, lesbian, and cohabiting heterosexual couples (Means-Christensen, Snyder, & Negy, 2003), (b) in an assessment of intimate relationships of Chinese couples in Taiwan (Lou et al., 2016), (c) in examining factors of marital satisfaction among young couples including various racial groups (MacKenzie et al., 2014), and (d) in validating the importance of evaluating both partners (Whisman, Uebelacker, & Weinstock, 2004).

Child Behavior Checklist (CBCL) The CBCL is a 118-item parent-report scale designed to measure parents' perceptions of the behavioral problems and symptoms of children ages 4–18 (Achenbach, 1991). A Teacher's Report Form and a Youth Self-Report Form are also available. In a family systems approach, requesting the perceptions of parents, teachers, and youths is an important part of the assessment process. A computerized profile as well as the instruments and manual are available from the University Associates in Psychiatry, Burlington, VT 05401.

Several studies attest to the use of CBCL as well as its reliability and validity (e.g., Macmann, Barnett, & Lopez, 1993). These studies include: (a) comparing the CBCL with the Behavior Rating Inventory of Executive Function (BRIEF) for Children in Uganda and finding the structural overlap (Familiar et al., 2015), (b) assessing symptom differentiation of anxiety and depression across youth development and clinic-referred/nonreferred samples (Price et al., 2013), (c) evaluating children with attention-deficit hyperactivity disorder (Wiedenhoff, 1994), and (d) the clinical status of children in state's custody (Heflinger, Simpkins, & Combs-Orme, 2000).

Effective Interventions

The Premarital Relationship Enhancement Program (PREP) was used by Van Widenfelt, Hosman, Schaap, and van der Staak (1996) as a preventative intervention program. The PREP is a cognitive-behaviorally oriented intervention derived from a behavior-competency model of marital success (for a more comprehensive description, refer to Renick, Blumberg, & Markham, 1992). Although the program was originally designed for couples who are marrying for the first time, it is also applicable to remarital couples. Special issues can be incorporated into the treatment that help integrate children from a previous marriage into a new family system (Carroll & Doherty, 2003; Markman, Floyd, Stanley, & Lewis, 1986).

Cognitive Marital Therapy (CMT) was the treatment used by Waring, Stalker, Carver, and Gitta (1991) in a study of 41 couples with severe marital discord. CMT is a structured, time-limited intervention that includes marital self-disclosure. The treatment includes a nine-step protocol of things not to do. The *CMT Training Manual* and videotapes of the techniques are available from the authors (Waring et al., 1991).

A study using behavioral marital therapy was designed by Gray-Little, Baucom, and Hamby (1996). The researchers examined the association of marital power type to marital adjustment and response to behavioral marital therapy in distressed couples. Besides receiving behavioral marital therapy, couples received various combinations of emotional expressiveness training and cognitive restructuring. Results indicated that wife-dominant couples improved the most, reporting increased marital satisfaction and demonstrating improved communication.

In addition to the content of PREP, the Australian Self-PREP program provided an additional self-regulation component (Halford, Sanders, & Behrens, 2001). Research showed that following the completion of the Australian Self-PREP program, couples at high risk of relationship problems are more likely to be satisfied with their relationship at 4-year follow-up than couples who are not participating in the program (Hahlweg & Richter, 2010).

The Children First Program (CFP) was evaluated by Kramer and Washo (1993). This program was developed to help groups of divorcing parents become more sensitive to their children's needs. Parents attend two 90-min sessions, conducted 1 week apart, in which they view videotaped vignettes. Also included in the program is a talk by a local judge and discussions led by a trained moderator. The program was found to have both positive and negative outcomes. On the positive side, parents found the CFP to be helpful and thought it would benefit other divorcing parents. Negative aspects presented themselves at follow-up—when parents perceived their children to be better adjusted to divorce. Respondents related these findings to the passage of time since marital separation rather than to participation in the program. The study suggested that the CFP may hold greater benefits for parents who report higher levels of conflict with their former spouses.

Another evaluation was conducted by Hughes, Clark, Schaefer-Hernan, and Good (1994) determining the effectiveness of a newsletter intervention for divorced mothers. The intervention consisted of a series of several newsletters that addressed issues identified as important to single mothers immediately following divorce. Each newsletter provided information based on current research knowledge that would help children adjust to the divorce. Specific practical suggestions were given to mothers as well as suggestions for further reading. Results indicated that over half of the participants read the newsletter from cover to cover and reported that they felt more hopeful and confident as a result of reading this material. The authors pose an important challenge to researchers and family life educators to create newsletters that are effective in helping families through this difficult transition.

Symons (2010) and Cookro (2009) evaluated the long-term effects of divorce mediation and resolution of child custody disputes. Symons (2010) provides an overview of guidelines, the assessment process, and the empirical basis for child custody and access assessment.

Nine years previous to the study, separated parents were randomly assigned to either a mediation group or to a traditional adversarial group. Results indicated that noncustodial parents assigned to mediation reported having more frequent current contact with their children as well as greater involvement in current decisions about them. Parents in the mediation group also reported more frequent communication about their children during the period since dispute resolution. This study supports a growing trend in the laws that are forcing parents to determine their own custody arrangements, which opens the door to even more divorce and family mediation, an area in which many family social workers are well-trained.

Intimate Partner Violence

Definition

For the purposes of this chapter, intimate partner violence is "violence committed by a spouse, ex-spouse, or current or former boyfriend or girlfriend and includes both heterosexual and same-sex couples" (National Center for Injury Prevention and Control, 2003, p. 3). This definition excludes violence toward elders and children. Other terms in the literature include spouse abuse, domestic violence, and relationship violence (Holt, Buckley, & Whelan, 2008). Recently, the term *intimate partner violence* (IPV) has replaced the use of *domestic violence* in order to differentiate from other types of familial violence (McClennen, 2005). The term *intimate partner violence* is also more inclusive of gay and lesbian couples and non-married partners (McClennen, 2005). There is little consensus on a standard definition of domestic violence or intimate partner violence. The Centers for Disease Control and Prevention launched a national project in hopes of creating a standardized definition of intimate partner violence (National Center for Injury Prevention and Control, 2003). The terms *domestic violence* and *intimate partner violence* will be used interchangeably throughout this chapter.

Prevalence, Incidence, and Costs

There are startling statistics pertaining to domestic violence. It is estimated that 5.3 million women are victims of intimate partner rape, physical assault, and/or stalking each year (National Center for Injury Prevention and Control, 2003). According to the National Intimate Partner and Sexual Violence Survey, one in four women and one in seven men have experienced physical violence by an intimate partner (National Center for Injury Prevention and Control, 2010). Women are five to eight times more likely than men to be victimized by an intimate partner (Basile et al., 2011). Domestic violence is the leading cause of injuries to women ages 15–44. These figures convert to financial costs to American businesses at the rate of $8.3 billion per year, leaving 21–60% of victims of intimate partner violence lose their jobs due to reasons stemming from the abuse (Rothman, Hathaway, Stidsen, & de Vries, 2007).

There are approximately 20 people who are experiencing intimate abuse every single minute in the USA. During 1 year, this equates to over ten million individuals including both genders (Walters, Chen, & Breiding, 2013). Chen and Ullman (2014) estimated that the annual incidence rate of physical assault on a spouse was 161 victims per 1000 couples in their study of 5349 couples. The rate of wife beating, defined as one or more violent acts that pose a serious risk of injury, was 34 victims per 1000 couples or an estimated 1.8 million seriously assaulted wives per year in the USA. Nonreporting does not always happen as a result of the dependency of the victims on the abusers. Due to the fact of nonreporting, researchers argue that the estimates of cost could be higher when nonreporting is taken into consideration (Carlson, 2010; Gelles & Straus, 1990). Numerous studies have supported that intimate partner violence is a gendered issue based on the fact that women experience and report more injuries (Caldwell, Swan, & Woodbrown, 2012), sexual victimization (Daigle & Mummert, 2014; Waal, Dekker, Kikkert, Kleinhesselink, & Goudriaan, 2017), and stalking (Dunlap, Lynch, Jewell, Wasarhaley, & Golding, 2015; Nobles, Reyns, Fox, & Fisher, 2014) from their intimate partners. One explanation for the staggering numbers regarding incidents of domestic violence is that women are rarely ready to terminate an abusive relationship and oftentimes return to the abuse (Shurman & Rodriguez, 2006).

The cost of domestic violence is staggering in terms of marital dissatisfaction and psychological and physical health problems (Black, 2011). Domestic violence can have lasting effects on physical health status, mental health status, and quality of life. Domestic violence also contributes to a higher use of health services (Campbell, 2002, p. 1331). Chronic health problems such as post-traumatic stress disorder (PTSD), depression, gastrointestinal disorders, and gynecological problems can result from experiencing domestic violence (Black, 2011). These chronic health issues can also be costly in terms of employment. Victims of domestic violence lose approximately 5.8 million days of paid work each year in the USA and $1.16 billion in Canada. Research indicates that the cost of violence against women is equivalent to 1.5 trillion, which is approximately the size of the economy of

Canada (United Nations Women, 2016). Other costs that must be accounted for include police services, social services, legal services, and imprisonment or other type of institutionalization.

Social Work's Involvement

A social worker is legally obligated to become involved in domestic violence cases. The Code of Ethics, outlined by the National Association of Social Workers, states that social workers are to intervene in cases of abuse or when imminent harm is evident (NASW Code of Ethics, 2012). If a social worker has knowledge of incidents of abuse, he or she is ethically and legally bound to report the abuse to the appropriate authorities. In the event a social worker does not uphold the Code of Ethics, he or she is legally liable for lack of involvement. For a more comprehensive review of the legal issues related to domestic violence, the reader is directed to Saunders (1995).

Many sources (Conner, 2016; Ford, 2016; Roark, Knight, Olson, & DeSandre, 2016) explain that an individual's exposure to domestic violence as a child increases the likelihood that they will, in turn, inflict violence on a partner. The Constructivist Self Development Theory discusses the possibility that negative experiences in childhood provides a template for what one considers normal or tolerable behavior (Berzenski & Yates, 2010; Ford, Chapman, Connor, & Cruise, 2012). The development of poor and unhealthy cognitive schemas with significant caregivers could result in the acceptance of unhealthy relationships which may lead to domestic violence. Corvo (2006) proposes the theoretical basis of intergenerational transmission models (ITM) of family violence by assessing variables from attachment theory with exposure to violence in family of origin. Childhood exposure to domestic violence is important in determining what the child deems as "normal" and it is important for a social worker to realize these traumas and risks.

Assessment Methods

In an article by Aldarondo and Straus (1994), five self-report instruments that assess physical violence in couple relationships were reviewed. An additional self-report instrument found in the literature was the Abusive Behavior Inventory (ABI). These assessments are described in the following sections.

Conflict Tactics Scales One of the most widely used assessments is the self-report Conflict Tactics Scales (CTS) developed by Straus (1979, 1990). The CTS has been used in numerous studies involving more than 70,000 participants from diverse cultural backgrounds and in at least 20 countries (Straus, Hamby, Boney-McCoy, & Sugarman, 1996).

Based on conflict theory, the CTS measures both the extent to which partners in a dating, cohabiting, or marital relationship engage in psychological and physical attacks on each other and also their use of reasoning or negotiation to deal with conflicts. The CTS does not measure attitudes about conflict or violence nor the causes and consequences of using different tactics (Straus & Mickey, 2012).

The original CTS had 19 items that represented a total scale and four subscales: minor violence, severe violence, verbal aggression, and reasoning. The CTS has been later revised (Straus et al., 1996) to include 39 items that represent five subscales: physical assault, psychological aggression, negotiation (both emotional and cognitive), injury, and sexual coercion. The new version is referred to as the Revised Conflict Tactics Scales (CTS2) and has: (a) additional items to enhance content validity and reliability, (b) revised wording to increase clarity and specificity, (c) better differentiation between minor and severe levels of each scale, (d) new scales to measure sexual coercion and physical injury, and (e) a new format to simplify administration and reduce response sets. According to Straus et al. (1996), permission to reproduce the CTS2 will be granted without charge for research purposes if a researcher agrees to carry out and report psychometric analyses or to provide the authors with the data.

The Index of Spouse Abuse (ISA)   The ISA, developed to quickly measure both physical and nonphysical abuse, consists of 30 items and has good reported reliability and validity (Hudson & McIntosh, 1981). While this assessment provides useful information about the psychological maltreatment of women, it offers limited information concerning physical violence and does not detect minor forms of physical violence (Aldarondo & Straus, 1994). Readers interested in this assessment are directed to Hudson and McIntosh's (1981) article. This assessment method is used in the Zeoli, Malinski, and Turchan (2016) article.

A newer version of the assessment, renamed the Partner Abuse Scales, has been developed and measures both physical and nonphysical abuse on the Partner Abuse Scale: Physical (PASPH) and Partner Abuse Scale: Non-physical (PASNP), respectively (Hudson, 1990). Both the PASPH and the PASNP each contain 25 items with 7-point Likert-type scaling. Initial reliability and validity estimates are good, including the ability to discriminate between abused and nonabused women (Attala, Hudson, & McSweeney, 1994).

The Wife Abuse Inventory (WAI)   The WAI, designed to identify both men and women at risk of abuse (Lewis, 1985), asks women to rate their partners and themselves on a number of "family management matters" that primarily focus on causes and consequences of abuse rather than on abusive behavior (Aldarondo & Straus, 1994). Readers interested in this assessment are directed to Lewis's (1985) article.

The Severity of Violence Against Women Scales (SVAWS)   The SVAWS (Marshall, 1992), as the name indicates, were developed to assess the severity of violence against women. Initial factor analysis of this 49-item assessment yielded nine scales: symbolic violence, mild threats, moderate threats, serious threats, minor violence, mild violence, moderate violence, sexual violence, and serious violence (Marshall,

1992). Although SVAWS are potentially useful to researchers and clinicians, there is presently no information on their validity and reliability (Straus & Mickey, 2012). Readers interested in this assessment are directed to Marshall's (1992) article.

The Relationship Conflict Inventory (RCI) The RCI (Bodin, 1992), developed as part of the efforts of the Task Force on Diagnosis and Classification of the Family, a division of the American Psychological Association, consists of 114 items that measure levels of verbal and physical abuse among couples in treatment. Although the psychometric properties of the RCI are unknown, the RCI should be of interest to systemic family therapists, given the clinical and theoretical basis of its development (Ronan, Dreer, Maurelli, Ronan, & Gerhart, 2014). The RCI is available from its author, Bodin, at the Mental Research Institute in Palo Alto, California.

The Abusive Behavior Inventory (ABI) The ABI (Shepard & Campbell, 1992) was developed for the Domestic Abuse Intervention Project (DAIP) because existing assessments such as the CTS did not conceptualize abuse in terms of power and control. The ABI is a 30-item self-report instrument that women complete concerning their partners' behavior 6 months prior to the intervention. According to its authors, initial research suggests that the ABI is a reliable and valid assessment (Shepard, 1993) and is still used in many studies, including one by Mills and Malley-Morrison (1998). The ABI is available for duplication as an appendix in Pence and Paymer's (1993) book.

Effective Interventions

According to Slabbert (2010), couple or family therapy is usually useful only when the violence behavior is under control or when the abuser is receiving separate treatment. Once the violence is brought under control (as verified by the victim), couple counseling focuses on replacing mutual dependency with respect, teaching stress and anger management skills, and improving communication. Cognitive restructuring techniques have been found helpful for both abusive husbands and abused wives (Slabbert, 2010).

Many critics contend that conjoint counseling places women at risk of violence. In spite of this criticism, Gelles advocates conjoint therapy. He reported success rates in excess of 90% for couples staying in treatment for a 2-year period (Gelles & Conte, 1990). Yegidis (1992) advocates the use of support groups for all types of family abuse victims, while other scholars (e.g., Dwyer, Smokowski, Bricout, & Wodarski, 1995; Edelson & Tolman, 1992) champion the use of an ecological approach.

In 1992, The Family Violence Project of the National Council of Juvenile and Family Court Judges identified 18 "State-of-the Art" programs. Their report describes each program and includes whom to contact for further information. Exemplary comprehensive programs identified were Minneapolis's Domestic Abuse Project, Baltimore's House of Ruth, Cleveland's Templum project, Denver's Project

Safeguard, and Maui's Family Court of the Second Circuit and Alternatives to Violence program. These programs all included (a) services to victims, (b) services to batterers, (c) teamwork with prosecutorial units and law enforcement, (d) coordination of or participation in community response, (e) advocacy to change laws and procedures affecting victims of domestic violence and their children and abusers.

To date, many recently developed violence programs and models have not been empirically evaluated, including developments by Cornelius and Resseguie (2007), LaFree, Dugan, and Korte (2009), and Guo, Roettger, and Cai (2008). In a follow-up evaluation of 12 support groups for women victims of domestic assault, Stover, Meadows, and Kaufman (2009) found significant improvements in self-esteem, belonging support, locus of control, less traditional attitudes toward marriage and the family, perceived stress, and marital functioning. They also found significant decreases in both physical and nonphysical abuse for women currently living with their spouses.

Group Therapy   Group therapy interventions tend to focus on anger management or anger control. One such intervention was developed by Deschner, McNeil, and Moore (1986) to treat couples by group methods to control anger in order to break battering cycles. The groups, limited to 14–16 members, met weekly for 10 weeks for approximately 2½ h.

The authors note that time out is an appropriate strategy at most phases. An evaluation of the program indicated that it was successful in lowering the number of arguments, decreasing the anger intensity of batterers, and improving marital quality. An overwhelming majority of the couples (over 85%) contacted for follow-up (at both 8-month and 1-year intervals) had avoided further battering (Hooper, 2013).

Pence and Paymer (1993) developed a group education model for men who batter. Referred to as the Duluth Model, or Domestic Abuse Intervention Project (DAIP), both batterers (men) and victims (their partners) participated in weekly educational sessions. To complement their Power and Control Wheel with the spokes of intimidation; emotional abuse; isolation; minimizing, denying, and blaming; children; male privilege; and economic abuse, and Equality Wheel was developed with the spokes of negotiation and fairness, nonthreatening behavior, respect, trust and support, honesty and accountability, responsible parenting, shared responsibility, and economic partnership. The curriculum was developed around these spokes and involves the use of control logs and action plans. As with many intervention programs, DAIP has had short-term effectiveness, but limited long-term success. In later phases of DAIP, both men and women reported lower rates of abuse, and lower rates of abuse were reported at a 1-year follow-up of battered women. In an examination of abusive behavior as documented by police and court records over a 5-year follow-up period, however, 40 out of 100 men were identified as recidivists.

Community Interventions   A variety of community interventions have evolved to address the problem of domestic violence. One such intervention developed to implement the Illinois Domestic Violence Act is Family Options. This program refers 911 calls involving domestic violence to the Family Options Program. The

Family Options team is composed of two social workers, two community advocates, and one lawyer (Caputo & Moynihan, 1986).

The social workers assess a family's problems and identify its needs. The social workers also review service needs, such as job training, substance abuse treatment, and child care, and help a family identify support services that could be obtained through the extended family and community (Caputo & Moynihan, 1986).

The community advocates help victims with the complicated legal process. The community advocates work in conjunction with the assistant state's attorney in helping a victim obtain orders of protection or any other type of order necessary for assistance. The lawyers represent the victims during the actual court proceedings (Caputo & Moynihan, 1986).

Prevention Thus far, the empirical evidence shows that there is very little prevention of domestic violence, providing a challenge for family social workers to work the larger systems (health care, legal, community resources, multimedia, etc.) researching and implementing effective domestic and family violence prevention programs. While not a primary prevention approach, screening for family violence is certainly advisable for all types of therapeutic interventions. There are several factors associated with family violence, including gender, social class, stress, unemployment, history of violence, dependence or jealousy, social isolation, poverty, substance abuse, and mental illness including depression and low self-esteem (Antunes-Alves & Stefano, 2014).

Intimate Partner Violence and Conflict in Gay and Lesbian Couples

While most of the literature focuses on male perpetrators and female victims/survivors, domestic violence involving same-sex partners is also prevalent. Intimate partner violence is one of the most prevalent public health concerns for gay men following only HIV/AIDS and substance abuse (Strasser et al., 2012). A prevalent myth is that when violence does occur in same-sex couples it is mutual with both parties engaging in the violence (Macdonald, 1998). However, it is estimated that the prevalence of domestic violence among gay and lesbian partners is comparable to the prevalence in heterosexual partners (Seelau & Seelau, 2005; Strasser et al., 2012). Protection for gay and lesbian victims is only stated explicitly in the laws of four states (Hawaii, Illinois, Kentucky, and Ohio) (Seelau & Seelau, 2005, p. 363). According to a literature review by McClennen (2005), 21 states still have laws stating sodomy as a criminal offense (p. 152). This poses a conundrum for same-gender victims. If they report their perpetrator, they are potentially confessing to the crime of sodomy (McClennen, 2005).

Another barrier for gay and lesbian couples obtaining services is the current definition of "marriage" and "spouse" as it is identified in the Defense of Marriage Act

(1996). The Defense of Marriage Act (DOMA) defines marriage as "a legal union between one man and one woman as husband and wife." DOMA defines spouse as referring "only to a person of the opposite sex who is a husband or a wife." These definitions are not inclusive and can impede gay and lesbian couples from rendering services. While DOMA has come under increased scrutiny in the past few years, it is still largely upheld. In fact, in 2012 the U.S. House of Representatives voted to cease the use of taxpayer funds to oppose DOMA (Kim, 2012). President Barack Obama has come forward explicitly supporting the right for gay and lesbian couples to legally marry. However, without Congress acting, change is not likely to occur.

Social Work's Involvement

When working with gay and lesbian couples, it is important that social workers are self-aware of their own biases and judgments. Couples therapy must be conducted in an accepting and understanding environment. It is important that social workers familiarize themselves with norms of gay and lesbian culture (Bepko & Johnson, 2000; Mitchell, 2016). Working with gay and lesbian couples may produce unique needs that therapists are not familiar with. For example, Bepko and Johnson (2000) outline four external factors that can have an impact on gay and lesbian couples: (1) homophobia and heterosexism; (2) gender norms; (3) issues around coming out to others; and (4) social support from family of origin and family of choice (p. 409).

Other implications for social workers go beyond therapy situations. Advocacy and education are also important contributions for social workers. Social workers need to educate their communities on the prevalence of gay and lesbian couple violence in hopes of normalizing reporting (Mitchell, 2016). Social workers should also advocate with local, state, and federal government to ensure that inclusive language is used in legal definitions.

Conclusions

The purpose of this chapter was to examine the empirical literature concerning family preservation. Included in this chapter were studies that involved empirically based interventions. Certainly, many empirically based, but not clinical, studies of family preservation exist, as do studies of nonempirically based interventions.

Although this chapter has focused on dysfunctional aspects of family life, we conclude by discussing functional aspects of family life. In an analysis by Previti and Amato (2003), 1424 married individuals were asked the question, "what are the most important factors keeping your marriage together?" This was part of a 17-year longitudinal study of Marital Instability over the Life Course (Booth, Amato, & Johnson, 1998). Among the participants, the most common reasons for remaining married included: (a) having strong feelings of love and affection, (b) respecting the spouse and the spouse's needs, (c) being honest with each other, trusting the spouse, (d) understanding, listening, and talking about concerns, (e) having a shared past, joined lives, and being married for many years, (f) feeling comfortable together, (g) happiness, (h) emotional security, (i) commitment to the partner, and (j) enjoying the sexual relationship. These reasons correlate with the nine basic dimensions of a strong, healthy family developed by family therapists: (a) adaptive ability, (b) commitment to family, (c) communicativeness, (d) encouragement of individuals, (e) expression of appreciation, (f) religious or spiritual orientation, (g) social connectedness, (h) clear roles, and (i) shared time (Family Therapy News, 1990, p. 8). Three additional dimensions included in the literature are: (a) clear boundaries, (b) cooperation, and (c) task negotiations (Kaslow & Robinson, 1996).

It seems to us that individuals, therapists, and scholars may take one of two views, pessimistic or optimistic, concerning the future of the American family. Rigorous empirical support for either view is sorely lacking. A person with a pessimistic view focuses on dysfunctional aspects of family life and believes that American families are declining. A person with an optimistic view, on the other hand, focuses on functional aspects of family life and believes that American families are changing. The authors definitely hold and optimistic view of the strength and resiliency of the American family and believe in an unlimited potential for positive growth and change. Which view do you hold concerning the future of the family?

Acknowledgement We would like to recognize the major contribution of Dr. Keresman (1935–2012) to the first edition of this chapter.

References

Achenbach, T. M. (1991). *Manual for the Child Behavior Checklist/4-18 and 1991 profile.* Burlington, VT: University of Vermont Department of Psychiatry.

Aldarondo, E., & Straus, M. A. (1994). Screening for physical violence is couple therapy: Methodological, practical, and ethical considerations. *Family Process, 33,* 425–439.

Antunes-Alves, S., & Stefano, J. D. (2014). Intimate partner violence: Making the case for joint couple treatment. *The Family Journal, 22*(1), 62–68.

Attala, J. M., Hudson, W. W., & McSweeney, M. (1994). A partial validation of two short-form partner abuse scales. *Women & Health, 21*(2/3), 125–139.

Bagarozzi, D. A. (1995). Evaluation, accountability and clinical expertise in managed mental health care: Basic considerations for the practice of family social work. *Journal of Family Social Work, 1*(2), 101–116.

Balderrama-Durbin, C., Snyder, D. K., & Balsis, S. (2015). Tailoring assessment of relationship distress using the Marital Satisfaction Inventory—brief form. *Couple and Family Psychology: Research and Practice, 4*(3), 127.

Banks, K. M., & Scott, A. M. (2016). *The National Historic Preservation Act: Past, present, and future.* New York, NY: Routledge.

Basile, K. C., Black, M. C., Breiding, M. J., Chen, J., Merrick, M. T., Smith, S. G., … Walters, M. L. (2011). *National Intimate Partner and Sexual Violence Survey: 2010 summary report.* Atlanta, GA: National Center for Injury Prevention and Control.

Bélanger, C., Laporte, L., Sabourin, S., & Wright, J. (2015). The effect of cognitive-behavioral group marital therapy on marital happiness and problem solving self-appraisal. *The American Journal of Family Therapy, 43*(2), 103–118.

Bepko, C., & Johnson, T. (2000). Gay and lesbian couples in therapy: Perspectives for the contemporary family therapist. *Journal of Marital and Family Therapy, 26*(4), 409–419.

Berzenski, S. R., & Yates, T. M. (2010). A developmental process analysis of the contribution of childhood emotional abuse to relationship violence. *Journal of Aggression, Maltreatment & Trauma, 19*(2), 180–203.

Black, M. C. (2011). Intimate partner violence and adverse health consequences: Implications for clinicians. *American Journal of Lifestyle Medicine, 5*(5), 428–439.

Bodin, A. M. (1992). *Relationship conflict inventory*. Palo Alto, CA: Mental Research Institute.

Booth, A., Amato, P. R., & Johnson, D. R. (1998). *Marital instability over the life course: Methodology report for fifth wave*. Lincoln, NE: Bureau of Sociological Research.

Boughner, S. R., Hayes, S. F., Bubenzer, D. L., & West, J. D. (1994). Use of standardized assessment instruments by marital and family therapists: A survey. *Journal of Marital and Family Therapy, 20*(1), 69–75.

Busby, D. M., Christensen, C., Crane, D. R., & Larson, J. H. (1995). A revision of the dyadic adjustment scale for use with distressed and nondistressed couples: Construct hierarchy and multidimensional scales. *Journal of Marital and Family Therapy, 21*(3), 289–308.

Caldwell, B. E., Woolley, S. R., & Caldwell, C. J. (2007). Preliminary estimates of cost-effectiveness for marital therapy. *Journal of Marital and Family Therapy, 33*(3), 392–405.

Caldwell, J. E., Swan, S. C., & Woodbrown, V. D. (2012). Gender differences in intimate partner violence outcomes. *Psychology of Violence, 2*(1), 42.

Campbell, J. C. (2002). Health consequences of intimate partner violence. *The Lancet, 359*, 1331–1336.

Caputo, R. K., & Moynihan, F. M. (1986). Family options: A practice/research model in family violence. *Social Casework, 67*, 460–465.

Carlson, B. E. (2010). Intimate partner violence and its effects. In N. R. Heller & A. Gitterman (Eds.), *Mental health and social problems: A social work perspective*. London, England: Routledge.

Carroll, J. S., & Doherty, W. J. (2003). Evaluating the effectiveness of premarital prevention programs: A meta-analytic review of outcome research. *Family Relations, 52*, 105–118.

Centers for Disease Control and Prevention (CDC). (2010). *National survey of family growth*. Atlanta, GA: CDC.

Chen, Y., & Ullman, S. E. (2014). Women's reporting of physical assaults to police in a national sample: A brief report. *Journal of Aggression, Maltreatment & Trauma, 23*(8), 854–868.

Choi, H., & Marks, N. F. (2008). Marital conflict, depressive symptoms, and functional impairment. *Journal of Marriage and Family, 70*, 377–390.

Christensen, A., Atkins, D. C., Berns, S., Wheeler, J., Baucom, D. H., & Simpson, L. E. (2004). Traditional versus integrative behavioral couple therapy for significantly and chronically distressed married couples. *Journal of Consulting and Clinical Psychology, 72*(2), 176–191.

Conner, D. H. (2016). Polyvictimized children & intimate partner violence: Promoting healthy outcomes for children. *Widener Law Review, 22*, 215.

Cookro, N. A. (2009). *Divorce mediation in Northeast Ohio: Perceptions of legal and social services professionals*. Akron, OH: University of Akron.

Cornelius, T. L., & Resseguie, N. (2007). Primary and secondary prevention programs for dating violence: A review of the literature. *Aggression and Violent Behavior, 12*(3), 364–375.

Corvo, K. (2006). Violence, separation, and loss in the families of origin of domestically violent men. *Journal of Family Violence, 21*(2), 117–125.

Cui, M., & Fincham, F. D. (2010). The differential effects of parental divorce and marital conflict on young adult romantic relationships. *Personal Relationships, 17*(3), 331–343.

Daigle, L. E., & Mummert, S. J. (2014). Sex-role identification and violent victimization: Gender differences in the role of masculinity. *Journal of Interpersonal Violence, 29*(2), 255–278.

Deschner, J. P., McNeil, J. S., & Moore, M. G. (1986). A treatment model for batterers. *Social Casework, 67*, 55–60.

Doss, B. D., Thum, Y. M., Sevier, M., & Atkins, D. C. (2005). Improving relationships: Mechanisms of change in couple therapy. *Journal of Consulting and Clinical Psychology, 73*(4), 624–633.

Dunlap, E. E., Lynch, K. R., Jewell, J. A., Wasarhaley, N. E., & Golding, J. M. (2015). Participant gender, stalking myth acceptance, and gender role stereotyping in perceptions of intimate partner stalking: A structural equation modeling approach. *Psychology, Crime & Law, 21*(3), 234–253.

Dwyer, D. C., Smokowski, P. R., Bricout, J. C., & Wodarski, J. S. (1995). Domestic violence research: Theoretical and practice implications for social work. *Clinical Social Work Journal, 23*, 185–197.

Edelson, J. L., & Tolman, R. M. (1992). *Intervention for men who batter: An ecological approach.* Newbury Park, CA: Sage.

Familiar, I., Ruisenor-Escudero, H., Giordani, B., Bangirana, P., Nakasujja, N., Opoka, R., & Boivin, M. (2015). Use of the behavior rating inventory of executive function and Child Behavior Checklist in Ugandan children with HIV or a history of severe malaria. *Journal of Developmental & Behavioral Pediatrics, 36*(4), 277–284.

Family Therapy News. (1990, July/August). Healthy families featured in Washington conference, p. 8.

Ford, J. D., Chapman, J., Connor, D. F., & Cruise, K. R. (2012). Complex trauma and aggression in secure juvenile justice settings. *Criminal Justice and Behavior, 39*(6), 694–724.

Ford, K. (2016). Children's exposure to intimate partner sexual violence. In L. McOrmond-Plummer, J. Y. Levy-Peck, & P. W. Easteal (Eds.), *Perpetrators of intimate partner sexual violence: A multidisciplinary approach to prevention, recognition, and intervention* (Vol. 21). New York, NY: Routledge.

Ganong, L. H., Coleman, M., Markham, M., & Rothrauff, T. (2011). Predicting postdivorce coparental communication. *Journal of Divorce and Remarriage, 52*(1), 1–18.

Gelles, R. J., & Conte, J. R. (1990). Domestic violence and sexual abuse of children. *Journal of Marriage and the Family, 52*, 1045–1058.

Gelles, R. J., & Straus, M. A. (1990). The medical and psychological costs of family violence. In M. A. Straus & R. J. Gelles (Eds.), *Physical violence in American families: Risk factors and adaptations to violence in 8,145 families* (pp. 425–430). New Brunswick, NJ: Transaction.

Gray-Little, B., Baucom, D. H., & Hamby, S. L. (1996). Marital power, marital adjustment, and therapy outcome. *Journal of Family Psychology, 10*, 292–303.

Guo, G., Roettger, M. E., & Cai, T. (2008). The integration of genetic propensities into social-control models of delinquency and violence among male youths. *American Sociological Review, 73*(4), 543–568.

Hahlweg, K., & Richter, D. (2010). Prevention of marital instability and distress. Results of an 11-year longitudinal follow-up study. *Behaviour Research and Therapy, 48*(5), 377–383.

Halford, W. K., Sanders, M. R., & Behrens, B. C. (2001). Can skills training prevent relationship problems in at-risk couples? Four-year effects of a behavioral relationship education program. *Journal of Family Psychology, 15*(4), 750.

Heflinger, C. A., Simpkins, C. G., & Combs-Orme, T. (2000). Using the CBCL to determine the clinical status of children in state custody. *Children and Youth Services Review, 22*(1), 55–73.

Herrington, R. L., Mitchell, A. E., Castellani, A. M., Joseph, J. I., Snyder, D. K., & Gleaves, D. H. (2008). Assessing disharmony and disaffection in intimate relationships: Revision of the Marital Satisfaction Inventory Factor Scales. *Psychological Assessment, 20*(4), 341–350.

Holt, S., Buckley, H., & Whelan, S. (2008). The impact of exposure to domestic violence on children and young people: A review of the literature. *Child Abuse & Neglect, 32*(8), 797–810.

Hooper, C.-A. (2013). *Mothers surviving child sexual abuse.* New York, NY: Routledge.

Hudson, W. W. (1990). *Partner abuse scales.* Tempe, AZ: Walmyr Publishing.

Hudson, W. W., & McIntosh, S. R. (1981). The assessment of spouse abuse: Two quantifiable dimensions. *Journal of Marriage and the Family, 43*, 873–888.

Hughes, R., Clark, C. D., Schaefer-Hernan, P., & Good, E. S. (1994). An evaluation of a newsletter intervention for divorced mothers. *Family Relations, 43*, 298–304.

Kaslow, F., & Robinson, J. A. (1996). Long-term satisfying marriages: Perceptions of contributing factors. *The American Journal of Family Therapy, 24*, 153–170.

Kim, S. M. (2012). House strikes back on gay marriage. *Politico*. Retrieved from http://www.politico.com/news/stories/0512/76147.html

Kramer, L., & Washo, C. A. (1993). Evaluation of a court-mandated prevention program for divorcing parents. *Family Relations, 42*, 179–186.

LaFree, G., Dugan, L., & Korte, R. (2009). The impact of British counterterrorist strategies on political violence in Northern Ireland: Comparing deterrence and backlash models. *Criminology, 47*(1), 17–45.

Lewis, B. Y. (1985). The wife abuse inventory: A screening device for identification of abused woman. *Social Work, 30*, 32–35.

Lin, C.-H., & Lee, M.-J. (2016). A comparative policy analysis of family preservation programs in the US and in Taiwan. *Journal of Child and Family Studies, 25*(4), 1131–1144.

Lou, Y.-C., Lin, C.-H., Chen, C.-M., Balderrama-Durbin, C., & Snyder, D. K. (2016). Assessing intimate relationships of Chinese couples in Taiwan using the marital satisfaction inventory–revised. *Assessment, 23*(3), 267–278.

Macdonald, B. J. (1998). Issues in therapy with gay and lesbian couples. *Journal of Sex and Marital Therapy, 24*(3), 165–190.

MacKenzie, J., Smith, T. W., Uchino, B., White, P. H., Light, K. C., & Grewen, K. M. (2014). Depressive symptoms, anger/hostility, and relationship quality in young couples. *Journal of Social and Clinical Psychology, 33*(4), 380–396.

Macmann, G. M., Barnett, D. W., & Lopez, E. J. (1993). The Child Behavior Checklist/4-18 and related materials: Reliability and validity of syndromal assessment. *School Psychology Review, 22*, 322–333.

Markman, H. J., Floyd, F. J., Stanley, S. M., & Lewis, H. C. (1986). Prevention. In N. S. Jacobson & A. S. Gurman (Eds.), *Clinical handbook of marital therapy* (pp. 173–195). New York, NY: Guilford Press.

Marshall, L. L. (1992). Development of the severity of violence against women scales. *Journal of Family Violence, 7*, 103–121.

McClennen, J. C. (2005). Domestic violence between same-gender partners: Recent findings and future research. *Journal of Interpersonal Violence, 20*(2), 149–154.

Means-Christensen, A. J., Snyder, D. K., & Negy, C. (2003). Assessing nontraditional couples: Validity of the Marital Satisfaction Inventory—revised with gay, lesbian, and cohabiting heterosexual couples. *Journal of Marital and Family Therapy, 29*(1), 69–83.

Mills, R. B., & Malley-Morrison, K. (1998). Emotional commitment, normative acceptability, and attributions for abusive partner behaviors. *Journal of Interpersonal Violence, 13*, 682–699.

Mitchell, V. (2016). 17 couple therapy with same-sex and gender-variant (LGBT) couples: Sociocultural problems and intrapsychic and relational consequences. In K. T. Sullivan & E. Lawrence (Eds.), *The Oxford handbook of relationship science and couple interventions* (p. 241). New York, NY: Oxford University Press.

Moore, A. M., & Crane, D. R. (2014). Relational diagnosis and psychotherapy treatment cost effectiveness. *Contemporary Family Therapy, 36*(2), 281–299.

Morgan, M. (2008). Cancer patients with pain: Examination of the role of the spouse/partner relationship in mediating quality of life outcomes for the couple. *Graduate School Theses and Dissertations*. Paper 415. Retrieved from http://scholarcommons.usf.edu/etd/415

NASW Code of Ethics. (2012). Washington, DC: NASW Publications.

National Center for Injury Prevention and Control. (2003). *Costs of intimate partner violence against women in the United States*. Atlanta, GA: Centers for Disease Control and Prevention.

National Center for Injury Prevention and Control. (2010). *National intimate partner and sexual violence survey*. Atlanta, GA: Centers for Disease Control and Prevention.

Nobles, M. R., Reyns, B. W., Fox, K. A., & Fisher, B. S. (2014). Protection against pursuit: A conceptual and empirical comparison of cyberstalking and stalking victimization among a national sample. *Justice Quarterly, 31*(6), 986–1014.

Pence, E., & Paymer, M. (1993). *Education groups for men who batter: The Duluth model.* New York, NY: Springer.

Previti, D., & Amato, P. R. (2003). Why stay married? Rewards, barriers, and marital stability. *Journal of Marriage and Family, 65,* 561–573.

Price, M., Higa-McMillan, C., Ebesutani, C., Okamura, K., Nakamura, B. J., Chorpita, B. F., & Weisz, J. (2013). Symptom differentiation of anxiety and depression across youth development and clinic-referred/nonreferred samples: An examination of competing factor structures of the Child Behavior Checklist DSM-oriented scales. *Development and psychopathology, 25*(4pt1), 1005–1015.

Renick, M. J., Blumberg, S. L., & Markham, H. J. (1992). The prevention and relationship enhancement program (PREP): An empirically based preventive intervention program for couples. *Family Relations, 41,* 141–147.

Riggio, H. R. (2004). Parental marital conflict and divorce, parent-child relationships, social support, and relationship anxiety in young adulthood. *Personal Relationships, 11,* 99–114.

Roark, J., Knight, K. E., Olson, H., & DeSandre, H. (2016). Predictors of child abuse charges within the context of domestic violence arrests. *Crime & Delinquency.* https://doi.org/10.1177/0011128716661141

Ronan, G. F., Dreer, L., Maurelli, K., Ronan, D. W., & Gerhart, J. (2014). Measures of violence. In *Practitioner's guide to empirically supported measures of anger, aggression, and violence* (pp. 157–261). Cham, Switzerland: Springer.

Rothman, E. F., Hathaway, J., Stidsen, A., & de Vries, H. F. (2007). How employment helps female victims of intimate partner violence: A qualitative study. *Journal of Occupational Health Psychology, 12*(2), 136.

Saunders, D. G. (1995). Domestic violence: Legal issues. In *Encyclopedia of social work* (Vol. 1, 19th ed., pp. 789–795). Washington, DC: National Association of Social Workers Press.

Schindler, I., Berg, C. A., Butler, J. M., Fortenberry, K. T., & Wiebe, D. J. (2010). Late-midlife and older couples' shared possible selves and psychological well-being during times of illness: The role of collaborative problem solving. *Journal of Gerontology: Psychological Sciences, 65B*(4), 416–424.

Seelau, S. M., & Seelau, E. P. (2005). Gender-role stereotypes and perceptions of heterosexual, gay and lesbian domestic violence. *Journal of Family Violence, 20*(6), 363–371.

Shepard, M. (1993). Evaluation of domestic abuse intervention programs. In E. Pence & M. Paymer (Eds.), *Education groups for men who batter: The Duluth model* (pp. 163–168). New York, NY: Springer.

Shepard, M., & Campbell, J. (1992). The abusive behavior inventory: A measure of psychological and physical abuse. *Journal of Interpersonal Violence, 7,* 291–305.

Shurman, L. A., & Rodriguez, C. M. (2006). Cognitive-affective predictors of women readiness to end domestic violence relationships. *Journal of Interpersonal Violence, 21*(11), 1417–1439.

Slabbert, I. (2010). *The experiences of low-income female survivors of domestic violence.* Stellenbosch, South Africa: University of Stellenbosch.

Snyder, D. K., Heyman, R. E., & Haynes, S. N. (2005). Evidence-based approaches to assessing couple distress. *Psychological Assessment, 17*(3), 288–307.

Snyder, D. K., Wills, R. M., & Keiser, T. W. (1981). Empirical validation of the marital satisfaction inventory: An actuarial approach. *Journal of Consulting and Clinical Psychology, 49,* 262–268.

South, S. C., Krueger, R. F., & Iacono, W. G. (2009). Factorial invariance of the Dyadic Adjustment Scale across gender. *Psychological Assessment, 21*(4), 622–628.

Spanier, G. B. (1976). Measuring dyadic adjustment: New scales for assessing the quality of marriage and similar dyads. *Journal of Marriage and the Family, 32,* 15–28.

Spanier, G. B. (1989). *Manual for the dyadic adjustment scale.* North Tonawanda, NY: Multi-Health Systems.

Stover, C. S., Meadows, A. L., & Kaufman, J. (2009). Interventions for intimate partner violence: Review and implications for evidence-based practice. *Professional Psychology: Research and Practice, 40*(3), 223.

Strasser, S. M., Smith, M., Pendrick-Denney, D., Boos-Beddington, S., Chen, K., & McCarty, F. (2012). Feasibility study of social media to reduce intimate partner violence among gay men in metro Atlanta, Georgia. *Western Journal of Emergency Medicine, 13*(3), 298–304.

Straus, M. A. (1979). Measuring intrafamily conflict and violence: The Conflict Tactics (CT) Scales. *Journal of Marriage and the Family, 39*, 75–88.

Straus, M. A. (1990). The Conflict Tactics Scale and its critics: An evaluation and new data on validity and reliability. In M. A. Straus & R. J. Gelles (Eds.), *Physical violence in American families: Risk factors and adaptations to violence in 8,145 families* (pp. 49–73). New Brunswick, NJ: Transaction.

Straus, M. A., Hamby, S. L., Boney-McCoy, S., & Sugarman, D. B. (1996). The revised Conflict Tactics Scales (CTS2): Developmental and preliminary psychometric data. *Journal of Family Issues, 17*, 283–316.

Straus, M. A., & Mickey, E. L. (2012). Reliability, validity, and prevalence of partner violence measured by the conflict tactics scales in male-dominant nations. *Aggression and Violent Behavior, 17*(5), 463–474.

Symons, D. K. (2010). A review of the practice and science of child custody and access assessment in the United States and Canada. *Professional Psychology: Research and Practice, 41*(3), 267.

United Nations Women. (2016). *The economic costs of violence against women.* Retrieved from http://www.unwomen.org/en/news/stories/2016/9/speech-by-lakshmi-puri-on-economic-costs-of-violence-against-women

Van Widenfelt, B., Hosman, C., Schaap, C., & van der Staak, C. (1996). The prevention of relationship distress for couples at risk: A controlled evaluation with nine-month and two-year follow-ups. *Family Relations, 45*, 156–165.

Waal, M. M., Dekker, J. J., Kikkert, M. J., Kleinhesselink, M. D., & Goudriaan, A. E. (2017). Gender differences in characteristics of physical and sexual victimization in patients with dual diagnosis: A cross-sectional study. *BMC Psychiatry, 17*(1), 270.

Walters, M. L., Chen, J., & Breiding, M. J. (2013). *The National Intimate Partner and Sexual Violence Survey (NISVS): 2010 findings on victimization by sexual orientation* (Vol. 648(73), p. 6). Atlanta, GA: National Center for Injury Prevention and Control, Centers for Disease Control and Prevention.

Ward, P. J., Lundberg, N. R., Zabriskie, R. B., & Berrett, K. (2009). Measuring marital satisfaction: A comparison of the revised dyadic adjustment scale and the satisfaction with married life scale. *Marriage and Family Review, 45*(4), 412–429.

Waring, E. M., Stalker, C. A., Carver, C. M., & Gitta, M. Z. (1991). Waiting list controlled trial of cognitive marital therapy in severe marital discord. *Journal of Marital and Family Therapy, 17*, 243–256.

Whisman, M. A., Uebelacker, L. A., & Weinstock, L. M. (2004). Psychopathology and marital satisfaction: The importance of evaluating both partners. *Journal of Consulting and Clinical Psychology, 72*(5), 830–838.

Wiedenhoff, A. R. (1994). Use of two behavior rating scales with mothers and teachers in the evaluation of children with attention-deficit hyperactivity disorder. *Dissertation Abstracts International, 54*(10-B), 5415.

Yegidis, B. L. (1992). Family violence: Contemporary research findings and practice issues. *Community Mental Health Journal, 28*, 519–530.

Zeoli, A. M., Malinski, R., & Turchan, B. (2016). Risks and targeted interventions: Firearms in intimate partner violence. *Epidemiologic Reviews, 38*(1), 125–139.

Chapter 12
Practice Approaches with Older Clients

Nancy P. Kropf and Sherry Cummings

Overview

Since the turn of the last century, the increase in the number of older adults has been dramatic. In the early 1900s, when the current cohort of elders was born, only 5% of the population was over the age of 65 (*Aging America*, 1991). In 2010, there were nearly 50 million people over the age of 62, which is 16.2% of the population. That is a 21.1% increase from 2000 (U.S. Census Bureau, 2010). The trend toward an increasingly older population is expected to continue, as a greater number of adults live into late life. Because of their multiple needs that often include medical, social, and financial assistance, social work practitioners in all service settings can expect to work with greater numbers of older adults in coming years.

 This chapter will provide an overview of empirical practice approaches with older adults. Due to the diversity of practice issues in work with older clients, various approaches focus on different practice outcomes. The important question is determining is what intervention administered in what format is effective with which population of older adults (Cummings & Kropf, 2009; Kropf & Cummings, 2017). Certain interventions have prevention objectives, with goals of keeping older adults as physically, socially, and psychologically healthy as possible. Other intervention approaches are remedial, with the goal of restoring functioning after the onset of a certain type of problematic condition (e.g., death of a spouse, onset of chronic health problem). Finally, some approaches provide support in progressive and irreversible situations such as dementia care or terminal illness. Intervention

N. P. Kropf (✉)
Georgia State University, Atlanta, GA, USA
e-mail: nkropf@gsu.edu

S. Cummings
College of Social Work, University of Tennessee, Knoxville, TN, USA

© Springer Nature Switzerland AG 2019
J. S. Wodarski, L. M. Hopson (eds.), *Empirically Based Interventions Targeting Social Problems*, https://doi.org/10.1007/978-3-030-28487-9_12

approaches discussed in this chapter are practice with individual clients, groups, and families of older adults, and community prevention programs.

Assessment Methods

Due to the number of different treatment programs for older adults, numerous assessment methods and instruments are found in outcome research with these clients. While some of the instruments used in assessment are specifically constructed for use with an older population (e.g., the Geriatric Depression Scale), the majority are used with adults of various age groups. This section will summarize assessment procedures by outcome, organized in the categories of health and physical functioning, psychiatric conditions, and social functioning and well-being.

Health and Physical Functioning

Overall physical functioning of older adults is commonly measured by the Physical Activities of Daily Living (Hanna-Pladdy, Heilman, & Foundas, 2003), which measures an older adult's level of functioning across several physical domains. This instrument can be administered to older adults or their care providers, or observational assessment can be performed by a rater. Physical health status has been measured by several self-report instruments. These include the Sickness Impact Profile (McEntee, Vowles, & McCracken, 2016) and the Perceived Health Questionnaire (Jones, Duffy, Flanagan, & Foster, 2012), both of which measure the impact of health conditions on an individual.

For specific health problems, self-reports tend to be used. These methods include sleep or headache journals that calculate the incidence of a condition over the course of a specified time period. Entries may also include the perceived severity or duration of the condition.

In sleep disorders, polysomnography (PSG) is also used. A PSG rates brain wave activities, respiration, and limb movement. These assessments are performed in a sleep laboratory and evaluated by an experienced technician. Because of the high expense of polysomnography, however, other screening tools for sleep disorders are currently being explored. In one 2008 study, the validity of the Observation-based Nocturnal Screening Inventory (ONSI) was assessed. The ONSI is a tool in which nurses record the hourly sleep status of a patient ($N = 115$). Each hourly visit lasts for 5 min, and the nurse observes the patient for symptoms of sleep apnea, including snoring, interrupted breathing, gasping, and choking. Of the 68 patients determined through use of polysomnography, 61 were correctly diagnosed using the ONSI measure (89.7%). The suggestions derived from this study suggest that measure such as ONSI may have utility as pre-screening tools for sleep disorders such as sleep apnea (Onen et al., 2008).

Psychiatric Conditions

The two most common psychiatric conditions that are included in outcome studies of older adults are depression and anxiety. Numerous instruments have been used to measure both diagnostic conditions, the majority of which are self-rating scales or indexes. A listing of the instruments that were used in the research studies included in this chapter is presented in Table 12.1.

Social Functioning

Several measures have also been used to assess areas of social competence with older adults. Many use self-report methods that measure a dimension of social connection or quality of life.

Table 12.2 lists those instruments that have been included in the research reported in this chapter.

Table 12.1 Measurement of depression and anxiety

Instrument	Reference
Depression	
Beck Depression Inventory	Beck, Ward, Mendelson, Mock, and Erbaugh (1971)
Beck Depression Inventory Second Edition	Beck, Steer, and Brown (1996)
Brief Symptom Inventory (BSI)	Derogatis and Spencer (1993)
Components of Depression	Beck, Rush, Shaw, and Emery (1987)
Epidemiological Studies Depression Scale	Radloff (1977)
Geriatric Depression Scale	Yesavage et al. (1983)
Hamilton Depression Scale	Hamilton (1967)
Profile of Mood States (POMS)	McNair, Lorr, and Droppleman (1971)
Schedule for Affective Disorders and Schizophrenia	Endicott and Spitzer (1978)
Tripartite Model	Clark, Watson, and Mineka (1994)
Wakefield Self-Rating Depression Scale	Snaith, Ahmed, Mehta, and Hamilton (1971)
Zung Depression Scale	Zung (1965)
Anxiety	
Adult Manifest Anxiety Scale—Elderly Version	Reynolds, Richmond, and Low (2003)
Affective Adjective Checklist Anxiety Index	Zuckerman and Lubin (1960)
Beck Anxiety Inventory	Beck, Epstein, Brown, and Steer (1988)
Hamilton Anxiety Scale	Hamilton (1959)
Spielberger Self-Evaluation Questionnaire	Spielberger, Gorsuch, and Lushene (1967)
State-Trait Anxiety Inventory	Spielberger, Gorsuch, and Luchene (1970)
Tripartite Model	Clark, Watson, and Mineka (1994)

Table 12.2 Measures of social functioning

Dimension	Instrument	Reference
Coping	Folkman and Lazarus Ways of Coping	Folkman and Lazarus (1980)
	Health-Specific Family Coping Index	Choi, LaVohn, and Christensen (1983)
	Revised Ways of Coping Scale	Vitaliano, Russo, Carr, Maiuro, and Becker (1985)
	Proactive Coping	Greenglass, Schwarzer, Jakubiec, Fiksenbaum, and Taubert (1999)
Life satisfaction	Life Satisfaction Index	Neugarten, Havighurst, and Tobin (1961)
Loneliness	UCLA Loneliness Scale	Russell, Peplau, and Ferguson (1978)
	MOS Social Support Survey	Sherbourne and Stewart (1991)
Morale	Philadelphia Geriatric Center Morale Scale	Lawton (1975)
Self-esteem		
Stress	Perceived Stress Scale	Cohen, Kamarck, and Mermelstein (1983)
Well-being	Bradburn's Affect Balance Scale	Bradburn (1969)
Worrying	Multidimensional Measures of Religious Involvement and Well-Being Penn State Worry Questionnaire—Past Week	Levin, Taylor, and Chatters (1995) Ryff and Essex (1992) Stober and Bittencourt (1998)

Other competencies are measured by certain types of outcome conditions as a result of participating in a treatment protocol or training situation. Examples of these measures are higher degree of knowledge about a certain subject (e.g., late-life alcoholism, accident prevention) or obtaining a particular outcome such as securing a job.

Effective Social Work Interventions

Interventions with Older Individuals

As people age, they often experience some type of physical health problem. Psychosocial interventions are used to help older clients in relieving health symptoms or increasing positive health behaviors. Psychiatric concerns are also areas for intervention, especially depression and anxiety. (Chronic mental illness in older adults, including dementia, will be specifically covered in another chapter.) In addition, older clients may face difficulties in adjusting to new environments, such as moving into a nursing home facility.

Health Conditions One health problem that affects older adults is chronic headache. Researchers found that of those living in a community setting had headaches on average 8.4 days a month (Fuh et al., 2008). Another study looked at 14 older adults (mean age $M = 66.7$ years) who suffered from migraine or tension headaches combined cognitive therapy with biofeedback and relaxation training to reduce pain (Nicholson & Blanchard, 1993). Each participant attended twelve 90-min sessions. Cognitive therapy included instruction and practice of techniques to reduce stress and increase problem-solving abilities. Headache activity was measured by a daily diary in which each participant scored headache activities four times per day ($0 = no$ *headache* to 5 = *incapacitating headache*). At the conclusion of the treatment, 50% of the sample achieved clinically significant reductions in headache activities. The importance of addressing chronic headaches and other forms of chronic pain is underscored in one study, which showed positive associations between chronic pain, including chronic headaches, and psychiatric comorbidity, particularly depression (Blay, Andreoli, Dewey, & Gastal, 2007).

A second health-related area involves sleep disturbances. Approximately 40% of the population of older adults report having difficulty sleeping. This can cause mental health and health risks such as poor cognition, poor physical functioning, pain, risk of falling, and lack of sleep can affect their relationships with others (Chen, Hayman, Shmerling, Bean, & Leveille, 2011). Sleep disturbances are overwhelmingly common in older adults and are associated with a variety of conditions ranging from neurodegenerative conditions, such as Parkinson's and Alzheimer's diseases, to depression (Dauvilliers, 2007). Furthermore, the economic costs of treating insomnia in the United States have reached epic proportions, largely due to the treatment of geriatric insomnia. Recent research estimates the annual cost of insomnia-related health care to be \$12–\$14 billion, including medical appointment, over-the-counter sleep aids, and prescription medication (Blaivas, Ancoli-Israel, Neubauer, and Sheldon, 2014).

Unfortunately, sleep disorders are commonly treated by medications, which can cause problems for older adults, including dependence, drug interactions, and increased potential for falls. One study even suggested that non-depressed older women using SSRIs were more likely than a non-drug using cohort to experience sleep disturbance and insomnia. In the study, consisting of 2853 women and 2337 women without depression, the women using SSRIs were actually found to be more likely to experience various forms of sleep disturbance, including decreased sleep duration, sleep latency of 1 h or more, and decreased sleep efficiency (Ensrud et al., 2006). In order to alleviate certain potentially harmful consequences, a sample of older adults ($n = 7$, $M = 61.9$ years) with insomnia was treated individually with relaxation therapy (4 weeks duration, then discontinued) followed by cognitive-behavioral therapy for 4 weeks (Edinger, Hoelscher, Marsh, Lipper, and Ionescu-Pioggia, 1992). Outcomes included objective measures such as number of awakenings, total sleep time, and time in bed, and subjective measures included perception of sleep difficulty and sleep quality. The findings indicated that relaxation therapy had little effect on either objective or subjective sleep outcomes. However, cognitive-behavioral therapy produced significant positive changes in sleep patterns. Furthermore, these gains were maintained at 3-month posttreatment.

Other studies have also presented findings that suggest that Cognitive-Behavioral Therapy may alleviate insomnia in older adults. For example, one study compared the use of CBT to the use of Zoplicone, a sleep medication, in the treatment of insomnia in older adults. The results suggested that CBT was more effective than pharmacological treatment in the treatment of chronic primary insomnia (Silvertsen et al., 2006).

In another study, however, relaxation was effective in treating sleep disorders. Soeffing et al. (2008) conducted cognitive-behavioral intervention with three components including relaxation training, stimulus control, and sleep hygiene instructions. Participants reported statistically significant and clinical meaningful improvement in sleep variables, which is unusually not accompanied by comparable gains in daytime function.

Depression and Anxiety Other studies have investigated outcomes of interventions on psychiatric conditions of older clients. Depression is a large problem for aging adults. As these demographic increases, this further expands the public mental health problem for western countries. In a study of nine European countries, it was found that the prevalence rate was 12% for depression in those over 64 years old (Klug et al., 2010). In research on depression, one study compared two treatment modalities (Cognitive-Behavioral Therapy and Psychodynamic Therapy) on depressive episodes (Driessen et al., 2013). A total of 341 participants who were diagnosed with a major depressive episode were randomly assigned to two groups: a 16-session cognitive-behavioral therapy (CBT) group and a short-term psychodynamic supportive therapy. Participants who were identified as serve patients were also supplemented with receiving antidepressant medication. There were no statistically significant treatment differences found between the two outcome measures. The findings extend the evidence base of psychodynamic therapy for depression but also indicate that time-limited treatment is insufficient for a substantial number of patients encountered in psychiatric outpatient clinics. One study compared the use of paroxetine drug therapy and the use of Interpersonal Psychotherapy in 52 adults (17 men and 35 women), aged 70 and older, in remission of depression, and of varying level of cognitive functioning. Over the course of the 2 year study, in cognitively impaired subjects, IPT demonstrated a higher level of effectiveness in preventing and prolonging relapse in the subjects than did drug therapy. In subjects of normal cognitive functioning, the effectiveness of IPT was equal to that of drug therapy (Carreira et al., 2008).

Lapid and Rummans (2003) assert that minor depression can ultimately have just as many negative effects as major depression if left untreated in the elderly. They both are associated with high mortality rates if left untreated as well. They suggest that improved detection of depression in older people and earlier interventions with treatment by primary care physicians are crucial to preventing disability and suicide (2003).

Anxiety is large mental health problem for aging populations which carries over effects in to their physical health as well. Approximately 5.5% of elderly have anxiety disorders in the United States and up to over 10% in Europe. The added stress of the anxiety has been shown to have health implication on the heart and other areas of the body (Alwahhabi, 2003). Cognitive-behavioral treatment has been found to be effective with anxiety in older clients.

With the purpose of reviewing the magnitude, duration, and factors that might impact the effect of cognitive-behavioral therapy (CBT) for older people with anxiety disorder, Gould, Coulson, and Howard (2012) searched the electronic literature databases and conducted a systematic critical review, random-effects meta-analysis, and meta-regression of randomized-controlled trials. This study confirmed the effectiveness of CBT for anxiety disorder treatment in older people. CBT was significantly more effective at reducing anxiety symptoms than other treatments or being on a waiting list at a period of 0–6 months.

Carek, Laibstain, and Carek (2011) discussed the role of exercise when incorporated in cognitive-behavioral therapy. Exercise and physical activity has been consistently supported by researchers about its association with improved physical health, life satisfaction, cognitive function, and psychological well-being. Exercise has more favorably effects on mild to moderate depression and anxiety when comparing to antidepressant medications. However, exercise has not been shown to have the effectiveness of reducing anxiety to the level of psychopharmaceuticals.

Puentes (2003) iterates the importance of disciplines integrating to find the common good for a population. In this instance the aim is to integrate two distinct psychotherapeutic approaches into one coherent mental health nursing intervention for the treatment of affective symptoms in older adults (2004). The use of life review through a case study was applied. The findings suggest that using the two different disciplines joined together can have successful outcomes by having a clear understanding of the dynamics of the various psychotherapeutic approaches, the skill level of the practitioner, the psychosocial sophistication of the client, and the pathology being treated (2004). The author asserts that cognitive therapy with added life review techniques is an excellent example of effective, eclectic treatment approach of affective disorders in the elder.

Lawton, Moss, Winter, & Hoffman in 2002 conducted a study concerning motivation in later life (Lawton, Moss, Hoffman, & Winter, 2002). The study revealed that personal projects are part of an open motivational system in which social position, cognitive ability, health, and positive mental health are mutually interacting members. The members of the study were 600 community residents over the age of 70. The most common activities of daily living were active recreation, other-oriented activities, intellectual activities, home planning, and spiritual/moral activities. The authors at this time believe that more research is needed to address some of the important dimensions of the elderly living. Other studies could also include starting goals that are psychological, ethical, self-enhancing, or spiritual. The individuals in the study who had self motivating projects had less depression.

A desensitization approach was successful in treating a dog phobia of a 70-year-old woman (Thyer, 1991). The woman had two harmful encounters with large dogs (an attack and an incident in which she fell), which resulted in a phobia that prevented her from walking in her neighborhood. The client engaged in five sessions with a therapist who gradually exposed her to anxiety-evoking stimuli, beginning with exposure to a small dog. By the last session, the client was exposed to two large dogs without significant anxiety. Telephone contact at 3 and 6 months after termination determined that the client remained symptom free. Calamari, Faber, Hitsman, and Poppe (1994) reported the effectiveness of exposure treatment in treating obsessive compulsive disorder (OCD) in old people. They described a case of OCD treatment in an 80-year-old man and concluded that old people appear to benefit from exposure treatment.

Suicide has also become a growing problem in the elderly population, and as the over 65 demographic increases, much recent research has attempted to isolate prominent suicide risk factors that may help to predict the likelihood of suicidal behavior in older adults. One study highlighted several significant risk factors associated with elder suicide, including a life long history of substance abuse, a history of mood disorders, recent (within 1 year) inpatient psychiatric hospitalization, social isolation, and a lack of social support (Beautrais, 2002). A study in Japan evaluated outcomes of a community-based program to prevent suicide among the elderly using a quasi-experimental design with a neighboring reference group. The program included depression screening with follow-up and health education through primary care and public health nursing. Changes in the suicide risk were noted and were reduced among women by 70%. The findings suggest that a community intervention against suicide using management of depression with non-psychiatric, primary health care would be effective for elderly females, but not males. The authors, Oyama, Goto, Fujita, Shibuya, and Sakashita (2006) suggest that programs acting on suicidal plan and impulsivity would be effective for males. For prevention, identifying risk factors and the practice of improving protective factors have promising results. Increasing supportive relationships (family members or friends), this includes using technology such as telephone counseling outreach programs (TeleHelp-TeleCheck services) are important focuses for interventions (Lapierre, Erlangsen, Waern, De Leo, & Oyama, 2011).

Reminiscence is an evidence-based therapeutic and nursing intervention used in a variety of settings (Stinson, Long, Kireuk, Peraza-Smith, & Flanagan, 2014). Reminiscence is a structured process of recalling and talking about individual's life and past events. Bohlmeijer, Roemer, Cuijpers, and Smit (2007) conducted a meta-analysis of 15 controlled outcome studies to evaluate the effectiveness of reminiscence on psychological well-beings. This study founded a moderate influence of reminiscence on life satisfaction and emotional well-beings on senior adults and a significant effect on community-dwelling adults. It is also recommended that there should be well-developed protocols.

Yet in another study by Smalbrugge et al. (2006) the objective was to determine the impact of depression and anxiety on well-being, disability, and use of health care services among nursing patients. The study consisted of 350 elderly nursing home patients who were 55 years or older. The use of the Philadelphia Geriatric Center Morale Scale (PGCMS) for well-being, a subpart of the Sickness Impact Profile for disability, as well as the Activities of Daily Living to note use of health care services. Presence of depression and/or anxiety was associated with significantly less well-being, but not with more disability. Presence of depression and/or anxiety was also significantly associated with four of the seven indicators of health care service use measured in this study. Depression and anxiety have a statistically and clinically negative impact on well-being but not on disability.

However, in a study in Canada, researchers, Streiner, Cairney, and Veldhuizen (2006), found that despite the negative changes that accompany old age—losses owing to death and physical limitations—the elderly are psychologically healthier than younger people. Their results were consistent with earlier results from past work suggesting that the observed pattern is not a change finding. They suggest that now efforts should focus on why disorder declines with age.

Counteracting this study, however, Teachman (2006) suggests that those studies that find lower rates of anxiety and mood disorders among the elderly may have missed the dynamic relationship between symptoms and aging. Teachman asserts that anxiety and depression symptoms among older populations reflect a serious, but understudied or mistake full, health problem. She further iterates that anxiety and depression result from symptoms of negative affect and have harmful consequences for physical health. She conducted a study to evaluate neuroticism, anxiety, and depression in a cross-sectional community sample of 335 individuals. The study's results displayed that symptom levels increased during early adulthood and then held a small decline until older adulthood (mid 70s), when the symptoms again increase with age. The results point to a strong relationship between age and psychological distress. The study suggest that the current data of other studies may suggest that there is a reduction, yet this study indicates that there is still a need to look for age differences that occur during late life.

Another consideration is to examine is where the treatment takes place. Many western countries have less developed services provided in the community or homes for elderly, compared to those who are of working age. Researchers discovered that when treatment for depression was provided in homes, symptoms were reduced and there was a reduction in admissions into nursing homes and psychiatric hospitals. This treatment is highly cost-effective (Klug et al., 2010).

Adjustment Disorders Adjustment difficulties of older adults, including schizophrenia, depression, stress and anxiety disorders, suicidal ideation and behavior, substance abuse, weight problems, offending behavior, relationship problems, cancer, and other problems, have also been successfully treated with cognitive-behavioral approaches (D'Zurilla & Nezu, 2010). With the purpose of testing the effectiveness of cognitive-behavioral therapy (CBT) intervention on PTSD, depression, and distress symptoms, DuHamel et al. (2010) conducted a randomized clinical trial. After a baseline assessment, participants were randomly assigned to a 10-session telephone-administered cognitive-behavioral therapy invention to reduce PTSD symptoms, depression, and general distress or a control group. This study revealed that participants who received CBT reported fewer illness-related PTSD symptoms. The effectiveness of CBT was consistent across follow-up assessments.

In order to apply CBT to older patients with acute physical illness and comorbid depression, Hummel et al. (2017) adopted a randomized-controlled trial with waiting-list control group in a in a geriatric day clinic. Researchers randomly selected 155 participants who were 76–88 years old were hospitalized for acute somatic illness, and scored more than 7 on the Hospital Anxiety and Depression Scale. Significant improvement in the intervention group, but not in the control group, was reported for the depression scales and other secondary outcome variables such as the Barthel and Karnofsky indexes. Researchers concluded that CBT is feasible and highly effective in improving physical and functional parameters.

Adjustment difficulties of elders in community settings have also been evaluated. In one outcome study, 52 elders of limited mobility were randomly assigned to one of three treatment protocols: a 6-week life review program, an equivalent number of "friendly visits," or neither intervention (Haight, 1992). The mean age of the sample was 76 years and all participants were receiving homebound services such as in-home meals. The study included the four outcome measures of life satisfaction measured by the Life Satisfaction Index, well-being measured by Bradburn's Affect Balance Scale, depression operationalized by the Zung Depression Scale, and the Activities of Daily Living Inventory. After 8 weeks, the participants who received life review showed significant gains on life satisfaction and well-being. Retesting after 1 year revealed that these participants continued to improve in life satisfaction, while the individuals who received the other treatment protocols remained the same.

Group Therapies

Group work is a common modality in the treatment of the elderly. Just as the elderly are a heterogeneous population, so are the groups that address their needs. While many elderly are healthy and seek to remain active in their postretirement years, others struggle with physical and cognitive disabilities, medical illness, and loss. In response, a large variety of groups have been developed and are currently used to address the challenges faced by the elderly and their family members. The following section will highlight those studies that utilized more rigorous research designs or those that demonstrated potential for creatively meeting elders' needs through a group modality.

Medical and Functional Disabilities   Researchers have found that of those 65 and older 59% report chronic pain from arthritis (Chen et al., 2011). An 8-week structured group to address the management of chronic pain was developed and tested by Subramanian (1991). The purpose of the group was to reduce participants' ($n = 32$, $M = 62$) subjective perception of pain and increase their physical and psychosocial functioning in spite of the actual presence of pain. Participants were randomly assigned to cognitive-behavioral treatment groups or to a wait-list group. The cognitive-behavioral groups, ranging in size from 5 to 7 members, met weekly for 2 h over a period of 8 weeks. Treatment groups incorporated relaxation training, cognitive restructuring, and social skills training. The Sickness Impact Profile and the Profile of Mood States were used to measure the impact of this treatment. Results showed that at posttest the treatment group improved significantly on measures of physical and psychosocial functioning and on mood status compared to the wait-list group and to pretest measures.

In a more recent study by McBee, Westreich, and Likourezos, a psychoeducational group therapy program for chronic pain, anxiety, and distress, modeled on the Mindfulness-Based Stress Reduction Program, was introduced into a nursing home. The therapy involved breathing exercises, meditation, visualization, guided imagery, music, and aromatherapy to create a calming effect. The author's pre and post tested the clients using the Coop scale. The findings revealed that after the treatment individuals had lower feelings of pain and felt less sad. The clients were able to reframe responses to difficult situations and began to feel more empowered (McBee, Westreich, & Likourezos, 2004).

A cognitive-behavioral group approach was also utilized for the treatment of late-life insomnia. Morin, Kowatch, Barry, and Walton (1993) randomly assigned 24 community-dwelling elders ($M = 67$ years) to a group treatment or to a wait-list control group. All participants had struggled with insomnia for an average of 13 years. The group treatment included a behavioral component (sleep restriction and stimulus control), a cognitive component (altering dysfunctional beliefs about sleep and the impact of sleep loss) and an educational component about food, nutrition, and exercise. Participants met weekly in groups of 4–6 persons for 8 weeks, in 90-min sessions. Polysomnography, sleep diaries, ratings by significant others and by the patients, and psychological measures such as the Beck Depression Scale (BDI), the Profile of Mood States, and the State-Trait Anxiety Scale were utilized to measure participant's pre- and posttest functioning. Those subjects participating in the cognitive-behavioral groups showed a significant decrease in the amount of awake time after sleep and greater sleep efficiency when compared to the control group. These improvements were maintained at 3- and 12-month follow-ups. In regards to the use of CBT, there is valid evidence that the success of CBT in treating sleep disorders is greatly affected by the patient's expectations and the strength of the therapeutic alliance. Constantino et al. (2007) found that for those patients who entered therapy with low expectations, the perception that the therapist was in high affiliation was associated with a greater reduction in sleep disorder symptoms.

However, in a review for evidence-based psychological treatments (EBTs) for insomnia in older adults by McCurry, Logsdon, Teri, and Vitiello, the findings suggest that only two meet EBT criteria: sleep restriction-sleep compression therapy and multicomponent cognitive-behavioral therapy. They further state that there is insufficient evidence to consider other psychological treatments such as cognitive therapy, relaxation, and sleep hygiene education as stand-alone interventions for older adults (McCurry, Logsdon, Teri, & Vitiello, 2007). They suggest that there is a link between physical and psychological health status, and this was not present in any but one study reviewed. They suggest that these are necessary to observe before any more research on insomnia is conducted.

In China, a study was conducted on insomnia and the impacts of a group intervention. They found that many people did not have the information or coping skills to deal with their insomnia. To deal with this problem, there needs to be an increase of psychoeducational programs that address sleep hygiene and insomnia. They also found that the members benefited from the group support (Ng & Chan, 2008).

Evans and colleagues tested the efficacy of telephone group therapy for disabled community elders. In separate studies, legally blind veterans (Evans & Jaureguy, 1982) and physically disabled outpatients (Evans, Smith, Werkhoven, Fox, & Pritzl, 1986) were randomly assigned to cognitive-behavioral telephone groups or to a control group condition. The average age of participants in the studies was 61.7 years and 62.4 years, respectively. In both studies, the treatment groups focused on the development of behavioral goals, goal achievement, the use of positive reinforcement, and problem solving. Three participants and a telephone counselor participated in group telephone therapy 1 h a week for 8 weeks. Before the designated appointment time, group participants were called and placed on the same trunk line so that a group discussion could follow. The Wakefield Self-Rating Depression Scale, the Ellsworth Personal Assessment of Role Skills (Ellsworth, 1975), the UCLA Loneliness Scale, and the Life Satisfaction Index were all used to measure treatment efficacy. Both studies revealed a significant decrease in loneliness. While there was also a decrease in depression, this did not reach a significant level. More recent studies and reviews of the literature have also found that telephone support groups which may link several patients with a therapist can be effective not only for the elderly, but also for their family caregivers. Furthermore, telephone therapy can be used in addressing a large variety of physical and mental health problems, giving it a wide applicability that could, no doubt, be useful as the number of older American increases (Toseland & Rivas, 2005).

Frazier, Mintz, and Mobley conducted a group study including the importance of religion in the lives of older African Americans and the psychological well-being. The study included 86 participants who completed multidimensional measures of religious involvement and well-being. The results indicated that religious involvement (including organizational, non-organizational, and subjective) and psychological well-being correlated. They found that there were positive relations with others, self-acceptance, environmental mastery, purpose in life, and personal growth. This study suggests that for African Americans, especially older African Americans, those who have religious behaviors and positive feelings about one's religion are related to increased psychological well-being (Frazier, Mintz, & Mobley, 2005).

Depression and Anxiety A variety of group methods are utilized to treat community-dwelling elders who suffer from depression and anxiety. Researchers have found that cognitive behavior group therapy reduces depressive symptoms and general functional impairment (Hsu et al., 2010). Most of the studies focusing on this topic have utilized a cognitive-behavioral approach. A research project conducted by Steuer et al. (1984) examined the impact of both cognitive-behavioral and psychodynamically oriented groups. Noninstitutionalized elders ($M = 66$ years), who had suffered from depression for 2 months to 15 years, were randomly assigned to cognitive-behavioral groups or to psychodynamic group psychotherapy. The former groups used cognitive and behavioral strategies to change behavior and modes of thinking. Techniques included the use of weekly activity schedules, mastery and pleasure logs, the recording and examination of cognitive distortions, and the generation of new ways of perceiving life. The latter groups were based on psychoanalytic concepts such as insight, transference, and resistance. All groups met twice a week for 10 weeks and then once a week for 26 weeks for a total of 46 sessions over a period of 9 months. Each session lasted 90 min. The Hamilton Depression Scale, the Hamilton Anxiety Scale, the Zung Self-Rating Depression Scale, and the BDI were administered as pretests and then again at 4, 8, 12, 26, and 36 weeks. Results revealed that participants in both types of group treatment experienced a significant decline in depression and anxiety across time.

Beutler et al. (1987) compared the impact of treating depressed elders with group cognitive therapy, with medication (alprazolam), and with a combination of the two. Elders assigned to cognitive therapy groups met for 90 min per week for a period of 20 weeks. Some of the elders in the therapy groups also received the medication, while others did not. Elders not in group treatment received either medication only or medication and support. Depression, using the Hamilton Rating Scale for Depression and the BDI, cognitive distortions using the Cognitive Error Questionnaire (Beck et al., 1987), and sleep efficiency based on polysomnographic recordings were all measured at pre- and posttest periods. A significant decrease in depression was found for all cognitive therapy groups, regardless of medication status. However, no significant change was revealed for those who received medication but did not participate in the therapy groups.

DeBerry, Davis, and Reinhard (1989) found that a relaxation-meditation group was effective in decreasing anxiety. Participants in a relaxation-meditation group received progressive relaxation combined with meditative imagery. A second treatment group received cognitive restructuring and assertiveness training, while a third group received no treatment and served as a control 32 participants ($M = 68.9$ years) met in treatment groups or a control group twice weekly for 10 weeks. The results of this study indicate that relaxation-meditation group treatment is effective in reducing anxiety. No significant change was found for the cognitive restructuring or control groups.

One study also examined the effects on depression and sense of well-being of two types of support groups as compared to a non-group treatment control group of women over 60. Segrist (2008) compared peer lead support groups, clinician lead support groups, and a non-group oriented treatment control group on measures of depression using The Philadelphia Geriatric Center Morale Scale (PGC Morale Scale) and The Geriatric Depression Scale (GDS). The study participants ranged from ages 60 to 90 ($N = 45$). Of the study participants, 23 participated in peer run groups, 13 in staff run groups, and the remaining 9 received individual services through an older adult oriented community organization. Significant differences in depression levels were found between the peer lead support group and the non-group treatment group, suggesting that peer lead support groups can be a beneficial intervention in the treatment of depression in older women.

Studies have also explored the efficacy of group treatment for depressed nursing home residents. Hussian and Lawrence (1981) tested the relative impact of problem-solving groups, social reinforcement of activity groups, and a group combination of the two. Group treatments were relatively brief, lasting for five sessions, 30 min per session, over a 2-week period. Participants in the problem-solving groups were taught problem definition and formulation, generation of alternatives, and decision making skills. Those in the social reinforcement groups received reinforcement from staff for attendance, participation, and interaction. The BDI was used to measure participants' levels of depression at pretest, after the first and second weeks of treatment, and at a 3-month follow-up. After 2 weeks, the problem-solving groups evidenced a significant decline in depression when compared with both of the other groups. However, the effects did not last posttreatment. At the 3-month follow-up, no significant difference was found between groups.

Husaini et al. (2004) also used a group therapy program targeting depression among elderly residents of subsidized high-rise apartments in Nashville, TN. The therapy included 303 women who attended 12 sessions. In the group therapy settings they worked on exercise and preventive health behaviors, cognitive and re-motivation therapy, reminiscence and grief therapy, and social skills development (2004). They found that group therapy could provide a supportive environment for elders to work out challenges they have had to come in contact with throughout their lives. The most difference was seen with the Caucasian women, those between the ages of 55 and 75, and those individuals who reported a greater number of symptoms consistent with minor clinical depression before the program. However, as far as minority's results, there is a need for further research.

Dhooper, Green, Huff, and Austin-Murphy (1993) also utilized a group problem-solving approach in the treatment of depressed nursing home residents. Sixteen depressed, cognitively intact residents ($M = 77.6$ years) were randomly assigned to a treatment or a control group. A combination of problem solving and reminiscence was used in the treatment group to counteract social isolation and increase participants' ability to cope with nursing home life. Groups met once a week over a 9-week period. Depression was measured through the administration of the Zung Depression Scale at pre- and posttest intervals. A significant difference was found in the depression levels of the problem-solving group when compared with the control group.

Greenglass, Fiksenbaum, and Eaton (2006) were interested in the relationship between coping, social support, functional disability, and depression in the elderly. Respondents were 224 community-residing older adults, mostly female. Volunteers were asked to participate in a study on reactions to day-to-day events, as well as complete a self-report questionnaire. Proactive coping was measured by the Proactive Coping subscale, depression by the Brief Symptom Inventory, physical health status by the Survey of Health Problems, and social support by the Social Support Behaviors Scale. The study offered an opportunity to test a synergistic model of social support and coping and its relationship to elderly functioning. The results showed that proactive coping was negatively associated with functional disability and with depression. Social support was positively associated with proactive coping techniques based on proactivity. Also there is a strong relationship between social support and coping where social support is positively related to improved coping skills. This study helps to show the importance of combined relationships of social support and coping to elderly functioning.

Quality of Life of Healthy Community-Dwelling Elders A variety of groups have emerged to meet the needs and enhance the lives of community-dwelling elders. While the goals and techniques utilized by these groups vary, the assumptions of such groups are based on the belief in elders' capacity for continued learning, growth, and development. Shin, Byeon, Kang, and Oak (2008) developed a study on physical symptom, activities of daily living, and health-related quality of life in the community-dwelling older adults. The purpose of this study is to explore and test the relationships among daily living activities, physical symptoms, and health-related life quality in the target population. The three variables were measured by three commonly used indexes. Physical symptoms were measured by the Physical Health Questionnaire; activities of daily living were measured by the Late-Life Functional and Disability Instrument; health-related quality of life was measured by the Medical Outcomes Short-Form Health Survey. Researchers adopted a stratified random sampling to recruit participants. A total of 242 community-dwelling elderly adults were recruited in this study. The results demonstrated that health-related life quality is significantly associated with the physical symptoms and daily living activities.

Daily living activities, physical symptoms, and health-related life quality. This study provided a better understanding of the relationship among physical symptoms, activities of daily living, and health-related life quality and providing the promising future of health programs that promotes older adults' health.

Xu and Chow (2011) conducted a case study to explore the community-based mutual aid group delivery model in China. This study not only provided an insight to the progress of community-based elderly service in China but also explores the community's role in this model. In this study, a new service delivery and community practice, a horizontal-vertical mixed model, was adopted. Vertical model are services that are funded by municipal governments. Most vertical services are free or nearly free. At the same time, horizontal model are services that are funded by multiple community and governmental resources, including personal donations, volunteers, organizations, schools, local businesses, and so forth. Horizontal model was designed for the elderly who can afford to pay for the services. In this study, we can see the role of the different levels of government in terms of mutual aid group for the aging group is developing and making progresses.

Groups for well-functioning older adults are promising approach for the treatment of subthreshold depression (Spek et al., 2007). Participants were 191 female and 110 male with subthreshold depression. Researchers randomly assign them into group cognitive behavior therapy, internet-based treatment, or a waiting-list control group. After participating 10 weeks, participants provided answers on the Beck Depression Inventory (BDI). A significant difference between the treatment groups and the control group was founded. The group cognitive-behavioral therapy was found to be at least as effective as the internet-based intervention.

Volunteers at senior centers were randomly assigned to multimodal behavioral therapy (MBT) groups or to a wait-list control group. The MBT groups met once a week for 75 minutes over an 8-week period. Problem identification, specification, and -solving skills were demonstrated and applied to participants' particular concerns. The Philadelphia Geriatric Center Morale Scale and a Problem Checklist designed for the study were administered at pre- and posttest intervals. Results revealed that MBT group participants experienced a significant decline in the number of problems and a significant gain in morale when compared with control group members.

Another area of concern for some older adults is the well-being after a job loss. Rife Mandal, Ayyagari, and Gallo (2011) conducted a secondary data analysis to reveal the relationship between unemployment and mental health status. The data used in this study were taken from the US Health and Retirement Study (HRS), which was a nationally representative sample of individuals who are 67 and 77 years old and their spouses regardless of age. This study found that the effect of unemployment on mental health status is significant on both age groups, and it is higher in magnitude in the 67 years old group. This study also revealed that old adults with lower education who experience unemployment reported worse mental health. Healthy relationship improved mental health while separation and divorce impacted mental health negatively for individuals who experience unemployment.

Older Family Members Over the past two decades there has been growing recognition of the unique dynamics present in late-life families. While all families undergo change related to members' aging processes, most studies have focused on those families struggling with caregiving responsibilities.

Gillespie, Mullan, and Harrison (2014) conducted a systematic review of the literature to describe the role of informal caregivers' medication management for older adults and people living with dementia in the community. Searched research articles written in 2000–2013, this study found 10 articles that described this topic. This study concluded that good medication management by informal caregivers improved the health outcomes and reduced institutional isolations. Specific medication management knowledge and skills are required for a better practice.

Blom, Zarit, Zwaaftink, Cuijpers, and Pot (2015) also explored the effectiveness of internet-based group treatment to assist Dementia' caregiver support. In this study, 251 caregivers were randomly assigned to a experimental group and a control group. The outcome variables were the scores of Center for Epidemiologic Studies Depression Scale: CES-D and Hospital Anxiety and Depression Scale: HADS-A. After the intervention, caregivers receiving the internet-based group treatment reported significantly lower symptoms of depression and anxiety comparing to their peers who were assigned to the control group. This intervention might become more promising because of the fact that future generations of caregivers will be more familiar with the Internet.

Dyck et al. (2016) evaluated the efficacy of an evidence-based psychosocial group treatment, Multi-Family Group (MFG) intervention, using a randomized-controlled design. A total of 32 individuals with SCI were recruited and randomly assigned to an MFG intervention group and a control group where participants receiving education. Participants received a baseline test, a post-program and a 6-month post-program test. Results demonstrated that MFG group treatment was superior to general education. The coping skills of participants and supportive strategies were improved after receiving this treatment.

A group program evaluated by Paukert, LeMaire, and Cully (2009) focused on care recipients rather than on the caregivers. The purpose of this study is to determine the role of some factors in predicting depressive symptoms. Veterans who at least 60 years old with heart failure were invited to attend this study. Participants provided demographic information, heart failure physical limitations, perception of heart failure intrusiveness, coping mechanisms, loss of control, self-efficacy, and social support. This study revealed that physical limitaitons from heart failure, perpections of heart failure intrusiveness, less-skilled coping skills, and heart failure efficacy are significantly associated with depressive symptoms.

A new intervention has increased with the influx of technology, called Computer Telephone Integrated System (CTIS). It is focused on the family caregivers of those who have dementia, who are at risk for depression. A computer and telephone connects the client to support among family members and their community. With the access to these resources family members can become involved in family therapy by using the phone or computer even if they are not in the same vicinity. The social worker is able to include the clients' support network and encourage the supportive behavior, often a missing ingredient in the caregiver's life. Supportive members of the caregiver's network may not be able to be in the same area, but they can still provide support (Eisdorfer et al., 2003).

Community Prevention Approaches

In order for older adults to remain functional in society, it is necessary for them to maintain an adequate level of psychosocial, economic, and physical well-being. Programs can maximize the quality of life by providing information and identifying lifestyle factors that can prevent or delay the onset of illnesses, disability, or other problems. This section includes community and prevention programs that have been found to be effective in promoting the health and well-being of older adults.

In one study involving community prevention approaches, there were positive outcomes. The study by Graff, Vernooij-Dassen, Hoefnagels, Dekker, and Witte in 2003 piloted a study to explore the effects of occupational therapy on the performance of daily activities by older individuals with cognitive impairments and on the sense of competence of their primary caregivers (Graff, Vernooij-Dassen, Hoefnagels, Dekker, & Witte, 2003). Included in the study were 12 older individuals with cognitive impairments alongside their primary caregivers and were randomized. A pre and posttest was given before and after 5 weeks of occupational therapy at home. The main outcome measures were older clients' motor and process skills, initiative, need for assistance, self-perception in occupational performance, and satisfaction with this performance in daily activities and primary caregivers' sense of competence. The results indicated that older adults' motor and process skills and self-perception in occupational performance improved and that they needed less help. This study helped to illuminate the effectiveness of occupational therapy in older individuals with cognitive impairments and their primary caregivers.

A major threat to older adults is home accidents. Sjösten and his research team described the implementation and the effects of a multifactorial fall prevention program. Researchers used a randomized-controlled trial. A total number of 591 participants were randomly assigned into two groups. One group received an intensive multifactorial prevention program and the other group received a one-time counseling on fall prevention. The prevention program included individual geriatric assessment, guidance and treatment, individual guidance on fall prevention, physical exercise, psychosocial group activities, lectures, home exercises, and home hazards assessment. This study demonstrated that this program can effectively improve the amount of regularly taken medicines. However, there were no other significant results founded.

Another problem faced by some older adults is alcoholism, yet awareness of this addiction in the older population is low. Moos, Schutte, Brennan, and Moos (2009) provided a 20-year perspective towards the older adults' alcohol consumption and drinking problems. There were 719 adults aged between 55 and 65 participating this study. A baseline survey was administered to them and then there was follow-up surveys 10 years and 20 years later. This study reported that adults were less likely to drink excessively over the 20-year interval. However, a substantial percentage of older adults reported excessive alcohol consumption. At ages 75–85, 27% women and 49% men still experience drinking problems.

Many older adults are involved with health care, yet often they do not have any advanced directives in case of an emergency situation. Brinkman-Stoppelenburg, Rietjens, and van der Heide (2014) conducted a systematic review to explore the effects of advance care planning on end-of-life care and gain insight in the effectiveness of different types of advance care planning. Researchers systematically searched and used 113 papers. Based on the review of these papers, the researchers drew a conclusion that there were intensive studies about the effects of different types of advance care planning. Existing literature provided evidence that advance care planning contributes to the improvements of the quality of end-of-life care.

Still another area of extreme importance that requires more research is that of Service-Learning (SL) projects. Lanana (2003) suggests that research populations seldom involve the elderly for purposes of improving their quality of life. To address the need to develop novel SL gerontology applications the study offers recommendations on ways to minimize the possible challenges of implementation of the new studies concerning SL. This further research would encompass some of the difficult topics such as elderly abuse and sexuality in older adults. Further research would benefit different professionals, quality of life for the elderly as well as lead to many positive outcomes.

Summary

In summary, various intervention approaches are helpful with older adults. Some methods have been successfully used in both individual treatment and group approaches, such as cognitive-behavioral therapy and relaxation. Outcome studies in physical and social functioning, as well as psychiatric conditions, indicate that practice with older adults can prevent and ameliorate problematic conditions that occur in late life. Demographics suggest that greater numbers of older adults will become clients of social work practitioners in coming years. Therefore, even greater efforts toward identifying and evaluating practice with older adults are necessary.

References

Aging America: Trends and projections. (1991). Washington, DC: U.S. Senate Special Committee on Aging, American Association of Retired Persons, the Federal Council on the Aging, and the U.S. Administration on Aging.

Alwahhabi, F. (2003). Anxiety symptoms and generalized anxiety disorder in the elderly: A review. *Harvard Review of Psychiatry, 11*(4), 180–193.

Beautrais, A. L. (2002). A case control study of suicide and attempted suicide in older adults. *Suicide and Life-Threatening Behavior, 32*(1), 1–9.

Beck, A. T., Epstein, N., Brown, G., & Steer, R. A. (1988). An inventory for measuring clinical anxiety: Psychometric properties. *Journal of Consulting and Clinical Psychology, 56,* 893–897.

Beck, A. T., Rush, A. J., Shaw, B. F., & Emery, G. (1987). *Cognitive therapy of depression.* New York, NY: Guilford Press.

Beck, A. T., Steer, R. A., & Brown, G. K. (1996). *Beck depression inventory-II manual.* San Antonio, TX: Psychological Connections.

Beck, A. T., Ward, C., Mendelson, M., Mock, J., & Erbaugh, J. (1971). An inventory for measuring depression. *Archives of General Psychiatry, 4,* 561–571.

Beutler, L. E., Scogin, F., Kirkish, P., Schretlen, D., Corbishley, A., Hamblin, D., … Levenson, A. I. (1987). Group cognitive therapy and alprazolam in the treatment of depression in older adults. *Journal of Consulting and Clinical Psychology, 55,* 550–556.

Blaivas, A. J., Ancoli-Israel, S., Neubauer, D., & Sheldon, S. H. (2014). *The future treatment of insomnia: Exploring the mechanisms of action.* http://www.cecity.com/aoa/monographs/oct_14/insomnia_oct14.pdf

Blay, S. L., Andreoli, S. B., Dewey, M. E., & Gastal, F. L. (2007). Co-occurrence of chronic physical pain and psychiatric morbidity in a community sample of older people. *International Journal of Geriatric Psychiatry, 22,* 902–908.

Blom, M. M., Zarit, S. H., Zwaaftink, R. B. G., Cuijpers, P., & Pot, A. M. (2015). Effectiveness of an internet intervention for family caregivers of people with dementia: Results of a randomized controlled trial. *PLoS One, 10*(2), e0116622.

Bohlmeijer, E., Roemer, M., Cuijpers, P., & Smit, F. (2007). The effects of reminiscence on psychological well-being in older adults: A meta-analysis. *Aging and Mental Health, 11*(3), 291–300.

Bradburn, H. (1969). *Structure of psychological well-being.* Chicago, IL: Aldine.

Brinkman-Stoppelenburg, A., Rietjens, J. A., & van der Heide, A. (2014). The effects of advance care planning on end-of-life care: A systematic review. *Palliative Medicine, 28*(8), 1000–1025.

Calamari, J. E., Faber, S. D., Hitsman, B. L., & Poppe, C. J. (1994). Treatment of obsessive compulsive disorder in the elderly: A review and case example. *Journal of Behavior Therapy and Experimental Psychiatry, 25*(2), 95–104.

Carek, P. J., Laibstain, S. E., & Carek, S. M. (2011). Exercise for the treatment of depression and anxiety. *International Journal of Psychiatry in Medicine, 41*(1), 15–28.

Carreira, K., Miller, M. D., Frank, E., Houck, P. R., Morse, J. Q., Dew, M. A., … Reynolds, C. F. (2008). A controlled evaluation of monthly maintenance Interpersonal Psychotherapy in late-life depression with varying levels of cognitive performance. *International Journal of Geriatric Psychiatry, 23*, 1110–1113.

Chen, Q., Hayman, L. L., Shmerling, R. H., Bean, J. F., & Leveille, S. G. (2011). Characteristics of chronic pain associated with sleep difficulty in older adults: The maintenance of balance, independent living, intellect, and zest in the elderly (MOBILIZE) Boston study. *Journal of the American Geriatrics Society, 59*(8), 1385–1392.

Choi, T., LaVohn, J., & Christensen, M. (1983). Health specific family coping index for non-institutional care. *American Journal of Public Health, 73*, 1275–1277.

Clark, L. A., Watson, D., & Mineka, S. (1994). Temperament, personality, and the mood and anxiety disorders. *Journal of Abnormal Psychology, 103*(1), 103.

Cohen, S., Kamarck, T., & Mermelstein, R. (1983). A global measure of perceived stress. *Journal of Health and Social Behavior, 24*, 385–396.

Constantino, M. J., Manber, R., Ong, J., Kuo, T. F., Huang, J. S., & Arnow, B. A. (2007). Patient expectations and therapeutic alliance as predictors of outcome in group cognitive-behavioral therapy for insomnia. *Behavioral Sleep Medicine, 5*, 210–228.

Cummings, S. M., & Kropf, N. P. (Eds.). (2009). *Handbook of psychosocial interventions with older adults: Evidence-based treatment.* London, England: Routledge.

D'Zurilla, T. J., & Nezu, A. M. (2010). Problem-solving therapy. *Handbook of Cognitive-Behavioral Therapies, 3*, 197–225.

Dauvilliers, Y. (2007). Insomnia in patients with neurodegenerative conditions. *Sleep Medicine, 8*(4), 27–34.

Derogatis, L. R., & Spencer, P. M. (1993). *Brief symptom inventory: BSI* (Vol. 18). Upper Saddle River, NJ: Pearson.

DeBerry, S., Davis, S., & Reinhard, K. E. (1989). A comparison of meditation-relaxation and cognitive behavioral techniques for reducing anxiety and depression in a geriatric population. *Journal of Geriatric Psychiatry, 22*, 231–247.

Dhooper, S. S., Green, S. M., Huff, M. B., & Austin-Murphy, J. (1993). Efficacy of a group approach to reducing depression in nursing home elderly residents. *Journal of Gerontological Social Work, 20*, 87–100.

Driessen, E., Van, H. L., Don, F. J., Peen, J., Kool, S., Westra, D., … Dekker, J. J. (2013). The efficacy of cognitive-behavioral therapy and psychodynamic therapy in the outpatient treatment of major depression: A randomized clinical trial. *American Journal of Psychiatry, 170*(9), 1041–1050.

DuHamel, K. N., Mosher, C. E., Winkel, G., Labay, L. E., Rini, C., Meschian, Y. M., … Grosskreutz, C. L. (2010). Randomized clinical trial of telephone-administered cognitive-behavioral therapy to reduce post-traumatic stress disorder and distress symptoms after hematopoietic stem-cell transplantation. *Journal of Clinical Oncology, 28*(23), 3754–3761.

Dyck, D. G., Weeks, D. L., Gross, S., Smith, C. L., Lott, H. A., Wallace, A. J., & Wood, S. M. (2016). Comparison of two psycho-educational family group interventions for improving psycho-social outcomes in persons with spinal cord injury and their caregivers: A randomized-controlled trial of multi-family group intervention versus an active education control condition. *BMC Psychology, 4*(1), 40.

Edinger, J. D., Hoelscher, T. J., Marsh, G. R., Lipper, S., & Ionescu-Pioggia, M. (1992). A cognitive-behavioral therapy for sleep-maintenance insomnia in older adults. *Psychology and Aging, 7*, 282–289.

Eisdorfer, C., Czaja, S. J., Loewenstein, D. A., Rubert, M. P., Arguelles, S., Mitrani, V. B., & Szapocznik, J. (2003). The effect of a family therapy and technology-based intervention on caregiver depression. *The Gerontologist, 43*(4), 521–531.

Ellsworth, R. (1975). Consumer feedback in measuring the effectiveness of mental health programs. In M. Guttentag (Ed.), *Handbook of evaluation research* (pp. 239–274). London, England: Sage.

Endicott, J., & Spitzer, R. (1978). A diagnostic interview for affective disorders and schizophrenia. *Archives of General Psychiatry, 35*, 837–844.

Ensrud, K. E., Blackwell, T. L., Anscoli-Israel, S., Redline, S., Yaffe, K., Diem, S., ... Stone, K. L. (2006). Use of selective serotonin reuptake inhibitors and sleep disturbances in community dwelling older women. *Journal of the American Geriatrics Society, 54*, 1508–1515.

Evans, R. L., & Jaureguy, B. M. (1982). Phone therapy outreach for blind elderly. *The Gerontologist, 22*, 32–35.

Evans, R. L., Smith, K. M., Werkhoven, W. S., Fox, H. R., & Pritzl, D. O. (1986). Cognitive telephone group therapy with physically disabled elderly persons. *The Gerontologist, 26*, 8–10.

Folkman, S., & Lazarus, R. S. (1980). An analysis of coping in a middle-aged community sample. *Journal of Health and Social Behavior, 21*, 219–239.

Frazier, C., Mintz, L. B., & Mobley, M. (2005). A multidimensional look at religious involvement and psychological well-being among urban elderly African Americans. *Journal of Counseling Psychology, 52*(4), 583–590.

Fuh, J. L., Wang, S. J., Lu, S. R., Tsai, P. H., Lai, T. H., & Lai, K. L. (2008). A 13-year long-term study of elderly with chronic daily headache. *Cephalalgia, 28*, 1017–1022.

Gillespie, R., Mullan, J., & Harrison, L. (2014). Managing medications: The role of informal caregivers of older adults and people living with dementia. A review of the literature. *Journal of Clinical Nursing, 23*(23–24), 3296–3308.

Gould, R. L., Coulson, M. C., & Howard, R. J. (2012). Efficacy of cognitive behavioral therapy for anxiety disorders in older people: A meta-analysis and meta-regression of randomized controlled trials. *Journal of the American Geriatrics Society, 60*(2), 218–229.

Graff, M. J., Vernooij-Dassen, M. J., Hoefnagels, W. H., Dekker, J., & Witte, L. P. (2003). Occupational therapy at home for older individuals with mild to moderate cognitive impairments and their primary caregivers: A Pilot Study. *Occupation, Participation and Health, 23*(4), 155–164.

Greenglass, E., Fiksenbaum, L., & Eaton, J. (2006). The relationship between coping, social support, functional disability and depression in the elderly. *Anxiety, Stress, and Coping, 19*(1), 15–31.

Greenglass, E., Schwarzer, R., Jakubiec, D., Fiksenbaum, L., & Taubert, S. (1999). The proactive coping inventory (PCI): A multidimensional research instrument. In *20th International Conference of the Stress and Anxiety Research Society (STAR)*, Cracow, Poland (Vol. 12, p. 14).

Haight, B. K. (1992). Long-term effects of a structured life review process. *Journal of Gerontology, 47*, 312–P315.

Hamilton, M. (1959). The assessment of anxiety states by rating. *British Journal of Medical Psychology, 32*, 50–55.

Hamilton, M. (1967). Development of a rating scale for primary depressive illness. *British Journal of Social and Clinical Psychology, 6*, 287–296.

Hanna-Pladdy, B., Heilman, K., & Foundas, A. (2003). Ecological implications of ideomotor apraxia: Evidence from physical activities of daily living. *Neurology, 60*(3), 487–490.

Hsu, C., Weng, C., Kuo, C., Lin, C., Jong, M., Kuo, S., & Chen, P. (2010). Effects of a cognitive-behavioral group program for community-dwelling elderly with minor depression. *International Journal of Geriatric Psychiatry, 25*(6), 654–655.

Hummel, J., Weisbrod, C., Boesch, L., Himpler, K., Hauer, K., Hautzinger, M., ... Dutzi, I. (2017). AIDE–acute illness and depression in elderly patients. Cognitive behavioral group psychotherapy in geriatric patients with comorbid depression: A randomized, controlled trial. *Journal of the American Medical Directors Association, 18*(4), 341–349.

Husaini, B. A., Cummings, S., Kilbourne, B., Roback, H., Sherkat, D., LeVine, R., & Cain, V. A. (2004). Group therapy for depressed elderly women. *International Journal of Group Psychotherapy, 54*(3), 295–319.

Hussian, R. A., & Lawrence, P. S. (1981). Social reinforcement of activity and problem-solving training in the treatment of depressed institutionalized elderly. *Cognitive Therapy and Research, 5*, 57–69.

Jones, D., Duffy, M. E., Flanagan, J., & Foster, F. (2012). Psychometric evaluation of the functional health pattern assessment screening tool (FHPAST). *International Journal of Nursing Knowledge, 23*(3), 140–145.

Klug, G., Hermann, G., Fuchs-Nieder, B., Panzer, M., Haider-Stipacek, A., Zapotoczky, H. G., & Priebe, S. (2010). Effectiveness of home treatment for elderly people with depression: Randomised controlled trial. *The British Journal of Psychiatry, 197*(6), 463–467.

Kropf, N. P., & Cummings, S. M. (2017). *Evidence-based treatment with older adults: Theory, research & practice.* New York, NY: Oxford University Press.

Lanana, L. (2003). Using service learning research to enhance the elderly's quality of life. *Educational Gerontology, 29*, 685–701.

Lapid, M. I., & Rummans, T. A. (2003). Evaluation and management of geriatric depression in primary care. *Geriatric Depression in Primary Care, 78*, 1423–1429.

Lapierre, S., Erlangsen, A., Waern, M., De Leo, D., & Oyama, H. (2011). A systematic review of elderly suicide prevention programs. *Crisis, 32*(2), 88–98.

Lawton, M. P. (1975). The Philadelphia Geriatric Morale Scale: A revision. *Journal of Gerontology, 30*, 85–89.

Lawton, M. P., Moss, M. S., Hoffman, C., & Winter, L. (2002). Motivation in later life: Personal projects and well-being. *Psychology and Aging, 17*(4), 539–547.

Levin, J. S., Taylor, R. J., & Chatters, L. M. (1995). A multidimensional measure of religious involvement for African Americans. *The Sociological Quarterly, 36*(1), 157–173.

Mandal, B., Ayyagari, P., & Gallo, W. T. (2011). Job loss and depression: The role of subjective expectations. *Social Science & Medicine, 72*(4), 576–583.

McBee, L., Westreich, L., & Likourezos, A. (2004). A psychoeducational relaxation group for pain and stress management in the nursing home. *Journal of Social Work in Long-Term Care, 3*(1), 15–28.

McCurry, S. M., Logsdon, R. G., Teri, L., & Vitiello, M. V. (2007). Evidence-based psychological treatments for insomnia in older adults. *Psychology and Aging, 22*(1), 18–27.

McEntee, M. L., Vowles, K. E., & McCracken, L. M. (2016). Development of a chronic pain–specific version of the Sickness Impact Profile. *Health Psychology, 35*(3), 228.

McNair, D. M., Lorr, M., & Droppleman, L. F. (1971). *Manual for the profile of mood states (POMS).* San Diego: Educational and Industrial Testing Service.

Moos, R. H., Schutte, K. K., Brennan, P. L., & Moos, B. S. (2009). Older adults' alcohol consumption and late-life drinking problems: A 20-year perspective. *Addiction, 104*(8), 1293–1302.

Morin, C. M., Kowatch, R. A., Barry, T., & Walton, E. (1993). Cognitive-behavioral therapy for late-life insomnia. *Journal of Consulting and Clinical Psychology, 61*, 137–146.

Neugarten, B., Havighurst, R., & Tobin, S. (1961). The measurement of life satisfaction. *Journal of Gerontology, 16*, 134–143.

Ng, P., & Chan, K. (2008). Integrated group program for improving sleep quality of elderly people. *Journal of Gerontological Social Work, 51*, 366–378.

Nicholson, N. L., & Blanchard, E. B. (1993). A controlled evaluation of behavioral treatment of chronic headache in the elderly. *Behavior Therapy, 24*, 395–408.

Onen, S. H., Dubray, C., Decullier, E., Moreau, T., Chapuis, F., & Onen, F. (2008). Observation-based nocturnal sleep inventory: Screening tool for sleep apnea in elderly people. *Journal of the American Geriatrics Society, 56*, 1920–1925.

Oyama, H., Goto, M., Fujita, M., Shibuya, H., & Sakashita, T. (2006). Preventing elderly suicide through primary care by community-based screening for depression in rural Japan. *Crisis, 27*(2), 58–65.

Paukert, A. L., LeMaire, A., & Cully, J. A. (2009). Predictors of depressive symptoms in older veterans with heart failure. *Aging & Mental Health, 13*(4), 601–610.

Puentes, W. J. (2003). Cognitive therapy integrated with life review techniques: An eclectic treatment approach for affective symptoms in older adults. *Journal of Clinical Nursing, 13*, 84–89.

Radloff, L. S. (1977). The CES-D Scale: A self-report depression scale for research in the general population. *Applied Psychological Measurement, 1*, 385–401.

Reynolds, C. R., Richmond, B. O., & Lowe, P. A. (2003). The adult manifest anxiety Scale-.4dult version. Los Angeles: Western Psychological Services.

Russell, D., Peplau, L. A., & Ferguson, M. L. (1978). Developing a measure of loneliness. *Journal of Personality Assessment, 42*, 290–294.

Ryff, C. D., & Essex, M. J. (1992). The interpretation of life experience and well-being: The sample case of relocation. *Psychology and aging, 7*(4), 507.

Segrist, K. A. (2008). Impact of support groups on well-being of older women. *Journal of Gerontological Social Work, 51*(1/2), 42.

Sherbourne, C. D., & Stewart, A. L. (1991). The MOS social support survey. *Social science & medicine, 32*(6), 705–714.

Shin, K. R., Byeon, Y. S., Kang, Y., & Oak, J. (2008). A study on physical symptom, activity of daily living, and health-related quality of life (HRQoL) in the community-dwelling older adults. *Journal of Korean Academy of Nursing, 38*(3), 437–444.

Silvertsen, B., Omvik, S., Pallesen, S., Bjorvatn, B., Havik, O. E., Kvale, G., … Nordhus, I. H. (2006). Cognitive behavioral therapy vs zopiclone for treatment of chronic primary insomnia in older adults: A randomized controlled trial. *JAMA, 295*(24), 2851–2858.

Smalbrugge, M., Pot, A. M., Jongenelis, L., Gundy, C. M., Beekman, A. T., & Eefsting, J. A. (2006). The impact of depression, and anxiety, on well being, disability and use of health care services in nursing home patients. *International Journal of Geriatric Psychiatry, 21*, 325–332.

Snaith, R. P., Ahmed, S., Mehta, S., & Hamilton, M. (1971). Assessment of the severity of primary depressive illness. *Psychological Medicine, 1*, 143–149.

Soeffing, J. P., Lichstein, K. L., Nau, S. D., McCrae, C. S., Wilson, N. M., Aguillard, R. N., … Bush, A. J. (2008). Psychological treatment of insomnia in hypnotic-dependant older adults. *Sleep Medicine, 9*(2), 165–171.

Spek, V., Nyklíček, I., Smits, N., Cuijpers, P. I. M., Riper, H., Keyzer, J., & Pop, V. (2007). Internet-based cognitive behavioural therapy for subthreshold depression in people over 50 years old: A randomized controlled clinical trial. *Psychological Medicine, 37*(12), 1797–1806.

Spielberger, C. D., Gorsuch, R., & Lushene, R. E. (1967). *State-trait anxiety inventory, preliminary manual for form B*. Unpublished manual. Tal-lahassee, FL: Florida State University.

Spielberger, C. D., Gorsuch, R. L., & Luchene, R. E. (1970). *Manual for the state-trait anxiety inventory*. Palo Alto, CA: Consulting Psychologists Press.

Steuer, J. L., Mintz, J., Hammen, C. L., Hill, M. A., Jarvik, L. F., McCarley, T., … Rosen, R. (1984). Cognitive-behavioral and psychodynamic group psychotherapy in treatment of geriatric depression. *Journal of Consulting and Clinical Psychology, 52*, 180–189.

Stinson, C., Long, E. M., Kireuk, T., Peraza-Smith, G. B., & Flanagan, N. M. (2014). Reminiscence: Improving the quality of life for older adults. *Geriatric Nursing, 35*(5), 399–404.

Stober, J., & Bittencourt, J. (1998). Weekly assessment of worry: An adaptation of the Penn State Worry Questionnaire for monitoring changes during treatment. *Behavior Research and Therapy, 36*, 645–656.

Streiner, D. L., Cairney, J., & Veldhuizen, S. (2006). The epidemiology of psychological problems in the elderly. *Canadian Journal of Psychiatry, 51*(3), 185–191.

Subramanian, K. (1991). Structured group work for the management of chronic pain: An experimental investigation. *Research on Social Work Practice, 1*, 32–45.

Teachman, B. (2006). Aging and negative affect: The rise and fall and rise of anxiety and depression symptoms. *Psychology and Aging, 21*(1), 201–207.

Thyer, B. A. (1991). Diagnosis and treatment of child and adolescent anxiety disorders. *Behavior Modification, 15*(3), 310–325.

Toseland, R., & Rivas, R. (2005). *An introduction to group work practice* (5th ed.). Needham Heights, MA: Allyn & Bacon.

U.S. Census Bureau. (2010). *Age and sex composition: 2010* (2010 Census briefs). Washington, DC: Government Printing Office.

Vitaliano, P. P., Russo, J., Carr, J. E., Maiuro, R. D., & Becker, J. (1985). The ways of coping checklist: Revision and psychometric properties. *Multivariate Behavioral Research, 20*(1), 3–26.

Xu, Q., & Chow, J. C. (2011). Exploring the community-based service delivery model: Elderly care in China. *International Social Work, 54*(3), 374–387.

Yesavage, J. A., Brink, T. L., Lum, O., Huang, V., Adey, M. B., & Leivor, V. O. (1983). Development and validation of a geriatric depression rating scale: A preliminary report. *Journal of Psychiatric Research, 17*, 27–49.

Zuckerman, M., & Lubin, W. (1960). *Affect adjective checklist*. New York, NY: Educational and Industrial Testing Service.

Zung, W. W. K. (1965). A self-rating depression scale. *Archives of General Psychiatry, 12*, 63–70.

Chapter 13
Promoting Self-Management of Chronic Medical Problems

Jan Ligon

Chronic Medical Problems

A 1996 study published by the Harvard School of Public Health (Murray & Lopez, 1996) forecasted that chronic medical conditions would replace infectious diseases as the primary global health concern by the year 2020. Indeed, chronic health conditions, also known as noncommunicable diseases (NCDs) now account for 71% of all deaths worldwide (World Health Organization, 2018). As the world's population continues to age and medical technology advances, health-related expenditures are likely to move from infectious to chronic conditions.

The combined influences of a shift in emphasis to chronic medical conditions, an aging population, and a continuing reform of the health care system may significantly change the role of social workers in health care. Regardless of future changes in the health care system, former US Surgeon General C. Everett Koop (1996) believes that "one thing seems certain; the economics of health care will mean that patients are going to have less time with their doctors" (p. 69).

Changing Roles in Health Care

According to Wodarski, Wodarski, Nixon, and Mackie (1991), prior to the 1960s "reliance on the family physician as primary change agent was reasonable and necessary" (p. 20) because of the focus on infectious diseases. However, the authors

Original chapter written by Jan Ligon in *Handbook of Empirical Social Work Practice: Social Problems and Practice Issues* (1998), John S. Wodarski and Bruce A. Thyer, Eds.

J. Ligon (✉)
School of Social Work, Andrew Young School of Policy Studies, Georgia State University, Atlanta, GA, USA
e-mail: jligon@gsu.edu

© Springer Nature Switzerland AG 2019
J. S. Wodarski, L. M. Hopson (eds.), *Empirically Based Interventions Targeting Social Problems*, https://doi.org/10.1007/978-3-030-28487-9_13

note that as the predominant area of health problems began shifting to chronic conditions, which are often related to unhealthy lifestyles, the health care system began "to include active client responsibility in the treatment of disease and the maintenance of health" (p. 20). As noted by Wodarski et al. (1991), "interdisciplinary fields are forming as traditional boundaries between disciplines break to accommodate the biopsychosocial model" (p. 21). Instead of waiting for a physician's instructions, patients are actively participating as informed partners in tandem with other resource persons, including medical personnel, social workers, psychologists, dietary and exercise consultants, and other paraprofessionals and volunteers.

This chapter provides information concerning methods that have been found to be effective in the self-management of four common chronic medical problems: (a) diabetes, (b) arthritis, (c) headache and low back pain, and (d) asthma. While these four chronic conditions are the focus of this chapter, research has shown that self-management can be effective for a wide variety of chronic conditions, and for a range of demographics, such as age, including children and their families (Henry & Schor, 2015), culture, and language spoken (Ritter, Lee, & Lorig, 2011).

Promoting Self-Management

As the role of the patient moves away from that of relying on the professional as expert and the predominant area of medical problems shifts to chronic conditions, the ability to self-manage a wide range of health problems will become increasingly important. Social workers Ivanoff and Stem (1992) define self-management as "the naturally occurring process by which individual identify and solve problems in the absence of external intervention" (p. 32). As noted earlier by Vattano, although patients "may be taught by professionals, the client assumes major responsibility for their operation in helping himself or herself' (Vattano, 1978, p. 113). Lorig (1996) agrees and describes self-management as being more complex than education alone, "in that it assists patients in gaining skills and, more important, gaining the confidence to apply these skills on a day-to-day basis" (p. xiv). Towle and Godolphin (2011) propose that chronic disease self-management is being largely ignored in medical education, which has resulted in a significant gap between medical professional's understanding of chronic disease self-management and patient expertise. This research suggests that future medical education should correct this problem by requiring better support of self-management.

Coleman and Newton (2005) explain self-management as the chronic conditions that many people struggle with today for example, "deciding what to eat, whether to exercise, if and when they will take medications" (p. 1). They define self-management support as a technique that professionals mainly use to contribute and motivate their clients in order to provide information, and help work in partnership with "patients to make medical decisions in collaborative manner (encouraging the patients to become activated)" (p. 1). Bodenheimer (2005) confirms that physicians may not produce enough information in any decision-making in multiple-agenda visit.

In order for them to provide high-quality, guidelines-compliant care in a 15-minute visit can not productive unless they have well teaching tool(s) for the patient to have accurate self-management/assessment. However, a 15-min physician's visit can produce weak result in patients with chronic conditions such as diabetes, arthritis, and back pain and so on. Research has shown that shortage of the 15-min visit make patients have incomplete information that they need in order to educate themselves. Furthermore, research also show that of 50% of patients who have type 2 diabetes earn limited or have no education on their condition because they have less time with their doctors. These situations give or create less opportunity for them to learn how to education more on self-management. Research shows that in addition to achieving the primary goal of preventing or delaying disease progression, self-management of chronic disease can improve general well-being, quality of life, and psychological-emotional states of patients (Conn, 2011).

Bodenheimer's article on "Planned Visit to Help Patients Self-manage Chronic Conditions" (Bodenheimer, 2005) suggests that self-management cannot be effective without planned visits that provide good education for the management of a patient with chronic condition. In addition to physicians, patients need additional supportive team members including nurses, social workers, and others or pharmacist other than the patient's regular physicians. Wagner, Baker, Bundorf, and Singer (2004) assessed the use of the Internet to obtain health information for people who have one to five different major chronic illnesses. The study proves found that using the Internet provides an opportunity for many clients to promote their self-management skills. A study conducted by Zheng, Nugent, McCullagh, Huang, and Zhang (2010) presents another way in which self-management of chronic disease can be assisted by technology. Patients are provided with an accelerometer, which measures and records levels of activity. Heart rate, blood pressure, and weight are also monitored and recorded by the device, allowing patients to constantly view feedback regarding their level of activity and health statistics, which was found to assist patients in achieving their health goals.

Key Aspects of Self-Management Programs

Clark et al. (1991) identify three elements that are essential to the effective self-management of chronic medical problems: (a) adequate information, (b) "activities aimed at management of the condition," and (c) the ability to "maintain adequate psychosocial functioning" (p. 6) through the management of feelings associated with the medical condition. In addition, patients must deal with a number of specific tasks, which are also noted (Clark et al., 1991).

Adequate patient information must be made available to patients so that informed self-management decisions can be made. Such information is available in many different forms and languages. Although written materials are the most common, valuable information is available through other formats, including audio and videotapes and the Internet. This information will help patients accomplish such tasks as understanding symptoms and triggers, using medication correctly, and managing crises.

It is important that social workers address any impairments to patient understanding, such as language, poor reading ability, visual or hearing impairments, or cognitive limitations, in order that the patient understands the information to the fullest possible extent. Physicians may not provide adequate coverage of this essential element of patient care. In a 1995 study, patients experiencing chronic medical problems were interviewed to gather information that would help to "enrich the approach to patient education through the views of patients" (Lacroix, Jacquemet, & Assal, 1995, p. 301). Medical problems addressed in the study included hypertension, back pain, asthma, chronic obstructive pulmonary disease, diabetes, and several other conditions. Numerous patients identified poor communication with physicians as a significant barrier to their treatment.

Patients interviewed in the study reported that physicians used that language that was not comprehensible, that there was a lack of access to relevant information, and that they experienced poor communicated with physicians (Lacroix et al., 1995). For example, one patient reported feeling "like a person relegated to the side," while another patient reported that nurses, on the other hand "are lists and lend us support" (p. 303). In addition to nurses, social workers and other health professionals are increasingly involved in the role of educating patients about their chronic medical conditions.

Self-management activities are behavioral steps or actions that are taken by patients based on the knowledge they have obtained about their conditions. Stretcher, DeVellis, Becker, and Rosenstock (1986) note that it is important for self-management programs to remove "the mysticism of change" (p. 90) by keeping programs simple and understandable. The social worker's role is to enhance the patient's ability to self-manage. Therefore, the patient, not the social worker, should become the expert on his or her condition. Self-management activities are helpful in dealing with a number of tasks, including eating properly, exercising, making decisions about symptoms and medications, and avoiding such harmful behaviors as smoking or abuse of alcohol and other substances.

Psychosocial functioning must be maintained in order for the patients to continue to self-manage his or her medical condition. Vattano (1978), a social worker, wrote about the need for self-management skills in dealing with stress and anxiety. In addition, people with chronic medical problems may also experience feeling of isolation, depression, and hopelessness. Interventions may be helpful to patients in accomplishing such tasks as adapting to work, managing emotions and enhancing relationships with others (Clark et al., 1991).

Self-Management Treatment Components

Patient education, medical self-management skills, and psychosocial self-management skills are three common components of many effective self-management programs. Social workers will likely experience a great deal of variance in their patients, not only with respect to their specific medical problems, but also relative to levels of functioning, cognitive ability, and motivation to self-manage their problems. Therefore, it is important to understand the subtleties of each medical problem and to work with patients at their own pace and level of motivation to change.

Patient Education

In order to self-manage a chronic medical problem, the patient must first acquire sufficient medical knowledge about the problem to be able to make treatment decisions when the condition exacerbates. Lorig (1996) provides extensive information on patient education and its role in self-management and status. She goes on to note that "just because someone has correct knowledge does not mean he or she will change" (p. xiv). The social worker can contribute greatly to the effort to educate the patient. First, information can be provided that is not only adequate but is also in a form that tie person ran comprehend. Second, social workers can assist in any obtaining necessary equipment that is needed to monitor medical conditions as well as in teaching the patient how to use it correctly. Third, supportive resources can be provided, such as telephone help lines or emergency services, for the patient to use as a backup when needed. Finally social workers ran support their patients providing feedback and positive reinforcement as the medical knowledge is mastered.

Medical Self-Management Skills

Although medical self-management skills will vary by specific problem, Clark et al. (1991) found that there were categories that were common to many programs. The correct use of medication is a common challenge in managing chronic medical problems and should begin with patient education about the medications. Next, programs may teach patients to use such tools as self-monitoring logs, daily medication dispensers, and devices to measure symptoms. These skills target medical symptoms and often involve teaching not only patients but also other supportive persons. The data obtained can be used to decide whether to alter medication, connect with backup resources, or go to an emergency facility. A wide range of mobile telephone applications are also available that can help patients manage their medications.

Psychosocial Self-Management Skills

In addition to managing medical symptoms, many self-management programs incorporate skills for with chronic medical problems. Wodarski et al. (1991) provide information concerning a number of effective techniques that social workers might teach to patients, including biofeedback, exercise, relaxation training, and systematic desensitization. Social workers Ivanoff and Stem (1992) report that, of 14 studies with follow-ups of 6 months or longer, "identified self-monitoring as an ongoing intervention component" (p. 33), and they further note that cognitive restructuring, self-instruction, and planning were used in the majority of the 14 studies. Certainly there may be overlap between medical and psychosocial techniques. In other words, becoming proficient at using a medical device to monitor symptoms may boost the patient's confidence. At the same time, learning to use relaxation techniques may help with the management of both physical symptoms and emotional characteristics.

Studies evaluating self-management programs have found that patients can be helped with a number of common chronic medical problems. As they become educated about their problems, learn medical and psychosocial management techniques, apply the knowledge on their own, and receive coaching and positive reinforcement from their social workers, patients can learn to effectively self-manage a wide range of conditions.

Community Interventions

Community interventions can used to help support patient self-management and also provide information about community resources. These could include local health departments, the YMCA, the Arthritis Foundation, or the American Lung Association. Any clients with arthritis, asthmas, diabetes, and any other chronic illness will have the opportunity to improve or upgrade their level in mastery of skills through learning and practice. Some community organizations continue to give to clients' programs that build up their self-management skills through exercise programs, self-help groups, and patient education classes. A specific example of community-based chronic disease self-management is Move More for Diabetes, a program which encourages physical activity in patients with Type II diabetes. Research found that this program was successful largely due to its community-based format, where patients found social support in other members of their community (Richert, Webb, Morse, O'Toole, & Brownson, 2007).

Self-Managing Specific Chronic Medical Problems

Social workers need a repertoire of potential tools and techniques in order to develop self-management programs that are congruent with patients' needs. However, a working knowledge of chronic medical conditions and the self-management programs that have been found to be effective for specific medical problems is also essential. Although not exhaustive, the following review of effective programs for

Table 13.1 Studies of self-management of chronic medical problems

Authors	Intervention components	Outcomes
Asthma		
Boulet, Boutin, Cote, Leblanc, and Laviolette (1995)	Self-management training for adults	Increased asthma knowledge and fewer visits to emergency room
Colland (1993)	Communication skills, education, and problem-solving	Reduced anxiety, improved sleep, and fewer school absences
Harver (1994)	Verbal feedback	Improved ability to detect flow resistance to breathing
Wilson et al. (1993)	Small-group or individualized education program	Improved use of inhalers and better ability to control symptoms
Arthritis		
Davis, Busch, Lowe, Taniguchi, and Djkowich (1994)	Group instruction	Improved knowledge and perceived ability to self-manage
Keefe et al. (1990)	Relaxation, imagery, and cognitive restructuring	Lower levels of pain and less psychosocial disability
Lorig and Holman (1993)	Education, pain management, problem-solving, and exercise	Lower pain, increased knowledge, and improved ability to self-manage
Taal et al. (1993)	Weekly contracting, goal-setting, and feedback	More practice of physical and relaxation exercises
Diabetes		
Glasgow et al. (1992)	Self-management training for patients over 60	Reduced calorie intake and reduced intake of fat
Glasgow, Toobert, Hampson, and Noell (1995)	Goal setting, feedback, and computer assistance	Weekly dietary goals achieved at a rate of 90% or higher
Pichert, Snyder, Kinzer, and Boswell (1994)	Anchored instruction for diabetics ages 9–15	Improved ability to link problem-solving to decision rationales
Holroyd and Penzien (1994)	Biofeedback and relaxation training,	Significant reduction in levels of pain
Turner and Clancy (1988)	Goal setting, relaxation, imagery and spouse training	Decreased physical and psychosocial disability

diabetes, arthritis, asthma, headache, low back pain, provides strong support for the potential benefits of self-managing chronic medical problems. In addition, Table 13.1 provides a brief summary by problem.

Diabetes

Diabetes is caused by absent or ineffective insulin in the body, which causes high levels of glucose to appear in the blood. Diabetes can lead to serious complications, including high blood pressure, kidney disease, blindness, and the necessity of amputations. The condition affects over 25 million people in the USA with annual healthcare costs that exceed $250 billion (NIH, 2017). It is the number one cause of blindness and the seventh leading cause of death in the USA (NIH, 2017). The American Diabetes Association is an information resource at both the national and local levels (www.diabetes.org).

Treatment emphasizes blood-glucose level and diet monitoring, physical activity, and attention to medical and psychosocial factors. Jenkins (1995) provides an overview of behavioral management techniques used in a number of diabetes programs. Self-management skills can be successfully learned by patients and several studies have indicated that these skills can be improved, although patient differences may affect the choice of intervention such as family treatment groups, and individual groups. Education group that will provide good outcome for patients and teach them what to eat and will also include the right medications. For example, Bradley (1994) identifies earlier studies that indicate that stress management may improve the psychological well-being of diabetics. On the other hand, a 10-week support group targeted to "improve blood sugar control and improve means of social support" (Oren, Carella, & Helma, 1996, p. 2) did not indicate significant results. Other programs that target specific populations and problems have been found to be significantly helpful to diabetics.

Pichert et al. (1994) studied the benefit of two 45-min small-group teaching sessions using an anchored instruction technique for participants ages 9–15 who were recruited from a summer diabetes camp. Campers who received the instruction were able to link the rationale for disease-management guidelines to their sick-day management decisions at a significantly higher rate than were controls.

A 10-session self-management training program for patients over age 60 having Type 11 (non-insulin-dependent) diabetes was helpful to "a relatively hardcore group of patients who had a long history of diabetes and a number of chronic diseases besides diabetes" (Glasgow et al., 1992, p. 71). Participants were reached through an aggressive community effort that included free testing materials and a coupon that could be redeemed for free walking shoes. Weekly groups focused on dietary and exercise self-care issues and used goal setting, logs, weekly assignments, and problem-solving activities. Participants reduced total calorie intake levels as well as the percent of fat calories at significantly higher rates than did controls.

Diabetic patients who utilized an office-based program to improve dietary self-care were able to achieve their goals at a very high level of success (Glasgow et al., 1995). Using computer technology, including interactive video, patients received a behavioral intervention program followed by immediate feedback and goal setting specifically tailored to the individual patient. At 1-week follow-up, 90% of the patients reported achieving their goal and 96% were successful after 3 weeks.

Technology can play an important role in self-management of chronic diseases, including diabetes. Bull, Gaglio, McKay, and Glasgow (2005) reviewed 87 websites that provide self-help for patients with diabetes. This research revealed that while most websites provided current and accurate information about diabetes, very few provided any interactive elements or social support networks, which have been found to be very effective in successful self-management of diabetes. Researchers suggest that websites implement these features in order to be of more use to patients. The addition of family support has also been found to improve self-management outcomes (Pamungkas, Chamroonsawasdi, & Vatanasomboon, 2017).

Arthritis

Arthritis is a common chronic medical problem and is "the major cause of disability in the elderly and of admission to skilled nursing facilities" (Lorig & Holman, 1993, p. 18). As the older adult population continues to grow in the USA, it has been estimated that over 25% of the population will be diagnosed with arthritis by 2040, the year 2040 (CDC, 2018a). There are different types of arthritis. Rheumatoid arthritis involves joint inflammation, with swelling, stiffness, and tenderness. Osteoarthritis, a degenerative joint disease, is the most common form of arthritis. The Arthritis Foundation is a resource for additional information at both the national and local levels (www.arthritis.org). Several studies have demonstrated the effectiveness of arthritis self-management that focus on learning to cope and live with the condition.

The Arthritis Self-Management Program (ASMP) is a well-established patient education program developed at Stanford University in 1979 (Lorig, 1992) that consists of six 2-h weekly sessions. Volunteers in the community are trained to teach the course, which is offered through local chapters of the Arthritis Foundation. The ASMP has been held in a wide range of community settings, including "senior centers, libraries, mobile home parks, churches, and shopping centers" (Lorig & Holman, 1993, p. 19).

The ASMP educates patients about the different forms of arthritis, the types and use of medications, exercises, cognitive pain management, and problem-solving skills. The Arthritis Help book (Lorig & Fries, 2006), a paperback text, provides additional information on the types of arthritis and medications and on goal setting and contracting, illustrates various exercises, and provides numerous tips on how to make daily tasks more manageable. In addition, the book can serve as a reference text for use by teachers and trainers.

Outcome studies have found the ASMP to be very helpful to arthritis patients. An earlier outcome study (Lorig, Lubeck, Kraines, Seleznick, & Holman, 1985) found that after 4 months, patients randomized to the ASMP exceeded those in a control group in their knowledge and practice of self-management techniques and experienced lower levels of pain. The investigation also included a 20-month longitudinal study that found that frequency of exercise and "a significant decline in pain was sustained at 20 months" (p. 682). Lorig and Holman (1993) published a 12-year review of the ASMP noting that the outcomes of replication studies in Australia and Canada were "similar to those in the original experimental setting with a reasonable range of variability" (p. 25).

Although Kraaimaat, Brons, Geenen, and Bijlsma (1995) did not find a 20-h cognitive-behavioral therapy group to be significantly helpful to rheumatoid arthritis patients. A 37-h group instruction program in Canada was found to improve both knowledge about arthritis and the perceived ability to self-manage the condition (Davis et al., 1994). The Canadian program is conducted by professionals, including social workers, rather than by trained volunteers like the ASMP (Lorig, 1992).

Patients with osteoarthritis knee pain who received pain-coping skills training were found to have significantly lower levels of pain and psychosocial disability than those in a control group who received patient education (Keefe et al., 1990). The intervention was conducted in small groups of 6–9 people and included training in a number of techniques, including relaxation, imagery, distraction, and cognitive restructuring. Participants also were taught how to break tasks into time periods of activity followed by rest, as well as how to schedule pleasant activities.

A group program for rheumatoid arthritis patients who participated in 10 h of instruction was found to be significantly more helpful than controls (Taal et al., 1993). Participants demonstrated higher levels of knowledge, of practice of physical and relaxation exercises, of self-management behaviors, and of positive outcome expectations. The program was delivered by social workers and other professionals and included weekly contracting, goal setting, and feedback. Follow-up data indicate that after 14 months the researchers "still found strong effects on knowledge and the practice of physical exercises and a small effect on self-efficacy function" (Taal et al., 1993, p. 184).

While chronic disease self-management has been found to be effective for people of all ages, a recent study found that older men are more likely to take advantage of self-management techniques for arthritis than are younger men. Researchers found that this was due to the fact that younger men are very aware of social stigma, and consider arthritis to be a disease that only affects the elderly; therefore, they were ashamed to participate in self-management programs. Older men, however, were not sensitive to the same social stigma, and were more likely to participate in the self-management programs (Gibbs, 2008). This study indicates that efforts should be made to reduce social stigma and ageism surrounding arthritis in order to increase participation in younger men.

Headache and Low Back Pain

Chronic low back pain and recurrent headache disorders are two common health problems that can account for large numbers of outpatient medical visits and serious economic losses, including the inability of patients to work (Holroyd & Penzien, 1994; Lackner, Carosella, & Feuerstein, 1996). Several behavioral techniques have been found to be helpful for both problems. For tension headaches, Holroyd and Penzien (1994) summarized 37 studies and found that biofeedback and relaxation training are equally effective and "have each yielded a nearly 50% reduction in tension headache activity" (p. 58). For migraine headaches, the researchers reported that a combination of biofeedback and relaxation training "yielded significantly larger reductions in migraine activity than either relaxation training or thermal biofeedback training alone" (p. 58). In a subsequent article, Penzien and Holroyd

(1994) provide a practical summary of techniques involved in both relaxation and biofeedback training.

For chronic low back pain, Turner and Clancy (1988) reported that, at 12-month follow-up, patients who had received 16 h of either operant behavioral or cognitive-behavioral treatment were helped equally. The operant behavioral group addressed pain and well behaviors and instructed spouses on how to positively reinforce well behaviors. Patients set behavioral goals, including exercises that were progressively increased using a quota system. The cognitive-behavioral group received training in progressive relaxation, in the use of imagery, and in methods for altering maladaptive thoughts.

A component analysis conducted by Turner, Clancy, McQuade, and Cardenas (1990) compared the outcomes of patients who were randomly assigned to 16 h of behavior therapy, to aerobic exercise, to a combination of both, or to a waiting-list control group. All three groups were found to have benefited at 6-month and 12-month follow-ups, although the groups receiving the combined behavioral and aerobic intervention reported the most significant reductions in self-reported levels of pain as well as in psychosocial disability. Behavioral treatment consisted of exploring pain and well behaviors, goal setting, homework assignments, and social reinforcement for completion.

Lackner et al. (1996) tested the influence of self-efficacies expectations on the treatment outcome of patients having chronic low back pain. The study investigated "functional self-efficacy expectations which refer to confidence judgments regarding the ability to execute or achieve tasks of physical performance" (p. 213). Results indicated that "performance-specific cognition may have greater explanatory power over disability than pain-specific ones" (p. 212). Keefe, Dunsmore, and Burnett (1992) provide additional information on the efficacy of behavioral interventions for chronic pain.

Technology also plays an important role in the current state of self-management of chronic back pain. PainACTION-Back Pain (https://www.painaction.com/) is a website dedicated to implementing self-management of chronic back pain. Chiauzzi, Pujol, Wood, Bond, and Black (2010) conducted a study to determine the efficacy of this website, and found that participants reported less pain, lower stress, increased coping skills, and increased social support when compared to the control participants.

Asthma

Asthma is a chronic medical problem caused by airflow obstruction in the bronchioles, which may lead to shortness of breath, wheezing, coughing, and tightness in the chest. The Centers for Disease Control and Prevention (CDC, 2017) report that asthma affects over 8% of the population at all ages. As the most common chronic childhood disease, it is the third leading cause of hospitalizations, and a common reason for emergency department visits (Johnson, Chambers, & Dexheimer, 2016).

The CDC (1995) notes that "morbidity and mortality associated with asthma may be affected by patient compliance, patient education, and medical management" (p. 954). Buist and Vollmer (1994) report the need for the increased use of objective measures, for improved efforts in environmental control, and for "a partnership between patients and healthcare providers that includes health education" (p. 1585). At the national and local levels, the American Lung Association (www.kung.org) provides information and support concerning the growing problem of asthma. Programs to improve the self-management of asthma have been found to be effective for both adults and children.

Asthma affects 9 million children in the USA and causes approximately 14 million missed school days annually (Johnson et al., 2016). Interventions and studies of programs to improve the self-management of asthma in children are extensive and are beyond the scope of this chapter. Rachelefsky (1987) provides a review of several self-management programs that have been helpful to children with asthma in reducing the frequency of asthma attacks, the numbers of school absences, and the numbers of both hospital emergency room visits and hospital inpatient days.

Children ages 8–13 who participated in a 10-h educational training program (Colland, 1993) experienced significant changes when compared to controls, including a higher level of knowledge about asthma, a greater reduction in anxiety, a higher level of ability to use inhaled medications correctly, fewer sleep interruptions, and fewer school absences. The program used behavioral techniques and group therapy to teach self-management activities. A positive reward system was used for individuals and for the group as a whole to reinforce the completion of homework. In addition to self-management skills, participants learned how to communicate their needs when exposed to triggers, such as tobacco smoke. Problem-solving skills were practiced in role-plays and in homework assignments. One year after the program ended, the experimental-group children demonstrated clinically significant differences in their ability to manage their asthma. Colland (1993) also reported that for parents of the children, "the burden of having a chronically ill child had been reduced as a result of the child's participation in the training program" (p. 150).

The Centers for Disease Control and Prevention (1996) notes the need for environmental controls in conjunction with patient education and medical management. Buist and Vollmer (1994) further note that "environmental factors should be taken seriously" (p. 1585) in controlling asthma, particularly in poverty areas. Social workers can provide patients with a wide range of helpful information (Ingram & Heymann, 1993), including using plastic mattress covers, controlling dust mites, applying household cleaning tips, exterminating cockroaches, and reducing of numerous triggers, including cat allergen and cigarette smoke. One study (Huss et al., 1994) found that children ages 5–12 who had plastic covers on their mattresses had significantly fewer emergency room visits than children without the mattress covers. Zap Asthma (www.asthmacommunitynetwork.org/) focuses on childhood asthma in poor communities where the incidence of childhood asthma is higher.

The ability to detect flow resistance in breathing, an important factor in asthma self-assessment, was "improved significantly as a function of feedback experience" (Harver, 1994, p. 60). Boulet et al. (1995) compared participants and controls 1 year before and 1 year after a 2-h education and self-management training program for adult asthma patients and found that the intervention group had significant increases in asthma knowledge and the means to control it, as well as a significant reduction in emergency room visits.

Wilson et al. (1993) studied adult asthma patients who were randomly assigned to one of four groups, including a 6-h small-group education program, three to five individually tailored sessions, a self-study workbook group, or a control group that did not include asthma education. Patients in the two treatment groups (small group or individual sessions) were found to report significant improvements in the bedroom environment, in the use of inhaler medications, in the control of symptoms, and in adherence to treatment. Although the use of a self-study workbook was not found to be helpful, small groups were found to "have significant beneficial effect for modest cost" (p. 575).

Ahmad and Grimes (2011) conducted a meta-analysis on the impact of self-management of asthma on school-aged children (ages 5–18) diagnosed with asthma. Their investigation of nine studies revealed that children who participated in self-management education about asthma were significantly less likely to miss school and be admitted to the hospital for asthma-related complications.

There is also evidence that self-management treatment of asthma can have a positive impact above and beyond physical health results. Tousman, Zeitz, and Taylor (2010) found that a group-style self-management program for asthmatic patients not only led to an improvement of asthma symptoms, but it also led to an increase in the quality of life, increased self-efficacy, and decreased depression.

Supplementary Information

General overviews concerning patient education and self-management programs, including theoretical perspectives are available (Araújo-Soares, Hankonen, Presseau, Rodrigues, & Sniehotta, 2018; Clark et al., 1991; Lorig, 1996; Stretcher et al., 1986). Additional information on the techniques used in self-management programs can be accessed elsewhere, including the use of goals and homework assignments (Shelton & Levy, 1981) and progressive relaxation training (Bernstein & Borkovec, 1973). Patient outcomes can be measured by using reliable and valid instruments available from original publications or from a two volume sourcebook (Corcoran & Fischer, 2013). Self-anchored scales, the use of client logs, and behavioral observations are also described by the authors.

Additional information concerning specific medical problems, as well as other helpful resources and patient education materials, are available from numerous organizations and the Internet. The Centers for Disease Control and Prevention offers its Chronic Disease Self-Management Program (Centers for Disease Control and Prevention, 2018b) with access to materials and workshops. The American Lung Association offers extensive information about asthma and has offices at both the national and local levels (www.lung.org) while the Arthritis Foundation provides resources and support across the USA (www.arthritis.com).

Conclusion

Former Attorney General C. Everett Koop, commenting on managed care and the sweeping changes in the delivery of health care, states that he is "convinced that patient education will help us solve the problems that lie before us" (Koop, 1996, p. 69). Many chronic medical problems have a more adverse effect on poor and disadvantaged groups traditionally served by social workers, including children, minority groups, disabled people, and elderly people. Patient education alone is not sufficient and may not reach these vulnerable and needy populations.

Social workers offer a unique perspective, practical skills, and a commitment to helping others that is congruent to the assessment, development, implementation, and evaluation of effective programs to help patients with the self-management of chronic medical problems. Dissemination of information through publishing, workshops, conferences, and teaching opportunities is essential as the expertise to help patients continues to expand.

References

Ahmad, E., & Grimes, D. E. (2011). The effects of self-management education for school-age children on asthma morbidity: A systematic review. *Journal of School Nursing, 27*(4), 282–292.

Araújo-Soares, V., Hankonen, N., Presseau, J., Rodrigues, A., & Sniehotta, F. F. (2018). Developing behavior change interventions for self-management in chronic illness: An integrative overview. *European Psychologist*. https://doi.org/10.1027/1016-9040/a000330

Bernstein, D. A., & Borkovec, T. C. (1973). *Progressive relaxation training: A manual for the helping professions*. Champaign, IL: Research Press.

Bodenheimer, T. (2005). Planned visits to help patients self-manage chronic conditions. *American Family Physician, 72*, 1454–1456.

Boulet, L. P., Boutin, H., Cote, J., Leblanc, P., & Laviolette, M. (1995). Evaluation of an asthma self-management education program. *Journal of Asthma, 32*, 199–206.

Bradley, C. (1994). Contributions of psychology to diabetes management. *British Journal of Clinical Psychology, 33*, 11–21.

Buist, A. S., & Vollmer, W. M. (1994). Preventing deaths from asthma. *The New England Journal of Medicine, 331*, 1584–1585.

Bull, S. S., Gaglio, B., McKay, H., & Glasgow, R. E. (2005). Harnessing the potential of the internet to promote chronic illness self-management: Diabetes as an example of how well we are doing. *Chronic Illness, 1*(2), 143–155.

Centers for Disease Control and Prevention. (1995). Asthma-United States, 1982–1992. *MMWR, 43*, 952–955.

Centers for Disease Control and Prevention. (1996). Asthma mortality and hospitalization among children and young adults-United States, 1980-1993. *MMWR, 45*, 350–353.

Centers for Disease Control and Prevention. (2017). *Asthma*. Retrieved from https://www.cdc.gov/nchs/fastats/asthma.htm

Centers for Disease Control and Prevention. (2018a). *Arthritis*. Retrieved from https://www.cdc.gov/arthritis/index.htm

Centers for Disease Control and Prevention. (2018b). *Chronic disease self-management program (CDSMP)*. Retrieved from https://www.cdc.gov/arthritis/marketing-support/1-2-3-approach/docs/pdf/provider_fact_sheet_cdsmp.pdf

Chiauzzi, E., Pujol, L. A., Wood, M., Bond, K., & Black, R. (2010). PainACTION back pain: A self-management website for people with chronic back pain. *Pain Medicine, 11*(7), 1044–1058.

Clark, N. M., Becker, M. H., Janz, N. K., Lorig, K., Rakowski, W., & Anderson, L. (1991). Self-management of chronic disease by older adults. *Journal of Aging and Health, 3*, 3–27.

Coleman, M. T., & Newton, K. S. (2005). Supporting self-management in patients with chronic illness. *American Family Physician, 72*(8), 1503–1510.

Colland, V. T. (1993). Learning to cope with asthma: A behavioral self-management program for children. *Patient Education and Counseling, 22*, 141–152.

Conn, V. S. (2011). Helping patients help themselves: Chronic disease self management interventions. *Western Journal of Nursing Research, 33*(2), 159–160.

Corcoran, K., & Fischer, J. (2013) *Measures for clinical practice and research* (5th Ed., Vols. 1–2). Oxford, England: Oxford University Press.

Davis, P., Busch, A. J., Lowe, J. C., Taniguchi, J., & Djkowich, B. (1994). Evaluation of a rheumatoid arthritis patient education program: Impact on knowledge and self-efficacy. *Patient Education and Counseling, 24*, 55–61.

Gibbs, L. (2008). Men and chronic arthritis: Does age make men more likely to use self-management services? *Generations, 32*(1), 78–81.

Glasgow, R. E., Toobert, D. J., Hampson, S. E., Brown, J. E., Lewinsohn, P. M., & Donnelly, J. (1992). Improving self-care among older patients with type II diabetes: The "sixth something …" study. *Patient Education and Counseling, 19*, 61–74.

Glasgow, R. E., Toobert, D. J., Hampson, S. E., & Noell, J. W. (1995). A brief office-based intervention to facilitate diabetes dietary self-management. *Health Education Research, 10*, 467–478.

Harver, A. (1994). Effect of feedback on the ability of asthmatic subjects to detect increases in the flow-resistive component to breathing. *Health Psychology, 13*, 52–62.

Henry, H. K., & Schor, E. L. (2015). Supporting self-management of chronic health problems. *Pediatrics, 135*(5), 789–792.

Holroyd, K. A., & Penzien, D. B. (1994). Psychosocial interventions in the management of recurrent headache disorders: 1. Overview and effectiveness. *Behavioral Medicine, 20*, 53–63.

Huss, K., Rand, C. S., Butz, A. M., Eggleston, P. A., Murigande, C., Thompson, L. C., … Malveaux. (1994). Home environmental risk factors in urban minority asthmatic children. *Annals of Allergy, 72*, 173–177.

Ingram, J. M., & Heymann, P. W. (1993). Environmental controls in the management of asthma. *Immunology and Allergy Clinics of North America, 13*, 785–801.

Ivanoff, A., & Stern, S. B. (1992). Self-management interventions in health and mental health settings: Evidence of maintenance and generalization. *Social Work Research and Abstracts, 28*, 32–38.

Jenkins, C. D. (1995). An integrated behavioral medicine approach to improving care of patients with diabetes mellitus. *Behavioral Medicine, 21*, 53–65.

Johnson, L. H., Chambers, P., & Dexheimer, J. W. (2016). Asthma-related emergency department use: Current perspectives. *Emergency Medicine, 8*, 47–55.

Keefe, F. J., Caldwell, D. S., Williams, D. A., Gil, K. M., Mitchell, D., Robertson, C., … Helms, M. (1990). Pain coping skills training in the management of osteoarthritis knee pain: A comparative study. *Behavior Therapy, 21*, 19–62.

Keefe, F. J., Dunsmore, J., & Burnett, R. (1992). Behavioral and cognitive-behavioral approaches to chronic pain: Recent advances and future directions. *Journal of Consulting and Clinical Psychology, 60*, 528–536.

Koop, C. E. (1996). Manage with care. *Time, 148*(14), 69.

Kraaimaat, F. W., Brons, M. R., Geenen, R., & Bijlsma, J. W. J. (1995). The effect of cognitive behavior therapy in patients with rheumatoid arthritis. *Behavior Research and Therapy, 33,* 487–495.

Lackner, J., Carosella, A. M., & Feuerstein, M. (1996). Pain expectancies, pain, and functional self-efficacy expectancies as determinants of disability in patients with chronic low back disorders. *Journal of Consulting and Clinical Psychology, 64,* 212–220.

Lacroix, A., Jacquemet, S., & Assal, J. (1995). Patients' experiences with their disease: Learning from the differences and sharing the common problems. *Patient Education and Counseling, 26,* 301–312.

Lorig, K., & Fries, J. F. (2006). *The arthritis helpbook: A tested self-management program for coping with arthritis and fibromyalgia* (6th Ed.). Cambridge, MA: Da Capo Press.

Lorig, K. (1992). *Arthritis self-help course.* Atlanta, GA: Arthritis Foundation.

Lorig, K. (1996). *Patient education: A practical approach.* Thousand Oaks, CA: Sage.

Lorig, K., & Holman, H. (1993). Arthritis self-management studies: A twelve-year review. *Health Education Quarterly, 20,* 17–28.

Lorig, K., Lubeck, D., Kraines, E. G., Seleznick, M., & Holman, H. R. (1985). Outcomes of self-help education for patients with arthritis. *Arthritis and Rheumatism, 28,* 680–685.

Murray, C. J., & Lopez, A. D. (1996). *The global burden of disease.* Cambridge, MA: Harvard University Press.

National Institutes of Health. (2017). *National diabetes statistics report.* Washington, DC. Retrieved from https://www.cdc.gov/diabetes/pdfs/data/statistics/national-diabetes-statistics-report.pdf

Oren, M. L., Carella, M., & Helma, T. (1996). Diabetes support group-study results and implications. *Employee Assistance Quarterly, 11,* 1–20.

Pamungkas, R., Chamroonsawasdi, K., & Vatanasomboon, P. (2017). A systematic review: Family support integrated with diabetes self-management among uncontrolled type II diabetes mellitus patients. *Behavioral Sciences, 62,* 1–17.

Penzien, D. B., & Holroyd, K. A. (1994). Psychosocial interventions in the management of recurrent headache disorders: 2. Description of treatment techniques. *Behavioral Medicine, 20,* 64–73.

Pichert, J. W., Snyder, G. M., Kinzer, C. K., & Boswell, E. J. (1994). Problem solving anchored instruction about sick days for adolescents with diabetes. *Patient Education and Counseling, 23,* 115–124.

Rachelefsky, G. S. (1987). Review of asthma self-management programs. *Journal of Allergy and Clinical Immunology, 80,* 506–511.

Richert, M. L., Webb, A. J., Morse, N. A., O'Toole, M. L., & Brownson, C. A. (2007). Move more diabetes: Using lay health educators to support physical activity in a community-based chronic disease self-management program. *The Diabetes Educator, 33,* 179–184.

Ritter, P. L., Lee, J., & Lorig, K. (2011). Moderators of chronic disease self management programs: Who benefits? *Chronic Illness, 7*(2), 162–172.

Shelton, J. L., & Levy, R. L. (1981). *Behavioral assignments and treatment compliance.* Champaign, IL: Research Press.

Stretcher, V. J., DeVellis, B. M., Becker, M. H., & Rosenstock, I. M. (1986). The role of self-efficacy in achieving health behavior change. *Health Education Quarterly, 13,* 73–91.

Taal, E., Riemsma, R. P., Brus, H. L., Seydel, E. R., Rasker, J. J., & Wiegman, O. (1993). Group education for patients with rheumatoid arthritis. *Patient Education and Counseling, 20,* 177–187.

Tousman, S., Zeitz, H., & Taylor, L. D. (2010). A pilot study assessing the impact of a learner-centered adults asthma self-management program on psychological outcomes. *Clinical Nursing Research, 19*(1), 71–88.

Towle, A., & Godolphin, W. (2011). The neglect of chronic disease self-management in medical education: Involving patients as educators. *Academic Medicine, 86*(11), 1350.

Turner, J., Clancy, S., McQuade, K. J., & Cardenas, D. D. (1990). Effectiveness of behavioral therapy for chronic low back pain: A component analysis. *Journal of Consulting and Clinical Psychology, 59*, 573–579.

Turner, J. A., & Clancy, S. (1988). Comparison of operant behavioral and cognitive-behavioral treatment for low back pain. *Journal of Consulting and Clinical Psychology, 56*, 261–266.

Vattano, A. J. (1978). Self-management for coping with stress. *Social Work, 23*, 113–199.

Wagner, T. H., Baker, L. C., Bundorf, M. K., & Singer, S. (2004). Use of the internet for health information by the chronically ill. *Centers for Disease Control and Prevention, 1*(4), 1–13.

Wilson, S. R., Scamages, P., German, D. F., Hughes, G. W., Lulla, S., Coss, S., … Arsham, G. M. (1993). A controlled trial of two forms of self-management education for adults with asthma. *The American Journal of Medicine, 54*, 564–576.

Wodarski, J. S., Wodarski, L. A., Nixon, S. C., & Mackie, C. (1991). Behavioral medicine: An emerging field of social work practice. *Journal of Health and Social Policy, 3*, 19–43.

World Health Organization. (2018). *Noncommunicable diseases*. Retrieved from http://www.who.int/en/news-room/fact-sheets/detail/noncommunicable-diseases

Zheng, H., Nugent, C., McCullagh, P., Huang, Y., & Zhang, S. (2010). Smart self management: Assistive technology to support people with chronic disease. *Journal of Telemedicine & Telecare, 16*(4), 224–227.

Index

Druck:
Customized Business Services GmbH
im Auftrag der
KNV Zeitfracht GmbH
Ein Unternehmen der Zeitfracht - Gruppe
Ferdinand-Jühlke-Str. 7
99095 Erfurt